Samuel Barber

Recent titles in
Bio-Bibliographies in Music
Series Advisers: *Donald L. Hixon and Adrienne Fried Block*

Thea Musgrave: A Bio-Bibliography
Donald L. Hixon

Aaron Copland: A Bio-Bibliography
JoAnn Skowronski

Samuel Barber

A Bio-Bibliography

DON A. HENNESSEE
Donald L. Hixon, Series Adviser

Bio-Bibliographies in Music, Number 3

Greenwood Press
Westport, Connecticut • London, England

Library of Congress Cataloging in Publication Data

Hennessee, Don A.
  Samuel Barber : a bio-bibliography.

  (Bio-bibliographies in music, ISSN 0742-6968 ; no. 3)
  Bibliography: p.
  Includes index.
  1. Barber, Samuel, 1910- —Bibliography.
2. Barber, Samuel, 1910- —Discography.   3. Music—
Bio-bibliography.   4. Composers—United States—
Biography.   I. Title.   II. Series.
ML134.B175H4   1985   016.78′092′4   84-29017
ISBN 0-313-24026-4 (lib. bdg.)

Library of Congress Catalog Card Number: 84-29017
ISBN: 0-313-24026-4
ISSN: 0742-6968

First published in 1985

Greenwood Press
A division of Congressional Information Service, Inc.
88 Post Road West, Westport, Connecticut 06881

Printed in the United States of America

10   9   8   7   6   5   4   3   2   1

CONTENTS

Contents

PREFACE

This volume consists of four main sections, as follows:

(1) a brief <u>biography</u>;
(2) a complete list of <u>works and performances</u> classified by genre and then arranged alphabetically by title
of composition. Following each title is a listing of
premiere and other selected performances cited in the "Bibliography." Each work is preceded by the mnemonic "W" (W1,
W2, etc.) and each performance of that work is identified
by successive lowercase letters (W1a, W1b, etc.) Information concerning the location of manuscripts, sketches,
holographs, etc., is included here (see remarks at the end
of this "Preface"), as are details of instrumentation,
duration, commissions, dedications, and publication.
Reference is made to commentaries on the performances cited
in the "Bibliography";
(3) a <u>discography</u> of commercially-produced sound
recordings except cassettes and cartridges. Each recorded
work is preceded by the mnemonic "D" (D1, D2, D3, etc.).
Reference is made to commentaries on the recordings cited
in the "Bibliography"; and
(4) an annotated <u>bibliography</u> of writings by and
about Samuel Barber, his style, and his music, with annotations often taking the form of quotations extracted from
performance reviews. Each citation is preceded by the
mnemonic "B," except that citations to general critical and
biographical material unrelated specifically to particular
works precede the more specialized citations and are preceded by the mnemonic "BG." Entries in the bibliography
refer to the "Works and Performances" and "Discography"
sections. Because of space limitations, names of performers often were omitted in the "Bibliography" except
when such names appeared in either the title of the source
cited or in the annotation. However, the cross references
to the appropriate listings in "Works and Performances,"

e.g. _See_: W61c, will aid in the identification of all performers and performing groups.

Mnemonics for the "Works and Performances," the "Discography," and the "Bibliography" sections are consistent to the degree possible. For example, Barber's _Adagio for Strings_ appears in the "Works and Performance" section under the mnemonic W61; recordings of this work may be found under the number D61 in the "Discography," and citations to published material concerning the work appear in the "Bibliography" under the number B61. Of course, not all of Barber's works have been recorded, which means that some compositions listed in the "Works and Performances" section do not appear in either the "Discography" or the "Bibliography." The numeric arrangement, therefore, occasionally is interrupted. This interruption is evident most often in the "Vocal Music" section. Many reviewers in major American newspapers and music journals appear only grudgingly to acknowledge the existence of American song literature. All too often, a long review of a vocal program will end with a passing remark of the kin of, "The program concluded with a selection of American songs by Barber, Ives, and Rorem." It is thus often impossible to identify the individual songs performed.

For decades, record collectors have been driven to distraction by the seemingly indiscriminate reissuing of recorded selections by a composer, with record companies offering different pairings of works, "enhancing" older recordings, and, most heinously, not acknowledging that they indeed represent identical performances. A lack of thoroughness on the part of some discographers has contributed to this confusion. There is no reason, for example, to suspect that Howard Hanson and the Eastman Rochester Symphony Orchestra recorded Barber's works more than once. Nevertheless, there are a large number of Hanson recordings in this discography. The same situation exists with Horowitz's recording of the _Piano Sonata_. In the "Bibliography," the record label number given corresponds to that given in the review itself; the only change in number was made with the detection of typographical errors in the cited source. In the "Discography," however, an attempt was made to document all recordings, whether or not they appear in the "Bibliography." Identical recordings generally are listed separately only when distinguished by different pairings.

Finally, _appendixes_ provide alphabetical and chronological listings of Barber's works. A complete _index_ of names (personal and corporate) and titles concludes the volume.

MANUSCRIPT COLLECTIONS

Most of Samuel Barber's manuscripts have been deposited with the Library of Congress in Washington, D.C., although some are located at the Curtis Institute of Music (Philadelphia), the University of Oregon (Eugene), and the Chester County Historical Society (West Chester, Penn.). The collections of the last-named also include numerous sketches, fragments, juvenalia, some bearing Roman-numeral opus numbers, and some of which have not been identified. The holdings of identifiable Barber manuscripts at the Chester County Historical Society are listed below:

1. Christmas Eve: a Trio With Solos [including a Shepherd's Solo]
2. Selections from The Rose Tree: "Gypsy Dance," "Gypsy Song," "Dialogue for Act 1, Scene 1," and "Serenade, Act 1, Scene 2"]
3. Let Down the Bars, O Death, op. 8, no. 2.
4. Invocation to Youth.
5. October Mountain Weather.
6. Main Street.
7. Sonata in Modern Form, op. XVI.
8. An Old Song (1921)
9. Petite Berceuse.
10. Thy Will Be Done, op. V, no. 1 (1923; a rev. ed. of The Wanderer, see below)
11. Themes, op. X, no. 2 (April 1923)
12. Hunting Song.
13. Music, When Soft Voices Die.
14. The Wanderer (1920)

Unfortunately, it has not always been possible to determine the whereabouts of Barber's manuscripts. Some no doubt are housed in scattered locations in this country and abroad while others undoubtedly are in Gian-Carlo Menotti's private collection in Scotland. Readers able to provide assistance in locating such manuscripts are encouraged to contact the author through Greenwood Press.

PUBLISHERS DIRECTORY

G. Schirmer, 866 Third Avenue, New York, New York, 10022

For territories outside the United States, inquiries about Barber's orchestral music should be addressed to the following:

For Australia and New Zealand: Allan & Company, 276-78 Collins Street, Melbourne
For Germany, Austria, the Netherlands, and Switzerland: Anton J. Benjamin, Werderstrasse 44, 2 Hamburg 13
For Italy: G. Ricordi & Co., Via Salamone 77, Milan
For France, Monaco, Luxembourg, Belgium, Spain, Portugal, Hungary, Poland, Czechoslovakia, Yugoslavia, Greece, and Israel: Editions Salabert, 22, rue Chauchat, Paris 75009

Preface

For the United Kingdom and Irish Free State: G. Schirmer, Ltd., 140 Strand, London WC2R 1HH
For Canada: Gordon V. Thompson Ltd., 29 Birch Avenue, Toronto, Ontario M4V 1E3

ACKNOWLEDGMENTS

Many persons and institutions contributed to the preparation of this volume. In particular, I should like to extend special thanks to the following:

Rita M. Moore, Assistant Librarian, Chester County Historical Society, West Chester, Pennsylvania;
William C. Parsons, Reference Librarian, Library of Congress, Washington, D.C.;
Eugenia Quigley, Secretary to Rev. Thomas D. Bowers, Rector, St. Bartholomew's Church, New York, New York;
Elizabeth Ostrow, Vice President and Director of Artists and Repertoire, New World Records, New York, New York; and
Elizabeth Walker, Librarian, Curtis Institute of Music, Philadelphia, Pennsylvania

In addition, I should like to acknowledge the valuable assistance of the following persons and organizations:

Library of the Coleman Chamber Concerts, Pasadena, California;
Hilary Cummings, Curator of Manuscripts, Special Collections, University of Oregon, Eugene;
Bruce MacCombie, Vice President and Director of Publications, G. Schirmer, Inc., New York, New York;
Emilie W. Mills, Special Collections, Walter Clinton Jackson Library, University of North Carolina, Greensboro;
Mary Moldenhauer of the Moldenhauer Archives, Spokane, Washington;
Milford Myhre, Carillonneur, Bok Tower Gardens, Mountain Lake Sanctuary, Lake Wales, Florida;
Administrative staff of the Van Cliburn Foundation, Inc., Fort Worth, Texas;
Lucretia Wolfe, Librarian, San Francisco Conservatory of Music.

Acknowledgments

Finally, special thanks must be extended to Helen Birkmann (Dept. of German), Richard Frank (Dept. of Classics), Herbert Lehnert (Dept. of German), and Linda McMichael (University Library), all from the University of California, Irvine, for providing Enlish translations of annotations originally in German, Italian, and French, and to Roger B. Berry, Department of Special Collections, University Library, University of California, Irvine, for specialized editorial assistance.

Samuel Barber

BIOGRAPHY

There is no way to predict the place of Samuel Barber in American music fifty or one hundred years from now. It is possible that he may be completely forgotten. More likely, however, he will be remembered by scholars and musicians as a composer with integrity, and his works will continue to be performed, some retaining their places in the repertoire of orchestras, opera companies, dance and ballet troupes, and soloists. In terms of stylistic classification, he will be recalled as a neo-Romantic.

When future researchers look back, they will find that, along with George Gershwin and Aaron Copland, Barber was one of the three most recorded and performed of American composers of the twentieth century. They will also discover that almost all of his works were introduced by major performers of their time--Leontyne Price, Eleanor Steber, John Browning, Arturo Toscanini, Serge Koussevitzky, and Bruno Walter, to name only a few. Also, they will discover that Barber was possibly the only American composer of the twentieth century who was able to earn his living entirely by composing; he did not need to teach or lecture.

Samuel Barber was born at West Chester, Pennsylvania, on March 9, 1910. Although his father was a physician, music was a part of his early life: his mother was a pianist and her sister was the noted contralto Louise Homer. His parents did not particularly encourage his musical interest, preferring instead that he assume a more active role in athletics. At an early age, his own determination was expressed in a letter to his mother: "I was meant to be a composer, and will be, I'm sure...Don't ask me to try to forget this and go and play football, Please!"

Parental recognition of his desires came when he was six and began studying piano with William Hatton Green, a former pupil of Leschetizky. At ten he attempted his first opera, The Rose Tree. Only the first act was completed because the cook, Annie Sullivan Brosius Noble, who was writing the libretto, left the family employment. Manuscripts of several early songs from this period may be found in the Library of the Chester County Historical Society in West Chester, Pennsylvania. In high school, Barber organized an orchestra and played the organ at the Westminster Church. In 1923 his song, Thy Will Be Done, a revised edition of The Wanderer, composed in 1920, was first sung by Mrs. Fred Dutt. At about this time, he played for the director of the Peabody Conservatory of Music in Baltimore, Harold Randolph, who was impressed and encouraged him to apply for admission to the then new Curtis Institute of Music in Philadelphia. While still in high school, Barber became a charter student at Curtis (1924), attending both schools concurrently until his high school graduation in 1926. He remained at Curtis eight years, studying piano with Isabelle Vengerova, composition with Rosario Scalero, and voice with Emilio de Gogorza.

A program devoted entirely to Barber's songs was presented at his home on April 25, 1926. The program for this event may be found in the jacket notes to the New World Records NW 229 album in the series Recorded Anthology of American Music. During the period 1927-1928, he wrote a set of songs to texts of A. E. Housman and James Stephens; these later were published as his Songs, op. 2. His Violin sonata, never published, won for him in 1928 the prestigious Bearns Prize of $1200.00. Dover Beach, for soprano and string quartet, set to a poem by Matthew Arnold, was composed in 1931 and received its New York premiere in 1931 in a recital by Rose Bampton and the New York String Quartet. His own version of this work, recorded with the Curtis String Quartet, was made May 13, 1935, and issued as a 78 rpm on Victor 8998. It has long been a collector's item as it represents the only appearance of Samuel Barber as a vocalist on records. He received a second Bearns Prize for his Overture to "The School for Scandal," which had its premiere in Philadelphia in 1933 and was the first of his works to receive public attention. During this same year he completed work on his Music For a Scene from Shelley, based on Shelley's Prometheus Unbound. It was introduced in 1935 by the New York Philharmonic Orchestra conducted by Werner Janssen.

While at Curtis, Barber was introduced to Gian-Carlo Menotti, who had come to the Institute from Italy and spoke no English. He was fluent in French, and as Samuel Barber used French with ease, it was natural that they would become close friends, a friendship that lasted for the rest of Barber's life. They worked together as composer and librettist and as composer and director, and until 1974 they maintained a home, Capricorn, at Mt. Kisco, New York, where much of their most productive work was done.

The money from the first Bearns Prize made it possible for Barber to travel to Europe. On this voyage, made on the liner De Grasse, he played the piano to earn a little extra money. It is noted that he performed a Brahms Cello Sonata with David Freed. In Europe, he traveled in France and Austria. While visiting Salzburg, he heard a performance of <u>Parsifal</u> and later described the work as a "melée of sickening chords hiding under a masque of pseudo religion." In the summer of 1932, Barber and Menotti took a nine-day walking tour from Innsbruck to Lake Como. During that time, Barber started work on the <u>Violoncello Sonata</u>. Two weeks after arriving at Menotti's home at Cadegliano, he had finished the first movement and had begun the scherzo. It was completed in November after he had returned to the United States; the <u>Sonata</u> won for him the the American Prix de Rome. He next received a Pulitzer Traveling Scholarship, which made another trip to Europe possible. He settled in Rome at the American Academy and completed work on his first symphony, which had its premiere in Rome in 1936 with the Augusteo Orchestra conducted by Bernardino Molinari. The American premiere followed the next month with the Cleveland Orchestra conducted by Artur Rodzinski. It was also in 1936 that Barber received the Pulitzer Traveling Scholarship a second time. In the summer of 1937, Rodzinski conducted the symphony at the Salzburg Festival, the first time an American symphony had been performed at this prestigious festival. The work was revised in 1942, the new version receiving its premiere in 1944 with Bruno Walter conducting the New York Philharmonic.

While in Italy, Barber and Menotti visited Arturo Toscanini, who reminisced about Barber's aunt, Louise Homer, and her singing in Gluck's <u>Orfeo</u>. This contact proved valuable, for on November 5, 1938, Arturo Toscanini conducted the NBC Symphony Orchestra in the premiere of two new works by Samuel Barber: his first <u>Essay for Orchestra</u> and the <u>Adagio for Strings</u>. This performance stirred great controversy in musical circles, and the letters column in the <u>New York Times</u> was filled for several weeks with pro and con arguments on the relative merits of the Barber works. Regardless of the controversy, the <u>Adagio for Strings</u>, arranged from the second movement of his <u>String Quartet</u>, has become one of the most popular works in the string ensemble repertoire. Some will remember that it was played on April 14, 1945, immediately after the official announcement of the death of President Roosevelt. Others will recall it as part of the score for the recent motion picture, <u>The Elephant Man</u>. In both the <u>Adagio</u> and the first <u>Essay</u>, lyricism and attention to melody and structure were of utmost importance and simplicity was preferred to complexity of any kind. This was to be characteristic of many of Barber's works. In his first <u>Essay</u>, moreover, Barber "borrowed a literary form for music to suggest an architectonic structure in which a thought is projected at the opening and then permitted to develop to a logical conclusion in the same way that a central thought unfolds in an essay."

It has been remarked that Barber made his living by composing and that he was not required to teach or lecture. Nevertheless, he did join the faculty of the Curtis Institute of Music in 1939. He taught conducting and or-

5

chestration and also conducted a choir. During this time, Barber was commissioned by industrialist Samuel Fels to compose a _Violin Concerto_ for violinist Iso Briselli. When Briselli saw the score, he said that the final movement, a moto perpetuo, was unplayable, and Fels refused to pay Barber the $500 still outstanding on the commission. The story is told in some detail that Herbert Baumel, violinist and faculty member of the Curtis Institute of Music, was asked if he could perform the concerto. After practicing it several hours, he returned to Curtis and performed it for Barber, Menotti, and others in Joseph Hoffmann's studio. Barber was then able to claim the rest of his commission. The _Violin Concerto_ was premiered by violinist Albert Spalding and the Philadelphia Orchestra, with Eugene Ormandy conducting, on February 7, 1941. Later it was to win one of two $3000 awards for original works by contemporary composers played by the Philadelphia Orchestra during the 1957-58 season. The winning compositions were selected by the first chair players of the Orchestra. One of the two works was Barber's _Violin Concerto_; his co-recipient of the award was Arthur Honegger.

In 1943, Barber was inducted into the Army and assigned a clerical position, due to his limited service classification. Although never specifically identified by name, Barber became a mild _cause célèbre_ when Lawrence Tibbett stated that the Army had refused a "distinguished young composer" permission to write a special American musical greeting to the Russian people. A short time later, Barber was transferred to the Air Force. One of his earliest wartime efforts was _Commando March_, scored for band. After this, he was comissioned to write a new symphony. To facilitate the writing, Barber was taken on flights and shown air force equipment and its uses. The result was his _Symphony No. 2_, op. 19, which in its original form employed electronic sounds such as he had been exposed to while touring from base to base. The first performance of the second symphony was given in 1944, with Serge Koussevitzky conducting the Boston Symphony Orchestra. A week later it was transmitted throughout the world by short wave radio under the auspices of the Office of War Information. Barber was never satisfied with this work, and in 1947 it was revised extensively and all the programmatic flight references were removed. The new version was premiered in January 1948 with the Philadelphia Orchestra under the baton of Alexander Hilsberg. Several years later, still not satisfied with the symphony, even in its revised form, Barber went with Hans Heinsheimer to the warehouse of G. Schirmer and together they destroyed all copies of the work. Robert Layton, the British critic for _Gramophone_, when he heard about this, called it a "kind of artistic infanticide."

In 1945, the year of his piano suite entitled _Excursions_, Barber completed his military service and returned to Capricorn. His _Violoncello Concerto_ received its premiere in 1946 with soloist Raya Garbousova and the Boston

Symphony Orchestra under Koussevitzky. The work had been commissioned by John Nicholas and Anne Brown of Providence, Rhode Island, and was created with Miss Garbousova in mind. Even though the Concerto was awarded the fifth annual New York Music Critics' Circle award, there was reluctance on the part of record companies to record this work. When Barber received an offer from Decca of London to record the work with Zara Nelsova as cellist, he gladly accepted, despite a stipulation that he conduct the orchestra. A preview performance was given in Copenhagen in 1950 and the work was later recorded in London.

Conducting was not a new experience to Barber. He had studied with Fritz Reiner (who considered him untalented as a conductor) and also in Vienna in 1933. On January 4, 1934, he had made his conducting debut with a program consisting of works by Corelli, Vivaldi, Haydn, Sibelius, and Menotti.

The years after the war were most productive. For Martha Graham he created a ballet, Medea, originally called The Serpent Heart but later renamed Cave of the Heart. This work had been commissioned by the Alice M. Ditson Fund of Columbia University for Martha Graham and her dancers, and its premiere was given May 10, 1946. Two orchestral works emerged from this ballet: the Medea Suite, which was introduced by Eugene Ormandy and the Philadelphia Orchestra in December 1947, and later Medea's Meditation and Dance of Vengeance, which was first performed by the New York Philharmonic Orchestra with Dimitri Mitropoulos conducting in February 1956.

Also during this period, soprano Eleanor Steber commissioned Barber to write a work for her, and his choice of text was the last part of an autobiographical essay by James Agee. The result, Knoxville: Summer of 1915, was premiered April 9, 1948, in Boston, with Eleanor Steber and the Boston Symphony Orchestra under Serge Koussevitzky. The work has had a lasting popularity and has been recorded numerous times, frequently appearing on vocal recitals.

A particularly significant work was the Piano Sonata, commissioned by the League of Composers with funds provided by Richard Rodgers and Irving Berlin. The premiere was entrusted to Vladimir Horowitz in Havana, Cuba, on December 9, 1949. An unofficial United States premiere was given at the Trustees Room of G. Schirmer on January 5, 1950 before a select group of invited guests, again with Horowitz at the keyboard. The first public performance in the United States, also by Horowitz, was given at Carnegie Hall on January 23, 1950. The sonata gained instant popularity and soon became a work that any aspiring young pianist had to include in his or her repertoire.

Not all of Barber's time was spent at Capricorn, for these were years of travel too. He had made trips to Europe in 1945 and again in 1948 and 1949. In 1950-51, he performed his own works in Denmark, Italy, and Germany. In Frankfurt and Berlin, for instance, he conducted three movements from Medea, the Violin Concerto, the Adagio for

<u>Strings</u>, and the <u>Second</u> <u>Symphony</u>.

One of Barber's major compositions in the early 1950s was <u>Hermit</u> <u>Songs</u> (1952-53), a group of songs commissioned by the Elizabeth Sprague Coolidge Foundation for the Founder's Day Concert and drawn from Irish texts of anonymous monks and scholars of the eighth to thirteenth centuries. These received an invitational premiere with soprano Leontyne Price and Samuel Barber at the Library of Congress on October 30, 1953; in November, 1954, the same artists offered the first public performance in New York City's Town Hall. The next month saw the premiere of <u>Prayers</u> <u>of</u> <u>Kierkegaard</u>, a work for mixed chorus, soprano soloist, and orchestra based on the writings of the Danish philosopher Søren Kierkegaard. It was presented by the Boston Symphony Orchestra, Charles Münch, conductor, and once more with Leontyne Price as soloist.

By now, Barber's style was well established. He combined strong lyrical and emotional elements with modern harmonies and rhythms. Critic Arthur Cohn has remarked, "Barber is never academic; he is merely concerned with earlier times, though he is of the twentieth century."

One area of composition that Barber had not yet attempted was opera. This would have seemed natural for him, particularly in view of his interest in vocal composition. Several times it appeared that an opera project was underway, but the great point of difficulty always seemed to center around the libretto. Several discussions about such projects had been held with Thornton Wilder, Stephen Spender, and Dylan Thomas, but no story suitable to Barber could be found. Edward Johnson of the Metropolitan Opera was interested, as was the Koussevitzky Foundation, but the problem of a suitable libretto remained a basic obstacle. Ironically, the librettist would be found in his own home, and finally it was announced that Menotti would write the text for a four-act opera. The Metropolitan for a long time had thought of Samuel Barber as a logical person to compose an American opera, and so it was that <u>Vanessa</u> came to the stage of the Met on the night of January 15, 1958. Instead of an opera with an American setting, <u>Vanessa</u> was set in a "northern country," presumably somewhere in Scandinavia. The opera won an enthusiastic reception by the audiences, but the critics were mixed in their reviews. The major disappointment seemed to be in Barber's choice of subject: why had he not picked an American locale and subject matter? Some critics even quibbled about the title, <u>Vanessa</u>, when quite plainly the most sympathetic character was Erika. Nevertheless, the opera was honored with a Pulitzer Prize. It was also scheduled for a performance at the Salzburg Festival in the Summer of 1958, the first American opera to be presented at this prestigious international festival. Although it was popular with the public, the critics, especially those from Germany and Austria, were unanimous in their frequently vitriolic criticism. Possibly <u>Vanessa</u> elicited a certain hostility of the European intelligentsia to American music. Barber reworked the opera, tightening it up a bit, but somehow it never really established a firm hold on the public. Shortly afterward, in May 1958, Barber was awarded the Henry Hadley Medal for American Composers and Conductors, and in 1959, he received an honorary doctorate from Harvard University.

A second Barber-Menotti collaboration was A Hand of Bridge, a nine-minute chamber opera. This work brings together two married couples playing a hand of bridge. In a series of asides, they reveal their true characters and the often brutal, grasping nature of their relationships. It had its premiere at Menotti's Festival of Two Worlds, in Spoleto, Italy, on June 17, 1959 and was presented in the United States for the first time on April 6, 1960. Next came Toccata Festiva, written for the inauguration of a new organ at the Philadelphia Academy of Music. It was later recorded by E. Power Biggs on the Columbia label.

The year 1962 was important for two chief reasons. Samuel Barber was invited to the Soviet Union to address the Biennial Congress of Soviet Composers, held in Moscow, March 26-31. He also met with Premier Khrushchev, and, in a friendly and constructive conversation, Mr. Barber remarked that he was pleased and surprised to find a number of his works being performed in the Soviet Union but disappointed that he did not receive the royalties due him from such performances. The Premier agreed that he was certainly entitled to his royalties and from that time on they were paid; Barber was one of few foreign composers to receive royalties from the Soviet Union. The second important event of the year was the premiere of his Piano Concerto, written on commission to celebrate the 100th anniversary of Barber's publisher, G. Schirmer. The work had its first performance during the opening week of New York's Lincoln Center for the Performing Arts on September 24, 1962, whereupon it achieved immediate popularity. John Browning was the pianist and the Boston Symphony orchestra was conducted by Erich Leinsdorf. In the Spring of 1965, George Szell featured the Piano Concerto in a European tour of the Cleveland Orchestra; John Browning was the soloist at each concert. The Piano Concerto won Barber his second Pulitzer Prize, and in May 1964 it received the New York Music Critics' Circle Award for an orchestral composition for the musical seasons of 1962-63 and 1963-64.

A commission from the New York Philharmonic soon followed, resulting in Andromache's Farewell, the premiere of which was presented on April 4, 1963, at Lincoln Center with Martina Arroyo, soprano, and the New York Philharmonic Orchestra under Thomas Schippers. It was a most successful performance, which added even more luster to the reputation Barber had been accumulating for his vocal compositions.

At this same time, a new opera house was rising at Lincoln Center to replace the aging Metropolitan Opera House. A natural concern, of course, revolved around the choice of the first opera to open this most modern of opera houses. Were a work in the standard repertoire deemed unsuitable, who would be commissioned to compose a new one? There seemed little doubt that the inaugural season would have to open with a new American opera, and the logical person to compose it was Samuel Barber. Many proposals were discussed, but Barber knew only that it had to feature Leontyne Price. It was finally decided that Antony and Cleopatra, based on Shakespeare's play of the same title, would be the new opening opera. Barber worked on the opera for two years, and it received its premiere, amongst much glitter and glamour, on the evening of September 16, 1966. There are indications that Barber had some fears about the work, not necessarily about the music, but rather the production. This was a new opera house, the most modern in the world, with all the mechanical gadgetry possible to assemble under one roof. The temptation was too much, and Franco Zeffirelli, the director and designer, became carried away with the spectacularly extravagant use of such equipment and the massing of people on stage. The costumes were lavish, but in many cases totally unsuitable. Leontyne Price was described by one critic as looking like Sitting Bull. With so much glamour in the audience and so much continually happening on stage, the music assumed less prominence than anything else. The reviews were most damning, with a good deal of the criticism heaped upon the Metropolitan itself and particularly on Zeffirelli.

The Alcoa Foundation commissioned Barber to write a work for the opening of Pittsburgh's Heinz Hall in 1971. The result was Fadograph of a Yestern Scene, the title derived from a line in James Joyce's Finnegan's Wake. William Steinberg conducted the Pittsburgh Symphony Orchestra in the first performance, which took place in Heinz Hall on September 10, 1971.

After the disappointment of Antony and Cleopatra, Barber spent some time abroad. In 1973 he made one of the major decisions of his life: to sell Capricorn. After this, he often described himself as homeless, although he maintained an apartment in New York City. Urban life had never appealed to him, and it is certain that he was never really happy there. A commission from the Chamber Music Society of Lincoln Center in New York was the creative urge he needed at this time, and the result was his Four Songs, op. 45. The premiere was scheduled for 1973, but the indisposition of the soloist, Dietrich Fischer-Dieskau, delayed the premiere until April 30, 1974.

On the morning of November 7, 1974, fire gutted the Metropolitan Opera warehouse, destroying costumes for 41 productions, including all those for Vanessa and Antony and Cleopatra. In this same year Barber and Menotti spent a great deal of time reworking Antony and Cleopatra. More than an hour of the opera was removed from the original and several additions were made. This revised version had its premiere at the Juilliard Theatre on February 6, 1975, in a production by the Juilliard American Opera Company. The production was done with simplicity and this time the costumes were beautiful but not exaggerated. Critical reception was favorable, but the work was still not totally successful. On June 28 and 29 of the same year, the Spoleto Festival honored Barber with a number of programs made up from his works. His opera Vanessa had had a more successful history, having been produced at Spoleto in 1961, in Washington in 1963, and again at the Metropolitan in 1965. In 1975 it was presented at Indiana University and in 1978 at the Spoleto Festival, U.S.A. at Charleston, South Carolina. A filmed version of this production was shown over PBS television on January 31, 1979. In the fall of 1979, Vanessa was given by the Kansas City Lyric Opera.

Barber continued to compose orchestral works and his Third Essay, op. 47, received its first performance on September 14, 1978, on a commission from the Merlin Foundation. According to a Billboard survey, it was the most-performed orchestral work by a living composer during the 1979-80 symphony season.

Later, in 1979, the Girard Bank of Philadelphia commissioned The Lovers, for baritone, chorus, and orchestra. The Bank's conservative Board of Directors at first objected to the choice of a work by the Chilean poet Pablo Neruda, an avowed Communist. The objection seemed to be based more on the content of the love poems than on the politics of the poet. Samuel Barber is reported to have asked the Board if love affairs did not occur in Philadelphia! One can be sure there must have been a twinkle in his eye as he asked the question. The Board agreed that such things did happen in Philadelphia and approved the commission. The premiere was given on September 22, 1980, by the Philadelphia Orchestra under the baton of Eugene Ormandy, with Tom Krause, baritone, and the Temple University Choirs. This was the same year that Pablo Neruda won the Nobel Prize.

On January 13, 1980, the Chamber Music Society of New York celebrated, somewhat prematurely, Barber's seventieth birthday by performing his Summer Music for wind octet. On Barber's actual date of birth (March 9), the Curtis Institute of Music presented two all-Barber programs. On this occasion, Efrem Zimbalist, Jr., remarked: "Sam was born with a song in his heart. We live by change, yet some things endure. Samuel Barber is acclaimed throughout the world today. We look forward to more to come from him. With lifted glass let us proclaim, Happy birthday, Sam!" A few days later he was honored by Rosalyn Carter, wife of the President, with the Wolf Trap Award, presented at the White House. In July an all-Barber program was presented in London, and on August 24th he was presented the Mac-Dowell medal. Throughout the year Barber's music was performed across the country in honor of his birthday.

Barber's last composition, dating from 1978, was an eight-minute piece for oboe and string orchestra completed in short score. It had originally been intended to form the middle movement of an oboe concerto, commissioned by the New York Philharmonic for its own members to perform. The outer movements were never written. Charles Turner,

11

Barber's pupil and friend, completely orchestrated the inner movement. It was premiered on December 17, 1981 as the <u>Canzonetta</u>, op. 48, by the New York Philharmonic under conductor Zubin Mehta at Lincoln Center with Harold Gomberg, the orchestra's first oboist from 1943 to 1977, as soloist.

Barber suffered from cancer the last several years of his life and composition became increasingly difficult. After a period of hospitalization, he was released on January 18, 1981, and returned to his apartment in New York City. He died there five days later, January 23, 1981.

A memorial service was held for Barber on February 9, 1981, at St. Bartholomew's Church in New York City. Close friends of the composer attended and a program of Barber's works was presented. Some of those performing had worked with Barber over the years and included Leontyne Price, Rosalind Elias, Esther Hinds, and John Browning. The Reverend Thomas D. Bowers conducted the service.

Barber's style is characterized by a romantic lyricism. While his melodies are chiefly tonal, his later works employ considerable chromaticism, sometimes bordering on atonality. His harmonic textures often display polytonality, and his contrapuntal scores exhibit significant canonic and fugal elements. His writing for solo instruments is sometimes idiomatic but always requires considerable virtuosity. Three years after his death his music still appears frequently on programs from coast to coast and abroad. What is the secret? Perhaps it is a very simple one: to the average concert-goer, his music is listenable, it has beauty and can be understood. We can still be moved by <u>Knoxville, Summer of 1915</u>, and probably Samuel Barber would ask no more than this.

WORKS AND PERFORMANCES

"See" references, e.g., <u>See</u>: B61d, identify citations in the "Bibliography" section.

OPERAS

W1. **ANTONY AND CLEOPATRA, OP. 40.** (1965-66; revised 1975; Schirmer; full evening; Library of Congress has (a) full score dated August 29, 1966, pencil, irregular paging and (b) piano-vocal score, pencil, a few pages bearing excerpts taken from proof sheets on which the composer made extensive corrections) <u>See</u>: B1c, B1d, B1n, B1w, B1cc, B1qq

Opera in three acts, revised 1975.
Libretto by Franco Zeffirelli based on Shakespeare's play of the same title; revised version libretto by Gian-Carlo Menotti.
3-3-2-3; 4-3-3-1; timp; perc, hp, pno, cel, str.
Commissioned by the Metropolitan Opera Association under a grant from the Ford Foundation.

<u>Premiere</u>

W1a. 1966 (Sep 16) [original version]: New York; Metropolitan Opera House; Cleopatra: Leontyne Price; Antony: Justino Diaz; Enobarbus: Ezio Flagello; Caesar Octavius: Jess Thomas; Maecenas: Russell Christopher; Agrippa: John Macurdy; Mardian: Andrea Velis; Charmian: Rosalind Elias; Octavia: Mary Ellen Pracht; Lepidus: Robert Nagy; Soothsayer: Lorenzo Alvary; Metropolitan Opera Orchestra; Thomas Schippers, conductor; Kurt Adler, chorus master; Franco Zeffirelli, director and designer; Alvin Ailey, choreographer. See: B1a, B1b, B1e, B1f, B1g, B1h, B1j, B1k, B1l, B1m, B1o, B1p, B1q, B1r, B1s, B1t, B1u, B1y, B1z, B1bb, B1dd, B1ff, B1gg, B1hh, B1ii, B1jj, B1kk, B1ll, B1nn, B1rr, B1tt, B1vv, B1xx, B1yy, B1aaa, B1bbb

W1b.   1975 (Feb 6-7, 9-10) [revised version]: New York; Juilliard Theatre; Juilliard American Opera Company; Cleopatra: Esther Hinds; Antony: Ronald Hedlund; Enobarbus: Joseph McKee; Caesar Octavius: Enoch Sherman; Agrippa: Albert DeRuiter; Charmian: Faith Esham; Octavia: Linda Burt; James Conlon, conductor; staged by Gian-Carlo Menotti. See: B1l, B1v, B1x, B1aa, B1ee, B1oo, B1pp, B1ww, B1zz

Other Selected Performances

W1c.   1980 (Sep 23): Paris; Radio France; Théâtre des Champs Elysées; Cleopatra: Mary Shearer; Antony: Norman Phillips; Caesar Octavius: Harry Theyard; also with Patricia Miller, Joyce Castle, and John Paul Bogart; Jean-Pierre Marty, conductor [revised version]

W1d.   1982 (Mar 27): London; Logan Hall; Abbey Opera; Cleopatra: Susan Bingemann; Caesar Octavius: Donald Stephenson; Antony: David Wilson-Johnson (Camden Festival) [concert performance of revised version] See: B1uu

W1e.   1983 (May 28-30, June 4): Charleston, S.C.; Gaillard Municipal Auditorium; Cleopatra: Esther Hinds; Antony: Jeffrey Wells; Edobardus: Eric Halfvarson; Caesar Octavius: Robert Grayson; Messenger: Steven Cole; Eros: David Hickox; Iras: Jane Bunnell; Charmian: Kathryn Cowdrick; Maecenas: Mark Cleveland; Agrippa: Charles Damsel; Dolabella: David Hamilton; Thidias: Kent Weaver; Senator: Ian Clark; Alexas: Dale Stine; Soothsayer: Philip Skinner; First Guard: Robert Swensen; Second Guard: Charles Damsel; Third Guard: David Hamilton; Fourth Guard: Philip Skinner; First Soldier: Rob Phillips; Second Soldier: Alan Arak; Soldier of Caesar: Robert Swensen; Rustic: Philip Skinner; Guardsman: David Dik; Zack Brown, sets; directed by Gian-Carlo Menotti; Westminster Choir; Joseph Flummerfelt, chorus master; Spoleto Festival Orchestra; Christian Badea, conductor; Robert Hart Baker, assistant conductor (Spoleto Festival USA) [revised version]

W1f.   1983 (Jun 25, 28, Jul 1, 3, 7, 9): Spoleto, Italy; Cleopatra: Esther Hinds; Caesar Octavius: Robert

Grayson; Antony: Jeffrey Wells; Enobarbus: Eric
Halfvarson [for remainder of cast, see W1e]
Christian Badea, conductor (Spoleto Festival of
Two Worlds) [revised version] See: B1ss

W2. **ANTONY AND CLEOPATRA. ON THE DEATH OF ANTONY.** (1968;
Schirmer)

For three-part chorus of women's voices and piano,
arranged by the composer.
Text by Shakespeare.

W3. **ANTONY AND CLEOPATRA.   ON THE DEATH OF CLEOPATRA.**
(1968; Schirmer)

For four-part chorus of mixed voices and piano, arranged by the composer.
Text by Shakespeare.

W4. **ANTONY AND CLEOPATRA. TWO SCENES.** (1965-66; Schirmer;
16 min.; Library of Congress has manuscript to "Give
Us Some Music," Act 1, Scene 4, full score, pencil,
incomplete; the 18 pages are reproductions of holograph with holograph annotations; this excerpt, with
piano acc., published 1968 by G. Schirmer in Samuel
Barber's "Music for Soprano and Orchestra.")

Originally for soprano and orchestra. 3-3-3-3; 4-3-3-
1; timp,perc,2 hp,pno,str.
Arrangement for soprano and piano also available.
Contents: Give Me Some Music -- Give Me My Robe
(Death of Cleopatra).

Premiere

W4a.   1968 (Jun 23): Columbia, Md.; Merriweather Post
Pavilion; Cleopatra: Ella Lee; National Symphony
Orchestra; Howard Mitchell, conductor (Fourth
Inter-American Music Festival) See: B4e

Other Selected Performances

W4b.   1970 (Feb 9-10): Seattle; Opera House; Leontyne
Price, soprano; Seattle Symphony Orchestra; Mil-
ton Katims, conductor [Give Me My Robe (Death of
Cleopatra) only]

W4c.   1971 (Apr 17-18): Cincinnati; Music Hall; Beverly
Wolff, mezzo-soprano; Chicago Symphony Orchestra;
Thomas Schippers, conductor [Give Me My Robe
(Death of Cleopatra) only] See: B4h

W4d.　1971 (Dec 9): New York; Lincoln Center for the Performing Arts; Philharmonic Hall; Martina Arroyo, soprano; New York Philharmonic Orchestra; Leonard Bernstein, conductor. See: B4c, B4i

DEATH OF CLEOPATRA　　See:　ANTONY AND CLEOPATRA. TWO SCENES.

DO NOT UTTER A WORD See:　VANESSA. DO NOT UTTER A WORD.

GIVE ME MY ROBE (Death of Cleopatra)　　See:　ANTONY AND CLEOPATRA. TWO SCENES.

GIVE ME SOME MUSIC See: ANTONY AND CLEOPATRA. TWO SCENES.

W5. **A HAND OF BRIDGE, OP. 35.**　(1958; Schirmer; 9 min.; Library of Congress has (a) pencil score, 1 p.l., 51 [i.e. 53] p., (b) piano-vocal score, pencil, [1], 17 p., and (c) first draft, piano-vocal score, pencil, 30 p.) See: B5e, B5i

For four solo voices and chamber orchestra.
1-1-1-1; 0-1-0-0; perc (1 player, 2 or 3 players preferable), pno, str (1-1-1-1-1)
Libretto by Gian-Carlo Menotti.

Premiere

W5a.　1959 (Jun 17): Spoleto, Italy; Festival of Two Worlds.

Other Selected Performances

W5b.　1960 (Apr 6): New York; Mannes College of Music; Fashion Institute of Technology Auditorium; David: John Fiorito; Geraldine: Donna Murray Porteous; Bill: Stanley Storch; Sally: Jean Stawski; Opera Production Workshops and Orchestra of the Mannes College of Music; Carl Bamberger, conductor (U.S. premiere) See: B5a, B5h

W5c.　1970 (Apr 5): Los Angeles; Immaculate Heart College; Immaculate Heart College Opera Workshop; soloists Stella Lopez, Nelda Nelson, Joseph Gole, and Roger Winnel; staging by Pat Madsen; sets by Thurston James; Robert Cole, cond. See: B5d

W5d.　1982 (Nov 18): Boston; Boston University; Concert Hall; Warren George Wilson, music director.

INTERMEZZO _See_: VANESSA. INTERMEZZO.

MUST THE WINTER COME SO SOON _See_: VANESSA. MUST THE
WINTER COME SO SOON.

QUINTET FROM VANESSA, ACT III, SCENE II _See_: VANES-
SA. QUINTET, ACT III, SCENE II.

W6. **THE ROSE TREE.** (1920; incomplete (only first act fin-
ished and unpublished; manuscript for "Gypsy Dance,"
"Gypsy Song," "Dialogue for Act I, Scene 1," and
"Serenade for Act I, Scene 2" at Chester County
Historical Society, West Chester, Pa.))

Written when Barber was ten years old.
Libretto by Annie Sullivan Brosius Noble, the family's Irish cook, left unfinished when Mrs. Noble
left the Barber kitchen.

UNDER THE WILLOW TREE _See_: VANESSA. UNDER THE WILLOW
TREE.

W7. **VANESSA, OP. 32.** (1957; Schirmer; full evening; Library of Congress has manuscript material: (a) full
score, pencil, 1 p.l., 5 p., 6-476 numb. l., leaf 247
numbered twice, 2 extra leaves inserted between 245
and 246; (b) piano-vocal score, pencil, [218] p.; (c)
pencil sketcches, [345] p.; (d) reproduction of copyist's piano-vocal score (247 p.) with composer's
holograph corrections and 2 leaves of holograph data;
(e) first draft of libretto (40 l., typed) with
holograph corrections and changes by both composer
and librettist) _See_: B7e, B7f, B7h, B7i, B7m, B7o,
B7p, B7s, B7ee, B7hh, B7rr, B7ddd, B7ggg, B7hhh,
B7kkk, B7ppp, B7bbbb, B7pppp, B7rrrr, B7ccccc

Opera in three acts.
Libretto by Gian-Carlo Menotti.
3-3-3-2; 4-3-3-1; timp, perc, hp, str.
Funds provided by Francis Goelet Foundation.
Received the 1958 Pulitzer Prize in Music.

Premiere

W7a. 1958 (Jan 15): New York; Metropolitan Opera House;
Vanessa: Eleanor Steber; Anatol: Nicolai Gedda;
Erika: Rosalind Elias; Old Doctor: Giorgio Tozzi;
Old Baroness: Regina Resnik; Major-Domo: George
Cehanovsky; Footman: Robert Nagy; Metropolitan
Opera Orchestra; Dimitri Mitropoulos, conductor;

17

Kurt Adler, chorus master; Zachary Solov, choreo-
grapher; Cecil Beaton, sets and costumes; staged
by Gian-Carlo Menotti. See: B7b, B7c, B7g, B7k,
B7q, B7r, B7y, B7z, B7aa, B7mm, B7pp, B7xx,
B7ccc, B7eee, B7mmm, B7ooo, B7uuu, B7xxx, B7yyy,
B7aaaa, B7ffff, B7gggg, B7jjjj, B7llll, B7mmmm,
B7qqqq, B7ssss, B7tttt, B7xxxx, B7zzzz, B7aaaaa

Other Selected Performances

W7b.   1958 (Feb 11): Philadelphia; Academy of Music; same
        cast as in W7a above.

W7c.   1958 (Aug 16, 22, 26): Salzburg; Festspielhaus;
        Vanessa: Eleanor Steber; Anatol: Nicolai Gedda;
        Erika: Rosalind Elias; Old Doctor: Giorgio Tozzi;
        Old Baroness: Ira Malaniuk; Nicholas: Alois Per-
        nerstorfer; Servant: Norman Foster; Vienna Phil-
        harmonic Orchestra and Chorus; Ballet of the
        Vienna State Opera; Dimitri Mitropoulos, conduc-
        tor (Salzburg Festival) See: B7j, B7n, B7w,
        B7gg, B7kk, B7mm, B7nn, B7ss, B7aaa, B7bbb,
        B7nnn, B7ttt, B7www, B7nnnn, B7vvvv, B7wwww

W7d.   1959 (Jan 7-8): New York; Metropolitan Opera House;
        same cast as in W7a above. See: B7iiii, B7kkkk

W7e.   1961 (Jun 15): Spoleto, Italy; Vanessa: Ivana Tosi-
        ni; Anatol: Alvino Misciano; Erika: Mietta Sig-
        hele; Old Doctor: Giulio Bardi; Grandmother:
        Giovanna Fioroni; Major-Domo: Harold Lara; Chorus
        of the Liceo Morlacchi of Perugia; Rolando Masel-
        li, chorus master; Werner Torkanowsky, conductor
        (for this production, the text was translated
        into Italian by Fedele D'Amico; Barber changed
        the setting to the Hudson River, so "Baroness"
        was inappropriate and was renamed "Grandmother")
        (4th Festival of Two Worlds) See: B7a, B7ff,
        B7iii, B7yyyy, B7bbbbb

W7f.   1963 (Nov 9): Washington, D.C.: Howard University;
        Cramton Auditorium; Washington Opera Society;
        Vanessa: Francesca Roberto; Anatol: Frank Porre-
        ta; Erika: Beverly Wolff; Old Doctor: John Rear-
        don; Footman: Lee Cass; National Symphony Orches-
        tra; Paul Callaway, conductor; Richard Pearlman,
        director; Ben Schecter, sets and costumes; James
        D. Waring, lighting. See: B7v, B7bb

W7g.   1965 (Mar 13): New York; Metropolitan Opera House;
        Vanessa: Mary Costa; Anatol: John Alexander;
        Erika: Rosalind Elias; Old Doctor: Giorgio Tozzi;
        Old Baroness: Blanche Thebom; Footman: Arthur
        Graham; Nicholas: Russell Christopher; William
        Steinberg, conductor (performance repeated and

broadcast over the Texaco-Metropolitan Opera Radio Network on April 3, 1965) See: B7x, B7zz, B7cccc, B7uuuu

W7h. 1975 (Mar 1): Bloomington; University of Indiana; Indiana University Opera Theater; Vanessa: Kathryn Montgomery; Anatol: Michael Ballam; Erika: Patricia Johnson Gilliland; Old Doctor: Scott Reeve; Old Baroness: Veronica August; Tibor Kozma, conductor [repeated March 8 and 15 with alternate casts] See: B7tt

W7i. 1978 (Jun 2, 4): Charleston, S.C.; Gaillard Municipal Auditorium; Spoleto USA; Vanessa: Johanna Meier; Anatol: Henry Price; Erika: Katherine Ciesinski; Old Doctor: Irwin Densen; Grandmother: Alice Garrott; Christopher Keene, conductor; Pasquale Grossi, sets; staged by Gian-Carlo Menotti (Spoleto Festival USA) See: B7cc, B7ll, B7oo, B7uu, B7lll, B7sss, B7vvv, B7zzz, B7hhhh

W7j. 1979 (Jan 31): Charleston, S.C.; PBS Television Network; taped live during the final performance of the 1978 Spoleto USA Festival; see W7i for further details. See: B7fff, B7qqq

W7k. 1979 (Oct 16, 18, 20, 24, 26): Kansas City, Missouri; Kansas City Lyric Opera; Vanessa: Elizabeth Volkman; Anatol: Barry Busse; Erika: Brenda Boozer; Old Doctor: J.B. Davis; Old Baroness: Jocelyn Wilkes; Russell Patterson, conductor; James Goolsby, director; Harold Mack, designer. See: B7ii, B7jj

W8. VANESSA. DO NOT UTTER A WORD. (1964, c1957; Schirmer)

For voice and piano.

W9. VANESSA. INTERMEZZO. (1957; Schirmer)

3-3-3-2; 4-2-3-1; timp,perc,hp,str.

Premiere

W9a. 1958 (Mar 15): New York; Carnegie Hall; New York Philharmonic Orchestra; André Kostelanetz, conductor. See: B9c

W10. VANESSA. MUST THE WINTER COME SO SOON. (195-?; Schirmer)

For voice and piano.

Selected Performances

W10a.   1960 (Dec 2): New York; Carnegie Recital Hall;
        Barbara Metropole, mezzo-soprano; David Stimer,
        piano.

W10b.   1982 (Oct 17): West Chester, Pa.; West Chester
        State College; Swope Hall; Leslie Ann Belcher,
        soprano; Robert Dodd Greene, piano.

W11. **VANESSA. QUINTET, ACT III, SCENE II** (1957; Schirmer)

Selected Performances

W11a.   1981 (Feb 9): New York; St. Bartholomew's Church;
        Marilyn Zschau, soprano; Rosalind Elias and
        Alice Garrott, mezzo-sopranos; John Aler, tenor;
        Irwin Densen, bass-baritone; John Browning,
        piano (part of program for the memorial services
        honoring Samuel Barber)

W11b.   1983 (Oct 22): New York; Lincoln Center for the
        Performing Arts; Metropolitan Opera; Johanna
        Meier, Rosalind Elias, Regina Resnik, John Al-
        exander, John Macurdy]; Metropolitan Opera Or-
        chestra; Thomas Fulton, conductor (Metropolitan
        Opera Centennial Gala)

W12. **VANESSA.   UNDER THE WILLOW TREE.** (1961; Schirmer;
        Library of Congress has (a) pencil manuscript, piano
        acc., [10] p.) and (b) country dance, 17 numb. l.,
        for orchestra, pencil manuscript; Elizabeth Walker,
        Librarian of the Curtis Institue of Music, reports
        that the Institute has a "pencil manuscript of
        song...presented to Mrs. Zimbalist in 1956.   In-
        scribed by the composer, "For Mary--souvenir of
        wonderful waltzes! Philadelphia, Oct. 8, 1956.")

        For SATB chorus and piano.

Selected Performance

W12a.   1982 (Oct 17): West Chester, Penn.; West Chester
        State College; Swope Hall; Leslie Ann Belcher,
        soprano; Robert Dodd Greene, piano.

CHORAL MUSIC

W13. **AD BIBINEM CUM ME ROGARET AD CENAM.** (1943?; Library of

Congress has pencil holograph and Barber's note
about alterations in the words (p. [6]), as a gift
from G. Schirmer, January 10, 1944)

For SATB chorus.
Slightly altered version of a poem by Venantius For-
tunatus.
Unavailable in octavo, but contained in A Birthday
Offering to Carl Engel, a collection of articles
and compositions written in honor of Carl Engel's
sixtieth birthday, comp. and ed. by Gustave Reese,
privately printed in an edition of 300 copies and
published by G. Schirmer in 1943 (233 p.)

W14. **AGNUS DEI.** (1967; Schirmer)   See: B14a, B14b

For SATB chorus and piano or organ.
A 1967 transcription for chorus of Barber's Adagio
for Strings, op. 11; see W61.
For an English-texted version under the title Lamb of
God, see W17.

ANTHONY O'DALY   See: **REINCARNATIONS, OP. 16.**

THE COOLIN   See: **REINCARNATIONS, OP. 16.**

W15. **EASTER CHORALE.** (1964; Schirmer)   See: B15a

For SATB chorus, brass, timpani, and organ.
Text from poem by Pack Browning.
Written for the dedication of the Bell Tower of the
National Cathedral, Washington, D.C., May 7, 1964.

W16. **GOD'S GRANDEUR.** (1938; unpublished)

Performance

W16a.   1938 (May 23): Princeton, N.J.; Princeton High
School Auditorium; members of church choirs
under the Westminster Choir School's direction;
John Finley Williamson, conductor (Westminster
Festival Week) (The Talbott and Contemporary
American Music Festivals)

HEAVEN-HAVEN   See: **SONGS (4), OP. 13. CHORAL TRANS-
CRIPTIONS. A NUN TAKES THE VEIL (HEAVEN-HAVEN)**

W17. **LAMB OF GOD.** (1967; Schirmer)

    For SATB chorus and piano.
    An English-texted version of <u>Agnus Dei</u>; see W14.

W18. **LET DOWN THE BARS, O DEATH, OP. 8, NO. 2.** (1935-36; Schirmer; Library of Congress has pencil holograph close score ([1] p.) in portfolio with Barber's <u>Reincarnations</u>, dated "Wolfgang. June 25-[19]36, in addition to unidentified beginnings of choral work on verso of leaf; manuscript at Chester County Historical Society, West Chester, Pa.) <u>See</u>: B18a, B18b, B18c

    For SATB chorus.
    Text by Emily Dickinson.

    <u>Selected Performances</u>

W18a. 1952 (Apr 22): Vienna; Schönbrunn Palace; Imperial Theatre; Vienna State Academy Orchestra, soloists, and the Wiener Kammerchor; Ferdinand Grossman and William Strickland, conductors (A Concert of American Music in Schönbrunn) [Note: part of the concert, including the Barber work, was issued on Vox PL 7750]

W18b. 1981 (Feb 9): New York; St. Bartholomew's Church; Choir of St. Bartholomew's Church; Jack H. Ossewaarde, choirmaster (part of program for the memorial services honoring Samuel Barber)

W18c. 1982 (Oct 17): West Chester, Penn.; West Chester State College; Swope Hall; West Chester State College Concert Choir; Lois M. Williams, director.

W19. **THE LOVERS, OP. 43.** (1971; Schirmer) <u>See</u>: B19d

    For baritone solo, SATB chorus, and orchestra.
    4-3-3-2; 4-2-3-1; timp,perc,hp,cel,pno,str.
    Commissioned by the Girard Bank of Philadelphia.
    Based on <u>Twenty Poems of Love and a Song of Despair</u> by Pablo Neruda, trans. by W.S. Merwin.

    <u>Premiere</u>

W19a. 1971 (Sep 22): Philadelphia; Academy of Music; Tom Krause, baritone; Philadelphia Orchestra; Temple University Choirs; Eugene Ormandy, conductor. <u>See</u>: B19a, B19b, B19c, B19e, B19f, B19g

    <u>Other Selected Performances</u>

W19b. 1971 (Oct 4): Washington, D.C.; Kennedy Center for the Performing Arts; same performers as in W19a above.

W19c. 1971 (Oct 5): New York; Lincoln Center for the Performing Arts; Philharmonic Hall; same performers as W19a above. See: B19h, B19i

MARY HYNES See: **REINCARNATIONS, OP. 16.**

THE MONK AND HIS CAT See: **HERMIT SONGS, OP. 29. CHORAL TRANSCRIPTIONS. THE MONK AND HIS CAT.**

A NUN TAKES THE VEIL See: **SONGS (4), OP. 13. CHORAL TRANSCRIPTIONS. A NUN TAKES THE VEIL.**

W20. **PRAYERS OF KIERKEGAARD, OP. 30.** (1954; Schirmer; 20 min.; Library of Congress has (a) pencil sketches ([72] p.), (b) pencil holograph (31 p.), and (c) pencil holograph (57 (i.e. 59) l.); in caption: To the memory of Serge and Natalie Koussevitzky; at end: January 1954) See: B20a, B20b, B20j, B20q, B20r, B20x

For mixed chorus, soprano soloist, and orchestra (3-3-3-2; 4-3-3-1; perc,pno,str.)
For soprano, four-part chorus: S,A ad lib, T ad lib, chorus, orchestra.
Text by Søren Kierkegaard from his writings of 1847-55, his journals, The Unchangeableness of God, and Christian Discoveries.
Commissioned by the Library of Congress' Serge Koussevitzky Music Foundation and dedicated to the memory of Serge and Natalie Koussevitzky.

Premiere

W20a. 1954 (Dec 3-4): Boston; Symphony Hall; Leontyne Price, soprano; Jean Kraft, alto; Edward Munro, tenor; Boston Symphony Orchestra; Cecilia Society, prepared by Hugh Ross; Charles Münch, conductor. See: B20d

Other Selected Performances

W20b. 1954 (Dec 8, 10): New York; Carnegie Hall; Leontyne Price, soprano, Mary McMurray, contralto, and Earl Ringland, tenor; Boston Symphony Orchestra; Charles Münch, conductor; Schola Cantorum; Hugh Ross, director. See: B20c, B20e, B20g, B20l, B20n, B20p, B20t

W20c. 1955 (Jun 10): London; Royal Festival Hall; London
Philharmonic Orchestra; Edgar Fleet, Evelyn Cut-
hill, and Eileen Poulter, soloists; London Philharmonic Choir; Massimo Freccia, conductor. See:
B20f, B20k, B20m

W20d. 1969 (May 20): Vienna; Grosser Saal des Mozarteums;
Cincinnati Symphony Orchestra; Joan Marie
Molnagh, soprano; A Cappella Chorus of Miami
University; Max Rudolph, conductor. See: B20u

W20e. 1976 (Apr 26): New York; Carnegie Hall; Brenda
Valente, soprano; Philadelphia Orchestra; Singing
City Choir; Eugene Ormandy, conductor. See: B20w

W20f. 1977 (Oct 28): New York; Carnegie Hall; Evelyn
Lear, soprano; Milwaukee Symphony Orchestra;
Rutgers University Choir; F. Austin Walter, di-
rector; Kenneth Schermerhorn, conductor. See:
B20o, B20s

W20g. 1981 (Feb 9): New York; St. Bartholomew's Church;
Esther Hinds, soprano; Marie Bogart, mezzo-soprano; Will Caplinger, tenor; Choir of St. Bartholomew's Church; Jack H. Ossewaarde, choirmaster; Dennis Keene, organist (part of program
for the memorial services honoring Samuel Barber)

W20h. 1981 (Mar 19): New York; Abraham Goodman House;
Jeannette Walters, soprano; Brooklyn Philharmonia
Chorus and Chamber Orchestra; Alexander Dashnaw,
conductor. See: B20l

W20i. 1982 (Oct 17): Bloomington; Indiana University;
Indiana University Singers; Indiana University
Chamber Orchestra; Jan Harrington, conductor.

W21. **REINCARNATIONS, OP. 16.** (1936-42; Schirmer; 8 min.,
40 sec.; Library of Congress has ink holograph on
transparent paper; at end of no. 1, St. Wolfgang.
Aug. 8-[19]37, no. 2, Dec. 17-[19]'40, and no. 3,
Nov. 10-[19]'40, in addition to pencil holograph
sketches laid in; in portfolio wtih Barber's Let
Down the Bars, O Death) See: B21e, B21j

For SATB chorus a cappella.
Text from Reincarnations by James Stephens, after
the Irish of Antoine O'Raftery (London: Macmillan,
1948), p. 3, 13, 14.)
Contents: No. 1, Mary Hynes; No. 2, Anthony O'Daly;
No. 3, The Coolin.

Selected Performances

W21a. 1956 (Nov 17): New York; Town Hall; The Master
       Singers; Joseph Liebling, conductor [Mary Hynes
       only]

W21b. 1963 (Apr 7): New York; Town Hall; Oberlin College
       Choir; Robert Fountain, cond. [Anthony O'Daly
       only] See: B21b

W21c. 1970 (Jan 18): Pasadena, Calif.; California Insti-
       tute of Technology; Beckman Auditorium; Nether-
       lands Chamber Choir; Felix de Nobel, conductor
       (Coleman Chamber Concert)

W21d. 1981 (Mar 19): New York; Abraham Goodman House;
       Brooklyn Philharmonia Chorus; Alexander Dashnaw,
       conductor. See: B21d

W21e. 1981 (Apr 30): New York; Abraham Goodman House;
       Indiana University Chamber Choir; Robert Price,
       conductor.

W21f. 1982 (Oct 17): West Chester, Penn.; West Chester
       State College; Swope Hall; West Chester State
       College Concert Choir; Lois M. Williams, di-
       rector.

W21g. 1982 (Oct 22): New York; Carnegie Recital Hall;
       The New York Motet Choir; Stephen Sturk, music
       director.

W22. **A STOPWATCH AND AN ORDNANCE MAP, OP. 15.** (1940;
     Schirmer; 6 min.; Library of Congress has manu-
     scripts in two versions: (a) four-part male chorus
     and three tympani (published in 1942 by G. Schir-
     mer), having neither date nor title, and (b) an
     arrangement for four horns, three trombones, and
     tuba consisting of the original printed score cut up
     and mounted below holograph additions, in pencil and
     ink, published in 1954 by G. Schirmer) See: B22a,
     B22b, B22e, B22h, B22i, B22k, B22m

     For TTBB chorus, 4 horns, 3 trombones, tuba, and 3
       timpani.
     Text from "Stopwatch and an Ordnance Map" by Stephen
       Spender from his Collected Poems (New York: Random
       House, 1955), p. 87.

     Premiere

     W22a. 1940 (Apr 23): Philadelphia; Curtis Institute of
           Music; Casimir Hall; Men's voices from the Cur-
           tis Institute; Madrigal Chorus; David Stephens,

25

tympani; Samuel Barber, conductor [original version] (Historical Series of Solo and Chamber Music, Second Season; repeated Apr 24 on Curtis Institute of Music Radio Program, Columbia Broadcasting System)

W22b.   1945 (Dec 16): New York; Carnegie Hall; Collegiate Chorale; David Machtel, tenor; Saul Goodman, tympani; Robert Shaw, conductor [a cappella version] See: B22f, B22l

SURE ON THIS SHINING NIGHT See: **SONGS (4), OP. 13. CHORAL TRANSCRIPTIONS. SURE ON THIS SHINING NIGHT.**

W23. **TO BE SUNG ON THE WATER, OP. 42, NO. 2.** (1969; Schirmer; Library of Congress has pencil manuscript dated December 14, 1968, 1 p.l., [5] p. and also first draft, pencil, [3] p.) See: B23a

For SATB chorus a cappella.
Also arranged for women's voices a cappella by the composer.
Text by Louise Bogan.

Selected Performances

W23a.   1981 (Feb 9): New York; St. Bartholomew's Church; Choir of St. Bartholomew's Church; Jack H. Ossewaarde, choirmaster (part of program for the memorial services honoring Samuel Barber)

W24. **TWELFTH NIGHT, OP. 42, NO. 1.** (1969; Schirmer; Library of Congress has (a) pencil manuscript dated "Xmas '68" and also (b) sketches and first draft, pencil, 10 l.) See: B24a

For SATB chorus a cappella.
Text by Laurie Lee.

W25. **THE VIRGIN MARTYRS, OP. 8, NO. 1.** (1935; Schirmer; 3 min., 30 sec.; Library of Congress has pencil manuscript, [5] p., including sketches) See: B25a

For SSAA chorus a cappella.
Text from Helen Waddell's English version of an old text after the Latin of Sigebert of Gemblous [Gemblow]

VOCAL MUSIC

W26. **ANDROMACHE'S FAREWELL, OP. 39.** (1962; Schirmer; 12 min.; Library of Congress has pencil holograph, accompanied by preliminary sketches ([28] p.) and sketches of a piano-vocal score (11 (i.e. 16) p.); gift of the composer, December 23, 1966) <u>See</u>: B26c, B26k

Originally for soprano and orchestra, but reduction for soprano and piano also exists.
3-3-3-2; 4-3-3-0; timp,pno,str.
From Euripides, trans. by John Patrick Creagh.

<u>Premiere</u>

W26a. 1963 (Apr 4, 7): New York; Lincoln Center for the Performing Arts; Philharmonic Hall; Martina Arroyo, soprano; New York Philharmonic Orchestra; Thomas Schippers, conductor. <u>See</u>: B26b, B26f, B26g, B26h, B26i

<u>Other</u> <u>Selected</u> <u>Performance</u>

W26b. 1967 (Nov 12-13): New York; Carnegie Hall; Martina Arroyo, soprano; American Symphony Orchestra; Joseph Eger, conductor. <u>See</u>: B26a, B26i

AT SAINT PATRICK'S PURGATORY <u>See</u>: **HERMIT SONGS, OP. 29.**

W27. **AU CLAIR DE LA LUNE.** (192-?; unpublished)

For voice and piano.
"A modern setting."

<u>Premiere</u>

W27a. 1926 (Apr 25): West Chester, Pa.; Home of Samuel Barber; Lilian McD. Brinton, mezzo-soprano; Samuel Barber, piano.

W28. **THE BEGGAR'S SONG** (192-?; unpublished)

For voice and piano.

<u>Premiere</u>

W28a. 1936 (Apr 22): Rome; American Academy (Accademia Americana); Villa Aurelia; Samuel Barber, vocalist and piano.

Other Selected Performances

W28b. 1937 (Mar 7): Philadelphia; Curtis Institute of
       Music; Casimir Hall; Benjamin de Loache, bari-
       tone; Edith Evans Braun, piano.

BESSIE BOBTAIL See: SONGS (2), OP. 2.

CHRISTMAS EVE: A TRIO WITH SOLOS, OP. XIII See:
Preface

CHURCH BELL AT NIGHT See: HERMIT SONGS, OP. 29.

LE CLOCHER CHANTE See: MELODIES PASSAGERES, OP. 27.

THE CRUCIFIXION See: HERMIT SONGS, OP. 29.

UN CYGNE See: MELODIES PASSAGERES, OP. 27.

THE DAISIES See: SONGS (3), OP. 2.

W29. THE DANCE (1927; unpublished)

For voice and piano.
Text by James Stephens.

Selected Performances

W29a. 1937 (Mar 7): Philadelphia; Curtis Institute of
       Music; Casimir Hall; Rose Bampton, soprano;
       Edith Evans Braun, piano.

DEPART See: MELODIES PASSAGERES, OP. 27.

W30. DERE TWO FELLA JOE. (192-?; unpublished)

For voice and piano.

Premiere

W30a. 1926 (Apr 25): West Chester, Pa.; Home of Samuel
       Barber; Gertrude K. Schmidt, soprano; Samuel
       Barber, piano.

THE DESIRE FOR HERMITAGE See: HERMIT SONGS, OP. 29.

W31. **DESPITE AND STILL, OP. 41.** (1969; Schirmer; Library
of Congress has (a) pencil first draft, (b) pencil
second draft with dedication "To my friend Leontyne
Price," (c) second holograph dated June 1968 of A
Last Song transposed a half tone higher, and (d)
incomplete pencil manuscript with Solitary Hotel
lacking) See: B31c

Song cycle for high or medium voice and piano.
Written for Leontyne Price.
Contents: No. 1, A Last Song, text by Robert Graves
-- No. 2, My Lizard, text by Theodore Roethke --
No. 3, In the Wilderness, text by Robert Graves --
No. 4, Solitary Hotel, text by James Joyce -- No.
5, Despite and Still, text by Robert Graves.

Premiere

W31a. 1969 (Apr 27): New York; Lincoln Center for the
Performing Arts; Philharmonic Hall; Leontyne
Price, soprano; David Garvey, piano. See: B31a,
B31b

Other Selected Performance

W31b. 1981 (Feb 9): New York; St. Bartholomew's Church;
Leontyne Price, soprano; David Garvey, piano
(part of program for the memorial services honoring Samuel Barber)

DOVER BEACH, OP. 3 See: W86

W32. **FANTASY IN PURPLE.** (192-?; unpublished)

For voice and piano.

Premiere

W32a. 1926 (Apr 25): West Chester, Pa.; Home of Samuel
Barber; Lilian McD. Brinton, mezzo-soprano;
Samuel Barber, piano.

A GREEN LOWLAND OF PIANOS See: SONGS (3), OP. 45.

THE HEAVENLY BANQUET See: HERMIT SONGS, OP. 29.

W33. **HERMIT SONGS, OP. 29.** (1952-53; Schirmer; 20 min.;

Library of Congress has pencil sketches, [42] p. and
black-line print from copyist's manusript, in addition to reproduction of a copyist's manuscript,
including many penciled holograph corrections and
performance indications) See: B33a, B33j, B33l,
B33n, B33s, B33t, B33y

For voice and piano.
Translated from Irish texts of anonymous monks and
    scholars of the eighth to thirteenth centuries.
Commissioned by the Elizabeth Sprague Coolidge Foun-
    dation for the Founder's Day Concert.
Contents: No. 1, At Saint Patrick's Purgatory, 13th
    cent., trans. by Sean O'Faolain -- No. 2, Church
    Bell at Night, 12th cent., trans. by Howard Mum-
    ford Jones -- No. 3, Saint Ita's Vision, 8th
    cent., trans. by Chester Kallman -- No. 4, The
    Heavenly Banquet, 10th cent., trans. by Sean O'-
    Faolain -- No. 5, The Crucifixion, from "The Spec-
    ked Book," 12th cent., trans. Howard Mumford Jones
    -- No. 6, Sea-Snatch, 8th and 9th cent. anonymous,
    from Kenneth Jackson's "A Celtic Miscellany" --
    No. 7, Promiscuity, 8th and 9th cent. anonymous,
    from Kenneth Jackson's "A Celtic Miscellany" --
    No. 8, The Monk and His Cat, 8th or 9th cent.,
    trans. W.H. Auden -- No. 9, The Praises of God,
    11th cent., trans. W.H. Auden -- No. 10, The De-
    sire for Hermitage, 8th or 9th cent., based on a
    trans. by Sean O'Faolain.

Premiere

W33a.   1953 (Oct 31): Washington, D.C.; Library of Con-
         gress; Leontyne Price, soprano; Samuel Barber,
         piano (Coolidge Festival; Founders' Day Concert)

Other Selected Performances

W33b.   1954 (Nov 14): New York; Town Hall; Leontyne
         Price, soprano; Samuel Barber, piano. See:
         B33r, B33u

W33c.   1956 (Nov 13): New York; Town Hall; Wayne Conner,
         tenor; Vladimir Sokoloff, piano [Nos. 8-9 only]

W33d.   1958 (May 12): New York; Carnegie Recital Hall;
         Phyllis Antognini, soprano; Norman Johnson,
         piano. See: B33b

W33e.   1959 (Nov 1): New York; Town Hall; Ksenia Bidina,
         mezzo-soprano; Bela Szilagi, piano [No. 8 only]

W33f.   1960 (Nov 27): New York; Carnegie Recital Hall;
         Frances McDaniel, soprano; John Moriarty, piano
         [sang five selections]

W33g.   1965 (Apr 23): New York; Carnegie Recital Hall;
        Geraldine Overstreet, soprano; Jonathan Brice,
        piano.

W33h.   1966 (Jul 27): Long Beach, Calif.; California
        State College at Long Beach; Little Theater;
        Frank Barney Spencer, baritone; Samuel Posthuma,
        piano.

W33i.   1969 (Apr 23): Brooklyn; Academy of Music; Alvin
        Ailey American Dance Theatre. See: B33m

W33j.   1971 (Dec 14): New York; City Center 55th Street
        Theater; Alvin Ailey American Dance Theater.
        See: B33c

W33k.   1975 (Mar 4): San Francisco; War Memorial Opera
        House; Leontyne Price, soprano; David Garvey,
        piano. See: B33x

W33l.   1980 (Jul 4): London; Christ Church, Spitalfields;
        Vivien Townley, soprano; John Constable, piano
        (Fourth Summer Festival of Music; in commemora-
        tion of Barber's 70th birthday)

W33m.   1981 (Feb 9): New York; St. Bartholomew's Church;
        Leontyne Price, soprano; David Garvey, piano
        [Nos. 5 and 10 only] (part of program for the
        memorial services honoring Samuel Barber)

W33n.   1984 (Feb 25): Torrance, Calif.; El Camino Col-
        lege; Stuart E. Marsee Auditorium; Marvellee
        Cariaga, soprano; Daniel Cariaga, piano.

W34. **HERMIT SONGS, OP. 29. CHORAL TRANSCRIPTIONS. THE MONK
     AND THE CAT.** (1967; Schirmer) See: B34a, B34b

     For SATB chorus and piano, arranged by the composer.

     HUNTING SONG See: Preface

     I HEAR AN ARMY See: **SONGS (3), OP. 10.**

     IN THE WILDERNESS See: **DESPITE AND STILL, OP. 41.**

W35. **INVOCATION TO YOUTH.** (192-?; unpublished; manuscript
     at Chester County Historical Society, West Chester,
     Pa.)

     For voice and piano.

31

W35a.   1926 (Apr 25): West Chester, Pa.; Home of Samuel
        Barber; Lilian McD. Brinton, mezzo-soprano;
        Samuel Barber, piano.

W36. **KNOXVILLE: SUMMER OF 1915, OP. 24.** (1947; Schirmer;
        16 min.; Library of Congress has pencil holograph
        dated April 4, 1947, together with pencil holograph
        of incomplete score without the words; gift of Bar-
        ber, December 28, 1956; Library of Congress also has
        pencil holograph of arrangement for voice and piano,
        dated April 4, 1947; gift of Barber, December 28,
        1956) See: B36a, B36d, B36l, B36m, B36n, B36y,
        B36dd, B36ee, B36ff, B36pp

        Originally for soprano and orchestra, and reduction
          for voice and piano available.
        1-1-1-1; 2-1-0-0; trgl,hp,str.
        Taken from the last part of an autobiographical
          essay by James Agee.
        Commissioned by Eleanor Steber.

        Premiere

W36a.   1948 (Apr 9-10): Boston; Eleanor Steber, soprano;
        Boston Symphony Orchestra; Serge Koussevitzky,
        conductor. See: B36f, B36ll

        Other Selected Performances

W36b.   1956 (Feb 29): New York; Carnegie Hall; Sylvia
        Stahlman, soprano; Robert Dean, baritone; Boy
        Choristers of the Cathedral of St. John the
        Divine and of St. Thomas Church; Oratorio Socie-
        ty of New York; William Strickland, conductor.
        See: B36gg

W36c.   1958 (Oct 10): New York; Carnegie Hall; Eleanor
        Steber, soprano; Edwin Biltcliffe, piano. See:
        B36e

W36d.   1959 (Nov 13, 15): New York; Carnegie Hall; Leon-
        tyne Price, soprano; New York Philharmonic Or-
        chestra; Thomas Schippers, conductor. See:
        B36s, B36mm, B36nn

W36e.   1969 (Apr 22): Brooklyn; Academy of Music; Alvin
        Ailey American Dance Theater. See: B36w

W36f.   1973 (Jul 1): Los Angeles; University of Califor-
        nia, Los Angeles; Royce Hall; Delcina Stevenson,
        soprano; Camerata of Los Angeles; H. Vincent
        Mitzelfelt, conductor. See: B36o

W36g.   1974 (Mar 15-16): Cincinnati; Music Hall; Evelyn Lear, soprano; Cincinnati Symphony Orchestra; Thomas Schippers, conductor. See: B36hh

W36h.   1980 (Mar 9): Philadelphia; Academy of Music; Marianne Casiello, soprano; Curtis Symphony Orchestra; Calvin Simmons, conductor (The Curtis Institute of Music's Fourth Faculty Commemorative Series honoring Samuel Barber on the occasion of his seventieth birthday, evening concert)

W36i.   1980 (Jul 4): London; Christ Church, Spitalfields; Vivien Townley, soprano; John Constable, piano (Fourth Summer Festival of Music; in commemoration of Barber's 70th birthday)

W36j.   1981 (Dec 9): Bloomington; Indiana University; Julia Blair-Battle, soprano; Davis Hart, piano.

W36k.   1982 (Mar 30): London; Queen Elizabeth Hall; Sheila Armstrong, soprano; English Chamber Orchestra; Michael Tilson Thomas, conductor.

W36l.   1982 (Nov 5): Bloomington; Indiana University; Marilyn Bulli, soprano; Davis Hart, piano.

W37. LADY, WHEN I BEHOLD THE ROSES.   (192-?; (unpublished)

For voice and piano.

Premiere

W37a.   1926 (Apr 25): West Chester, Pa.; Home of Samuel Barber; Lilian McD. Brinton, mezzo-soprano; Samuel Barber, piano.

A LAST SONG   See: **DESPITE AND STILL, OP. 41.**

W38. LITTLE CHILDREN OF THE WIND. (192-?; unpublished)

For voice and piano.

Premiere

W38a.   1926 (Apr 25): West Chester, Pa.; Home of Samuel Barber; Lilian McD. Brinton, mezzo-soprano; Samuel Barber, piano.

W39. LONGING. (192-?; unpublished)

For voice and piano.

<u>Premiere</u>

W39a. 1926 (Apr 25): West Chester, Pa.; Home of Samuel
Barber; Lilian McD. Brinton, mezzo-soprano;
Samuel Barber, piano.

W40. MAN. (192-?; unpublished)

For voice and piano.

<u>Premiere</u>

W40a. 1926 (Apr 25): West Chester, Pa.; Home of Samuel
Barber; Gertrude K. Schmidt, soprano; Samuel
Barber, piano.

W41. MELODIES PASSAGERES, OP. 27. (1950-1951; Schirmer;
Library of Congress has pencil holographs: no. 1
dated January 1950, no. 2, April 21, 1951, no. 3,
April 26, 1951, no. 4, February 16, 1952, and no. 5,
February 10, 1950) <u>See</u>: B41a, B41b, B41c, B41e,
B41g, B41h

For voice and piano.
Dedicated to Pierre Bernac and Francis Poulenc.
From <u>Poèmes Français</u> by Rainer Maria Rilke.
Contents: No. 1, <u>Puisque tout passe</u> -- No. 2, <u>Un
cygne</u> -- No. 3, <u>Tombeau dans un parc</u> -- No. 4, <u>Le
clocher chanté</u> -- No. 5, <u>Départ</u>.

<u>Premiere</u>

W41a. 1950 (Apr 1): Washington, D.C.; Eileen Farrell,
soprano; Samuel Barber, piano [Nos. 1 and 4-5
only]

W41b. 1952 (Feb 10): New York; Town Hall; Pierre Bernac,
baritone; Francis Poulenc, piano [first complete
performance] <u>See</u>: B41d

<u>Other Selected Performance</u>

W41c. 1964 (Nov 12): New York; Carnegie Recital Hall;
Jeanne Beauvais, soprano

THE MONK AND HIS CAT <u>See</u>: **HERMIT SONGS, OP. 29.**

MONKS AND RAISINS _See_: **SONGS (2), OP. 18.**

W42. **MOTHER GOOSE SONGS.** (1920; unpublished)

 For voice and piano.
 "Dedicated to Sara, 1920."

 Premiere

 W42a. 1926 (Apr 25): West Chester, Pa.; Home of Samuel
   Barber; Gertrude K. Schmidt, soprano; Samuel
   Barber, piano.

W43. **MUSIC, WHEN SOFT VOICES DIE.** (192-?; unpublished;
  manuscript at Chester County Historical Society,
  West Chester, Pa.)

 For voice and piano.

 Premiere

 W43a. 1926 (Apr 25): West Chester, Pa.; Home of Samuel
   Barber; Lilian McD. Brinton, mezzo-soprano;
   Samuel Barber, piano.

W44. **MY FAIRYLAND.** (192-?; unpublished)

 For voice and piano.

 Premiere

 W44a. 1926 (Apr 25): West Chester, Pa.; Home of Samuel
   Barber; Gertrude K. Schmidt, soprano; Samuel
   Barber, piano.

 MY LIZARD _See_: **DESPITE AND STILL, OP. 41.**

 NOCTURNE _See_: **SONGS (4), OP. 13.**

 NOW I HAVE FED AND EATEN UP THE ROSE _See_: **SONGS (3),
 OP. 45.**

W45. **LA NUIT.** (192-?; unpublished)

 For voice and piano.

Premiere

W45a.   1926 (Apr 25): West Chester, Pa.; Home of Samuel
         Barber; Lilian McD. Brinton, mezzo-soprano;
         Samuel Barber, piano.

A NUN TAKES THE VEIL See: SONGS (4), OP. 13.

W46. **NUVOLETTA, OP. 25.** (1947; Schirmer; 5 min., 15 sec.;
     Library of Congress has pencil holograph dated Octo-
     ber 17, 1947) See: B46a, B46c, B46d, B46e

     For voice and piano.
     Text from a passage from Finnegan's Wake by James
     Joyce.

     Selected Performances

W46a.   1953 (Nov 20): New York; Lincoln Center for the
         Performing Arts; Juilliard Concert Hall; Gayle
         Pierce, soprano.

W46b.   1959 (Apr 5): New York; Carnegie Recital Hall;
         Georgia Dell, soprano; Miriam LeMon, piano.

W46c.   1959 (May 26): New York; Carnegie Recital Hall;
         Patricia Neway, soprano; Robert Colston, piano
         (the entire program was composed of vocal set-
         tings on texts of James Joyce)

W46d.   1983 (Jul 9): Bloomington; Indiana University;
         Marilee David Skidmore, soprano; Davis Hart,
         piano.

O BOUNDLESS, BOUNDLESS EVENING See: SONGS (3), OP.
45.

W47. **OCTOBER-WEATHER.** (192-?; unpublished; manuscript for
     October Mountain Weather at Chester County Histori-
     cal Society, West Chester, Pa.)

     For voice and piano.

     Premiere

W47a.   1926 (Apr 25): West Chester, Pa.; Home of Samuel
         Barber; Gertrude K. Schmidt, soprano; Samuel
         Barber, piano.

AN OLD SONG See: Preface

PRAISES OF GOD <u>See</u>: HERMIT SONGS, OP. 29.

PROMISCUITY <u>See</u>: HERMIT SONGS, OP. 29.

PUISQUE TOUT PASSE <u>See</u>: MELODIES PASSAGERES, OP. 27.

THE QUEEN'S FACE ON THE SUMMERY COIN <u>See</u>: SONGS (2), OP. 18.

RAIN HAS FALLEN <u>See</u>: SONGS (3), OP. 10.

SAINT ITA'S VISION <u>See</u>: HERMIT SONGS, OP. 29.

SEA-SNATCH <u>See</u>: HERMIT SONGS, OP. 29.

SECRETS OF THE OLD <u>See</u>: SONGS (4), OP. 13.

W48. **SLUMBER SONG OF THE MADONNA.** (192-?; unpublished)

For voice and piano.

<u>Premiere</u>

W48a. 1926 (Apr 25): West Chester, Pa.; Home of Samuel Barber; Lilian McD. Brinton, mezzo-soprano; Samuel Barber, piano.

SOLITARY HOTEL <u>See</u>: DESPITE AND STILL, OP. 41.

W49. **SOMETIME.** (1917; unpublished)

For voice and piano.
"Dedicated to Mother, 1917."

<u>Premiere</u>

W49a. 1926 (Apr 25): West Chester, Pa.; Home of Samuel Barber; Lilian McD. Brinton, mezzo-soprano; Samuel Barber, piano.

W50. **SONG FOR A NEW HOUSE.** (1940; unpublished; Elizabeth Walker, Librarian of the Curtis Institute of Music, reports that the Institute has a "holograph manuscript...with dedication to Mrs. Zimbalist. Presented to her in 1940 on the occasion of her moving to Philadelphia from Merion.")

For voice, flute, and piano.

W51. SONGS (3), OP. 2. (1927-1934; Schirmer)

For voice and piano.
Contents: No. 1, The Daisies (1927; Schirmer; text by James Stephens from his Collected Poems (New York: Macmillan, 1926), p. 53 (Library of Congress has manuscript dated July 20, 1927, pencil, 1 leaf)); No. 2, With Rue My Heart is Laden (1928; Schirmer; text by A.E. Housman from a poem of the same title; Library of Congress has ink holograph dated January 25, 1928; Elizabeth Walker, Librarian of the Curtis Institute of Music, reports that the Institute has "holograph in ink, signed...At end: Jan 25, 1928, (from 'Three Arkwright Songs'). Ms. was a presentation copy from the composer to Gama Gilbert (Curtis '34), to whom the song is dedicated. Purchased Oct. 29, 1981 from Paul Erfer, a friend to whom Gilbert had given the ms. Published: New York: G. Schirmer, c1936, not in this key but in transpositions one whole step higher and lower."); No. 3, Bessie Bobtail (1934; Schirmer; 2 min., 20 sec.; text by James Stephens from his Collected Poems (New York: Macmillan, 1926), p. 143) See: B51b, B51e

Selected Performances

W51a.　1936 (Apr 22): Rome; American Academy (Accademia Americana); Villa Aurelia; Samuel Barber, piano and vocalist [Nos. 1-2 only]

W51b.　1937 (Mar 7): Philadelphia; Curtis Institute of Music; Casimir Hall; Rose Bampton, soprano; Edith Evans Braun, piano [No. 1 only]

W51c.　1937 (Mar 7): Philadelphia; Curtis Institute of Music; Casimir Hall; Benjamin de Loache, baritone; Edith Evans Braun, piano [Nos. 2-3 only]

W51d.　1982 (Oct 17): West Chester, Penn.; West Chester State College; Swope Hall; Leslie Ann Belcher, soprano; Robert Dodd Greene, piano [No. 1only]

W51e.　1982 (Oct 21): Louisville, Ky.; Southern Baptist Theological Seminary; Heeren Recital Hall; Mark A. Logsdon, baritone; Dale A. Moore, piano [No. 1 only]

W51f.　1983 (Jul 9): Bloomington; Indiana University;

Marilee David Skidmore, soprano; Davis Hart, piano [No. 2 only]

W52. **SONGS (3), OP. 10.** (1936; Schirmer) See: B52b, B52c, B52d, B52e

For voice and piano.
Complete title: Three Songs to Poems From Chamber Music by James Joyce.
All texts by James Joyce from "Chamber Music" in his Collected Poems, The Portable James Joyce (New York: Viking Press, 1947).
Contents: No. 1, Rain Has Fallen (1936; Schirmer; 2 min., 20 sec.; Library of Congress has two versions in ink holograph, dated Nov. 21-[19]35. Rome); No. 2, Sleep Now (1936; Schirmer; 2 min., 30 sec.; Library of Congress has ink holograph dated Nov. 29-[19]35); No. 3, I Hear an Army (1936; Schirmer; 2 min., 30 sec.; Library of Congress has holographs in pencil and also ink versions, dated July 13-[19]36. St. Wolfgang)

Selected Performances

W52a.   1936 (Apr 22): Rome; American Academy (Accademia Americana); Villa Aurelia; Samuel Barber, vocalist and piano [Nos. 1-2 only]

W52b.   1937 (Mar 7): Philadelphia; Curtis Institute of Music; Casimir Hall; Rose Bampton, soprano; Samuel Barber, piano.

W52c.   1940 (Apr 23): Philadelphia; Curtis Institute of Music; Casimir Hall; Willa Stewart, soprano; Samuel Barber, piano (Historical Series of Solo and Chamber Music, Second Season)

W52d.   1941 (Apr 23): New York; Town Hall; John Walsh, baritone; Martin Rich, piano [No. 3 only]

W52e.   1947 (Feb 26): New York; Times Hall; Freeda Cluff, soprano; Arpad Sandor, piano [No. 3 only]

W52f.   1958 (Oct 18): New York; Carl Fischer Concert Hall; Harold S. Johnson, tenor; Joy Pottle, piano [Nos. 2-3 only]

W52g.   1959 (Apr 5): New York; Carnegie Recital Hall; Dwain de Paul, baritone; Stuart Ross, piano [No. 3 only]

W52h.   1960 (Oct 18): New York; Town Hall; McHenry Boatwright, baritone; Paul Ulanowsky, piano [No. 3 only]

W52i.   1974 (Apr 30): New York; Lincoln Center for the
         Performing Arts; Alice Tully Hall; Chamber Music
         Society of Lincoln Center; Dietrich Fischer-
         Dieskau, baritone; Charles Wadsworth, piano [No.
         3 only]

W52j.   1983 (Jul 9): Bloomington; Indiana University;
         Marilee David Skidmore, soprano; Davis Hart,
         piano [No. 1 only]

W53. **SONGS (4), OP. 13.** (1937-40; Schirmer; Library of
     Congress has ink holographs on transparent paper; at
     end of no. 1, 1937, no. 2, September 1938, no. 3,
     September 1938, and no. 4, February 11, 1940; holo-
     graph sketches in pencil laid in) See: B53e, B53f,
     B53h, B53j

         Originally for voice and piano; Barber arranged the
         songs for voice and orchestra and also for four-
         part chorus of mixed voices a cappella (SATB,
         TTBB, or SSAA); cf. W54-55.
         Contents: No. 1. A Nun Takes the Veil (Heaven-
         Haven). Text by Gerald Manley Hopkins from Poems
         of Gerald Manley Hopkins (London: Oxford Univer-
         sity Press, 1931), p. 8 -- No. 2. The Secrets of
         the Old. Text by W.B. Yeats from The Collected
         Poems of W.B. Yeats (New York: Macmillan, 1951),
         p. 221 -- No. 3. Sure on This Shining Night. Text
         by James Agee from his Permit Me Voyage (New
         Haven: Yale University Press, 1934), p. 14 -- No.
         4. Nocturne. Text by Frederic Prokosch from his
         Chosen Poems (New York: Doubleday, 1947), p. 13.

         Premiere

W53a.   1939 (Feb 12): New York; additional information
         unavailable [No. 2 only]

         Other Selected Performances

W53b.   1941 (Apr 7): New York; Town Hall; Povla Frijsh,
         soprano; Celius Dougherty, piano [No. 1 only]
         See: B53b

W53c.   1943 (Oct 24): New York; Town Hall; Povla Frijsh,
         soprano; Celius Dougherty, piano. See: B53c,
         B53g

W53d.   1947 (Jan 12): New York; Town Hall; Camilla
         Williams, soprano; Fritz Kramer, piano [No. 3
         only]

W53e.   1950 (Jan 15): New York; Carnegie Hall; Marian
         Anderson, contralto; Franz Rupp, piano [No. 4

only]

W53f.   1952 (Nov 25): Brooklyn; Academy of Music; Jan
        Peerce, tenor [No. 3 only]

W53g.   1955 (Dec 13): New York; Town Hall; Mary MacKen-
        zie, contralto; Paul Ulanowsky, piano [No. 3
        only]

W53h.   1959 (Apr 21): Brooklyn; Academy of Music; Marian
        Anderson, contralto; Franz Rupp, piano [No. 4
        only]

W53i.   1960 (Oct 14): New York; Town Hall; Carol Wilder,
        soprano; Lawrence Smith, piano [No. 1 only]

W53j.   1963 (Oct 10): New York; Carnegie Recital Hall;
        Esther Admor, mezzo-soprano; Leo Taubman, piano
        [No. 1 only]

W53k.   1965 (Apr 18): New York; Carnegie Hall; Marian
        Anderson, contralto; Franz Rupp, piano [No. 4
        only; Marian Anderson's farewell recital] See:
        B53m

W53l.   1974 (Apr 30): New York; Lincoln Center for the
        Performing Arts; Alice Tully Hall; Chamber Music
        Society of Lincoln Center; Dietrich Fischer-
        Dieskau, baritone; Charles Wadsworth, piano
        [No. 4 only]

W53m.   1982 (Oct 17): West Chester, Penn.; West Chester
        State College; Swope Hall; Leslie Ann Belcher,
        soprano; Robert Dodd Greene, piano.

W53n.   1983 (Jul 9): Bloomington; Indiana University;
        Marilee David Skidmore, soprano; Davis Hart,
        piano [No. 4 only]

W54. **SONGS (4), OP. 13. CHORAL TRANSCRIPTIONS. A NUN TAKES
      THE VEIL (HEAVEN-HAVEN).** (1937; Schirmer; Library of
      Congress has (a) pencil manuscript, piano for re-
      hearsal only, [3] p., (b) for men's chorus a cappel-
      la, as above, [3] p., and (c) for women's chorus a
      cappella, as above, [3] p.)) See: B54a

      For four-part chorus of mixed voices a cappella
        (SATB, TTBB, or SSAA)
      Transcription of the vocal-piano composition.

W55. **SONGS (4), OP. 13. CHORAL TRANSCRIPTIONS. SURE ON THIS
      SHINING NIGHT.** (1961; Schirmer; 2 min., 30 sec.;

Library of Congress has pencil manuscript, [7] p.)
See: B55a

For SATB chorus and piano, arranged by the composer.

W56. **SONGS (2), OP. 18.** (1943; Schirmer; for no. 1, Library of Congress has ink holograph on transparent
paper dated November 1942, in addition to pencil
holograph sketch ([4] p.) laid in; for no. 2, Library of Congress has manuscript) See: B56a, B56b,
B56c

For voice and piano.
Contents: No. 1, The Queen's Face on the Summery
Coin, text by Robert Horan; No. 2, Monks and
Raisins, text by José Garcia Villa, from his Have
Come, Am Here (New York, Viking Press, 1942), p.
62.

W57. **SONGS (3), OP. 45.** (1974; Schirmer)

For high or low voice and piano.
Written for Dietrich Fischer-Dieskau.
Commissioned by the Chamber Music Society of Lincoln
Center.
Contents: No. 1, Now I Have Fed and Eaten Up the
Rose, text by Gottfried Keller, trans. James Joyce
-- No. 2, A Green Lowland of Pianos, text by Jerzy
Harasymowicz, trans. Czeslaw Milosz -- No. 3, O
Boundless, Boundless Evening, text by Georg Heym,
trans. Christopher Middleton.

Premiere

W57a.   1974 (Apr 30): New York; Lincoln Center for the
Performing Arts; Alice Tully Hall; Chamber Music
Society of Lincoln Center; Dietrich Fischer-
Dieskau, baritone; Charles Wadsworth, piano [a
performance had been scheduled with Mr. Fischer-
Dieskau for January 23, 1973, but the event was
cancelled due to the illness of the vocalist]
See: B57a, B57c

Other Selected Performances

W57b.   1980 (Mar 9): Philadelphia; Curtis Institute of
Music; Curtis Hall Auditorium; Donald Collup,
baritone; Vladimir Sokoloff, piano (Collup
replaced Theodor Uppman who was scheduled to
sing but who became ill) (The Curtis Institute
of Music's Fourth Faculty Commemorative Series
Honoring Samuel Barber on the occasion of his
70th birthday; afternoon concert)

SURE ON THIS SHINING NIGHT <u>See</u>: **SONGS (4), OP. 13.**

W58. THY LOVE. (192-?; unpublished)

For voice and piano.

<u>Premiere</u>

W58a. 1926 (Apr 25): West Chester, Pa.; Home of Samuel Barber; Lilian McD. Brinton, mezzo-soprano; Samuel Barber, piano.

THY WILL BE DONE, OP. V, NO. 1 <u>See</u>: Preface

TOMBEAU DANS UN PARC <u>See</u>: **MELODIES PASSAGERES, OP. 27.**

THE WANDERER <u>See</u>: Preface

W59. THE WATCHERS. (192-?; unpublished)

For voice and piano.

<u>Premiere</u>

W59a. 1926 (Apr 25): West Chester, Pa.; Home of Samuel Barber; Lilian McD. Brinton, mezzo-soprano; Samuel Barber, piano.

<u>Other</u> <u>Selected</u> <u>Performances</u>

W59b. 1927 (Jan 29): New York; Carnegie Hall; Louise Homer, contralto; Ruth Emerson, piano. <u>See</u>: B59a

WITH RUE MY HEART IS LADEN <u>See</u>: **SONGS (2), OP. 2**

W60. YOUTH. (192-?; unpublished)

For voice and piano.

<u>Premiere</u>

W60a. 1926 (Apr 25): West Chester, Pa.; Home of Samuel Barber; Gertrude K. Schmidt, soprano; Samuel Barber, piano.

ORCHESTRAL MUSIC

W61. **ADAGIO FOR STRINGS, OP. 11.** (1936; Schirmer; 8 min.)
[Library of Congress has ink holograph ([7] p.);
according to typewritten copy of composer's letter,
laid in, to Harold Spivacke, dated July 28, 1943,
the red pencil markings on p. [5] were made by
Arturo Toscanini; gift of Barber, dated July 29,
1943; Library of Congress also has pencil holograph
(12-14 p.) dated "Sept. 19-[19]36. St. Wolfgang";
gift of the composer, December 28, 1954) _See_: B61y,
B61dd, B61pp, B61qq, B61tt, B61yy, B61aaa

Arrangement of the second movement from the _String_
Quartet, op. 11; see W91.
For a 1967 transcription for chorus, see W14.

Premiere

W61a. 1938 (Nov 5): New York; NBC Symphony Orchestra;
Arturo Toscanini, conductor [first performance
in orchestral arrangement] _See_: B61m, B61tt,
B61zz

Other Selected Performances

W61b. 1939 (Mar 3-4); Los Angeles; Philharmonic Auditorium; Los Angeles Philharmonic Orchestra; Otto
Klemperer, conductor. _See_: B61aa

W61c. 1940 (Jan 25-26); New York; Carnegie Hall; New
York Philharmonic-Symphony Orchestra; John Barbirolli, conductor. _See_: B61l

W61d. 1949 (Mar 18-19): Philadelphia; Academy of Music;
Philadelphia Orchestra; Eugene Ormandy, conductor.

W61e. 1953 (Feb 27-28): Boston; Symphony Hall; Boston
Symphony Orchestra; Charles Münch, conductor.

W61f. 1955 (Mar 19): New York; Carnegie Hall; New York
Philharmonic-Symphony Orchestra; Guido Cantelli,
conductor. _See_: B61jj

W61g. 1955 (Mar 30): New York; Carnegie Hall; Berlin
Philharmonic Orchestra; Herbert von Karajan,
conductor. _See_: B61ss, B61uu

W61h. 1956 (Jul 21): Lenox-Tanglewood, Mass.; Boston
Symphony Orchestra; Charles Münch, conductor
(Berkshire Festival)

W61i.   1967 (Mar 29): New York; City Center Theater; National Ballet of Washington [included in ballet entitled Through the Edge] See: B61b

W61j.   1967 (Jul 19): Liverpool; Liverpool Philharmonic Hall; Royal Liverpool Philharmonic Orchestra; Perino Gamba, conductor.

W61k.   1967 (Nov 7): New York; Broadway Theater; Harkness Ballet [included in ballet entitled Youth] See: B61ee

W61l.   1967 (Dec 2): Eastbourne, Eng.; Congress Theatre; London Philharmonic Orchestra; Constantin Silvestri, conductor.

W61m.   1968 (May 3): Aylesbury, Eng.; Borough Assembly Hall; Philomusica of London; Roger Norrington, conductor.

W61n.   1970 (Apr 19): Los Angeles; University of California, Los Angeles; Royce Hall; Tossy Spivakovsky and Henri Temianka, violins; California Chamber Symphony; Henri Temianka, conductor. See: B61d

W61o.   1973 (Feb 11): Pasadena, Calif.; California Institute of Technology; Beckman Auditorium; Paul Kuentz Chamber Orchestra; Paul Kuentz, conductor (Coleman Chamber Concert)

W61p.   1980 (Mar 8): New York; Lincoln Center for the Performing Arts; Avery Fisher Hall; New York Philharmonic Orchestra; Morton Gould, conductor. See: B61n

W61q.   1981 (Jan 12): New York; Carnegie Hall; Brooklyn Philharmonia; Lukas Foss, conductor. See: B61j

W61r.   1982 (Mar 24): London; Royal Festival Hall; Leipzig Gewandhaus Orchestra; Kurt Masur, conductor. See: B61w

W61s.   1982 (Oct 17): West Chester, Penn.; West Chester State College; Swope Hall; Sylvia Ahramjian and Molly Renninger, violins, Aino Wolfson, viola, and Eugene Klein, violoncello.

W61t.   1983 (Oct 11): Los Angeles; University of California, Los Angeles; Pauley Pavilion; National Symphony Orchestra; Mstislav Rostropovich, conductor.

W61u.   1983 (Nov 13): Pasadena, Calif.; Ambassador Auditorium; Victoria [British Columbia] Symphony; Paul Freeman, conductor.

W61v.   1984 (Feb 26): Pasadena, Calif.; Ambassador Audi-
         torium; Polish Chamber Orchestra; Jerzy Maksy-
         miuk, conductor.

W62. **ADVENTURE.** (1954; unpublished); 8 min.; Library of
    Congress has pencil holograph on transparent paper,
    dated November 25, 1954) _See_: B62a, B62b

    "The score...was completed on November 25, 1954.
    Aptly titled _Adventure_ it calls for an extraordi-
    nary orchestra of flute, clarinet, horn, harp, and
    a number of exotic 'instruments from the Museum of
    Natural History.' These include African sansas, a
    Balinese water drum, African xylophones, gourds
    filled with peas, hollow tree trunks, pressure
    drums, and still others for special effects."
    (Waters, Edward N. "Harvest of the Year: Selected
    Acquisitions of the Music Division." _Quarterly
    Journal of the Library of Congress_ 24:54-55 (Jan-
    uary 1967))

W63. **A BLUE ROSE.** (1952; Schirmer)

    Ballet using _Souvenirs_, op. 28, as the music.

    Premiere

  W63a.   1957 (Dec 26): London; Covent Garden; Royal Ballet
           (The Junior Company) _See_: B63a

W64. **CANZONETTA, OP. 48.** (1978; Schirmer; 8 min.)

    For oboe and string orchestra and intended as the
    middle movement of an oboe concerto commissioned
    by the New York Philharmonic; the other movements
    were never written.
    Orchestration by Charles Turner.

    Premiere

  W64a.   1981 (Dec 17): New York; Lincoln Center for the
           Performing Arts; Avery Fisher Hall; Harold Gom-
           berg, oboe; New York Philharmonic Orchestra;
           Zubin Mehta, conductor. _See_: B64b, B64c

    Other Selected Performance

  W64b.   1983 (May 28): Charleston, S.C.; Cathedral of St.
           Luke and St. Paul; Eric Ohlsson, oboe; orchestra
           conducted by Adrian Gnam (Piccolo Spoleto Festi-
           val) _See_: B64a

CAVE OF THE HEART   See: W71.

COMMANDO MARCH   See: W83.

W65. **CONCERTO FOR PIANO AND ORCHESTRA, OP. 38.** (1962;
Schirmer; 26 min.; Library of Congress has (a) full
score. 64 [i.e. 65] p.; 65-85, 1-57 numb l. Pencil, except solo piano part in ink in hand of
copyist, and lacking first 14 measures) and (b) two
piano version. Pencil score. 27, [20], 20 p. Together with pencil sketches and drafts, 46 l.) See:
B65c, B65d, B65f, B65g, B65i, B65r

3-3-3-2; 4-3-3-0; timp,pno,perc,str.
Commissioned by G. Schirmer in celebration of the
company's 100th anniversary in 1961.
Dedicated to Manfred Ibel.
The second movement was adapted by the composer to
form the Canzone for Flute and Piano, op. 38a.
Arranged for ballet under title Configurations,
commissioned by Mikhail Baryshnikov and performed
by Baryshnikov and Marianna Tcherkassky (National
Ballet of Washington) See: W65o, W65p

Premiere

W65a.   1962 (Sep 24): New York; Lincoln Center for the
Performing Arts; Philharmonic Hall; John Brown-
ing, piano; Boston Symphony Orchestra; Erich
Leinsdorf, conductor. See: B65u, B65ff, B65ll

Other Selected Performances

W65b.   1962 (Sep 28-29): Boston; Symphony Hall; John
Browning, piano; Boston Symphony Orchestra;
Erich Leinsdorf, conductor. See: B65e

W65c.   1963 (Jan 8): London; radio broadcast; John Brown-
ing, piano; Philharmonia Orchestra; Berthold
Goldschmidt, conductor. See: B65gg, B65jj,
B65pp, B65qq

W65d.   1963 (Jul): Spoleto, Italy; John Browning, piano;
Dietfried Bennet, conductor (Festival of Two
Worlds) See: B65o

W65e.   1963 (Aug 18): Lenox-Tanglewood, Mass.; John
Browning, piano; Boston Symphony Orchestra;
Erich Leinsdorf, conductor (Berkshire Festival)

W65f.   1963 (Nov 7): New York; Lincoln Center for the
Performing Arts; Philharmonic Hall; John Browning, piano; New York Philharmonic Orchestra;

Josef Krips, conductor. <u>See</u>: B65s, B65z, B65kk

W65g. 1964 (Mar 18-20): San Francisco; War Memorial
       Opera House; John Browning, piano; San Francisco
       Symphony; Josef Krips, conductor. <u>See</u>: B65l

W65h. 1965 (Jun 21): London; Royal Festival Hall; John
       Browning, piano; Cleveland Orchestra; George
       Szell, conductor. <u>See</u>: B65a

W65i. 1965 (Oct 7-8): Chicago; Orchestra Hall; John
       Browning, piano; Chicago Symphony Orchestra;
       Jean Martinon, conductor. <u>See</u>: B65rr

W65j. 1966 (Jan 24-25): Seattle; Opera House; John
       Browning, piano; Seattle Symphony Orchestra;
       Milton Katims, conductor.

W65k. 1969 (Nov 22): Brooklyn; Academy of Music; Alvin
       Ailey American Dance Theater [second movement
       included in ballet entitled <u>Poeme</u>] <u>See</u>: B65b

W65l. 1971 (Sep 22): Philadelphia; Academy of Music;
       John Browning, piano; Philadelphia Orchestra;
       Eugene Ormandy, conductor.

W65m. 1975 (Nov 6-8, 11): New York; Lincoln Center for
       the Performing Arts; Avery Fisher Hall; John
       Browning, piano; New York Philharmonic Orches-
       tra; Erich Leinsdorf, conductor. <u>See</u>: B65v

W65n. 1980 (Mar 11-13): Washington, D.C.; Kennedy Center
       Concert Hall; James Tocco, piano; National Sym-
       phony Orchestra; Antal Dorati, conductor. <u>See</u>:
       B65w

W65o. 1981 (Oct 9): Washington, D.C.; Lisner Auditorium;
       Mikhail Baryshnikov and the Washington Ballet
       and a guest ensemble from the American Ballet
       Theatre; Mary Day, founder/director; Choo San
       Goh, choreography (benefit performance) [under
       title "Configurations"] <u>See</u>: B65bb, B65oo

W65p. 1981 (Oct 15): Minneapolis; Mikhail Baryshnikov
       and the American Ballet Theatre; Choo San Goh,
       choreography [under title "Configurations"]

W65q. 1984 (Feb 11-12): Pasadena, Calif.; Pasadena Civic
       Auditorium; Tedd Joselson, piano; Pasadena Sym-
       phony Orchestra; Andrew Schenck, guest conduc-
       tor. <u>See</u>: B65m

W66. **CONCERTO FOR VIOLIN AND ORCHESTRA, OP. 14.** (1939;
     Schirmer; 22 min.; Library of Congress has orchestra

score, pencil, 88 p.) <u>See</u>: B66c, B66f, B66j, B66u, B66x, B66aa, B66ll, B66mm, B66nn

2-2-2-2; 2-2-0-0; timp,pno,str.
Reduction by the composer for violin and piano also
  exists.

<u>Premiere</u>

W66a.   1941 (Feb 7-8): Philadelphia; Academy of Music;
         Albert Spalding, violin; Philadelphia Orchestra;
         Eugene Ormandy, conductor [three performances
         took place before the above "official" premiere,
         all featuring violinist Herbert Baumel, once
         with pianist Ralph Berkowitz, once with Fritz
         Reiner conducting the Curtis Symphony, and once
         with Eugene Ormandy conducting the Philadelphia
         Orchestra] <u>See</u>: B66g, B66k, B66t, B66oo

<u>Other</u> <u>Selected</u> <u>Performances</u>

W66b.   1941 (Feb 11): New York; Carnegie Hall; Albert
         Spalding, violin; Philadelphia Orchestra; Eugene
         Ormandy, conductor. <u>See</u>: B66k

W66c.   1941 (Aug 14, 16-17): Lenox-Tanglewood, Mass.;
         Ruth Posselt, violin; Boston Symphony Orchestra;
         Serge Koussevitzky, conductor (Berkshire Festi-
         val)

W66d.   1944 (Jun 23): London; Royal Albert Hall; Eda
         Kersey, violin; London Promenade Orchestra;
         Basil Cameron, conductor (Promenade Concert)
         <u>See</u>: B66b, B66pp

W66e.   1960 (Oct 13, 14, 16): New York; Carnegie Hall;
         Aaron Rosand, violin; New York Philharmonic
         Orchestra; Leonard Bernstein, conductor. <u>See</u>:
         B66bb, B66ss

W66f.   1962 (Apr 13-14): Boston; Symphony Hall; Ruth
         Posselt, violin; Boston Symphony Orchestra;
         Richard Burgin, conductor.

W66g.   1976 (Jul 28): London; Royal Albert Hall; Ralph
         Holmes, violin; BBC Symphony Orchestra; Edward
         Downes, conductor (Promenade Concert) <u>See</u>:
         B66vv

W66h.   1980 (Mar 9): Philadelphia; Academy of Music;
         Jaime Laredo, violin; Curtis Symphony Orchestra;
         Calvin Simmons, conductor (The Curtis Institute
         of Music's Fourth Faculty Commemorative Series
         honoring Samuel Barber on the occasion of his
         seventieth birthday; evening concert)

W66i.   1982 (May 16): London; St. John's Smith Square;
        Christopher Warren-Green, violin; Young Musi-
        cians' Symphony Orchestra; James Blair, conduc-
        tor.

W66j.   1982 (Nov 5): London; Barbican Hall; Jaime Laredo,
        violin; Royal Philharmonic Orchestra; Sir Char-
        les Groves, conductor. See: B66d

W66k.   1983 (Oct 15): Santa Ana, Calif.; Santa Ana High
        School Auditorium; Ruggiero Ricci, violin; Paci-
        fic Symphony Orchestra; Keith Clark, conductor.
        See: B66i

W67. CONCERTO FOR VIOLONCELLO AND ORCHESTRA, OP. 22.
(1945; Schirmer; 26 min.; Library of Congress has
pencil holograph dated "Nov. 27, 1945. Capricorn";
gift of Barber, December 28, 1954; Hilary Cummings,
Curator of Manuscripts, Special Collections, University of Oregon, Eugene, reports that the University
has among the Alexander Merovich Papers "the manuscript score" of the Concerto) See: B67a, B67e,
B67k, B67n, B67q, B67x, B67aa

2-2-2(b cl)-2; 2-3-0-0; timp,perc,str.
Reduction by the composer for violoncello and piano
   also exists.
Commissioned by John Nicholas Brown and Anne Brown
   for Raya Garbousova.
Won fifth annual Music Critics' Circle of New York
   City award for a work for orchestra.

Premiere

W67a.   1946 (Apr 5): Boston; Raya Garbousova, violon-
        cello; Boston Symphony Orchestra; Serge Kousse-
        vitzky, conductor. See: B67j

Other Selected Performances

W67b.   1946 (Apr 12): Brooklyn; Academy of Music; Raya
        Garbousova, violoncello; Boston Symphony Orches-
        tra; Serge Koussevitzky, conductor.

W67c.   1946 (Apr 13): New York; Carnegie Hall; Raya Gar-
        bousova, violoncello; Boston Symphony Orchestra;
        Serge Koussevitzky, conductor. See: B67g

W67d.   1947 (Dec 4, 7): New York; Carnegie Hall; Raya
        Garbousova, violoncello; New York Philharmonic-
        Symphony Orchestra; Dmitri Mitropoulos, conduc-
        tor. See: B67h

W67e.   1959 (Jan 29-30): New York; Carnegie Hall; Leonard

Rose, violoncello; New York Philharmonic Orchestra; Leonard Bernstein, conductor. See: B67u, B67z

W67f.   1964 (Dec 19): New York; Grace Rainey Rogers Auditorium; Raya Garbousova, violoncello; Musica Aeterna Orchestra; Frederic Waldman, conductor. See: B67w

W67g.   1970 (Apr 17): Los Angeles; University of California, Los Angeles; Royce Hall; Paul Tobias violoncello; Debut Orchestra; John Waddell, conductor. See: B67o

CONFIGURATIONS See: **CONCERTO FOR PIANO AND ORCHESTRA, OP. 38.**

W68. **ESSAY FOR ORCHESTRA, OP. 12.** (1937; Schirmer; 8 min.) See: B68a, B68g, B68i, B68l

2-2-2-2; 4-3-3-1; timp,pno,str.
Later renamed "First Essay For Orchestra."

Premiere

W68a.   1938 (Nov 5): New York; NBC Symphony Orchestra; Arturo Toscanini, conductor. See: B68d, B68m

Other Selected Performances

W68b.   1939 (Mar 3-4): Los Angeles; Philharmonic Hall; Los Angeles Philharmonic Orchestra; Otto Klemperer, conductor. See: B68h

W68c.   1941 (Apr 25-26): Boston; Symphony Hall; Boston Symphony Orchestra; Serge Koussevitzky, conductor.

W68d.   1942 (Dec 7): Seattle; Music Hall; Seattle Symphony Orchestra; Edwin McArthur, conductor.

W68e.   1943 (Apr 3): New York; Carnegie Hall; Boston Symphony Orchestra; Serge Koussevitzky, conductor. See: B68b

W68f.   1950 (Dec 7): New York; Carnegie Hall; New York Philharmonic-Symphony Orchestra; Georg Szell, conductor. See: B68c

W68g.   1954 (Dec 7): Seattle; Orpheum Theatre; Seattle Symphony Orchestra; Milton Katims, conductor.

W68h.   1967 (Mar 6-7): Seattle; Opera House; Seattle

Symphony Orchestra; Milton Katims, conductor.

W68i. 1981 (Aug 31): Salzburg; Grosses Festspielhaus; Chicago Symphony Orchestra; George Solti, conductor.

W68j. 1981 (Sep 2): Lucerne; Grosser Kunsthausaal; Chicago Symphony Orchestra; George Solti, conductor.

W68k. 1981 (Sep 4): London; Royal Albert Hall; Chicago Symphony Orchestra; George Solti, conductor (simultaneously broadcast on Radio 3) See: B68e

W68l. 1981 (Sep 15): Brussels; Palais des Beaux Arts; Chicago Symphony Orchestra; George Solti, conductor.

ESSAY FOR ORCHESTRA NO. 2 See: **SECOND ESSAY FOR ORCHESTRA**

ESSAY FOR ORCHESTRA NO. 3 See: **THIRD ESSAY FOR ORCHESTRA**

W69. **FADOGRAPH OF A YESTERN SCENE, OP. 44.** (1971; Schirmer; 7 min.) See: B69a, B69c

3-3-3-2; 4-3-3-1; timp,perc,hp,pno,str.
After a line from Finnegan's Wake by James Joyce.
Commissioned by the Alcoa Foundation.

Premiere

W69a. 1971 (Sep 10-11): Pittsburgh; Heinz Hall for the Performing Arts; Pittsburgh Symphony Orchestra; William Steinberg, conductor [performed for the opening of Heinz Hall for the Performing Arts]

Other Selected Performance

W69b. 1971 (Nov 5): New York; Carnegie Hall; Pittsburgh Symphony Orchestra; William Steinberg, conductor. See: B69b

FIRST ESSAY FOR ORCHESTRA, OP. 12. See: **ESSAY FOR ORCHESTRA, OP. 12.**

GALOP See: **SOUVENIRS, OP. 28.**

HESITATION TANGO _See_: SOUVENIRS, OP. 28.

W70. **HORIZON.** (1945; the Library of Congress has positive photocopy of manuscript [10 numbered leaves])

Composed in Mt. Kisco, New York
Title from caption on manuscript.

W71. **MEDEA, OP. 23.** (1946; Schirmer; 22 min.; Library of Congress has pencil holograph; gift of the composer, December 30, 1957) _See_: B71b, B71d, B71g, B71i

Ballet.
2(pic)-3(E hn)-2-2; 2-2-2-0; timp,perc,hp,pno,str.
Commissioned by the Alice M. Ditson Fund of Columbia University and written for Martha Graham.
Sets created by Isamu Noguchi.
First produced under title _The Serpent Heart_ but after revision of the score titled _Cave of the Heart_.

Premiere

W71a. 1946 (May 10): New York; Columbia University; Macmillan Theatre; Martha Graham Dance Company (under the title _The Serpent Heart_) _See_: B71h

Other Selected Performances

W71b. 1947 (Feb 27): New York; Ziegfeld Theatre; Martha Graham Dance Company; Sorceress: Martha Graham; Adventurer: Erick Hawkins; Victim: Yuriko; Chorus: Mary O'Donnell (under the title _Cave of the Heart_)

W71c. 1947 (Dec 5-6, 8): Philadelphia; Academy of Music; Philadelphia Orchestra; Eugene Ormandy, conductor (7-movement suite)

W71d. 1965 (Nov 4, 7, 11, 19): New York; 54th Street Theatre; Martha Graham Dance Company; Medea: Helen McGhee; Jason: Robert Cohan; Princess: Yuriko; Chorus: Matt Turney. _See_: B71a

W72. **MEDEA'S MEDITATION AND DANCE OF VENGEANCE, OP. 23A.** (1955; Schirmer; 14 min.; Library of Congress has pencil score, 1 p.l., 50 [i.e. 51] p.; gift of the composer, December 23, 1966) _See_: B72k, B72l

3(pic)-3-4-3; 4-3-3-1; timp,perc,xyl,hp,pno,str.

Premiere

W72a. 1956 (Feb 2): New York; Carnegie Hall; New York
       Philharmonic-Symphony Orchestra; Dimitri Mitro-
       poulos, conductor. <u>See</u>: B72h, B72i, B72j, B72n

Other Selected Performances

W72b. 1956 (Dec 15): Boston; Symphony Hall; Boston
       Symphony Orchestra; Charles Münch, conductor.
       <u>See</u>: B72a

W72c. 1957 (Jan 31): London; Royal Festival Hall; Royal
       Philharmonic Orchestra; Thomas Schippers, con-
       ductor (Harold Holt Celebrity Concert) <u>See</u>:
       B72c, B72e, B72m

W72d. 1958 (Feb 24-25): Seattle; Orpheum Theatre;
       Seattle Symphony Orchestra; Milton Katims, con-
       ductor.

W72e. 1959 (Oct 30-31): Boston; Symphony Hall; Boston
       Symphony Orchestra; Thomas Schippers, conductor.

W72f. 1961 (Aug 15): Los Angeles; Hollywood Bowl; Los
       Angeles Philharmonic Orchestra; Howard Mitchell,
       guest conductor. <u>See</u>: B72f

W72g. 1962 (Jan 12): St. Louis, Mo.; Chase Hotel;
       Khorasson Room; St. Louis Symphony Orchestra;
       Werner Torkanowsky, conductor [repeated Jan 13
       in St. Louis' Kiel Auditorium Opera House]

W72h. 1962 (Feb 29, Mar 2): San Francisco; War Memorial
       Opera House; San Francisco Symphony Orchestra;
       Thomas Schippers, conductor. <u>See</u>: B72d

W72i. 1962 (Oct 29-30): Seattle; Opera House; Seattle
       Symphony Orchestra; Milton Katims, conductor.

W72j. 1965 (Nov 12-13): Boston; Symphony Hall; Boston
       Symphony Orchestra; Werner Torkanowsky, conduc-
       tor.

W72k. 1966 (Mar 22): New York; Carnegie Hall; Philadel-
       phia Orchestra; Stanislaw Skrowaczewski, conduc-
       tor.

W72l. 1966 (May 13): Caracas, Venezuela; Concha Acustica
       de Bello Monte; Philadelphia Orchestra; Eugene
       Ormandy, conductor.

W72m. 1966 (May 19): Rio de Janeiro; Teatro Municipal;
       Philadelphia Orchestra; Stanislaw Skrowaczewski,
       conductor.

W72n.   1966 (May 21): São Paolo; Teatro Municipal; Phila-
        delphia Orchestra; Stanislaw Skrowaczweski, con-
        ductor.

W72o.   1966 (Jun 1): Santiago de Chile; Teatro Caupoli-
        can; Philadelphia Orchestra; Stanislaw Skrowa-
        czewski, conductor.

W72p.   1966 (Jun 11): Mexico City; Palacio de Bellas
        Artes; Philadelphia Orchestra; Stanislaw Skrowa-
        czewski, conductor.

W72q.   1966 (Jun 14): Gainesville; University of Florida;
        University Gymnasium; Philadelphia Orchestra;
        Stanislaw Skrowaczewski, conductor.

W72r.   1980 (Mar 11-13): Washington, D.C.; Kennedy Center
        for the Performing Arts; Concert Hall; National
        Symphony Orchestra; Antal Dorati, conductor.
        See: B72g

W73. **MUSIC FOR A SCENE FROM SHELLEY, OP. 7.**   (1933;
        Schirmer; 8 min., 30 sec.) See: B73c, B73l

        3-3-3-3; 4-3-3-1; timp,perc,glock,hp,str.
        From Shelley's Prometheus Unbound, act 2, scene 5.
        Written in 1933 while Barber was living at Cadi-
        gliano, Italy.

        Premiere

W73a.   1935 (Mar 23-24): New York; Carnegie Hall; New
        York Philharmonic-Symphony Orchestra; Werner
        Janssen, conductor. See: B73d, B73e

        Other Selected Performances

W73b.   1936 (Aug 2): Ravinia Park, Ill.; Chicago Symphony
        Orchestra; Werner Janssen (Ravinia Festival)
        See: B73a, B73k

W73c.   1937 (Jul 23): Los Angeles; Hollywood Bowl; Los
        Angeles Philharmonic Orchestra; Werner Janssen,
        conductor. See: B73j

W73d.   1939 (Apr 23): Rome; Teatro Adriano; Orchestra
        Stabile della Regia Accade mia di Santa Cecilia;
        Bernardino Molinari, conductor.

W73e.   1939 (early): Helsinki; Helsinki Municipal Sympho-
        ny; Martti Similä, conductor. See: B73b

W74. **DIE NATALI: CHORAL PRELUDES FOR CHRISTMAS, OP. 37.**
(1960; Schirmer; 16 min.; Library of Congress has
condensed pencil score and sketches, [82] p.) and
pencil holograph (67 l.); dated at end: Santa Cris-
tina.   Sept. 3-[19]60) See: B74d, B74l

A sequence of chorale preludes, based on familiar
Christmas carols.
3-3-3-2; 4-3-3-1; timp,perc,hp,str.
Organ arrangement by the composer available.
Commissioned by Charles Münch in celebration of the
75th season of the Boston Symphony Orchestra,
Charles Münch, Music Director.
Dedicated to the memory of Serge and Natalie
Koussevitzky.
Separately arranged by Barber is his prelude on
Silent Night.

Premiere

W74a.   1960 (Dec 22-23): Boston; Symphony Hall; Boston
Symphony Orchestra; Charles Münch, conductor.
See: B74a, B74e, B74f, B74g, B74k, B74l

Other Selected Performances

W74b.   1961 (Jan 4): New York; Carnegie Hall; Boston
Symphony Orchestra; Charles Münch, conductor.

W74c.   1961 (Dec 30): London; radio broadcast on Network
Three; BBC Northern Orchestra; Stanford Robinson, conductor. See: B74b

W74d.   1963 (Feb 1-2): Boston; Symphony Hall; Boston
Symphony Orchestra; Charles Münch, conductor.

W74e.   1968 (Dec 19-21): Chicago; Orchestra Hall; Chicago
Symphony Orchestra; William Steinberg, conductor. See: B74h

W74f.   1970 (Jan 2-3, 6): Boston; Symphony Hall; Boston
Symphony Orchestra; William Steinberg, conductor.

W74g.   1971 (Dec 17-18): Cincinnati; Music Hall; Cincinnati Symphony Orchestra; Erich Kunzel, conductor. See: B74j

W75. **NIGHT FLIGHT, OP. 19A.** (1944; Schirmer; 8 min.;
Library of Congress has first draft, condensed pencil score, [4] p.)

Second movement of the Symphony no. 2, op. 19.
3-3-4-2; 4-3-3-1; perc,pno,str.

Premiere

W75a. 1964 (Oct 8): Cleveland; Severance Hall; Cleveland
       Orchestra; Georg Szell, conductor.

W76. **OVERTURE TO "THE SCHOOL FOR SCANDAL," OP. 5.** (1931-33;
     Schirmer; 8 min.) See: B76b, B76d, B76e, B76j, B76o

     3-3-3-2; 4-3-3-1; timp,perc,hp,cel,str.
     Arr. for band (trans. by Frank Hudson) available.
     Graduation thesis from Curtis Institute of Music,
     1932.
     With this work, Barber awarded the Joseph H. Bearns
     Music Prize for the second time.

     Premiere

W76a. 1933 (Aug 30): Philadelphia; Robin Hood Dell;
       Philadelphia Orchestra; Alexander Smallens, con-
       ductor.

     Other Selected Performances

W76b. 1938 (Mar 30-Apr 1): New York; Carnegie Hall; New
       York Philharmonic-Symphony Orchestra; John Bar-
       birolli, conductor. See: B76f

W76c. 1940 (Nov 15-16): Boston; Symphony Hall; Boston
       Symphony Orchestra; Serge Koussevitzky, conduc-
       tor.

W76d. 1941 (Feb 11): New York; Carnegie Hall; Philadel-
       phia Orchestra; Eugene Ormandy, conductor. See:
       B76k

W76e. 1941 (Feb 15): New York; Carnegie Hall; Boston
       Symphony Orchestra; Serge Koussevitzky, conduc-
       tor. See: B76g

W76f. 1950 (Feb 18): New York; Carnegie Hall; Boston
       Symphony Orchestra; Charles Münch, conductor.
       See: B76h

W76g. 1950 (Mar 30-31): Los Angeles; Philharmonic Audi-
       torium; Los Angeles Philharmonic Orchestra;
       Alfred Wallenstein, conductor. See: B76s

W76h. 1951 (Mar 18): New York; Carnegie Hall; New York
       Philharmonic-Symphony Orchestra; Victor de Saba-
       ta, conductor.

W76i. 1953 (May 4): Los Angeles; Shrine Auditorium;
       Boston Symphony Orchestra; Charles Münch, con-
       ductor. See: B76a

W76j.　1973 (Feb 10): New York; Carnegie Hall; Youth
　　　　Symphony Orchestra of New York; Gary Sheldon,
　　　　conductor. See: B76l

W76k.　1973 (Dec 7-8): Cincinnati; Music Hall; Cincinnati
　　　　Symphony Orchestra; Carmon De Leone, conductor.
　　　　See: B76q

W76l.　1975 (Feb 4): New York; Carnegie Hall; Cleveland
　　　　Orchestra; Lorin Maazel, conductor.

W76m.　1980 (Mar 9): Philadelphia; Academy of Music;
　　　　Curtis Symphony Orchestra; Calvin Simmons, con-
　　　　ductor (The Curtis Institute of Music's Fourth
　　　　Faculty Commemorative Series honoring Samuel
　　　　Barber on the occasion of his seventieth birth-
　　　　day; evening concert)

W76n.　1981 (Mar 27): Boston; Boston University; Boston
　　　　University Wind Ensemble; Thomas Evans, conduc-
　　　　tor (transcribed by Frank Hudson)

W76o.　1983 (Nov 10): Los Angeles; Music Center; Dorothy
　　　　Chandler Pavilion; Los Angeles Philharmonic
　　　　Orchestra; John Williams, conductor. See: B76c

PAS DE DEUX See: **SOUVENIRS, OP. 28.**

POEME See: **CONCERTO FOR PIANO AND ORCHESTRA, OP. 38**
(W65k)

SCHOTTISCHE See: **SOUVENIRS, OP. 28.**

W77. **SECOND ESSAY FOR ORCHESTRA, OP. 17.** (1942; Schirmer;
　　　10 min.; Library of Congress has first draft, con-
　　　densed pencil score and sketches, [20] p.) See:
　　　B77b, B77c, B77d, B77g, B77h, B77k

　　　3-3-3-2; 4-3-3-1; timp,perc,str.
　　　Written for the Centennial of the New York Philhar-
　　　　monic-Symphony Orchestra.
　　　Dedicated to Robert Horan.

　　　Premiere

W77a.　1942 (Apr 16): New York; Carnegie Hall; New York
　　　　Philharmonic-Symphony Orchestra; Bruno Walter,
　　　　conductor. See: B77r

　　　Other Selected Performances

W77b.   1943 (Jul 25): New York; Lewisohn Stadium; New
         York Philharmonic-Symphony Orchestra; Jascha
         Horenstein, conductor.

W77c.   1944 (Jan 6-7): Los Angeles; Philharmonic Audi-
         torium; Los Angeles Philharmonic Orchestra;
         Alfred Wallenstein, conductor. See: B77j

W77d.   1945 (Nov 2-3): Philadelphia; Academy of Music;
         Philadelphia Orchestra; Eugene Ormandy, conduc-
         tor.

W77e.   1952 (Oct 17-18): Philadelphia; Academy of Music;
         Philadelphia Orchestra; Eugene Ormandy, conduc-
         tor.

W77f.   1953 (Feb 19): Atlanta; Philadelphia Orchestra;
         Eugene Ormandy, conductor.

W77g.   1953 (May 3): Ann Arbor; University of Michigan;
         Philadelphia Orchestra; Eugene Ormandy, conduc-
         tor (60th May Festival)

W77h.   1959 (Oct 10): London; Royal Festival Hall; New
         York Philharmonic Orchestra; Leonard Bernstein,
         conductor. See: B77n

W77i.   1959 (Oct 24): New York; Carnegie Hall; New York
         Philharmonic Orchestra; Leonard Bernstein, con-
         ductor.

W77j.   1960 (Nov 16): New York; Carnegie Hall; Orchestra
         of America; Richard Korn, conductor. See: B77m

W77k.   1970 (Mar 20-21): Cincinnati; Music Hall; Cincin-
         nati Symphony Orchestra; Izler Solomon, con-
         ductor.   See: B77o

W77l.   1974 (Mar 15-16): Cincinnati; Music Hall; Cincin-
         nati Symphony Orchestra; Thomas Schippers, con-
         ductor.   See: B77p

W77m.   1975 (Jan 18-20): Seattle; Opera House; Seattle
         Symphony Orchestra; Guido Ajmone-Marsan, con-
         ductor.

W77n.   1975 (Apr 28): New York; Lincoln Center for the
         Performing Arts; Avery Fisher Hall; Philadelphia
         Orchestra; Eugene Ormandy, conductor. See: B77q

W77o.   1980 (Mar 9): Philadelphia; Academy of Music;
         Curtis Symphony Orchestra; Calvin Simmons, con-
         ductor The Curtis Institute of Music's Fourth
         Faculty Commemorative Series honoring Samuel
         Barber on the occasion of his seventieth birth-

day; evening concert)

W77p.   1980 (Oct 8): Philadelphia; Academy of Music;
         Philadelphia Orchestra; Eugene Ormandy, conduc-
         tor (The Children's Hospital of Philadelphia's
         125th Anniversary Benefit Concert)

W77q.   1983 (Oct 11, 13): Oakland, Calif.; Paramount
         Theatre; Oakland Symphony Orchestra; Richard
         Buckley, conductor. See: B77s

W77r.   1983 (Oct 12): Berkeley; University of California;
         Zellerbach Auditorium; Oakland Symphony Orches-
         tra; Richard Buckley, conductor.

THE SERPENT HEART See: **MEDEA, OP. 23 (W71)**

SILENT NIGHT See: **DIE NATALI...OP. 37.**

W78. **SOUVENIRS, OP. 28.** (1952; Schirmer; 19 min.; Library
       of Congress has two copies of a black-line print
       ed., with Barber's additions and corrections in
       colored pencil (37 p.) and his pencilled corrections
       for the holograph ([1] leaf) laid in, in addition to
       a pencil holograph with corrections in red ink of
       the orchestra arrangement) See: B78c, B78l, B78n

       2(pic)-2(E hn)-2-2; 4-3-3-0; timp,perc,hp,cel,str.
       Ballet suite in six movements: 1(pic)-1(E hn)-2-2;
         4-3-3-0; timp,perc,hp,cel,str.
       Contents: Waltz; Schottische; Pas de deux; Two-Step;
         Hesitation Tango; Galop.
       Originally a work for one piano, four hands; in
         1952, Barber arranged for solo piano; also arran-
         ged by Arthur Gold and Robert Fizdale for two
         pianos, four hands.
       Dedicated to Charles Turner.
       Lincoln Kirstein suggested orchestrating for use as
         a ballet score or an orchestral concert suite.
       For the adaptation entitled A Blue Rose, see W63.

       Premiere

    W78a.   1952 (Jul): NBC-TV; Arthur Gold and Robert Fiz-
             dale, duo pianists [two pianos, four hands]

    W78b.   1953 (Nov 12): Chicago; Chicago Symphony Orches-
             tra; Fritz Reiner, conductor [ballet suite]

    W78c.   1955 (Nov 15): New York; New York City Ballet;
             City Center; Todd Bolender, choreography; Rouben
             Ter-Arutunian, sets and costumes; Jean Rosen-

thal, lighting [complete ballet] <u>See</u>: B78o

<u>Other</u> <u>Selected</u> <u>Performances</u>

W78d.   1952 (Dec 12): London; Wigmore Hall; Arthur Gold
        and Robert Fizdale, duo pianists. <u>See</u>: B78m

W78e.   1953 (Mar 13): New York; Museum of Modern Art;
        Arthur Gold and Robert Fizdale, duo pianists.
        <u>See</u>: B78g

W78f.   1959 (Jan 12): New York; NBC-TV; Arthur Gold and
        Robert Fizdale, duo pianists (Bell Telephone
        Hour)

W78g.   1960 (Mar 9): Philadelphia; Curtis Institute of
        Music; Curtis Hall Auditorium; Vladimir and
        Eleanor Sokoloff, piano (Originally soprano
        Patti Jean Thompson had intended to perform
        Songs, opp. 13, 2, no. 1, and 10, no. 1; how-
        ever, when Ms. Thompson became indisposed, the
        Sokoloffs performed <u>Souvenirs</u> instead) (per-
        formed to honor Barber's 50th birthday).

W78h.   1960 (Mar 21): Seattle; Orpheum Theatre; Seattle
        Symphony Orchestra; Milton Katims, conductor.

W78i.   1960 (Nov 18): New York; New York City Ballet;
        City Center; Todd Bolender, choreography; Rouben
        Ter-Arutunian, sets and costumes [complete bal-
        let]

W78j.   1967 (Nov 13): New York; Carnegie Recital Hall;
        Marcia Klebanow and Johanna-Maria Fraenkel, duo
        pianists [two pianos, four hands]

W78k.   1969 (Nov 6): Brooklyn; Academy of Music; Harkness
        Ballet. <u>See</u>: B78a

W78l.   1982 (Oct 17): West Chester, Penn.; West Chester
        State College; Swope Hall; Richard K. Veleta and
        Robert Dodd Greene, duo-pianists; Thomas W.
        Sabatino, timpani; Richard F. Fitz and Thomas S.
        Whitmoyer, percussion.

"SYMPHONY DEDICATED TO THE ARMY AIR FORCES" <u>See</u>:
SYMPHONY NO. 2, OP. 19.

W79. **SYMPHONY NO. 1, OP. 9.** (1936, revised 1942; Schirmer;
        19 min.; Library of Congress has pencil score, 1,
        23, 36, 38-55 p., in caption: "To Gian Carlo Menot-
        ti," and at end: "Roquebrune Feb. 24-26 - 36.")
        <u>See</u>: B79b, B79m, B79o, B79s, B79t, B79v, B79y

3-3-3-3; 4-3-3-1; timp,perc,hp,str.
Version for concert band also exists.
Awarded Pulitzer Prize (1936) for music.
Dedicated to Gian-Carlo Menotti.

Premiere

W79a. 1936 (Dec 13): Rome; Adriano Theatre; Augusteo
       Orchestra; Bernardino Molinari, conductor. See:
       B79a, B79e

Other Selected Performances

W79b. 1937 (Jan 21, 23): Cleveland; Severance Hall;
       Cleveland Orchestra; Rudolph Ringwall, conductor
       [Ringwall replaced Artur Rodzinski due to the
       latter's illness]

W79c. 1937 (Mar 24-25, Apr 3-4): New York; Carnegie
       Hall; New York Philharmonic-Symphony Orchestra;
       Artur Rodzinski, conductor. See: B79g

W79d. 1937 (Jul 25): Salzburg; Mozarteum; Vienna
       Philharmonic Orchestra; Artur Rodzinski, conduc-
       tor (Salzburg Festival) See: B79bb

W79e. 1938 (Dec 2-3): Philadelphia; Academy of Music;
       Philadelphia Orchestra; Eugene Ormandy, conduc-
       tor. See: B79w

W79f. 1941 (Feb 20): Detroit; Masonic Temple; Detroit
       Symphony Orchestra; Albert Stoessel, conductor.

W79g. 1941 (Aug 5): London; Royal Albert Hall; London
       Symphony Orchestra; Sir Henry Wood, conductor
       (Promenade Concert) See: B79x

W79h. 1944 (Feb 18-19): New York; Carnegie Hall; New
       York Philharmonic-Symphony Orchestra; Bruno Wal-
       ter, conductor [revised version] See: B79aa

W79i. 1946 (Dec 2-3): Seattle; Moore Theatre; Seattle
       Symphony Orchestra; Carl Bricken, conductor.

W79j. 1953 (Jan 13): Seattle; Civic Auditorium; Seattle
       Symphony Orchestra; Milton Katims, conductor.

W79k. 1956 (Jan 13-14, 16): Philadelphia; Academy of
       Music; Philadelphia Orchestra; Paul Paray, con-
       ductor.

W79l. 1963 (Jan 10-11): San Francisco; War Memorial
       Opera House; San Francisco Symphony Orchestra;
       Howard Mitchell, guest conductor. See: B79i

W79m.   1963 (Sep 27-28): Boston; Symphony Hall; Boston
         Symphony Orchestra; Erich Leinsdorf, conductor.

W79n.   1964 (Aug 27): Los Angeles; Hollywood Bowl; Los
         Angeles Philharmonic Orchestra; André Vander-
         noot, guest conductor. See: B79n

W79o.   1969 (Jan 12): Seattle; Opera House; Seattle Sym-
         phony Orchestra; Howard Mitchell, conductor
         ("Olympia 'Stars of the Future' Concert 4")

W79p.   1981 (Feb 6-7): Chicago; Orchestra Hall; Chicago
         Symphony Orchestra; Erich Leinsdorf, conductor.
         See: B79u

W79q.   1982 (Nov 12): Boston; Boston University; Concert
         Hall; Boston University Wind Ensemble; Paul Gay,
         conductor [transcribed by Guy Duker]

W79r.   1984 (Feb 18): Santa Ana, Calif.; Santa Ana High
         School Auditorium; Pacific Symphony Orchestra;
         Keith Clark, conductor. See: B79h

W80. **SYMPHONY NO. 2, OP. 19.** (1944, revised 1947; Schir-
         mer; Library of Congress has pencil holograph (41,
         10 [i.e. 9], 31 l.) on transparent paper dated
         February 3, 1944; withdrawn by Barber in the early
         1960s]) See: B80b, B80g, B80i, B80j, B80k, B80m,
         B80n, B80q, B80s, B80t, B80u, B80w, B80y

         2 fl., 1 picc., 2 ob., 1 Engl hrn., 2 cl., E-flat
         bass cl., 2 bsn., 1 contra bsn., 4 hrn., 3 tpts, 3
         trmb., tuba, percussion, pf., electronic "tone
         generator," strings.
         Begun while at the Army Air Field at Fort Worth,
         Texas.
         Commissioned by the U.S. Air Forces.
         First performed as Symphony Dedicated to the Army
         Air Forces.
         A revised version of the slow movement has been
         published separately under the title of Night
         Flight, op. 19a; see W75.

         Premiere

W80a.   1944 (Mar 3-4): Boston; Symphony Hall; Boston
         Symphony Orchestra; Serge Koussevitzky, conduc-
         tor. See: B80a, B80b, B80d

         Other Selected Performances

W80b.   1944 (Mar 9): New York; Carnegie Hall; Boston
         Symphony Orchestra; Serge Koussevitzky, conduc-
         tor. See: B80e

W80c.   1949 (Jan 5): Philadelphia; Academy of Music;
         Curtis Symphony Orchestra; Alexander Hilsberg,
         conductor [revised version] (invitation concert
         for 25th anniversary of Curtis Institute of
         Music) See: B80r, B80x

W80d.   1949 (Jan 21-22): Philadelphia; Academy of Music;
         Philadelphia Orchestra; Alexander Hilsberg, con-
         ductor [revised version]

W80e.   1951 (Apr 6): Boston; Symphony Hall; Boston Sym-
         phony Orchestra; Samuel Barber, conductor [re-
         vised version] See: B80l

W81. **THIRD ESSAY FOR ORCHESTRA, OP. 47.** (1978; Schirmer)
     See: B81a

     Premiere

W81a.   1978 (Sep 14): New York; Lincoln Center for the
         Performing Arts; Avery Fisher Hall; New York
         Philharmonic Orchestra; Zubin Mehta, conductor.
         See: B81d

     Other Selected Performance

W81b.   1979 (Nov 15): London; Royal Festival Hall; Royal
         Philharmonic Orchestra; Leonard Slatkin, conduc-
         tor.

         THROUGH THE EDGE See: **ADAGIO FOR STRINGS, OP. 11**
         (W61i)

W82. **TOCCATA FESTIVA, OP. 36.** (1960; Schirmer; 16 min.;
     Library of Congress has first draft dated February
     13, 1960, pencil score for organ and piano, [52] p.)
     See: B82g, B82l, B82m

     For organ and orchestra; version for organ and piano
     available.
     3-3-3-2; 4-3-3-1; timp,perc,str.
     Work commissioned by Mary Curtis Zimbalist.
     Written for the opening of the new organ at the
     Philadelphia Academy of Music, September 30, 1960.

     Premiere

W82a.   1960 (Sep 30): Philadelphia; Academy of Music;
         Paul Callaway, organ; Philadelphia Orchestra;
         Eugene Ormandy, conductor. See: B82c, B82j,
         B82k, B82m

Other Selected Performances

W82b.   1962 (Oct 5-6, 15): Philadelphia; Academy of Mu-
        sic; E. Power Biggs, organ; Philadelphia Orches-
        tra; Eugene Ormandy, conductor.

W82c.   1973 (Nov 19): Los Angeles; University of Califor-
        nia, Los Angeles; Royce Hall; Thomas Harmon,
        organ; UCLA Symphony; Mehli Mehta, conductor.
        See: B82h

W82d.   1975 (Apr 13): New York; Lincoln Center for the
        Performing Arts; Alice Tully Hall; Catharine
        Crozier, organ; Musica Aeterna Orchestra; Fred-
        eric Waldman, conductor. See: B82d

   TWO-STEP See: SOUVENIRS, OP. 28.

   WALTZ See: SOUVENIRS, OP. 28.

   YOUTH See: ADAGIO FOR STRINGS, OP. 11 (W61k)

BAND MUSIC

W83. **COMMANDO MARCH.** (1943; Schirmer; 3 min., 30 sec.)
      See: B83b

      Composed while Barber was in the Army.
      Originally composed for band, but was prepared for
      orchestra by the composer at the suggestion of
      Serge Koussevitzky.

   Premiere

W83a.   1943 (Feb): Atlantic City, New Jersey; Army Air
        Force Band.

   Other Selected Performances

W83b.   1943 (Oct 29-30): Boston; Boston Symphony Orches-
        tra; Serge Koussevitzky, conductor [orchestral
        arrangement] See: B83g

W83c.   1981 (May 5): Louisville, Ky.; Southern Baptist
        Theological Seminary; Alumni Chapel; Seminary
        Winds; Douglas Smith, conductor.

W83d.   1981 (Oct 4): Milwaukee; Milwaukee County Per-

forming Arts Center; Vogel Hall; UWM Symphony
Band and Wind Ensemble; Thomas L. Dvorak, conductor.

OVERTURE TO "THE SCHOOL FOR SCANDAL," OP. 5. See:
W76.

CHAMBER MUSIC

W84. **CANZONE FOR FLUTE AND PIANO, OP. 38A.** (1963; Schirmer; Library of Congress has pencil manuscript, [4]
p.)

Composer's adaptation of the second movement of the
Piano Concerto, op. 38; cf. W65.

W85. **CAPRICORN CONCERTO, OP. 21.** (1944; Schirmer; 14 min.;
Library of Congress has pencil holograph on trans-
parent paper dated September 8, 1944; holograph
sketch in pencil ([11] p.) laid in; gift of Barber,
December 29, 1955) See: B85a, B85b, B85c, B85g,
B85h, B85j, B85o

For flute, oboe, trumpet, and strings.
Named after Barber's home on Croton Lake, Mt. Kisco,
New York.

Premiere

W85a. 1944 (Oct 8): New York; Town Hall; Mitchell Miller, oboe; John Wummer, flute; identification of
trumpeter not specified; Saidenberg Little Symphony; Daniel Saidenberg, conductor. See: B85h,
B85k, B85q

Other Selected Performances

W85b. 1954 (Feb 7): New York; Town Hall; Saidenberg
Little Symphony; Daniel Saidenberg, conductor
(program of the Concert Society of New York)

W85c. 1956 (Oct 18): New York; Carnegie Hall; New York
Philharmonic-Symphony Orchestra; Dimitri Mitropoulos, conductor. See: B85e

W85d. 1964 (Nov 11): New York; Carnegie Hall; Festival
Orchestra of New York; Thomas Dunn, conductor
[repeated Nov 13, Philharmonic Hall] See: B85d

W85e. 1984 (Jan 28): Pasadena; Ambassador Auditorium;
       Allan Vogel, oboe; David Shostac, flute; Mario
       Guaneri, trumpet; Los Angeles Chamber Orchestra;
       Gerard Schwarz, conductor. See: B85i

W86. **DOVER BEACH, OP. 3.** (1931; Schirmer; 8 min., 30 sec.;
     Library of Congress has manuscript dated May 7,
     1931, pencil score, [1], 7 p.) See: B86d, B86k

     For voice and string quartet, for voice and orches-
     tra, and for voice and piano.
     Text by Matthew Arnold from his Poems (New York:
     Macmillan, 1940), p. 211-212.

     Premiere

W86a. 1932 (May 12): Philadelphia; Curtis Institute of
       Music; Casimir Hall; Rose Bampton, contralto
       (later soprano); James Bloom and Frances Wiener,
       violins, Arthur Granick, viola, and Samuel Ge-
       schichter, violoncello (Twenty-Fifth Students'
       Concert)

     Other Selected Performances

W86b. 1937 (Mar 7): Philadelphia; Curtis Institute of
       Music; Casimir Hall; Rose Bampton, soprano;
       Curtis String Quartet.

W86c. 1955 (Aug 16): Marlboro, Vt.; Marlboro College
       Auditorium; Charles Crook, baritone; Ling Tung
       and Amnon Levy, violins; Lotte Hammerschlag,
       viola; Yuan Tung, violoncello (Marlboro Music
       Festival)

W86d. 1958 (Jul 23): Marlboro, Vt.; Marlboro College
       Auditorium; Charles Crook, baritone; Bjoern
       Andreasson and Patricia Grimes, violins; Rhoda
       Rhea, viola; Burton Dines, violoncello (Marlboro
       Music Festival)

W86e. 1960 (Mar 9): Philadelphia; Curtis Institute of
       Music; Curtis Hall Auditorium; Barry Hanner,
       baritone; Curtis String Quartet (Jascha Brodsky
       and Mehli Mehta, violins, Max Aronoff, viola,
       and Orlando Cole, violoncello) (performed to
       honor Barber's 50th birthday).

W86f. 1963 (Aug 31): Marlboro, Vt.; Marlboro College
       Auditorium; Ara Berberian, bass; Marc Gottlieb
       and Ling Tung, violins; Karen Tuttle, viola;
       Madeline Foley, violoncello (Marlboro Music
       Festival)

W86g. 1965 (Jul 24): Marlboro, Vt.; Marlboro College
        Auditorium; Lawrence Bogue, baritone; Oswald
        Lehnert and Felix Galimir, violins; Harry Zarat-
        zian, viola; Jay Humeston, violoncello (Marlboro
        Music Festival)

W86h. 1968 (Jul 3): Marlboro, Vt.; Marlboro College
        Auditorium; Leslie Guinn, baritone; Masuko Ush-
        ioda and Marc Gottlieb, violins; Martha Katz,
        viola; Gayle Smith, violoncello (Marlboro Music
        Festival)

W86i. 1969 (Nov 23): Los Angeles; Exposition Park; Coun-
        ty Museum of Natural History; Beverly Robinson,
        soprano; Valley String Quartet.

W86j. 1972 (Jul 19): Marlboro, Vt.; Marlboro College
        Auditorium; Evans Clough, baritone; Paul Biss
        and Miriam Fried, violins; Robert Vernon, viola;
        Denis Brott, violoncello (Marlboro Music Festi-
        val)

W86k. 1980 (Mar 9): Philadelphia; Curtis Institute of
        Music; Curtis Hall Auditorium; Casimir Hall;
        Rose Bampton, soprano; Curtis String Quartet
        (Jascha Brodsky and Yumi Ninomiya, violins, Max
        Aronoff, viola, and Orlando Cole, violoncello)
        (The Curtis Institute of Music's Fourth Faculty
        Commemorative Series honoring Samuel Barber on
        the occasion of his seventieth birthday; after-
        noon concert)

W86l. 1980 (Jul 4): London; Christ Church, Spitalfields;
        Vivien Townley, soprano; London Sinfonietta
        (Fourth Summer Festival of Music; in commemora-
        tion of Barber's 70th birthday) _See_: B86e

W86m. 1981 (Sep 29): Louisville, Ky.; Southern Baptist
        Theological Seminary; Heeren Recital Hall; War-
        ren Jaworski, baritone; Beverly Holder, piano.

W86n. 1982 (Oct 17): West Chester, Pa.; West Chester
        State College; Swope Hall; G. Alan Wagner, bari-
        tone; Sylvia Ahramjian and Molly Renninger,
        violins, Aino Wolfson, viola, and Eugene Klein,
        violoncello.

W87. **MUTATIONS FROM BACH.** (1968; Schirmer; Library of
        Congress has pencil score, 11 numb. l.) _See_: B87a,
        B87b, B87d

        For brass ensemble and timpani.
        Utilizes plain-song melody "Christe du Lamm Gottes"
          (cf. Bach's Cantata no. 23, "Du wahrer Gott und

Davids Sohn")
Sometimes called Meditations on a Theme of Bach.

Premiere

W87a.   1969: American Symphony Orchestra; Leopold Stokowski, conductor [additional information unavail-
able]   See: B87c

Other Selected Performances

W87b.   1981 (Mar 27): Cambridge, Mass.; Harvard University; Sanders Theatre; Empire Brass Quintet.

W87c.   1981 (Apr 7): Boston; Boston University; Boston
University Brass Ensemble; Paul Gay, conductor.

W87d.   1982 (Mar 17): Bloomington; Indiana University;
Indiana University Brass Choir; Charles Gorham,
conductor.

W88.   **SERENADE FOR STRINGS, OP. 1.** (1928; Schirmer (1942);
10 min.; Library of Congress has pencil score, [14]
p.) See: B88b, B88d, B88h

Originally for string quartet but also arranged for
string orchestra.
Written while Barber was a student at Curtis Institute of Music, Philadelphia.

Premiere

W88a.   1930 (May 5): Philadelphia; Curtis Institute of
Music; Casimir Hall; Swastika Quartet (Gama
Gilbert and Benjamin Sharlip, violins Max Aro-
noff, viola, and Orlando Cole, violoncello)

Other Selected Performances

W88b.   1936 (Nov 16): Rome; American Academy (Accademia
Americana); Villa Aurelia; Curtis String Quartet
(Jascha Brodsky and Charles Jaffe, violins, Max
Aronoff, viola, and Orlando Cole, violoncello)

W88c.   1937 (Mar 7): Philadelphia; Curtis Institute of
Music; Casimir Hall; Curtis String Quartet Jas-
cha Brodsky and Charles Jaffe, violins, Max
Aronoff, viola, and Orlando Cole, violoncello)

W88d.   1980 (Jul 4): London; Christ Church, Spitalfields;
London Sinfonietta (Fourth Summer Festival of
Music; in honor of Barber's 70th birthday)

W89. **SONATA FOR VIOLIN AND PIANO.** (1928; unpublished)

> Written for the Joseph H. Bearns Music Prize competition offered by Columbia University for the best composition submitted pseudonymously to its judges; Barber won the competition.

W90. **SONATA FOR VIOLONCELLO AND PIANO IN C MINOR, OP. 6.**
(1932; Schirmer, published 1936; 18 min., 30 sec.; Library of Congress has manuscript dated December 9, 1932, pencil, p. 4-16, pages 1-3 lacking; Emilie W. Mills, Special Collections Librarian, University of North Carolina at Greenboro, reports that the University has the <u>Sonata</u> "in manuscript" and also "performance notes in the hand of Luigi Silva" on the 1936 G. Schirmer printed edition inscribed to Silva by Barber) <u>See</u>: B90a, B90f, B90g, B90h, B90l, B90s, B90cc

> Dedicated to Rosario Scalero.
> Received, along with <u>Music For a Scene from Shelley, op. 7</u>, the Pulitzer Prize for Music (May 6, 1935) and Prix de Rome (May 9, 1935); judges granting awards included Deems Taylor, Carl Engel, Leo Sowerby, and Walter Damrosch.

<u>Premiere</u>

W90a. 1932: Orlando Cole, violoncello; Samuel Barber, piano.

<u>Other Selected Performances</u>

W90b. 1933 (Mar): Philadelphia; Mellon Galleries; Orlando Cole, violoncello; Ralph Berkowitz, piano (presented by the Society for Contemporary Music)

W90c. 1936 (Apr 22): Rome; American Academy (Accademia Americana); Villa Aurelia; Luigi Silva, violoncello; Samuel Barber, piano.

W90d. 1936 (Nov 9): Philadelphia; Curtis Institute of Music; Casimir Hall; Felix Salmond, violoncello; Ralph Berkowitz, piano.

W90e. 1937 (Feb 7): New York; Town Hall; Felix Salmond, violoncello; Ralph Berkowitz, piano.

W90f. 1937 (Mar 7): Philadelphia; Curtis Institute of Music; Casimir Hall; Felix Salmond, violoncello; Ralph Berkowitz, piano.

W90g. 1937 (Jun 21): London; Wigmore Hall; Felix Salmond, violoncello; Samuel Barber, piano. <u>See</u>: B90t, B90w

W90h.   1943 (Dec 8): Los Angeles; University of Southern California; Hancock Hall; Members of the Hancock Trio (Stephen De'ak, violoncello; John Crown, piano) <u>See</u>: B90p

W90i.   1947 (Feb 26): New York; Carnegie Hall; Gregor Piatigorsky, violoncello; Ralph Berkowitz, piano.

W90j.   1959 (Dec 18): New York; Carnegie Recital Hall; Jules Eskin, violoncello; John Thomas Covelli, piano. <u>See</u>: B90v

W90k.   1960 (Mar 9): Philadelphia; Curtis Institute of Music; Curtis Hall Auditorium; Orlando Cole, violoncello; Vladimir Sokoloff, piano (performed to honor Barber's 50th birthday)

W90l.   1963 (Oct 28): New York; Town Hall; Gregory Bemko, violoncello; Yoshiko Niiya, piano. <u>See</u>: B90r

W90m.   1968 (Sep 28): London; Wigmore Hall; Thaddeus Brys, violoncello; Jonathan Sack, piano. <u>See</u>: B90m

W90n.   1978 (Sep 26): Berkeley, Calif.; University of California; Hertz Hall; Celeste Winocur, violoncello; Marlene Rozofsky, piano.

W90o.   1979 (Aug 12): Vienna, Va.; Wolf Trap Farm Park for the Performing Arts; Charles Curtis, violoncello; Earl Wild, piano. <u>See</u>: B90o

W90p.   1980 (Mar 9): Philadelphia; Curtis Institute of Music; Curtis Hall Auditorium; Orlando Cole, violoncello; Vladimir Sokoloff, piano (The Curtis Institute of Music's Fourth Faculty Commemorative Series honoring Samuel Barber on the occasion of his 70th birthday; afternoon concert)

W90q.   1980 (Jul 2): London; Christ Church, Spitalfields; Susan Salm, violoncello; Daniel Epstein, piano (Fourth Summer Festival of Music)

W90r.   1982 (Oct 17): West Chester, Penn.; West Chester State College; Swope Hall; Eugene Klein, violoncello; Robert Dodd Greene, piano.

W90s.   1982 (Dec 11): Bloomington; Indiana University; Recital Hall; Karen Buranskas, violoncello; Masako Hayashi, piano.

W91. STRING QUARTET IN B MINOR, OP. 11. (1936; Schirmer; 17 min.; Library of Congress has ink holograph ([7] p.); according to typewritten copy of Barber's letter (laid in) to Harold Spivacke, dated July 28, 1943, the red pencil markings on p. [5] were made by Arturo Toscanini; gift of the composer, July 29, 1943)

Written during late summer and early fall of 1936 at St. Wolfgang, near Salzburg.

Written as a three-movement work, now regarded as a two-movement work with the molto allegro (p.14-16 of the first edition) omitted from performance.

Barber made a string orchestra arrangement of the second movement under the title Adagio for Strings; See: W61.

Premiere

W91a.   1936 (Dec): Rome; American Academy (Accademia Americana); Villa Aurelia; Pro Arte String Quartet.

Other Selected Performances

W91b.   1937 (Mar 7): Philadelphia; Curtis Institute of Music; Casimir Hall; Curtis String Quartet (Jascha Brodsky and Charles Jaffe, violins, Max Aronoff, viola, and Orlando Cole, violoncello) [two movements only]

W91c.   1937 (Apr 20): Washington, D.C.; Library of Congress; Chamber Music Auditorium; Gordon Quartet (Jacques Gordon and David Sackson, violins, William Lincer, viola, and Naoum Benditzky, violoncello) (presented by the Friends of Music in the Library of Congress; U.S. premiere)

W91d.   1938 (Mar 14): Philadelphia; Curtis Institute of Music; Casimir Hall; Curtis String Quartet (same performers as in W91b above) See: B91c, B91u

W91e.   1938 (May 15): New York; Town Hall; Curtis String Quartet (same performers as in W91b above)

W91f.   1964 (Nov 1): Pasadena, Calif.; Pasadena Playhouse; Borodin Quartet (Rosticlav Doubinsky and Yaroslav Alexandrov, violins, Dimitri Shebalin, viola, and Valentin Berlinsky, violoncello) (Coleman Chamber Concert)

W91g.   1980 (Jan 27): Pasadena, Calif.; California Institute of Technology; Beckman Auditorium; Napoca String Quartet (Stefan Ruha and Vasile Horvath, violins, Vasile Fulop, viola, and Jacob Dula, violoncello)   (Coleman Chamber Concert)

W91h.   1980 (Jul 4): London; Christ Church, Spitalfields;
Strings of the London Sinfonietta (Fourth Summer
Festival of Music; in commemoration of Barber's
70th birthday) See: B91i

W92. **SUMMER MUSIC, OP. 31.** (1956; Schirmer; 11 min., 30
sec.; Library of Congress has pencil score dated
November 5, 1955, 1 p.l., 25 [i.e. 26] p.) See:
B92a, B92n

For woodwind quintet.
Commissioned by the Chamber Music Society of Detroit
from contributions by members, "some as small as
$1.00."

Premiere

W92a.   1956 (Mar 20): Detroit; Detroit Institute of Arts;
first-desk men of the Detroit Symphony Orchestra.

Other Selected Performances

W92b.   1956 (Nov 16): New York; Carnegie Hall; New York
Woodwind Quintet (Samuel Baron, flute, David
Glazer, clarinet, Jerome Roth, oboe, Bernard
Garfield, bassoon, John Barrows, French horn)
See: B92q

W92c.   1958 (Jan 19): Pasadena; Pasadena Playhouse; New
York Woodwind Quintet (Samuel Baron, flute,
David Glazer, clarinet, Jerome Roth, oboe, Arthur Weisberg, bassoon, John Barrows, French
horn) (Coleman Chamber Concert)

W92d.   1965 (Jul 30): Marlboro, Vt.; Marlboro College
Auditorium; Ornulf Gulbransen, flute; John Mack,
oboe; Elsa Ludewig, clarinet; John Barrows,
horn; Ryohei Nakagawa, bassoon (Marlboro Music
Festival)

W92e.   1967 (Jun 9): London; Queen Elizabeth Hall;
Northern Sinfonia Orchestra; David Haslam, conductor.

W92f.   1967 (Jun 10): Lewisham, Eng.; Town Hall; same
performers as in W92e above.

W92g.   1967 (Jun 12): Croydon, Eng.; Fairfield Hall; same
performers as in W92e above.

W92h.   1968 (Oct 15): London; Queen Elizabeth Hall; Nash

Ensemble. See: B92i, B92j

W92i.   1969 (Jul 23): Marlboro, Vt.; Marlboro College
         Auditorium; Mardele Combs, flute; Joseph Turner,
         oboe; Richard Stoltzman, clarinet; John Barrows,
         horn; William Winstead, bassoon (Marlboro Music
         Festival)

W92j.   1980 (Jun 24): London; Queen Elizabeth Hall; Nash
         Ensemble.

W92k.   1980 (Jul 4): London; Christ Church, Spitalfields;
         Wind section of the London Sinfonietta (Fourth
         Summer Festival of Music; in commemoration of
         Barber's 70th birthday) See: B92f

W92l.   1981 (Feb 9): New York; St. Bartholomew's Church;
         Ransom Wilson, flute; Randall Wolfgang, oboe;
         Richard Vrotney, bassoon; Gary McGee, clarinet;
         David Jolley, French horn (part of program for
         the memorial services honoring Samuel Barber)

W92m.   1981 (Jun 25): Bloomington; Indiana University;
         Dorian Woodwind Quintet.

SOLO INSTRUMENTAL MUSIC

W93. BALLADE, OP. 46.   (1977; Schirmer; 5 min.)

For piano solo.
Commissioned by the Van Cliburn Foundation, Inc.,
   for the Fifth Van Cliburn International Quadrien-
   nial Piano Competition, made possible by a gift
   from Mrs. J. Lee Johnson, III. See: B93a, B93e,
   B93f

Premiere

W93a.   1977 (Sep 19-21): Fort Worth, Texas; Texas
         Christian University; Ed Landreth Auditorium;
         Semi-finalists: Christian Blackshaw (4th Prize
         Tied), Pi-Hsien Chen, Michel-Jean-Jacques Dal-
         berto (4th Prize Tied), Steven DeGroote (Grand
         Prize Winner), Youri Egorov, Abdel-Rahman El-
         Bacha, Ian Richard Hobson (5th Prize Tied),
         Yevgeny Dmitrievich Krushevsky, Steven Allan
         Mayer, Alexander Ashotovich Mndoyants (5th Prize
         Tied), Elaine Rodrigues (Nascimento), Eugene
         Rowley, Jeffrey Swan (Bronze Medal Winner),
         Alexander Toradze (Silver Medal Winner), and
         Geoffrey Tozer (Fifth Van Cliburn International

Quadrennial Piano Competition)

Other Selected Performance

W93b.   1977 (Nov 1): London; Purcell Room; Steven Allan
          Mayer, piano. See: B93b

W94. EXCURSIONS, OP. 20.   (1944; Schirmer; 11 min., 30
     sec.; Library of Congress has ink holograph on
     transparent paper, with holograph sketches of 1st,
     2nd, and 4th pieces, in pencil, dated at end June
     16, 1944 ([12] p.) laid in.) See: B94a, B94d, B94e,
     B94f, B94p

     Four piano pieces.
       Contents: No. 1. Un poco allegro -- No. 2. In slow
       blues tempo -- No. 3. Allegretto -- No. 4. Allegro
       molto.

     Premiere

W94a.   1945 (Jan 4): Philadelphia; Academy of Music;
          Vladimir Horowitz, piano [Nos. 1-2 and 4 only]

     Other Selected Performances

W94b.   1945 (Feb 12): Chicago; Orchestra Hall; Vladimir
          Horowitz, piano [Nos. 1-2 and 4 only]

W94c.   1945 (Mar 28): New York; Carnegie Hall; Vladimir
          Horowitz, piano [Nos. 1-2 and 4 only] See: B94g

W94d.   1946 (Jan 18): New York; Carnegie Hall; Rudolf
          Firkusny, piano [Nos. 1-2 and 4 only] See:
          B94q

W94e.   1950 (Jan 22): New York; Town Hall; Lucille Roth-
          man, piano [Nos. 3-4 only]

W94f.   1950 (Apr 13): Helsinki; University of Helsinki;
          Andor Foldes, piano (sponsored by the Finnish-
          American Society)

W94g.   1956 (Nov 17): New York; Town Hall; Thomas Darson,
          piano. See: B94c

W94h.   1957 (Nov 14): New York; Town Hall; Jose Kahan,
          piano.

W94i.   1959 (Apr 11): New York; Washington Irving High
          School; Ruth Slenczynska, piano.

W94j.   1959 (Nov 15): New York; Museum of the City of New
          York; Ethel Elfenbein, piano [Nos. 3-4 only]

W94k. 1960 (Mar 13): New York; Carnegie Hall; Robert Schrade, piano.

W94l. 1961 (Jul 31): Salzburg; Mozarteum; Shura Cherkassy, piano (Salzburg Festival)

W94m. 1969 (Oct 14): Evanston, III.; Northwestern University; Lutkin Hall; Nicolas Constantinidis, piano.

W94n. 1970 (Feb 8): Nashville; Tennessee State University; Recital Hall; Donald Barrett, piano.

W94o. 1974 (Jan 17): New York; Carnegie Hall; Zola Shaulis, piano. See: B94j

W94p. 1975 (Oct 18-19): New York; Newman Theater; Eliot Feld Ballet; Christe Sarry, Richard Fein, Michaela Hughes, Linda Miller, Jeff Satinoff, and Patrick Swayze; Gladys Celeste Mercader, piano (New York Shakespeare Festival) See: B94k

W94q. 1976 (Nov 5): Bristol; Virginia Intermount College; Harrison-Jones Memorial Hall; Ruth Slenczynska, piano.

W94r. 1982 (Oct 17): West Chester, Penn.; West Chester State College; Swope Hall; Patricia Taylor Lee, piano.

W94s. 1983 (Apr 5): South Bend; Indiana University at South Bend; Recital Hall; Ejnar Krantz, piano.

FIVE PIECES FOR A SINGING TOWER See: **SUITE FOR CARILLON**

W95. **INCIDENTAL MUSIC TO "ONE DAY OF SPRING."** (193-?)

Play by Mary Kennedy.

Performances

W95a. 1935 (Jan 24): Winter Park, Florida; Annie Russell Theatre [performers unidentifiable]

INTERLUDES (2) FOR PIANO See: **INTERMEZZI (2) FOR PIANO**

W96. **INTERMEZZI (2) FOR PIANO.** (1930-32; unpublished)

For solo piano.

Sometimes called "Two Interludes for Piano."
Nathan Broder, in his Samuel Barber (New York: G.
Schirmer, 1954), p. 16, assigns op. 4 to this
work, whereas other sources assign op. 4 to his
unpublished Violin and Piano Sonata (1931)

W96a.   1932 (May 12): Philadelphia; Curtis Institute of
Music; Casimir Hall; Samuel Barber, piano (Twen-
ty-Fifth Students' Concert)

Other Selected Performances

W96b.   1934 (Mar 1): Philadelphia; Foyer of the Academy
of Music; Jeanne Behrend, piano [No. 1 only]

W96c.   1939 (Mar 1): Philadelphia; Curtis Institute of
Music; Casimir Hall; Jeanne Behrend, piano.

LOVE SONG See: **THREE SKETCHES FOR PIANOFORTE**

MAIN STREET See: Preface

MINUET See: **THREE SKETCHES FOR PIANOFORTE**

DIE NATALI, OP. 37. See: W74.

W97. **NOCTURNE: HOMAGE TO JOHN FIELD, OP. 33.** (1959; Schirmer; 4 min.) See: B97b, B97h

Premiere

W97a.   1959 (Dec 11?): Cleveland?; John Browning, piano.

Other Selected Performances

W97b.   1968 (Sep 29): London; Wigmore Hall; Penelope
Spurrell, piano. See: B97a

W97c.   1976 (Nov 5): Bristol; Virginia Intermount College; Harrison-Jones Memorial Hall; Ruth Slenczynska, piano.

W97d.   1983 (Mar 18): Louisville, Ky.; Southern Baptist
Theological Seminary; Heeren Recital Hall; Ja-
nelle Ganey, piano.

"ONE DAY OF SPRING," INCIDENTAL MUSIC TO See: **INCI-
DENTAL MUSIC TO "ONE DAY OF SPRING"**

77

PETITE BERCEUSE _See_: Preface

W98. **PIANO SONATA, OP. 26.** (1949; Schirmer; 19 min.; Library of Congress has pencil holograph dated June 1949, together with two copies of a black-line print ed. of the work, with Barber's additions and corrections in colored pencil (37 p.) and Barber's penciled corrections for the holograph laid in ([1] l.), affecting the fourth movements; also at Library of Congress is a Moscow edition of the _Sonata_) _See_: B98a, B98i, B98k, B98m, B98n, B98o, B98w, B98cc, B98ww, B98xx, B98bbb, B98jjj, B98nnn, B98ppp, B98bbbb, B98eeee, B98ffff, B98kkkk

Commissioned by Irving Berlin and Richard Rodgers to honor the League of Composers 25th anniversary.

Premiere

W98a. 1949 (Dec 9): Havana, Cuba; Vladimir Horowitz, piano.

W98b. 1950 (Jan 4): New York; Trustees Room of G. Schirmer; Vladimir Horowitz, piano [first performance for an invited audience]

W98c. 1950 (Jan 23): New York; Carnegie Hall; Vladimir Horowitz, piano [first U.S. public performance] _See_: B98k, B98t, B98mm, B98eee

Other Selected Performances

W98d. 1950 (Mar 20): New York; Carnegie Hall; Vladimir Horowitz, piano.

W98e. 1950 (Nov 1): New York; Town Hall; Thomas Brockman, piano.

W98f. 1950 (Nov 17): London; Wigmore Hall; Robert Wallenborn, piano. _See_: B98ee

W98g. 1950 (Nov 18): New York; Town Hall; Marjorie Mitchell, piano.

W98h. 1951 (Oct 8): New York; Town Hall; Moura Lympany, piano. _See_: B98bb

W98i. 1951 (Nov 24): New York; Hunter College; Auditorium; Rudolf Firkusny, piano. _See_: B98ttt

W98j. 1952 (Nov 25): New York; Carnegie Hall; Robert Goldsand, piano. _See_: B98s

W98k.   1953 (Mar 20): New York; Town Hall; Frank Martori,
         piano.

W98l.   1953 (Nov 23): New York; Town Hall; Nikita Maga-
         loff, piano. See: B98g, B98uu

W98m.   1954 (Mar 13): New York; Town Hall; Roberto Eyza-
         guerre, piano.

W98n.   1954 (Oct 5): New York; Town Hall; William Dopp-
         mann, piano. See: B98f

W98o.   1956 (Nov 14): Urbana; University of Illinois;
         Recital Hall; Joseph Battista, piano.

W98p.   1956 (Dec 4): New York; Town Hall; Daniel Pollack,
         piano. See: B98h, B98x

W98q.   1957 (Apr 24): New York; Town Hall; Seymour
         Bernstein, piano. See: B98hhh

W98r.   1957 (Nov 7): New York; Town Hall; Miklos Schwalb,
         piano. See: B98fff

W98s.   1957 (Dec 4): New York; Town Hall; Daniel Pollack,
         piano.

W98t.   1957 (Dec 7): New York; Town Hall; Joseph Battis-
         ta, piano. See: B98ii, B98ss, B98rrr

W98u.   1957 (Dec 21): New York; Town Hall; Samuel Lipman,
         piano.

W98v.   1958 (Jan 17): Pasadena, Calif.; Pasadena Civic
         Auditorium; John Browning, piano. See: B98e

W98w.   1958 (Nov 2): New York; Kaufmann Concert Hall;
         Robert Goldsand, piano.

W98x.   1958 (Nov 5): New York; Town Hall; John Browning,
         piano. See: B98ggg, B98dddd, B98iiii

W98y.   1959 (Jan 18): New York; Town Hall; Thomas Brock-
         man, piano. See: B98ooo, B98zzz

W98z.   1959 (Nov 3): New York; Town Hall; Howard Aibel,
         piano (presented under the auspices of the Wal-
         ter W. Naumburg Musical Foundation) See: B98q,
         B98vv, B98xxx

W98aa.   1959 (Nov 17): Baton Rouge; Louisiana State Uni-
         versity; University Theatre; Ezra Rachlin, pi-
         ano.

W98bb.　1959 (Dec 3): New York; Town Hall; Zita Carno, piano. *See*: B98c, B98www

W98cc.　1960 (Mar 9): Philadelphia; Curtis Institute of Music; Curtis Hall Auditorium; Ruth Meckler (later Laredo), piano (performed to honor Barber's 50th birthday)

W98dd.　1960 (Mar 22): Warsaw; Filharmonia Narodowa; Michael Block, piano.

W98ee.　1960 (Jul 21): Nashville, Tenn.; George Peabody College; Nathaniel Patch, piano.

W98ff.　1961 (Jan 12): Columbus, Ohio; Ohio State University; Mershon Auditorium; John Browning, piano. *See*: B98llll

W98gg.　1961 (Feb 11): New York; Town Hall; Marjorie Mitchell, piano. *See*: B98tt

W98hh.　1962 (Jan 12): Los Angeles; Friday Morning Club Playhouse; John Browning, piano.

W98ii.　1962 (Mar 20): Nashville, Tenn.; Fisk University; John Browning, piano.

W98jj.　1963 (Oct 4): New York; Philharmonic Hall; Van Cliburn, piano. *See*: B98d, B98vvv

W98kk.　1964 (Mar 15): New Rochelle, N.Y.; Women's Club; Abbott Lee Ruskin, piano.

W98ll.　1964 (Jun 22): Los Angeles; University of California; Schoenberg Hall; Jeffrey Siegel, piano.

W98mm.　1964 (Aug 3): Salzburg; Mozarteum; Van Cliburn, piano (Salzburg Festival)

W98nn.　1964 (Sep 17): London; Wigmore Hall; Thomas Owen Mastroianni, piano.

W98oo.　1965 (Nov 4): New York; Carnegie Hall; Nicolai Petrov, piano ["Adagio" and "Fugue" only] *See*: B98yy

W98pp.　1966 (May 1): Johannesburg, South Africa; Civic Theater; John Browning, piano.

W98qq.　1967 (Nov 15): New York; Town Hall; Arliss Heukelekian, piano. *See*: B98cccc

W98rr.　1971 (Jan 8): New York; Carnegie Recital Hall; Thomas Owen Mastroianni, piano.

W98ss.   1971 (Apr 9): Winston-Salem; North Carolina
          School of the Arts; Main Auditorium; Marjorie
          Mitchell, piano.

W98tt.   1971 (Sep 3): Edinburgh; Freemason's Hall;
          Michael Block, piano.

W98uu.   1973 (Oct 20): Manitowoc, Wisc.; Silver Lake Col-
          lege; Pietro Spada, piano.

W98vv.   1975 (Feb 2): New York; Hunter College Assembly
          Hall; John Browning, piano. See: B98p

W98ww.   1975 (Nov 5): New York; Lincoln Center for the
          Performing Arts; Alice Tully Hall; Robert De
          Gaetano, piano. See: B98nn

W98xx.   1976 (Mar 23): New York; Juilliard Theater; Jane
          Carlson, piano. See: B98oo

W98yy.   1980 (Jan 25): Beijing; Daniel Pollack, piano.
          See: B98lll

W98zz.   1980 (Mar 9): Philadelphia; Curtis Institute of
          Music; Curtis Hall Auditorium; Ruth Laredo,
          piano (The Curtis Institute of Music's Fourth
          Faculty Commemorative Series honoring Samuel
          Barber on the occasion of his 70th birthday;
          afternoon concert) See: B98aaa

W98aaa.   1981 (Jan 18): Bloomington; Indiana University;
          Robert Goldsand, piano.

W98bbb.   1983 (Oct 9): Los Angeles; Wadsworth Theatre
          (sponsored by University of California, Los
          Angeles); Ruth Laredo, piano. See: B98u

W98ccc.   1983 (Oct 21): Torrance, Calif.; El Camino Col-
          lege; Stuart E. Marsee Auditorium; John Brown-
          ing, piano.

W98ddd.   1983 (Dec 11): San Francisco; San Francisco Con-
          servatory of Music; Hellman Hall; Steve War-
          zycki, piano.

   SILENT NIGHT See: W74.

   SKETCHES FOR PIANO See: THREE SKETCHES FOR PIANOFORTE

   SONATA IN MODERN FORM, OP. XVI See: Preface

SOUVENIRS, OP. 28. See: W78.

W99. SUITE FOR CARILLON. (1930-31; Schirmer)

For carillon.
Also called Five Pieces for a Singing Tower.
Commissioned by Edward Bok for Bok's carillon at the
  Mountain Lakes Bird Sanctuary in Lake Wales, Flor-
  ida. See: B99a

THEMES, OP. X, NO. 2 See: Preface

TO MY STEINWAY See: THREE SKETCHES FOR PIANOFORTE

TWO INTERMEZZI FOR PIANO See: INTERMEZZI (2) FOR
PIANO

TWO INTERLUDES FOR PIANO See: INTERMEZZI (2) FOR
PIANO

W100. THREE SKETCHES FOR PIANOFORTE (1923-24)

Presumably the first collection of Samuel Barber's
  compositions to appear in print and to receive a
  copyright. Published under the name Samuel O.
  Barber 2nd. Funding for the project was supplied
  by Samuel's grandfather, Samuel Osmond Barber, for
  whom the composer was named.
Contents: No. 1. Love Song -- No. 2. To My Steinway
  -- No. 3. Minuet.

W101. WONDROUS LOVE: VARIATIONS ON A SHAPE-NOTE HYMN, OP.
34. (1958; Schirmer; Library of Congress has pencil
  manuscript, 7 p.) See: B101a, B101b, B101e, B101f,
  B101g

For organ solo.
Composed for the dedication of a new organ at Christ
  Episcopal Church, Grosse Point Farms, Michigan.
Dedicated to Richard Roeckelein.
Hymn published in the Original Sacred Harp, Atlanta,
  Ga., 1869.

DISCOGRAPHY

This list includes all commercially-produced discs, whether or not currently available. "See" references, e.g., See: B61, identify citations in the "Bibliography" section. "LC card no" refers to numbers for the ordering Library of Congress catalog cards.

OPERAS

D1. ANTONY AND CLEOPATRA, OP. 40. [revised version]

  D1a. Esther Hinds, Jeffrey Wells, and Eric Halfvarson, soloists [for complete cast see W1e]
New World Records NW 322-324 (3 discs) 1984.
Aaron Baron, engineer; Elizabeth Ostrow, producer.
Recorded at the Festival of Two Worlds in Spoleto, Italy, June 1983.
See: W1e, W1f

D4. ANTONY AND CLEOPATRA. TWO SCENES. [No. 1, Give Me Some Music; No. 2, Give Me My Robe (Death of Cleopatra)]

  D4a. Leontyne Price soprano; New Philharmonia Orchestra; Thomas Schippers conductor
RCA Red Seal LSC 3062, RCA SB 6799 (Great Britain) 1969; in 1983, released as RCA Gold Seal AGL1 5221 ("digitally remastered analog recording")
Duration: 8 min., 58 sec., 9 min., 21 sec.
Program notes and text on slipcase.
With his Knoxville: Summer of 1915.
LC card no. R68-3658 (1969)
See: B4a, B4d, B4f, B4g

D4b.   Leontyne Price, soprano.
        RCA Red Seal ARL 1 4856. 1984.
        Album title: Opening Nights at the Met.
        With works by Verdi and Cilea. ["Give Me My Robe"
        only]
        See: B4b

D5. A HAND OF BRIDGE, OP. 35.

D5a.   Patricia Neway, soprano; Eunice Alberts, contralto;
        William Lewis, tenor; Philip Maero, baritone; The
        Symphony of the Air; Vladimir Golschmann, con-
        ductor.   Vanguard VRS 1065, VSL 11019 (Great
        Britain) 1961; later released as VSD 2083. 1968.
        Series: Landmarks of American Music (1961); West
        Projects Release (1968)
        Duration: 9 min., 26 sec.
        Program notes by Sidney Finkelstein, texts and
        biographical notes on slipcase.
        With his Second Essay For Orchestra, Music For a
        Scene From Shelley, A Stopwatch and an Ordnance
        Map, and Serenade For Strings.
        LC card no. R61-671 (1961)
        See: B5b, B5c, B5f, B5g

D7. VANESSA, OP. 32.

D7a.   Eleanor Steber, soprano; Rosalind Elias, Regina
        Resnik, mezzo sopranos; Nicolai Gedda, tenor;
        George Cehanovsky, baritone; Giorgio Tozzi, bass;
        supporting soloists (see W7a); Metropolitan Opera
        Chorus; Kurt Adler, chorus master; Ignace Stras-
        fogel, assistant conductor; Metropolitan Opera
        Orchestra; Dimitri Mitropoulos, conductor.
        RCA Red Seal LM 6138, LSC 6138, RL 02094 (Great
        Britain) (3 discs) 1958; later reissued as ARL2
        2094 (2 discs) 1977.
        Duration: ca. 1 hr., 44 min.
        Program notes by F. Robinson, synopsis, and libret-
        to in container.
        With selections by Donizetti, Ponchielli, and Mas-
        cagni (LM 6138 and LSC 6138 only)
        LC card no. R58-724 (1958), R58-458 (1958), 77-
        760993 (1977)
        See: B7d, B7i, B7u, B7dd, B7vv, B7ww, B7yy, B7jjj,
        B7rrr, B7oooo

D7b.   Eleanor Steber, soprano; Rosalind Elias, Regina
        Resnik, mezzo sopranos; Nicolai Gedda, tenor;
        George Cehanovsky, baritone; Giorgio Tozzi, bass;
        supporting soloists (see W7a); Metropolitan Opera
        Chorus; Kurt Adler, chorus master; Ignace Stras-
        fogel, assistant conductor; Metropolitan Opera

Orchestra; Dimitri Mitropoulos, conductor (abridged version) RCA Red Seal LM 6062, LSC 6062. 1959.
Program notes by F. Robinson, synopsis, and libretto in container.
LC card no.R59-161 (1959),R59-464 (1958)

D7c.   Leontyne Price, soprano; RCA Italian Opera Orchestra; Francesco Molinari-Pradelli, conductor [selections]
RCA Victor SB 6700 (Great Britain)
With works by Purcell, Mozart, Verdi, Massenet, Meyerbeer, and Charpentier.
See: B7qq

D8. VANESSA. DO NOT UTTER A WORD.

D8a.   Helen-Kay Eberley, soprano; Donald Isaak, piano.
EB-SKO 1007. 1984?
Album title: American Girl.
With works by Hoiby, Floyd, Copland, Menotti, and Moore.
See: B8b

D8b.   Leontyne Price, soprano; RCA Italian Opera Orchestra; Francesco Molinari-Pradelli, conductor.
RCA Victor LM 2898, LSC 2898.
Album title: Leontyne Price, Great Soprano Arias.
With works by Purcell, Mozart, Verdi, Meyerbeer, Massenet, Cilea, and Charpentier.
See: B8a, B8c

D9. VANESSA. INTERMEZZO.

D9a.   Columbia Symphony Orchestra; Thomas Schippers, conductor.
Columbia ML 5564, MS 6164. 1960.
Album title: Orchestral Music from the Opera.
Series: Columbia Masterworks.
Durations on labels.
With works by Bizet, Fauré, Prokofiev, Verdi, Puccini, Mascagni, Berg, and Humperdinck.
LC card no.: R60-1241.

D9b.   New York Philharmonic Orchestra; André Kostelanetz, conductor.
Columbia ML 5347, MS 6040. 1959; later ([197-?]) released under Columbia Special Service Records 91A 02007 as part of the Spoken word series.
Album title: Spirit of '76 (except 91A 02007)
Program notes on slipcase.
Duration: ca. 4 min., 17 sec.
With works by Copland and Schuman.

LC card no. R59-1006, R59-1009.
See: B9a, B9b

D9c.   New York Philharmonic Orchestra; André Kostelanetz,
          conductor.
       Columbia MG 33728 (2 discs)
       With works by Creston, Gershwin, Cowell, Griffes,
          Grofé, Hovhaness, Ives, and Rodgers.

D10. VANESSA.   MUST THE WINTER COME SO SOON.

D10a.   Rosalind Elias, soprano; Metropolitan Opera
          Orchestra; Dimitri Mitropoulos, conductor.
        RCA Victor SP 33 21.
        Album title: Meet the Artist [sampler]

D12. VANESSA.   UNDER THE WILLOW TREE.

D12a.   L. Ivanova, soprano.
        Melodiya D12261/2.
        With his Songs, op. 2, no.1, op. 10, nos. 1-3, and
          op. 13, no. 3.

CHORAL MUSIC

D18. LET DOWN THE BARS, O DEATH, OP. 8, NO. 2.

D18a.   Vienna State Academy Orchestra; vocal soloists;
          Wiener Kammerchor; Ferdinand Grossman, director;
          William Strickland, conductor.
        Vox PL 7750.
        Album title: A Concert of American Music in Schön-
          brunn.
        Duration: 3 min.
        With works by Copland, Piston, and Thomson.

D18b.   Washington Cathedral Choir of Men and Boys; Paul
          Callaway, conductor.
        Vanguard VRS 1036, VSD 2021.
        Album title: Music of the Protestant Episcopal
          Church: Music From the Washington Cathedral.
        With works by Morley, Tallis, Byrd, Gibbons,
          Palestrina, Victoria, Schütz, Davies, Sowerby,
          Warlock, Willan, and Parker.

D20. PRAYERS OF KIERKEGAARD, OP. 30.

D20a.   Gloria Capone, soprano; Chorus of the Southern

Baptist Theological Seminary; Louisville Orches-
tra; Jorge Mester, conductor.
Louisville Orchestra LS 763. 1977?
Series: Louisville Orchestra first edition re-
cords, [1976, no. 3]
Recorded Mar. 24, 1977, Macauley Theatre, Louis-
ville.
Program notes on slipcase.
Duration: ca. 17 min., 30 sec.
With works by Welcher and Johnson.
LC card no. 78-762423.
See: B20h, B20v

D21. REINCARNATIONS, OP. 16.

D21a.   C.W. Post College Chorus and Chamber Singers.
Golden Crest CCS 8050.
LC card no. 78-760073.

D21b.   Gregg Smith Singers.
Everest SDBR 3129, LPBR 6129. 1965.
Album title: An American Triptych.
Program notes and text on slipcase.
Duration: 10 min., 15 sec.
With works by Copland and Schuman.
LC card no. R65-1552.
See: B21a, B21c, B21f, B21g, B21h

D21c.   Hufstader Singers; Robert Hufstader, conductor.
Cook Laboratories 1092 (10"), 11312.
Series: Sounds of Our Times.
With works by Dowland, Jannequin, Lassus, Morley,
Pilkington, and Ravel.

D21d.   King Chorale; Gordon King, conductor.
Orion ORS 75205.
Album title: American Songs.
With works by Hennagin, Mennin, Pinkham, Rorem,
Stevens, Thompson, Berger, Persichetti, Adler,
and Chorbajian.
See: B21i, B21k

D21e.   Vancouver Chamber Choir; Jon Washburn, conductor.
Canadian Broadcasting Corporation SM 303. 1977.
Duration: 9 min., 37 sec.
With works by Handel and Debussy.

D22. A STOPWATCH AND AN ORDNANCE MAP, OP. 15.

D22a.   Gregg Smith Singers; Texas Boys' Choir; Columbia
University Men's Glee Club; Peabody Conservatory
Concert Singers; Gregg Smith, conductor.
Vox SVBX 5353 (3 discs)

87

Album title: America Sings, 1920-1950.
With works by Schuman, Carter, Riegger, Sessions,
Copland, Seeger, V. Thomson, R. Thompson, Pis-
ton, Fine, Talma, Bernstein, and Gershwin.

D22b.   Robert De Cormier Chorale; The Symphony of the
Air; Vladimir Golschmann, conductor.
Vanguard VRS 1065, VSL 11019 (Great Britain) 1961;
later released as VSD 2083. 1968.
Series: Landmarks of American Music (1961); West
Projects Release (1968)
Duration: 5 min., 44 sec.
Program notes by Sidney Finkelstein, texts and
biographical notes on slipcase.
With his Second Essay For Orchestra, Music For a
Scene From Shelley, A Hand of Bridge, and Sere-
nade For Strings.
LC card no. R61-671 (1961)
See: B22c, B22d, B22g, B22j

VOCAL MUSIC

D26. ANDROMACHE'S FAREWELL, OP. 39.

D26a.   Martina Arroyo, soprano; New York Philharmonic
Orchestra; Thomas Schippers, conductor.
Columbia ML 5912, MS 6512. 1963.
Columbia Masterworks.
Duration: 12 min., 10 sec.
Program notes by Edward Downes on slipcase.
With Schuman's Symphony No. 8.
LC card no.: R63-1349; R63-1351.
See: B26d, B26e, B26j

D31. DESPITE AND STILL, OP. 41. [No. 1, A Last Song -- No.
2, My Lizard -- No. 3, In the Wilderness -- No. 4,
Solitary Hotel -- No. 5, Despite and Still]

D31a.   Joan Patenaude, soprano; Mikael Eliasen, piano
[No. 4 only]
Musical Heritage Society MHS 3770. 1978.
Album title: Songs of the Great Opera Composers,
vol. II.
With his Songs, op. 2 (no. 2), op. 10, op. 13, and
songs by Alban Berg.
LC card no. 78-750276.

D33. HERMIT SONGS, OP. 29. [No. 1, At Saint Patrick's
Purgatory -- No. 2, Church Bell at Night -- No. 3,

Saint Ita's Vision -- No. 4, The Heavenly Banquet
-- No. 5, The Crucifixion -- No. 6, Sea-Snatch --
No. 7, Promiscuity -- No. 8, The Monk and His Cat --
No. 9, The Praises of God -- No. 10, The Desire for
Hermitage]

D33a.   Sandra Browne, mezzo-soprano; Michael Isador,
            piano.
         Enigma Classics VAR 1029 (Great Britain)
         With Copland's Twelve Songs by Emily Dickinson.
         See: B33w

D33b.   Leontyne Price, soprano; Samuel Barber, piano.
         Columbia ML 4988. 1955.
         Columbia Masterworks.
         Series: Modern American Music Series.
         Commissioned by the Elizabeth Sprague Coolidge
            Foundation in the Library of Congress and first
            performed there by the same artists, Oct. 30,
            1953.
         Recorded under the supervision of the composer.
         Program notes and English translation of the text
            on slipcase.
         Duration: 16 min., 5 sec.
         With Haieff's String Quartet No. 1.
         LC card no. R55-450.
         See: B33d, B33e, B33f, B33g, B33i, B33k, B33p,
            B33v

D33c.   Leontyne Price, soprano; Samuel Barber, piano.
         Odyssey 32 16 0230; previously issued as Columbia
            ML 4988.
         Duration: ca. 16 min., 5 sec.
         With his Knoxville: Summer of 1915 (in 1950 issued
            as Columbia ML 5483)
         See: B33q

D33d.   Eleanor Steber, soprano; Dumbarton Oaks Chamber
            Orchestra; William Strickland, conductor.
         Columbia ML 5843; previously ML 2174, ML 4940.
            1963; in 1968 released as Odyssey 32 16 0230.
         Series: Columbia Masterworks (1963), Legendary
            Performances (1968)
         Program notes by Eleanor Steber on slipcase; sup-
            plementary notes by David Johnson and text (2
            p.) inserted.
         With Berlioz's Les nuits d'été (1963) or Knox-
            ville: Summer of 1915.
         LC card nos.: R63-1072 (1963), R68-2562 (1968)

D33e.   Nancy Tatum, soprano; Geoffrey Parsons, piano
            [Nos. 5 and 8 only]
         London OS 26053, Decca SXL 6336 (Great Britain)
         Album title: Recital of American Songs.
         With works by MacDowell, Gold, Manning, Copland,

89

Bischoff, Guion, Thomson, and Griffes.
See: B33h, B33o

D36. KNOXVILLE: SUMMER OF 1915, OP. 24.

D36a. Molly McGurk, soprano; West Australian Symphony
Orchestra; David Measham, conductor.
Unicorn UNS 256 (in 1978 reissued as Unicorn UN1
72016)
Duration: 16 min., 38 sec.
Program notes by Richard Saxby on slipcase.
With his Music for a Scene from Shelley and the
Violin Concerto.
LC card no. 78-750413.
See: B36p, B36v, B36ll, B36kk, B36qq

D36b. Leontyne Price, soprano; New Philharmonia Orches-
tra; Thomas Schippers, conductor.
RCA Red Seal LSC 3062, SB 6799. 1969; in 1983,
released as RCA Gold Seal AGL1 5221 ("digitally
remastered analog recording")
Program notes and text on slipcase.
With his Two Scenes From Antony and Cleopatra.
LC card no. R68-3658 (1969)
See: B36h, B36j, B36bb, B36cc, B36jj

D36c. Leontyne Price, soprano; Samuel Barber, piano.
Odyssey 32 16 0230; in 1950 issued as Columbia ML
5483.
With his Hermit Songs.
See: B36c, B36x

D36d. Eleanor Steber, soprano; Dumbarton Oaks Chamber
Orchestra; William Strickland, conductor.
Columbia ML 5843; previously ML 2174 (10"), ML
4940. 1963; in 1968 released as Odyssey 32 16
0230; see also D36e below.
Series: Columbia Masterworks (1963), Legendary
Performances (1968)
Duration: 14 min., 2 sec.
Program notes by Eleanor Steber on slipcase; sup-
plementary notes by David Johnson and text (2
p.) inserted.
With Les nuits d'été by Hector Berlioz (1963) or
Hermit Songs (1968)
LC card no.: R63-1072 (1963), R68-2562 (1968)
See: B36b, B36g, B36k, B36q, B36t, B36u, B36z,
B36oo

D36e. Eleanor Steber, soprano; Dumbarton Oaks Chamber
Orchestra; William Strickland, conductor.
Columbia ML 2174 (10 in.); see also D36d above.
With his Excursions.

D36f.   Eleanor Steber, soprano; Greater Trenton Symphony
        Orchestra; Nicholas Harsanyi, conductor.
        St/and SLP 420, SLS 7420. 1962.
        Recorded during a performance in the War Memorial
        Building, Trenton, N.J., January 13, 1962.
        Duration: ca. 17 min.
        Program notes by Max de Schauensee on slipcase.
        With La Montaine's Songs of the Rose of Sharon.
        LC card no. R62-599 (SLP 420)
        See: B36l, B36z

D41. MELODIES PASSAGERES, OP. 27. [No. 1, <u>Puisque tout</u>
    <u>passe</u> -- No. 2, <u>Un cygne</u> -- No. 3, <u>Tombeau dans un</u>
    <u>parc</u> -- No. 4, <u>Le clocher chanté</u> -- No. 5, <u>Départ</u>]

D41a.   Pierre Bernac, baritone; Francis Poulenc, piano.
        New World Records NW 229. 1978.
        Album title: Songs of Samuel Barber and Ned Rorem.
        Series: Recorded Anthology of American Music.
        Recorded Feb. 15, 1952 in New York.
        Program notes and interviews with the composers by
            P. Ramey, with English translations of the
            French words, and bibliographies bound in.
        With his Dover Beach and songs by Ned Rorem.
        LC card no. 78-750041.
        See: B41f

D46. NUVOLETTA, OP. 25.

D46a.   Patricia Neway, soprano; Robert Colston, piano.
        Lyrichord LL 83.
        Album title: Songs to Texts by James Joyce.
        With works by De Hartmann, Buchbinder, Gruen,
            Citkowitz, and Barab.
        See: B46g

D46b.   Eleanor Steber, soprano; Edwin Biltcliffe, piano.
        Desto SLP 7411/2, DST 6411/2 (2 discs)
        Recording sponsored by the Alice M. Ditson Fund
            and Columbia University.
        With works by Diamond, Persichetti, Luening, Fine,
            Flanagin, Rorem, Ives, Moore, Beeson, Bowles,
            Edmunds, Carpenter, Bacon, Bergsma, Griffes, La
            Montaine, Thomson, Copland, Ward, Gruen, Pink-
            ham, Weber, and Cowell.
        See: B46b, B46f

D51. SONGS (3), OP. 2. [No. 1, <u>The Daisies</u> -- No. 2, <u>With</u>
    <u>Rue My Heart is Laden</u> -- No. 3, <u>Bessie Bobtail</u>]

D51a.   Anonymous vocalist [No. 3 only]
        Yaddo 8 (78 rpm)

With The Beggar's song.

D51b.   Donald Gramm, bass; R. Cumming, piano.
        Music Library 7033 [No. 1 only]

D51c.   John Kennedy Hanks, tenor; Ruth Friedberg, piano
          [No. 3 only]
        Duke University Press DWR 6417/8 (2 discs)
        Album title: The Art Song in America.
        With his Songs, op. 10 (no. 3), op. 13 (nos. 3-4),
          and songs by MacDowell, Chadwick, Loeffler,
          Ives, Hageman, Carpenter, Griffes, Josten, Duke,
          Bacon, Copland, Harris, Dougherty, Bowles, Fin-
          ney, Klenz, and Dello Joio.
        See: B51a, B51c

D51d.   L. Ivanova, soprano [No. 1 only]
        Melodiya D12261/2.
        With his Songs, op. 10 (nos. 1-3), op. 13 (no. 3),
          and Under the Willow Tree (from Vanessa)

D51e.   Dale Moore, baritone; Betty Ruth Tomfohrde, piano
          [Nos. 1-2 only]
        Cambridge CRS 2715. 1972.
        Album Title: On the Road to Mandalay & Other
          Favorite American Concert Songs From 1900 to
          1950.
        With his Songs, op. 10, op. 13 (nos. 3-4), op. 18
          (no. 2), and songs by Rogers, Homer, Stillman-
          Kelly, Hageman, Charles, Griffes, Duke, and
          Speaks.
        LC card no. 72-750716.
        See: B51d

D51f.   Joan Patenaude, soprano; Mikael Eliasen, piano
          [No. 2 only]
        Musical Heritage Society MHS 3770. 1978.
        Album title: Songs of the Great Opera Composers,
          vol. II.
        With his Songs, op. 10 (nos. 1-3), op. 13, op. 41
          (no. 4), and songs by Alban Berg.
        LC card no. 78-750276.

D52. SONGS (3), OP. 10. [No. 1, Rain Has Fallen -- No. 2,
        Sleep Now -- No. 3, I Hear an Army]

  D52a. Marilyn Cotlow, soprano; Claire Stafford, piano
          [No. 2 only]
        Victor V 1467 (10" 78 rpm)

  D52b. Dietrich Fischer-Dieskau, baritone; Charles Wads-
          worth, piano [No. 3 only]
        Musical Heritage Society MHS 824794K.
        Album title: The Chamber Music Society of Lincoln

Center.
Recorded live at Alice Tully Hall, New York City.
Program notes by Nancy Hager and Harris Goldsmith
  on slipcase.
Duration: 2 min., 12 sec.
With his Songs, op. 13 (no. 4), op. 45, and works
  by Handel, Britten, and Wolf.
LC card no. 83-743178.

D52c.   L. Ivanova, soprano.
Melodiya D12261/2.
With his Songs, op. 2 (no. 1) and op. 13 (no. 3),
  and Under the Willow Tree (from Vanessa)

D52d.   John Kennedy Hanks, tenor; Ruth Friedberg, piano
  [No. 3 only]
Duke University Press DWR 6417/8 (2 discs)
Album title: The Art Song in America.
With his Songs, op. 2 (no. 3), op. 13 (nos. 1-2),
  and songs by MacDowell, Chadwick, Loeffler,
  Ives, Hageman, Carpenter, Griffes, Josten, Duke,
  Bacon, Copland, Harris, Dougherty, Bowles, Fin-
  ney, Klenz, and Dello Joio.

D52e.   Paul King, baritone; Samuel Quincy, piano.
Classic Editions CE 1011.
Duration: ca. 2 min., 30 sec.
With his Dover Beach and Symphony No. 1.

D52f.   Glenda Maurice, mezzo-soprano; David Garvey, pi-
  ano [Nos. 2-3 only]
Etcetera/Conifer ETC 1002.
With his Songs, op. 13, op. 45 and work by Brit-
  ten.
See: B52a

D52g.   Dale Moore, baritone; Betty Ruth Tomfohrde, piano.
Cambridge CRS 2715. 1972.
Album Title: On the Road to Mandalay & Other
  Favorite American Concert Songs From 1900 to
  1950.
With his Songs, op. 2 (nos. 1-2), op. 13 (nos. 3-
  4), op. 18 (no. 2), and songs by Rogers, Homer,
  Stillman-Kelly, Hageman, Charles, Griffes, Duke,
  and Speaks.
LC card no. 72-750716.

D52h.   Joan Patenaude, soprano; Mikael Eliasen, piano
Musical Heritage Society MHS 3770. 1978.
Album title: Songs of the Great Opera Composers,
  vol. II.
With his Songs, op. 2 (no. 2), op. 13, op. 41 (no.
  4), and songs by Alban Berg.
LC card no. 78-750276.

D53. SONGS (4), OP. 13. [No. 1, A Nun Takes a Veil -- No. 2, The Secrets of the Old -- No. 3, Sure on This Shining Night -- No. 4, Nocturne]

    D53a.   Lucine Amara, soprano; David Benedict, piano [No. 3 only]
        Cambridge CRM 704, CRS 1704.
        With works by Donaudy, Del Paquino, Traetta, Debussy, Fourdrain, Schumann, Wolf, Brahms, Hageman, and Bliss.

    D53b.   Beverly Beardslee, soprano; Robert Helps, piano [No. 3 only]
        New World Records NW 243. 1977.
        Album title: But Yesterday Is Not Today.
        Series: Recorded Anthology of American Music.
        "The American Art Song From 1930 to 1960: a Personal Survey, by Ned Rorem," bibliography, and discography bound in.
        With works by Chanler, Bowles, Duke, Citkowitz, Copland, Sessions, and Helps.
        LC card no. 76-750908.
        See: B53k

    D53c.   Dietrich Fischer-Dieskau, baritone; Charles Wadsworth, piano [No. 4 only]
        Musical Heritage Society MHS 824794K.
        Album title: The Chamber Music Society of Lincoln Center.
        Recorded live at Alice Tully Hall, New York City.
        Program notes by Nancy Hager and Harris Goldsmith on slipcase.
        Duration: 2 min., 59 sec.
        With his Songs, op. 10 (no. 3), op. 45, and works by Handel, Britten, and Wolf.
        LC card no. 83-743178.

    D53d.   John Kennedy Hanks, tenor; Ruth Friedberg, piano [Nos. 3-4 only]
        Duke University Press DWR 6417/8 (2 discs)
        Album title: The Art Song in America.
        With his Songs, op. 2 (no. 3) and songs by MacDowell, Chadwick, Loeffler, Ives, Hageman, Carpenter, Griffes, Josten, Duke, Bacon, Copland, Harris, Dougherty, Bowles, Finney, Kienz, and Dello Joio.
        See: B53d

    D53e.   L. Ivanova, soprano [No. 3 only]
        Melodiya D12261/2.
        With his Songs, op. 2 (no. 1), op. 10 (nos. 1-3), and Under the Willow Tree (from Vanessa)

    D53f.   Glenda Maurice, mezzo-soprano; David Garvey, piano.

Etcetera/Conifer ETC 1002.
With his Songs, op. 10 (nos. 1-2), op. 45, and
work by Britten.
<u>See</u>: B53a

D53g. Dale Moore, baritone; Betty Ruth Tomfohrde, piano
[Nos. 3-4 only]
Cambridge CRS 2715. 1972.
Album Title: On the Road to Mandalay & Other
Favorite American Concert Songs From 1900 to
1950.
With his Songs, op. 2 (nos. 1-2), op. 10, op. 18
(no. 2), and songs by Rogers, Homer, Stillman-
Kelly, Hageman, Charles, Griffes, Duke, and
Speaks.
LC card no. 72-750716.

D53h. Joan Patenaude, soprano; Mikael Eliasen, piano.
Musical Heritage Society MHS 3770. 1978.
Album title: Songs of the Great Opera Composers,
vol. II.
With his Songs, op. 2 (no. 2), op. 10 (nos. 1-3),
op. 41 (no. 4), and songs by Alban Berg.
LC card no. 78-750276.
<u>See</u>: B53l

D53i. Frances Yeend, soprano; James Benner, piano.
DaVinci D 203.
Album title: Frances Yeend Sings.
With songs by Scarlatti, Strauss, Rachmaninoff,
Ravel, Russell, Quilter, Obradors, and Turina.
<u>See</u>: B53l

D56. SONGS (2), OP. 18. [No. 1, <u>The Queen's Face on The
Summery Coin</u> -- No. 2, <u>Monks and Raisins</u>]

D56a. Dale Moore, baritone; Betty Ruth Tomfohrde, piano
[No. 2 only]
Cambridge CRS 2715. 1972.
Album Title: On the Road to Mandalay & Other
Favorite American Concert Songs From 1900 to
1950.
With his Songs, op. 2 (nos. 1-2), op. 10, op. 13
(no. 3-4), and songs by Rogers, Homer, Stillman-
Kelly, Hageman, Charles, Griffes, Duke, and
Speaks.
LC card no. 72-750716.

D57. SONGS (3), OP. 45. [No. 1, <u>Now Have I Fed and Eaten
Up the Rose</u> -- No. 2, <u>A Green Lowland of Pianos</u> --
No. 3, <u>O Boundless, Boundless Evening</u>]

D57a. Dietrich Fischer-Dieskau, baritone; Charles Wads-

worth, piano.
Musical Heritage Society MHS 824794K.
Album title: The Chamber Music Society of Lincoln
  Center.
Recorded live at Alice Tully Hall, New York City.
Program notes by Nancy Hager and Harris Goldsmith
  on slipcase.
Duration: 6 min., 54 sec.
With his Songs, op. 10 (no. 3), op. 13 (no. 4),
  and works by Handel, Britten, and Wolf.
LC card no. 83-743178.

D57b. Glenda Maurice, mezzo-soprano; David Garvey, pi-
         ano.
       Etcetera/Conifer ETC 1002.
       With his Songs, op. 10 (nos. 1-2), op. 13, and
         work by Britten.
       See: B57b

ORCHESTRAL MUSIC

D61. ADAGIO FOR STRINGS, OP. 11.

D61a. Academy of St. Martin-in-the-Fields; Neville Mar-
         riner, conductor.
       Argo ZRG 845. 1976.
       Recorded October 1975 in St. John's, Smith Square,
         London.
       With works by Ives, Copland, Cowell, and Creston.
       See: B61e, B61f, B61u, B61gg

D61b. Baroque Strings Zürich.
       Denon PCM OX 7120 ND.
       Digital recording.
       With works by Grieg and Britten.

D61c. Beaux Arts String Quartet (Charles Libove and Alan
         Martin, violins, Peter Mark, viola, Bruce
         Rogers, violoncello)
       Columbia LC 3907; Columbia Subscription Service
         (sampler) MPS 11 Winter 1966/67.

D61d. Boston Festival Orchestra; Willis Page, conductor.
       Rondo ST502; Nixa 45EP651 (45 rpm, extended play,
         Great Britain)
       Duration: ca. 8 min.
       With works by Stravinsky and Honegger.

D61e. Boston Orchestra Society; Willis Page, conductor
         [cf. D61bb]

Cook 10683, 10683 S.
With works by Honegger and Debussy.

D61f.   Boston Symphony Orchestra (strings of); Charles
         Münch, conductor.
         Victor LM 2105, LSC 2105, ARL2 1421, RCA Victrola
            VICS 1540, VCS 2001 (Great Britain) 1957.
         Program notes by Fred Grunfeld on slipcase.
         With works by Tchaikovsky and Elgar.
         LC card no. R57-781 rev.
         See: B61t, B61z, B61kk, B61oo

D61g.   Boyd Neel String Orchestra; Boyd Neel, conductor.
         London LPS 298; Decca X 305 (Great Britain, 10")
         Album title: Music For the 20th Century.
         With works by Bloch and Copland.
         See: B61a, B61c, B61h, B61k, B61q

D61h.   Capitol Symphony Orchestra; Carmen Dragon, conduc-
            tor.
         Capitol P 8542, SP 8542.
         Album title: Romantique.
         With works by Niles, Elgar, Rubinstein, Bolzoni,
            Corelli, Friml, Tchaikovsky, Beethoven, and
            Grieg.
         See: B61xx

D61i.   Chicago Strings; Francis Akos, conductor.
         Janus JAS 19024; also released on Pirouette 19024,
            S 19024.
         Duration: ca. 6 min., 45 sec.
         With works by Telemann, Schubert, Wolf, and Tchai-
            kovsky.

D61j.   Concert Arts Orchestra; Vladimir Golschmann, con-
            ductor.
         Capitol P 8245.
         Album title: Contemporary American Music.
         Series: Capitol Classics.
         With works by Diamond, Copland, and Creston.
         LC card no. R54-237.
         See: B61o

D61k.   Eastman-Rochester Symphony Orchestra; Howard Han-
            son, conductor.
         Mercury MG 40002, MG 50075, MG 50420, SR 90420.
         With his Essay For Orchestra No. 1, Overture to
            "The School For Scandal," and Gould's Latin-
            American Symphonette.

D61l.   Eastman-Rochester Symphony Orchestra; Howard Han-
            son, conductor.
         Mercury MG 50148. 1958.
         Series: Olympian Series.
         Program notes on slipcase.

        Duration: ca. 7 min., 15 sec.
        With his Symphony No. 1.
        LC card no.: R60-674.

D61m.   Eastman-Rochester Symphony Orchestra; Howard Han-
            son, conductor.
        Mercury SRI 75012. 1974.
        Series: Golden Imports.
        Program notes by Nathan Broder on slipcase.
        With his Symphony No. 1, Overture to "The School
            For Scandal," and Medea Suite.
        LC card no.: 74-761433.

D61n.   Hollywood Bowl Symphony Orchestra; Felix Slatkin,
            conductor.
        Capitol P 8444, SP 8444 (reissued in 1975 as Angel
            S 36087)
        Album title: Strings by Starlight.
        With works by Bach, Borodin, Grainger, Sibelius,
            and Tchaikovsky.
        LC card no. 75-750396.

D61o.   Kapp Sinfonietta (strings of); Emanuel Vardi,
            conductor.
        Kapp 9059, KC 9059S, S 9059.
        With works by Mendelssohn, Arensky, Vaughan
            Williams, and Warlock.

D61p.   John Korman, Beverly Schiebler, violins, Thomas
            Dumm, viola; St. Louis Symphony Orchestra;
            Leonard Slatkin, conductor.
        Telarc DC 10059.
        With works by Vaughan Williams, Grainger, Faure,
            and Satie.

D61q.   Lansdowne Quartet.
        HMV HQS 1061.
        With Sibelius' String Quartet in D minor, op. 56.
        See: B61ff

D61r.   London Symphony Orchestra; André Previn, con-
            ductor.
        Angel S 37201, S 37409. 1974-1977.
        Album title, U.S.: Showpieces For Orchestra; Great
            Britain: André Previn's Music Night, v. 2.
        With works by Bernstein, Vaughan Williams, Enesco,
            Tchaikovsky, Glinka, Falla, Debussy, Butter-
            worth, and J. Strauss.
        LC card no. 74-750483.
        See: B61l, B61x

D61s.   London Symphony Orchestra; André Previn, con-
            ductor.
        20th Century Fox Records T 1000. 1980.
        The original soundtrack recording from the motion

picture _Elephant_ _Man_, with music chiefly com-
posed by John Morris.
Recorded June 5-8, 1980, at the Music Centre,
London.
Program notes on inner liner.
LC card no. 82-760398.

D61t. Los Angeles Philharmonic Orchestra; Leonard Bern-
stein, conductor.
DG 2532 085 (digital) 1983.
Program notes by Jack Gottlieb in English with
French translation on container.
With works by Schuman and Bernstein.
See: B61s

D61u. Melbourne Symphony Orchestra (strings of); Leonard
Dommett, conductor.
Chandos CBR 1007.
With works by Elgar, Wiren, and Mozart.

D61v. Milwaukee Symphony Orchestra; Lukas Foss, conduc-
tor.
Pro Arte PAD 102 (digital) 1983.
Album title: American Festival.
Program notes on container.
Duration: 9 min., 44 sec.
With works by Bernstein, Schuman, Ives, Ruggeri,
Copland, and Cowell.

D61w. I Musici.
Philips SABL 216, 900001, 500001. 1962; later re-
issued as Philips Festivo 6570 181; Philips
Universo 6580 045.
Album title: I Musici Play Music by Barber,
Bartok, Respighi, and Britten (900001, 500001);
Modern Music (SABL 216)
Program notes on slipcase.
Duration: 7 min., 12 sec.
LC card no. R62-483, R62-649 (1962)
See: B61g, B61p, B61hh, B61mm, B61nn, B61bbb

D61x. NBC Symphony Orchestra; Arturo Toscanini, conduc-
tor.
RCA Victor LM 7032 (2 discs); RCA Victor RB 6606-7
(2 discs, Great Britain)
Album title: Toscanini Concert Favorites.
With works by Bach, Gluck, Kay, Kabalevsky, Paga-
nini, Mendelssohn, Ravel, Sousa, Strauss, Jr.,
R. Strauss, Tchaikovsky, and Wagner.

D61y. NBC Symphony Orchestra; Arturo Toscanini, conductor.
Victor 11 8287; HMV DB 6180 (Great Britain) (78
rpm) 1936.
See: B61v, B61bb, B61ll, B61vv

D61z. National High School Orchestra; George C. Wilson,
conductor.
Interlochen, Mich., National Music Camp NMC 1960-
19. 1960.
Recorded during an outdoor performance.
Duration: 6 min., 23 sec.
Note concerning the National Music Camp on slip-
case.
With Tchaikovsky's Symphony No. 5.
LC card no. R61-2128

D61aa. National Philharmonic; Morton Gould, conductor.
Pro Arte Sinfonia SDS 627 (digital) 1983.
Recorded on May 20, 1981, at EMI Studios, London.
"Released by arrangement with Readers Digest."
Duration: 7 min., 25 sec.
Program notes by John Michel on slipcase.
With works by Gershwin and Gould.

D61bb. New Orchestral Society of Boston; Willis Page,
conductor [cf. D61e]
Cook 1068. [196-?]
Series: Sounds of Our Times.
With works by Honegger and Debussy.

D61cc. New York Philharmonic Orchestra; Leonard Bern-
stein, conductor.
Columbia M 30573.
Album title: Nocturne, Music For Quiet Listening.
With works by Offenbach, Humperdinck, Bizet,
Grieg, Vaughan Williams, Ravel.

D61dd. New York Philharmonic Orchestra; Leonard Bern-
stein, conductor.
CBS Great Performances MY 38 484; previously
issued as Columbia M 30573.
Album title: Romantic Favorites for Strings.
Series: CBS Great Performances, no. 92.
Duration: 9 min., 53 sec.
With works by Mahler, Vaughan Williams, and Tchai-
kovsky.
See: B61ll

D61ee. New York Philharmonic Orchestra; Thomas Schippers,
conductor.
Columbia Subscription Service (sampler) MPS 11
Winter 1966/67; CBS Masterworks 32 11 0005, 32
11 0006 (1966); in 1975 released as Odyssey Y
33230.
Album title: Four Melodic Masterpieces (1966);
Thomas Schippers Conducts Barber (1975)
Program notes by Nicolas Slonimsky on slipcase
(unsigned in 1975, but same notes as 1966 re-
lease)
Duration: ca. 9 min., 16 sec.

With his Medea's Meditation and Dance of Vengeance, Overture to "The School for Scandal," and Second Essay For Orchestra.
LC card no. R66-2667, R66-2668 (1966), 74-750609 (1975)
See: B61ww

D61ff. Norlin Salutes the Music in America; premiere recording [no label number] 1974.
Various artists.
Issued with the Norlin Corporation annual report for 1974.
With works by Gould, Copland, Bernstein, and Schuman.

D61gg. Orchestra; Leopold Stokowski, conductor.
Seraphim SIB 6094 (2 discs). 1977.
Album title: Stokowski Conducts.
With works by Sibelius, Strauss, Gluck, Bach-Stokowski, Purcell, Tchaikovsky, Debussy, Ravel, Moussorgsky, and Turina.
LC card no. 77-761913.

D61hh. Orchestra; Leopold Stokowski, conductor.
Capitol SAL 8385.
With: Dukas, Farberman, Moussorgsky, Persichetti, R. Strauss, Tchaikovsky, and Vaughan Williams.

D61ii. Philadelphia Orchestra (strings of); Eugene Ormandy, conductor.
Columbia ML 5187, ML 5624, ML 6224, MS 6224. 1957; M 30066; in 1961 re-released in Columbia Masterworks series.
Album title: Strings of the Philadelphia Orchestra.
Program notes by Charles Burr on slipcase.
With works by Borodin, Tchaikovsky, and Vaughan Williams, or by Mascagni, Tchaikovsky, Massenet, Grieg, Bizet, and MacDowell (M 30066)
LC card no. R57-1026 (1957), R60-1428, R60-1429 (1961)

D61jj. Philharmonia Orchestra; Anatole Fistoulari, conductor.
HMV Concert Classics SXLP 20058.
Album title: Music For Strings.
With works by Grieg, Bach, and Tchaikovsky.
See: B61r

D61kk. Philharmonia Orchestra; Paul Kletzki, conductor.
Columbia LX 1595 (Great Britain), 78 rpm
See: B61rr

D61ll. I Solisti di Zagreb; Antonio Janigro, conductor.
Vanguard VSD 2126, VRS 1095; VSL 11027 (Great

Britain)
Album title: Notturno.
With works by Respighi, Mozart, Vaughan Williams,
Pergolesi, and Sibelius.

D61mm. Stockholm Sinfonlette; Jan-Olay Wedin, conductor.
Bis LP 180.
With works by Rossini, Grandjany, Schubert, Alf-
ven, Sibelius, Blomdahl, and Lumbye.

D61nn. Stuttgart Chamber Orchestra; Karl Münchinger,
conductor.
London LL 1395; Decca Eclipse ECS 688 (from mono
BR 3039 and LXT 5153)
Album title, U.S.: Music For Strings; Great Brit-
ain: Contemporary Music For String Orchestra.
With works by Grieg (except LXT 5153), Berkeley,
Martin, and Hindemith.
See: B61cc

D61oo. USSR State Orchestra; Constantine Ivanov, conduc-
tor.
Melodiya D 6509/10, S6581/2.
With his Overture to "The School for Scandal."

D65. CONCERTO FOR PIANO AND ORCHESTRA, OP. 38.

D65a. John Browning, piano; Cleveland Orchestra; George
Szell, conductor.
Columbia ML 6038, MS 6638; excerpts appeared on
Spring 1965 Columbia Audition sampler MPS 4,
which included a brief spoken interview with
Samuel Barber; SAX 2575 (Great Britain), 33CX
1937. 1964.
Columbia Masterworks.
Duration: 25 min., 46 sec.
Program notes by Klaus G. Roy on slipcase.
With Schuman's A Song of Orpheus (except in samp-
ler)
LC card no. R64-1377, R64-1379.
See: B65j, B65p, B65y, B65aa, B65cc, B65ee, B65ii,
B65nn

D65b. John Browning, piano; Cleveland Orchestra; George
Szell, conductor.
CBS Classics 61621 (reissue of SAX 2575 (Great
Britain)
Duration: 25 min., 46 sec.
With his Violin Concerto.
See: B65h, B65dd, B65hh

D65c. S. Dorensky, piano; USSR State Orchestra; Dubrov-
sky, conductor.

Melodiya D 017965/6.
With his Violoncello Concerto.

D65d.   Abbott Ruskin, piano; MIT Symphony Orchestra;
          David Epstein, conductor.
        Turnabout QTV 34683. 1977.
        Recorded November 1976.
        Program notes by Barbara S. Kafka on slipcase.
        With Copland's Piano Concerto (1926)
        LC card no. 78-760144.
        See: B65n, B65q, B65x, B65mm

D66.   CONCERTO FOR VIOLIN AND ORCHESTRA, OP. 14.

D66a.   Claire Bernard, violin; L'Orchestre National de
          l'Opéra de Monte Carlo; Edouard van Remoortel,
          conductor.
        Philips PHC 9105. 1969.
        Series: World Series.
        Duration: 26 min., 37 sec.
        Program notes on slipcase.
        With Milhaud's Violin Concerto No. 2.
        LC card no. 73-760980.
        See: B66o, B66s

D66b.   Robert Gerle, violin; Vienna State Opera Orches-
          tra; Robert Zeller, conductor.
        Westminster WST 17045, XWN 19045, World Record
          Club SCM 59, CM 59. 1963.
        Recorded in Mozart Hall, Vienna, June 1963.
        Duration: 24 min., 16 sec.
        Program notes by Irving Kolodin on slipcase.
        With Delius' Violin Concerto.
        LC card no. RA66-22 (XWN 19045), 73-760716 (WST
          17045)
        See: B66a, B66m, B66w, B66z, B66tt

D66c.   Hans Girdach, violin; Berlin Radio Symphony Or-
          chestra; Franz Schultz, conductor.
        Regent Records MG 5024 (10 in.)

D66d.   Louis Kaufman, violin; Concert Hall Symphony; Wal-
          ter Goehr, conductor.
        Concert Hall CHS 1253; in 1959 reissued as Orion
          ORS 79355 (see D66e and D66f)
        With Vaughan Williams' Concerto Accademico.
        See: B66dd, B66rr

D66e.   Louis Kaufman, violin; Lucerne Festival Orchestra;
          Walter Goehr, conductor.
        Orion ORS 79355. 1979; previously issued as Con-
          cert Hall CHS 1253 (see D66d)
        Duration: ca. 25 min.

Program notes by A.L.K. on container.
With Bloch's Violin and Piano Sonata.
LC card no. 79-750386.
<u>See</u>: B66jj, B66kk

D66f.   Louis Kaufman, violin; Lucerne Festival Orchestra;
        Walter Goehr, conductor.
        Concert Hall E8; later released as Concert Hall
        CHS 1253 (see D66d)
        Duration: ca. 25 min.
        With Diamond's String Quartet No. 3 (Concert Hall
        E8) or Vaughan Williams' Concerto Accademico
        (Concert Hall CHS 1253)
        <u>See</u>: B66q

D66g.   Louis Kaufman, violin; Musical Masterpiece Sympho-
        ny Orchestra; Walter Goehr, conductor.
        Musical Masterpiece Society MMS 105 (10 in.)
        [1955?]
        Program notes on slipcase.
        With Copland's Piano Concerto.
        LC card no. R67-1516.
        <u>See</u>: B66p

D66h.   Wolfgang Stavenhagen, violin; Imperial Philhar-
        monic Symphony Orchestra; William Strickland,
        conductor.
        Composers Recordings CRI 137, SD 137. 1960.
        Program notes by David Hall on slipcase.
        Duration: 24 min.
        With his Symphony no. 1.
        LC card no. R61-63.
        <u>See</u>: B66y, B66ff

D66i.   Isaac Stern, violin; New York Philharmonic Orches-
        tra; Leonard Bernstein, conductor.
        Columbia ML 6113, MS 6713. 1965; CBS SBRG 72345,
        BRG 72345 (Great Britain)
        Album title: Two Twentieth Century Masterpieces.
        Series: Columbia Masterworks.
        Duration: 22 min., 40 sec.
        Program notes by Martin Bernheimer on slipcase.
        With Hindemith's Violin Concerto.
        LC card no.: R65-2095, R65-2097.
        <u>See</u>: B66e, B66h, B66r, B66cc, B66hh, B66uu

D66j.   Isaac Stern, violin; New York Philharmonic
        Orchestra; Leonard Bernstein, conductor.
        CBS Classics 61621 (Great Britain; previously CBS
        SBRG 72345)
        With his Piano Concerto (previously Columbia SAX
        2575)
        <u>See</u>: B66i, B66n, B66ee, B66qq

D66k.   Ronald Thomas, violin; West Australian Symphony

Orchestra; David Measham, conductor.
Unicorn UNS 256 (in 1978 reissued as Unicorn UN1
72016)
Duration: 22 min., 15 sec.
Program notes by Richard Saxby on slipcase.
With his Music for a Scene from Shelley and Knox-
ville: Summer of 1915.
LC card no. 78-750413.
See: B66v, B66gg

D67. CONCERTO FOR VIOLONCELLO AND ORCHESTRA, OP. 22.

D67a. Raya Garbousova, violoncello; Musica Aeterna Or-
chestra; Frederic Waldman, conductor.
Decca DL 10 132, DL 710 132. 1966; later released
as Varese Sarabande VC 81057 Program notes by
Joseph Braunstein on slipcase.
With Britten's Serenade for Tenor, Horn, and
String Orchestra.
LC card no. R66-2965, R66-2967.
See: B67b, B67c, B67d, B67f, B67i, B67m, B67v,
B67y

D67b. Zara Nelsova, violoncello; New Symphony Orchestra;
Samuel Barber, conductor.
London LPS 332 (10 in.) 1951.
Recorded at Kingsway Hall, London, December 1950.
Program notes on slipcase.
LC card no. RA55-93 rev.

D67c. Zara Nelsova, violoncello; New Symphony Orchestra;
Samuel Barber, conductor.
Decca Ace of Clubs ACL 264; previousy issued as
Decca Eclipse ECS 707 and LX 3048 (10") (see
D67d); orig. London LPS 332 (10") (see D67b)
Duration: 28 min.
With his Symphony No. 2.
See: B67i, B67p, B67s

D67d. Zara Nelsova, violoncello; New Symphony Orchestra;
Samuel Barber, conductor.
Decca Eclipse ECS 707; later reissued as Decca Ace
of Clubs ACL 264; see D67c
With Rawthorne's Piano Concerto No. 2.
See: B67r

D67e. V. Simon, violoncello; USSR State Radio Orchestra;
Gennady Rozhdestvensky, conductor.
Melodiya D017965/6.
With his Piano Concerto.

D67f. Raphael Wallfisch, violoncello; English Chamber
Orchestra; Geoffrey Simon, conductor.
Chandos ABRO 1085 (digital)

With Shostakovich's Violoncello Concerto No. 1.
<u>See</u>: B67†

D68. ESSAY FOR ORCHESTRA, OP. 12.

D68a. Eastman-Rochester Symphony Orchestra; Howard Han-
son, conductor.
Mercury MG 40002, 50075, 50148.
With his Adagio for Strings, Overture to "The
School For Scandal," and Gould's Latin-American
Symphonette.

D68b. London Symphony Orchestra; David Measham, conduc-
tor.
Unicorn UN1 72010. 1976; also Unicorn RHS 342.
Durations on labels.
Program notes by Robert Angles on container.
With his Second Essay for Orchestra, Symphony
no. 1, and Night Flight.
LC card no. 77-750475 (UN1 72010)

D68c. Philadelphia Orchestra; Eugene Ormandy, conductor.
Victor 18 062 (78 rpm) 1941.
<u>See</u>: B68f, B68j, B68k

D68d. Utah Symphony Orchestra; Ardeen Watts, conductor.

D68e. Warwick Symphony [i.e. Philadelphia Orchestra];
Eugene Ormandy, conductor.
Camden CAL 238; reissue of Victor V 18062.
Duration: 7 min.
With works by Menotti, McDonald, and Liszt.

D71. MEDEA, OP. 23.

D71a. Eastman-Rochester Symphony Orchestra; Howard Han-
son, conductor.
Mercury MG 50224, SR 90224. 1959; Mercury AMS
16096 (Great Britain)
Olympian Series.
Program notes by Nathan Broder on slipcase.
Duration: ca. 25 min.
With his Capricorn Concerto.
LC card no. R60-101.
<u>See</u>: B71c, B71f, B71n, B71o

D71b. Eastman-Rochester Symphony Orchestra; Howard Han-
son, conductor.
Mercury MG 50148, SR 90420. 1965; reissued as
Mercury SRI 75012 (see D71d below)
Album title: The Music of Samuel Barber.
Series: Great Music by American Composers.
Program notes by David Hall and Nathan Broder on
slipcase.

Duration: ca. 25 min.
With his Symphony No. 1, Overture to "The School
   For Scandal," and Adagio For Strings.
LC card no.: R65-957 (SR 90420)

D71c.   Eastman-Rochester Orchestra; Howard Hanson, con-
          ductor.
        Mercury SRI 75012. 1972; reissue of Mercury MG
          50148, SR 90420 (see D71b above)
        Series: Golden Imports.
        Program notes by Nathan Broder on slipcase.
        Duration: ca. 25 min.
        With his Symphony No. 1, Overture to "The School
          For Scandal," and Adagio For Strings.
        LC card no.: 74-761433.

D71d.   New Symphony Orchestra; Samuel Barber, conductor.
        London LPS 333 (10") 1951; Decca LX 3049 (10",
          Great Britain) (presumably same performance as
          D71e below)
        Program notes on slipcase.
        LC card no. RA55-48.
       See: B71e, B71j, B71k, B71l

D71e.   New Symphony Orchestra; Samuel Barber, conductor.
        London LL 1328, CM 9145; Everest 3282; reissue of
          10 in. London LPS 333 (1951) (see also D71d above)
        With his Symphony No. 2.

D72. MEDEA'S MEDITATION AND DANCE OF VENGEANCE, OP. 23A.

D72a.   Boston Symphony Orchestra; Charles Münch, conduct-
          or.
        RCA Victor LM 2197. 1958; in 1969 released as RCA
          Victrola VIC 1391 (see D72b below)
        Program notes by Herbert Weinstock on slipcase.
        With Prokofiev's Piano Concerto No. 2.
        LC card no. R58-355.
        See: B72b

D72b.   Boston Symphony Orchestra; Charles Münch, conduct-
          or.
        RCA Victrola VIC 1391. 1969; in 1958 released as
          RCA Victor LM 2197 (see D72a above)
        Program notes on slipcase.
        With Debussy's Images.
        LC card no. R68-3662.
        See: B72o

D72c.   New York Philharmonic Orchestra; Thomas Schippers,
          conductor.
        CBS Masterworks 32 11 0005, 32 11 0006 (1966), 73
          434; in 1975 released as Odyssey Y 33230.
        Album title: Four Melodic Masterpieces (1966);

Thomas Schippers Conducts Barber (1975)
Program notes by Nicolas Slonimsky on slipcase
(unsigned in 1975, but same notes as 1966 re-
lease)
Duration: ca. 12 min., 31 sec.
With his Second Essay For Orchestra, Adagio for
Strings, and Overture to "The School For Scan-
dal."
LC card no. R66-2667, R66-2668 (1966), 74-750609
(1975)
See: B72k

D73. MUSIC FOR A SCENE FROM SHELLEY, OP. 7.

D73a.   American Recording Society Orchestra [i.e. Vienna
Symphony Orchestra]; Walter Hendl, conductor.
American Recording Society ARS 26. 1953.
Series: 200 Years of American Music.
Program notes on slipcase.
With his Overture to "The School For Scandal" and
Copland's Appalachian Spring.
LC card no. R53-781.
See: B73f

D73b.   The Symphony of the Air; Vladimir Golschmann,
conductor.
Vanguard VRS 1065 (in 1968 reissued as VSD 2083),
VSL 11019 (Great Britain) (1961)
Series: Landmarks of American Music (1961); West
Projects Release (1968)
Duration: 8 min., 48 sec.
Program notes by Sidney Finkelstein, texts and
biographical notes on slipcase.
With his Second Essay For Orchestra, A Stopwatch
and an Ordnance Map, A Hand of Bridge, and
Serenade For Strings.
LC card no. R61-671 (1961)
See: B73g, B73h

D73c.   Vienna Symphony Orchestra; Walter Hendl, conduc-
tor.
American Recording Society ARS 26; in 1971 re-
issued as Desto D 418, DST 6418.
Series: American Composers Series.
"Electronically reprocessed from monaural tapes."
Program notes on slipcase.
With his Overture to "The School For Scandal" and
Copland's Music For the Theatre.
LC card no. 78-764715.

D73d.   West Australian Symphony Orchestra; David Measham,
conductor.
Unicorn UNS 256 (in 1978 reissued as Unicorn UN1
72016)

Duration: 10 min., 15 sec.
Program notes by Richard Saxby on slipcase.
With his Violin Concerto and Knoxville: Summer of
    1915.
LC card no. 78-750413.
See: B731, B731

D74. DIE NATALI: CHORAL PRELUDES FOR CHRISTMAS, OP. 37.

D74a.   Louisville Orchestra; Jorge Mester, conductor.
         Louisville Orchestra LS 745. 1975.
         "125th release."
         Recorded February 20, 1975.
         Duration: 17 min., 38 sec.
         Program notes (4 p.) inserted in slipcase.
         With Claus Adam's Violoncello Concerto.
         LC card no. 75-762217.
         See: B74c

D74b.   Walter Hillsman, organ ("Chorale Prelude on Silent
             Night" only; arr. by the composer)
         Vista VPS 1038. 1976.
         Album title: American Organ Music from Southwark
             Cathedral.
         Recorded May 10-11, 1976.
         Program notes by the organist. "A brief history of
             the organ" by Garrett O'Brien, and specifica-
             tions of the organ on container.
         With his Wondrous Love: Variations on a Shape-Note
             Hymn and works by Ives, Sessions, Copland, Buck,
             and Brenner.
         LC card no. 79-760978.

D75. NIGHT FLIGHT, OP. 19A.

D75a.   London Symphony Orchestra; David Measham, conduc-
             tor.
         Unicorn UN1 72010, RHS 342. 1976.
         Duration on label.
         Program notes by Robert Angles on container.
         With his Essay for Orchestra, Second Essay for
             Orchestra, and Symphony no. 1.
         LC card no. 77-750475 (UN1 72010)
         See: B75a, B75b, B75c

D76. OVERTURE TO "THE SCHOOL FOR SCANDAL," OP. 5.

D76a.   American Recording Society Orchestra [i.e., Vienna
             Symphony Orchestra]; Walter Hendl, conductor.
         American Recording Society ARS 26. 1953.
         Series: 200 Years of American Music.
         Program notes on slipcase.

With his Music For a Scene From Shelley and
Copland's Appalachian Spring.
LC card no. R53-781 rev.
See: B76i

D76b.   Eastman-Rochester Symphony Orchestra; Howard Han-
son, conductor.
Mercury MG 40002. 1953; in 1956, released as MG
50075 in the Olympian Series.
Series: American Music Festival Series, v. 3.
Golden Lyre Series.
Program notes on slipcase.
With his Adagio For Strings, Essay For Orchestra
No. 1, and Gould's Latin-American Symphonette.
LC card no. RA58-104 (1953), R60-565 (1956)
See: B76n

D76c.   Eastman-Rochester Symphony Orchestra; Howard Han-
son, conductor.
Mercury SR 90420, MG 50148, 50420. 1965.
Album title: The Music of Samuel Barber.
Series: Great Music by American Composers.
Program notes by David Hall and Nathan Broder on
slipcase.
Duration: 8 min.
With his Symphony No. 1, Medea Suite, and Adagio
For Strings.
LC card no.: R65-957.

D76d.   Eastman-Rochester Symphony Orchestra; Howard Han-
son, conductor.
Mercury SRI 75012. 1974.
Series: Golden Imports.
Program notes by Nathan Broder on slipcase.
With his Symphony no. 1, Medea Suite, and Adagio
For Strings.
LC card no.: 74-761433.

D76e.   Janssen Symphony of Los Angeles; Werner Janssen,
conductor.
RCA Camden CAL 205 (reissue of V 11 8591, 78 rpm)
Duration: 5 min.
Reissue with works by Kern, Hermann, Tansman, and
Raskin.
See: B76m, B76p

D76f.   New York Philharmonic Orchestra; Thomas Schippers,
conductor.
CBS Masterworks 32 11 0005, 32 11 0006 (1966); in
1975 released as Odyssey Y 33230.
Album title: Four Melodic Masterpieces (1966);
Thomas Schippers Conducts Barber (1975)
Program notes by Nicolas Slonimsky on slipcase
(unsigned in 1975, but same notes as 1966 release)

Duration: ca. 7 min., 31 sec.
With his Medea's Meditation and Dance of Ven-
    geance, Adagio for Strings, and Second Essay For
    Orchestra.
LC card no. R66-2667, R66-2668 (1966), 74-750609
    (1975)
See: B76r

D76g.   USSR State Orchestra; Constantine Ivanov, conduc-
    tor.
    Melodiya D6509/10, S6581/2.
    With his Adagio for Strings.

D76h.   Vienna Symphony Orchestra; Walter Hendl, conductor
    [see also D76a]
    Desto D 418, DST 6418. 1971.
    Series: American Composers Series.
    "Electronically reprocessed from monaural tapes."
    Program notes on slipcase.
    With his Music for a Scene from Shelley and Cop-
        land's Music For the Theatre.
    LC card no. 78-764715.

D77. SECOND ESSAY FOR ORCHESTRA, OP. 17.

D77a.   London Symphony Orchestra; David Measham, conduc-
    tor.
    Unicorn UN1 72010, RHS 342. 1976.
    Duration on label.
    Program notes by Robert Angles on container.
    With his Essay for Orchestra, Symphony no. 1, and
        Night Flight.
    LC card no. 77-750475 (UN1 72010)

D77b.   New York Philharmonic Orchestra; Thomas Schippers,
    conductor.
    CBS Masterworks 32 11 0005, 32 11 0006 (1966), 73
        434; in 1975 released as Odyssey Y 33230.
    Album title: Four Melodic Masterpieces (1966);
        Thomas Schippers Conducts Barber (1975)
    Program notes by Nicolas Slonimsky on slipcase
        (unsigned in 1975, but same notes as 1966 re-
        lease)
    Duration: ca. 10 min., 38 sec.
    With his Medea's Meditation and Dance of Ven-
        geance, Adagio for Strings, and Overture to "The
        School For Scandal."
    LC card no. R66-2667, R66-2668 (1966), 74-750609
        (1975)
    See: B77a, B77l

D77c.   Symphonie Canadiana; Yondani Butt, conductor.
    Orion Master Recordings ORS 82433. 1982.
    Album title: A Sound Spectacular.

Recorded Dec. 8-9, 1981, in Centennial Hall, N. Vancouver.
Duration: 10 min., 50 sec.
With works by Saint-Saëns, Liszt, and Sibelius.
LC card no. 81-750534.

D77d.   The Symphony of the Air; Vladimir Golschmann, conductor.
Vanguard VRS 1065, VSL 11019 (Great Britain) 1961; later released as VSD 2083. 1968.
Series: Landmarks of American Music (1961); West Projects Release (1968)
Duration: 8 min., 6 sec.
Program notes by Sidney Finkelstein, texts and biographical notes on slipcase.
With his Music For a Scene From Shelley, A Stopwatch and an Ordnance Map, A Hand of Bridge, and Serenade For Strings.
LC card no. R61-671 (1961)
See: B77e, B77l

D78. SOUVENIRS, OP. 28.

D78a.   Arthur Gold and Robert Fizdale, piano.
Columbia SL 198 (ML 4853-ML 4855) 1954.
Album title: Music For Two Pianos.
Recorded August 15, 1952, at Columbia's 30th St. Studio, New York.
Program notes by Charles Burr bound in album.
Duration: ca. 17 min., 30 sec.
With works by Stravinsky, Hindemith, Rieti, Milhaud, Satie, Debussy, Poulenc, and Haieff.
LC card no. R54-346.
See: B78b, B78d, B78j, B78p, B78q

D78b.   Grant Johannesen, piano ("Hesitation Tango" only)
Golden Crest CRS 4132. 1974.
Album title: Rags and Tangos.
Series: Laboratory series.
Program and biographical notes on container.
With: works by Stravinsky, Castro, Milhaud, and Thomson.
LC card no. 77-760686.

D78c.   Ruth Laredo, piano.
Nonesuch Digital D79032.
With his Piano Sonata and Nocturne.
See: B78h, B78l

D78d.   London Symphony Orchestra; José Serebrier, conductor.
Desto DC 6433.
Duration: ca. 18 min.
With Surinach's Spells and Rhymes for Dancers.

See: B78f, B78k

D78e. Philharmonia Orchestra; Efrem Kurtz, conductor.
EMI-Capitol G 7146. 1959; also issued as Columbia
G 7146 (Great Britain)
With Shostakovich's Ballet Suite from The Age of
Gold.
Program notes on slipcase.
LC card no. R59-580.
See: B78e, B78r

D78f. Arthur Whittemore and Jack Lowe, piano ("Pas de
Deux" only)
Personal Touch 88 WL.
With works by Copland, Gottschalk, Griffes, Ives,
Joplin, Rodgers, Russell, and Sousa.

D79. SYMPHONY NO. 1, OP. 9.

D79a. Eastman-Rochester Symphony Orchestra; Howard Han-
son, conductor. (revised version)
Mercury MG 40014, MG 50087 (later issued as MG
4020/23, SR 40420/23)
Duration: ca. 19 min.
With Hanson's Cherubic Hymn and Symphony No. 5.
See: B79j, B79z

D79b. Eastman-Rochester Symphony Orchestra; Howard Han-
son, conductor (revised version)
Mercury MG 4020/23, SR 40420/2 (reissued from
various Mercury recordings), MG 50420, SR 90420
Album title: Great Music by American Composers.
With works by Copland, Harris, MacDowell, Griffes,
Piston, Sessions, Hanson, and Hovhannes.

D79c. Eastman-Rochester Symphony Orchestra; Howard Han-
son, conductor (revised version)
Mercury MG 50148, 50420, 90420. 1958.
Series: Olympian series.
Recorded in the Eastman Theater, Rochester.
Program notes on slipcase.
Duration: ca. 19 min., 30 sec.
With his Overture to "The School For Scandal," and
Adagio For Strings.
LC card no. R60-673.

D79d. Eastman-Rochester Symphony Orchestra; Howard Han-
son, conductor (revised version)
Mercury MG 50087. 1956.
Album title: The Music of Samuel Barber.
Series: American Music Festival Series.
Recorded in the Eastman Theater, Rochester, 1954.
Program notes on slipcase.
With Hanson's Symphony No. 5.

LC card no.: R60-539.

D79e. Eastman-Rochester Symphony Orchestra; Howard Han-
son, conductor (revised version)
Mercury SRI 75012. 1974.
Series: Golden Imports.
Program notes by Nathan Broder on slipcase.
With his Overture to "The School For Scandal,"
Medea Suite, and Adagio For Strings.
LC card no.: 74-761433.

D79f. Japan Philharmonic Symphony Orchestra; William
Strickland, conductor.
Composers Recordings CRI 137; Rediffusion Com-
posers Recordings SD 137 (Great Britain)
Duration: ca. 19 min.
Program notes by David Hall on slipcase.
With his Concerto For Violin and Orchestra.
LC card no. R61-63.
See: B79q

D79g. London Symphony Orchestra; David Measham, conduc-
tor.
Unicorn RHS 342 (in 1976 released as UN1 72010)
Durations on labels.
Program notes by Robert Angles on container.
With his Essay for Orchestra, Second Essay for
Orchestra, and Night Flight.
LC card no. 77-750475 (UN1 72010)
See: B79d, B79f, B79l, B79r, B79dd, B79ee

D79h. Milwaukee Symphony Orchestra; Kenneth Schermer-
horn, conductor.
Turnabout TV S 34564, QTV 34564. 1974.
Series: The Contemporary Composer in the USA.
Duration: 19 min., 51 sec.
Program notes on container.
With Mayer's Octagon.
LC card no. 76-761873.
See: B79c, B79cc

D79i. New York Philharmonic Orchestra; Bruno Walter,
conductor.
Columbia LX 1077-78 (originally Columbia 12128/9D
Set (M)X 252, 78 rpm, 4 sides)
See: B79b

D79j. Stockholm Symphony Orchestra; Nils Lehmann, con-
ductor.
Classic Editions CE 1011.
With his Dover Beach and Songs, op. 10.
See: B79k, B79p

D80. SYMPHONY NO. 2, OP. 19.

    D80a.   New Symphony Orchestra; Samuel Barber, conductor.
             London LPS 334 (10"), Decca LX 3050 (10"), Great
                Britain; reissued as Decca Ace of Clubs ACL 264.
             With his Medea Suite (LPS 334) or his Violoncello
                Concerto (ACL 264)
             See: B80f, B80h, B80o, B80p, B80v

    D80b.   New Symphony Orchestra; Samuel Barber, conductor.
             London LPS 334 (10"), LL 1328, CM 9145; Everest
                3282 (rechanneled stereo from London CM 9145,
                1951)
             With his Medea Suite.
             See: B80c

D81. THIRD ESSAY FOR ORCHESTRA, OP. 47.

    D81a.   New York Philharmonic Orchestra; Zubin Mehta,
             conductor.
             New World Records NW 309. 1981.
             "Recorded Anthology of American Music, Inc."
             Recorded at Avery Fisher Hall.
             Program notes ([4] p., ill.) by Phillip Ramey
                inserted in slipcase.
             With Corigliano's Clarinet Concerto.
             LC card no. 80-750482.
             See: B81b, B81c

D82. TOCCATA FESTIVA, OP. 36.

    D82a.   E. Power Biggs, organ; Philadelphia Orchestra;
             Eugene Ormandy, conductor.
             Columbia ML 5798, 6038, MS 6398. 1963; CBS SBRG
                72364 (Great Britain)
             Album title: Music for Organ and Orchestra.
             Columbia Masterworks.
             Duration: 13 min., 48 sec.
             Recorded in the Academy of Music, Philadelphia.
             Program notes by Max de Schauensee and Edwin H.
                Schloss on slipcase.
             With works by Poulenc and R. Strauss.
             LC card no.: R62-1360, R62-1362.
             See: B82a, B82b, B82e, B82f, B82i

BAND MUSIC

D83. COMMANDO MARCH.

D83a. Cleveland Symphonic Winds; Frederick Fennell,
conductor.
Tel Arc DG 10043.
Digital recording.
With works by Leemans, Fucik, Seitz, King, Miles,
Zimmerman, Grafulla, J. Strauss, Sr., Vaughan
Williams, Ganne, and Sousa.
See: B83a, B83c, B83f

D83b. Cornell University Wind Ensemble; Maurice W.
Stith, conductor.
Silver Crest Custom CUWE 6. 1970.
With works by Erickson, Jenkins, Vaughan Williams,
and Copland.

D83c. Eastman Wind Ensemble; Frederick Fennell, conduc-
tor.
Mercury SRI 75086, MG 40006, MG 5007.
Album title: American Concert Band Masterpieces.
"Electronically altered to simulate stereo."
"Previously released by Mercury Records on MG
50079."
Program notes by David Hall on slipcase.
With works by Persichetti, Gould, Schuman, Ben-
nett, and Piston.
LC card no. 78-760231.
See: B83d, B83e

D83d. Harvard University Concert Band; Walker, cond.
INC 7. 1973?
With works by Jacob and Persichetti.

D83e. United States Coast Guard Band; Lt. Lewis J. Buck-
ley, director.
U.S. Coast Guard Academy MC 20203.
Album title: The Stars and Stripes Forever!
"Recording sessions took place the week of Septem-
ber 21, 1981 in Leamy Hall Auditorium at the
U.S. Coast Guard Academy in New London, Connec-
ticut."
Duration: 3 min., 32 sec.
Program notes on container.

D83f. United States Marine Band.
RCA Victor LSP 2687, LPM 2687.

D83g. United States Military Academy Band; Francis E.
Resta, conductor.
American Society of Composers, Authors and
Publishers CB 177. 1954.
"Authorized by American Federation of Musi-
cians...for non commercial use only."
At head of title: Pittsburgh International Contem-
porary Music Festival [1952]
With works by Still, Ravel, Stravinsky, and Mil-

haud.
LC card no. RA55-133.

CHAMBER MUSIC

D84. CANZONE FOR FLUTE AND PIANO, OP. 38A.

D84a. Ransom Wilson, flute; J. Villa, piano.
Musical Heritage Society MHS 1856. [1974?]
Album title: Flute Encores.
With works by Bach, Ravel, Couperin, Nicholson,
Mozart, Lancen, Beethoven, Gretry, Debussy,
Vivaldi, Schumann, Bartok, Damase, Handel, Cho-
pin, and Scarlatti.

D85. CAPRICORN CONCERTO, OP. 21.

D85a. Joseph Mariano, flute, Robert Sprenkle, oboe, and
Sydney Mear, trumpet; Strings of the Eastman-
Rochester Symphony Orchestra; Howard Hanson,
conductor.
Mercury MG 50224, SR 90224, AMS 16096. 1960; later
issued as Mercury SRI 75049 in the Golden Im-
ports series.
Series: Olympian Series.
Program notes by Nathan Broder on slipcase.
Duration: 15 min.
With his Medea Suite (MG 50224, SR 90224) or works
by Ginastera and Sessions (SRI 75049)
LC card no. R60-101rev (MG 50224, SR 90224)
See: B85f, B85n, B85p

D85b. Julius Baker, flute, Mitchell Miller, oboe, and
Harry Freistadt, trumpet; Saidenberg Little
Symphony; Daniel Saidenberg, conductor.
Concert Hall Society 1078; originally issued on 78
rpm in Concert Hall Limited Editions series,
later as CH A4 (4 sides)
With Schuman's Symphony for Strings.
See: B85l, B85m

D86. DOVER BEACH, OP. 3.

D86a. Samuel Barber, baritone; Curtis String Quartet
(Jascha Brodsky, Charles Jaffe, violins, Max
Aronoff, viola, Orlando Cole, violoncello)
New World Records NW 229. 1978.
Album title: Songs of Samuel Barber and Ned Rorem.
Series: Recorded Anthology of American Music.

> Originally issued as Victor 8898 (78 rpm)
> Recorded May 13, 1935 in Camden, N.J.
> Program notes and interviews with the composers by
>   P. Ramey, and bibliographies bound in.
> See: B86l

D86b. Samuel Barber, baritone; Curtis String Quartet
      (see D86a above for performers)
      RCA Victor LCT 1158.
      Album title: Paul Hume's Critics Choice.
      Reissue of twelve 78 rpm recordings chosen by Paul
        Hume, Music Editor of the Washington Post; ori-
        ginally issued as Victor 8898 (78 rpm)
      With works by Rachmaninoff, Mozart, Bach, Humper-
        dinck, Wylie-Thompson, Poulenc, Alfano, Schu-
        bert, Ponchielli, Verdi, and Gretchaninoff.
      See: B86b, B86f, B86g, B86h

D86c. Dietrich Fischer-Dieskau, baritone; Juilliard
      Quartet (Robert Mann, Earl Carlyso, violins,
      Raphael Hillyer, viola, Claus Adam, violon-
      cello)
      Columbia CSP 7131, CKS 7131, KS 7131. 1968; re-
        issued as AKS 7131; Great Britain, CBS 72687)
      Series: Columbia Masterworks.
      Text inserted in slipcase; program notes by Phil-
        lip Ramey on slipcase.
      Duration: 8 min., 20 sec.
      With Schoeck's Notturno, op. 47.
      LC card no. R68-2698 (1968)
      See: B86a, B86j, B86m, B86n, B86o, B86p

D86d. Leslie Guinn, baritone; Concord Quartet.
      Elektra/Asylum/Nonesuch 78017. 1983.
      Series: Nonesuch Silver Series.
      Program notes Phillip Ramey.
      With his String Quartet and Rochberg's String
        Quartet No. 7.
      See: B86q

D86e. Paul King, baritone; Hartt String Quartet; Samuel
      Quincy, piano.
      Classic Editions CE 1011.
      Duration: ca. 8 min.
      With his Symphony no. 1 and Songs, op. 10.
      See: B86c, B86l

D86f. John Langstaff, baritone; Hiroch String Quartet.
      HMV C 4201 (78 rpm)

D87. MUTATIONS FROM BACH.

D87a. Locke Brass Consort; James Stobart, conductor.
      Unicorn RHS 339.

Album title: Contrasts in Brass.
With works by Buxtehude, Grieg, Kauffman, Tcherep-
nin, Carr, and Haydn.
See: B87c

D88. SERENADE FOR STRINGS, OP. 1.

D88a.   Los Angeles Chamber Orchestra; Gerard Schwarz,
conductor.
Nonesuch D 79002. 1980.
Album title: American Music for Strings.
Duration: 10 min., 19 sec.
Recorded April 2, 1980 at Ambassador Auditorium,
Pasadena, California.
Digital recording.
Program notes by Eric Salzman on container.
With works by Fine, Carter, and Diamond.
LC card no. 82-760365.
See: B88a, B88c, B88e, B88f

D88b.   Rome Chamber Orchestra; Nicolas Flagello, conductor.
Peters International PLE 059.

D88c.   The Symphony of the Air; Vladimir Golschmann,
conductor.
Vanguard VRS 1065, VSL 11019 (Great Britain) 1961;
later released as VSD 2083. 1968.
Series: Landmarks of American Music (1961); West
Projects Release (1968)
Duration: 8 min., 44 sec.
Program notes by Sidney Finkelstein, texts and
biographical notes on slipcase.
With his Second Essay For Orchestra, Music For a
Scene From Shelley, A Stopwatch and an Ordnance
Map, and A Hand of Bridge.
LC card no. R61-671 (1961)
See: B88g

D90. SONATA FOR VIOLONCELLO AND PIANO IN C MINOR, OP. 6.

D90a.   Clark-Schuldmann Duo (Harry Clark, violoncello and
Sandra Schuldmann, piano).
Musical Heritage Society MHS 3378. 1976.
Duration: 22 min., 32 sec.
Program notes by H. Parsons on container.
With Diamond's Sonata For Cello and Piano.
LC card no. 76-750247.
See: B90c, B90y

D90b.   Eileen Croxford, violoncello; David Parkhouse,
piano.
Saga STXID 5272, XID 5272 (Great Britain)

With Rachmaninoff's Cello Sonata in G minor, op.
19.
See: B90d

D90c.   Gordon Epperson, violoncello; Frances Burnett,
piano.
Golden Crest 7026. 1968.
Series: Recital Series.
Program notes by Gordon Epperson on slipcase.
With Martinu's Sonata No. 2 For Violoncello and
Piano.
LC card no. R68-1504.

D90d.   Raya Garbousova, violoncello; Erich Itor Kahn,
piano.
Concert Hall Society 1092. 1951. (reissue of Con-
cert Hall Society Limited Set No. 1, Series B,
78 rpm, 4 sides)
Program notes by Moses Smith and Edward Tatnall
Canby on container.
With Thomson's String Quartet In D Minor.
See: B90e, B90j, B90u

D90e.   Lucille A. Greco, violoncello; Mary Mark Zeyen,
piano.
Orion ORS 7297. 1972.
Duration: ca. 19 min.
Program notes on slipcase.
With arrangements of selected Bach instrumental
works.
LC card no.: 72-750610.
See: B90x

D90f.   Charles McCracken, violoncello; Lucy Greene, pi-
ano.
Finnadar 90076 1. 1983.
Program notes by Doris Hays on container.
Duration: 12 min., 3 sec.
With Beethoven's Cello and Piano Sonata No. 5.
See: B90n, B90aa

D90g.   Leslie Parnas, violoncello; E. Dyachenko, piano.
Melodiya D010243/4.
With Schubert's "Arpeggione" Sonata.

D90h.   Gregor Piatigorsky, violoncello; Ralph Berkowitz,
piano.
RCA Victor LM 2013. 1956.
Program notes by Nathan Broder on slipcase.
With Hindemith's Sonata For Cello and Piano.
LC card no. R56-528.
See: B90b, B90i, B90q

D90i.   George Ricci, violoncello; Leopold Mittman, piano.
Stradivari STR 602.

With his String Quartet and Wolf's Italienische
   Serenade.
See: B90bb

D90j.   Jeffrey Solow, violoncello; Albert Dominguez,
          piano.
        Pelican Records LP 2010. 1979.
        Recorded May 26-27, 1977, Los Angeles.
        Duration: ca. 19 min.
        Program notes by Truman Fisher and biographical
          notes on the performers on container.
        With works by Kodaly and Dello Joio.
        LC card no. 76-750755.
        See: B90k, B90z

D91. STRING QUARTET IN B MINOR, OP. 11.

D91a.   Beaux-Arts String Quartet (Charles Libove, Alan
          Martin, violins, Peter Mark, viola, Bruce Ro-
          gers, violoncello)
        Columbia ML 3907, Epic LC 3907,BC1307. 1965.
        Duration: 14 min., 48 sec.
        Program notes by William Flanagan on slipcase.
        With: Diamond's String Quartet No. 4.
        LC card no.: R65-2584, R65-2586.
        See: B91b, B91e, B91g, B91h, B91j, B91m, B91p

D91b.   Borodin Quartet.
        Artia 1563 (Connoisseur MK 1563)
        With Weinberg's String Quartet No. 7.
        See: B91d, B91f, B91l

D91c.   Borodin Quartet.
        Melodiya D06173/4.

D91d.   Cleveland Quartet.
        RCA Victor Red Seal ARL1 1 1599, ARD1 1 1599.
          1976.
        Duration: ca. 18 min.
        Program notes by S. Fleming on container.
        Withworks by Ives.
        LC card no. 76-262251.
        See: B91a, B91n, B91q

D91e.   Concord Quartet.
        Elektra/Asylum/Nonesuch/Conifer 78017. 1983.
        Series: Nonesuch Silver Series.
        Program notes Phillip Ramey.
        With his Dover Beach and Rochberg's String Quartet
          No. 7.
        See: B91k, B91r

D91f.   Leningrad Philharmonic Quartet.
        Melodiya D16089/90.

D91g.   Stradivari Records String Quartet (Arnold Eidus,
        Louis Graeler, violins, David Mankowitz, viola,
        George Ricci, violoncello)
        Stradivari STR 602.
        With his Sonata For Cello and Piano and Wolf's
        Italienische Serenade.
        See: B91o, B91t

D92. SUMMER MUSIC, OP. 31.

D92a.   Barry Tuckwell Wind Quintet (Peter Lloyd, flute;
        Gervase de Peyer, clarinet; Derek Wickens, oboe;
        Martin Gatt, bassoon; Barry Tuckwell, French
        horn)
        Elektra/Asylum/Nonesuch 78022. 1984; In 1980 re-
        leased on the EMI label.
        Series: Silver Series (78022)
        Duration: 10 min., 2 sec.
        With works by Milhaud, Arnold, Ligeti, and Ibert.

D92b.   Dorian Woodwind Quintet (Karl Kraber, flute; Jerry
        Kirkbride, clarinet; Charles Kuskin, oboe; Jane
        Taylor, bassoon; Barry Benjamin, French horn)
        Vox Box SVBX 5307 (3 discs)
        Album title: Avant-Garde Woodwind Quintet in the
        U.S.A.
        Duration: ca. 12 min.
        With works by Berger, Carter, Berio, Fine, Foss,
        Davidovsky, Druckman, Schuller, and Husa.
        See: B92k, B92r

D92c.   Leningrad Philharmonic Quintet.
        Melodiya D10533/4, S357/8.
        With Rameau's Suite for Wind Quintet.

D92d.   New York Woodwind Quintet (Samuel Baron, flute,
        Jerome Roth, oboe, David Glazer, clarinet, Ar-
        thur Weisberg, bassoon, John Barrows, French
        horn)
        Concert-Disc CM 1216, CS 216. 1959.
        Series: Connoisseur series.
        Program notes on slipcase.
        Duration: ca. 12 min.
        With works by Dahl and Etler.
        LC card no. R64-870.
        See: B92b, B92d, B92e, B92p

D92e.   New York Woodwind Quintet (for members see D91d)
        Saga XIP 7009 (Great Britain)
        Album title: American Chamber Music.
        With works by Etler, Dahl, and Riegger.
        See: B92l

D92f.   Philadelphia Woodwind Quintet (Robert Cole, flute;

Anthony Gigliotti, clarinet; John de Lancie,
oboe; Sol Schoenbach, bassoon; Mason Jones,
horn)
Columbia ML 5441, MS 6114. 1960.
Columbia Masterworks.
Duration: 11 min., 40 sec.
Program notes on slipcase.
With Nielsen's Quintet for Woodwinds and Horn.
Duration: 11 min., 40 sec.
LC card no. R60-364, R60-366.
<u>See</u>: B92c, B92g, B92h, B92m, B92o

D92g. Soni Ventorum Wind Quintet (Felix Skowronek,
flute; William McColl, clarinet; Laila Storch,
oboe; Arthur Grossmann, bassoon; David Kappy,
horn)
Musical Heritage Society MHS 4782F. 1983.
Title on label: 20th-Century Works for Wind Ensemble.
Title on container: Summer Music.
Program notes by Rita H. Mead on container.
Duration: 12 min., 45 sec.
With works by Carter, Fine, and Goodman.
LC card no. 83-743167.

SOLO INSTRUMENTAL MUSIC

D93. BALLADE, OP. 46.

D93a. Jo Alfidi, piano.
Queen Elizabeth International Music Competition
1980-031.
Duration: 4 min., 55 sec.
With his Piano Sonata, Nocturne: Homage to John
Field, and Excursions.

D93b. Angela Brownridge, piano.
Hyperion A66016. 1980.
Album title: Piano Music of Samuel Barber.
Recorded July 13-14, 1980.
Program notes by Kenneth Dommett on container.
Duration: 6 min., 12 sec.
With his Piano Sonata, Excursions, and Nocturne:
Homage to John Field.
LC card no. 81-760358.
<u>See</u>: B93c, B93d

D94. EXCURSIONS, OP. 20.

D94a. Jo Alfidi, piano.
Queen Elizabeth International Music Competition

1980-031.
Duration: 12 min., 6 sec.
With his Piano Sonata, Nocturne: Homage to John
   Field, and Ballade.

D94b.   Leon Bates, piano.
        Orion ORS 76237. 1976.
        Album title: Leon Bates Explores Music of the New
           World.
        Duration: ca. 11 min.
        Program notes by J. Eschelman and biographical
           notes on the performer on container.
        With works by MacDowell and G. Walker.
        LC card no. 76-750467.
        See: B94l

D94c.   Angela Brownridge, piano.
        Hyperion A66016. 1980.
        Album title: Piano Music of Samuel Barber.
        Recorded July 13-14, 1980.
        Program notes by Kenneth Dommett on container.
        Duration: 11 min., 4 sec.
        With his Nocturne: Homage to John Field, Ballade,
           and Piano Sonata.
        LC card no. 81-760358.
        See: B94i

D94d.   Rudolf Firkusny, piano.
        Columbia ML 2174 (10 in.)
        With his Knoxville: Summer of 1915.
        See: B94m, B94n, B94o, B94r

D94e.   Andor Foldes, piano.
        Vox 174 (10 in., 78 rpm)

D94f.   Carol Honigsberg, piano.
        Musical Heritage Society MHS 4474. 1981.
        Album title: 20th Century Piano Music.
        Recorded in the G. Steurbaut Studio, Ghent.
        Program notes by Myrna Nachman on slipcase.
        With works by Griffes, Longque, Meester, and Poot.
        LC card no. 81-750410.

D94g.   André Previn, piano.
        Columbia ML 5639, MS 6239. 1961.
        Series: Columbia Masterworks.
        Duration: 11 min., 13 sec.
        With works by Hindemith and Martin.
        LCcard no.: R61-1023rev, R61-1026rev.
        See: B94b, B94h

D94h.   Zola Shaulis, piano.
        Composers Recordings CRI SD 295. 1972.
        Album title: Naumburg Piano Award Winners, 1971.
        Duration: 11 min., 45 sec.

Program notes on slipcase.
With works by Gruenberg andBloch.
LC card no.: 73-750287.

D94i.   Stanley Waldoff, piano.
        Musical Heritage Society MHS 3808.
        Album title: The Piano in America.
        With works by Brown, Gottschalk, Hoffman, Nevin,
            Dett, Griffes, Antheil, Thomson, Reinagle,
            Beach, MacDowell, Gershwin, Gould, Cumming, and
            Zaminelli.

D97. NOCTURNE: HOMAGE TO JOHN FIELD, OP. 33.

D97a.   Jo Alfidi, piano.
        Queen Elizabeth International Music Competition
            1980-031.
        Duration: 3 min., 30 sec.
        With his Piano Sonata, Ballade, and Excursions.

D97b.   Angela Brownridge, piano.
        Hyperion A66016. 1980.
        Album title: Piano Music of Samuel Barber.
        Recorded July 13-14, 1980.
        Program notes by Kenneth Dommett on container.
        Duration: 4 min., 7 sec.
        With his Piano Sonata, Ballade, and Excursions.
        LC card no. 81-760358.
        See: B97c, B97e

D97c.   Monique Duphil, piano.
        Conciertos Avila LPE 1018431. 1976.
        Album title: Joyas de America. Jewels of America.
        Biographical note by A. Abreu on container; pro-
            gram notes by I. Peña in Spanish and English
            inserted.
        With works by Castellanos, Hernandez Lopez, Carre-
            ño, Estevez, Gershwin, Ain, Villa Lobos, and
            Ginastera.
        LC card no. 77-760899.

D97d.   Grant Johannesen, piano.
        Golden Crest CR 4065.
        Album title: American Encores From a Russian Tour.
        With works by Gottschalk, Carpenter, Farwell,
            Gershwin, Shepherd, Mennin, Bowles, Thomson, and
            Johannesen.

D97e.   Ruth Laredo, piano.
        Nonesuch Digital D 79032.
        With his Piano Sonata and Souvenirs.
        See: B97f, B97g

D97f.   Robert Shields, piano.

Vox Box SVBX 5303.
Album title: Piano Music in America, v.2., 1900-
45.
With the "Fuga" from his Piano Sonata and works by
MacDowell, Cowell, Griffes, Antheil, Gershwin,
Riegger, Ruggles, Sessions, Schuman, Copland,
Piston, and Thomson.
See: B97d

D97g. Gary Wolf, piano.
Golden Crest Records RE 7092. 1980.
Recital Series.
Recorded April 20, 1980, Golden Crest Studios.
Duration: ca. 4 min.
Program notes on container.
With works by Brahms and Schumann.
LC card no. 81-760060.

D98. PIANO SONATA, OP. 26.

D98a. Jo Alfidi, piano.
Queen Elizabeth International Music Competition
1980-031
Duration: 18 min., 54 sec.
With his Nocturne: Homage to John Field, Ballade,
and Excursions.

D98b. Angela Brownridge, piano.
Hyperion A66016. 1980.
Album title: Piano Music of Samuel Barber.
Recorded July 13-14, 1980.
Program notes by Kenneth Dommett on container.
Duration: ca. 18 min., 46 sec.
With his Nocturne: Homage to John Field, Ballade,
and Excursions.
LC card no. 81-760358.
See: B98b, B98r, B98hh, B98aaaa

D98c. John Browning, piano.
Desto DC 7120.
With Cummings' 24 Preludes.
See: B98jj, B98kk, B98hhhh

D98d. John Browning, piano.
Peerless PRCM 204.
With Britten's Diversions on a Theme.
See: B98jjjj

D98e. Van Cliburn, piano.
RCA Red Seal LSC 3229. 1971; RCA LBS 4095 (Great
Britain)
Album title: Two Twentieth Century Masterpieces.
Program notes by Edward Jablonski on slipcase.
With Prokofieff's Piano Sonata No. 6.

LC card no. 76-752378.
See: B98z, B98jj, B98kk, B98pp, B98lll, B98kkk

D98f.   Robert Guralnik, piano.
        Mace MXX 90855, S 9085.
        With Ginastera's Piano Sonata.
        See: B98l, B98gggg

D98g.   Horacio Gutierrez, piano ("Fuga" only)
        Melodiya D028091/2.

D98h.   Vladimir Horowitz, piano.
        RCA Red Seal ARM 1 2952. 1978.
        Series: The Horowitz Collection.
        Duration: ca. 19 min.
        Recorded May 15, 1950.
        Program notes on container.
        With works by Prokofiev and Scriabin.
        LC card no. 78-763536.
        See: B98ll, B98rr

D98i.   Vladimir Horowitz, piano.
        RCA Victor LD 7021 (2 discs)
        Series: The Horowitz Collection.
        With works by Czerny, Mozart, Clementi, Schumann,
          Mendelssohn, and Saint-Saëns/Liszt/Horowitz.
        See: B98aa

D98j.   Vladimir Horowitz, piano.
        RCA Victor LM 1113.
        With Chopin's Piano Sonata No. 2.
        See: B98sss

D98k.   Vladimir Horowitz, piano.
        RCA Victor RB 6554-5 (Great Britain; 2 discs)
        With works by Czerny, Mozart, Clementi, Schumann,
          Mendelssohn, Chopin, Scriabin, Prokofiev, Mos-
          kowski, and Saint-Saëns.
        See: B98qqq, B98uuu

D98l.   Vladimir Horowitz, piano.
        RCA Victrola VH 1014 (Great Britain); reissued
          from RB 6555, RB 166019, and HMV ALP 1431.
        With works by Prokofiev and Scriabin.
        See: B98ff

D98m.   Vladimir Horowitz, piano.
        Victor WDM 2466 (45 rpm)
        Duration: ca. 19 min.

D98n.   Terence Judd, piano.
        Chandos DBR 3001. 1980 (3 discs)
        Album title: In Memory of Terence Judd, 1957-1979.
        Recorded 1976-78 in the Broadcasting House Concert
          Hall of the New Gallery, London.

Program notes by Bryce Morrison in container.
With works by Scarlatti, Chopin, Ginastera, Haydn,
    Ravel, Liszt, Liadov, Tchaikovsky, Prokofiev,
    and Balakirev.
LC card no. 81-760527.
<u>See</u>: B98gg

D98o.   Katrina Krimsky, piano.
        Transoner Records 3008.
        With works by Riley, Shaw, and Shaw/Krimsky.
        <u>See</u>: B98mmm

D98p.   Ruth Laredo, piano.
        Nonesuch Digital D79032.
        With his Nocturne and Souvenirs.
        <u>See</u>: B98zz, B98ddd

D98q.   Marjorie Mitchell, piano.
        Decca DL 10 136, DL 710 136. 1977.
        Series: Decca gold label series.
        Program notes by Charles Briefer on slipcase.
        With Delius' Piano Concerto in C minor.
        LC card no. R66-3500, R66-3502.
        <u>See</u>: B98j, B98qq, B98yyy

D98r.   Nikolai Petrov, piano.
        Melodiya D023027/8.
        With works by Bach, Haydn, and Prokofiev.

D98s.   Daniel Pollock, piano.
        Artia 04299. 1961?
        At head of title: Laureates of the Tchaikovsky
            International Contest.
        Serial no. on slipcase: MK 1513.
        "An Artia cultural exchange presentation."
        Program notes on slipcase.
        With Prokofiev's Piano Sonata No. 3.
        LC card no. RA67-162.

D98t.   Daniel Pollock, piano.
        Artia MK 1513.
        With Prokofiev's Piano Sonatas Nos. 3 and 7.
        <u>See</u>: B98v, B98dd, B98ccc

D98u.   Daniel Pollock, piano.
        Melodiya D04299-4318.

D98v.   Robert Shields, piano ("Fuga" only)
        Vox Box SVBX 5303.
        Album title: Piano Music in America, v.2., 1900-
            45.
        With his Nocturne and works by Ives, MacDowell,
            Cowell, Griffes, Antheil, Gershwin, Riegger,
            Ruggles, Sessions, Schuman, Copland, Piston, and

Thomson.
<u>See</u>: B98y

D101. WONDROUS LOVE: VARIATIONS ON A SHAPE-NOTE HYMN, OP. 34.

D101a.　Thomas Harmon, playing the Skinner Organ in the Royce Hall Auditorium, UCLA.
Orion ORS 76255. 1976 or 1977.
Album title: American Organ Music of Three Centuries.
Program notes and specifications of the organ on container.
With works by Selby, Moller, Kay, Sowerby, Paine, Parker, and Farnam.
LC card no. 76-750761.
<u>See</u>: B101a, B101d

D101b.　Walter Hillsman, organ.
Vista VPS 1038. 1976.
Album title: American Organ Music From Southwark Cathedral.
Recorded May 10-11, 1976.
Program notes by the organist, "A brief history of the organ" by Garrett O'Brien, and specifications of the organ on container.
With his Chorale Prelude on Silent night (from Die Natali), works by Ives, Sessions, Copland, Buck, and Brenner.
LC card no. 79-760978.

D101c.　Rollin Smith, playing the 1883 H.L. Roosevelt Organ, First Congregational Church, Great Barrington, Massachusetts.
Repertoire Recording Society RRS 12.
Album title: The American Collection.
With works by Shelley, Parker, Gibson, Ives, Buck, Thomson, Chadwick, Foote, Copland, and Sowerby.
<u>See</u>: B101c

BIBLIOGRAPHY

This Bibliography represents a contemporary view of criticism of Samuel Barber's music, while at the same time providing some concept of who performed his music, how it was performed, and how such performances were received by critics and the listening public. Some of the annotations, which generally assume the form of quotations of relevant passages from the sources cited, might appear inordinately long. In order to provide users of this Bibliography with as comprehensive a view of sources of contemporary criticism of Barber's music in general and of his individual works, however, it was felt that such quoted passages were required to be sufficiently substantial to present the often-differing perspectives of the original authors.

"See" references refer to individual works and particular performances of those works as described in the "Works and Performances" section (e.g., See: W61d) and in the "Discography" (e.g., See: D7).

GENERAL REFERENCES

BG1. "Acclaimed Composer Samuel Barber Dies." Chicago Tribune, January 24, 1981, sect. 2, p. 13.
   Obituary. "Perhaps no other American composer has ever enjoyed such early, persistent, and long-lasting acclaim."

BG2. Albertson, John Emery. A Study of the Stylistic Elements of Samuel Barber's 'Hermit Songs' and Franz Schubert's 'Die Winterreise'. Thesis (D.M.A.)--University of Missouri, Kansas City, 1969. 101 p.

"From about 1939, Barber's career was characterized by significant changes in his compositional style. The romanticism of his earlier compositions was modified by an obvious awareness of techniques used by contemporary composers. The change in style is revealed in the melodic structure of his music, in its harmonic and contrapuntal texture, and in its rhythms...The melodic quality of Barber's music may be attributed to his extensive vocal training. He is one of the few composers that aspired to a singing career." [p. 4-5]

BG3. "American Academy of Arts and Letters Elects Four." New York Times, December 6, 1958, p. 18.
    News article announcing that Samuel Barber had been elected to the American Academy of Arts and Letters, an honorary society of artists, writers, and composers. Membership is limited to fifty who are chosen for special distinction from the 260 members of the Academy's parent body, the National Institute of Arts and Letters.

BG4. Angles, Robert. "Samuel Barber" [album notes for Unicorn RHS 342 disc]
    "His music is notable for its memorable quality of sustained lyricism. Few 20th century composers can match his melodic gifts, its flow and its high degree of expressiveness. When, as in Barber's music, this is combined (a rare achievement) with a keen sense of musical design and logical development of dramatic content, the results are of unique distinction."

BG5. Ardoin, John. "Samuel Barber of Capricorn." Musical America 80:4-5+ (March 1960)
    An interview with Samuel Barber at his Mt. Kisco home, Capricorn, which provides an intimate glimpse of the composer at home.

BG6. Arvey, Verna. "From the Mail Pouch: West Coast Point of View." New York Times, December 25, 1938, sect. 9, p. 8.
    Miss Arvey, in reply to Ashley Pettis' letter, "Important American Music" in the New York Times for November 13, 1938: "The controversy over whether or not Samuel Barber is representative enough as an American composer to have his music played by Toscanini has interested a great many of us on the West Coast...It seems, however, that despite the relative merits, or demerits, of the various American composers whose names have been injected into the discussion, that the important fact to remember is that Toscanini did play an American composition and that he may be prevailed upon to play more of these in the future."

BG7. Autori, Franco. "From the Mail Pouch: A Question of Personal Taste." New York Times, November 27, 1938, sect. 9, p. 6.
    The author replies, in part to Ashley Pettis' letter,

"Important American Music" in the New York Times for November 13, 1938: "The real issue is whether the composer has a message to deliver, whether he is competent to deliver it, and whether, in delivering it, he is sincere and true to his purpose...If Mr. Pettis does not like these works, or the idiom in which they are conceived and written, he is entitled to his opinion; and so is Mr. Toscanini, and so are those many listeners who found the two works, and especially the first, full of 'youthful vigor, freshness, fire, and incidentally, quite contemporary.'"

BG8. "Barber, Samuel." Current Biography 1944:30-32.
General article covering Barber's early career.

BG9. -------. Current Biography 1963:17-19.
Useful biography giving in some detail his career and mention of his major works up to 1963.

BG10. -------. Current Biography 1981:458.
Contains Barber's obituary.

BG11. Bawden, J. L. "Drawn From the Mail Pouch: 'Both Your Houses' Argument." New York Times, November 20, 1938, sect. 9, p. 8.
In reply to Ashley Pettis' letter, "Important American Music" in the New York Times for November 13, 1938: "...setting aside the question of the importance of Mr. Barber's works, the letter unwittingly reveals the bankruptcy of the whole problem by submitting Aaron Copland, Roy Harris, Charles Ives, etc., as composers worthier of performance. Mr. Toscanini probably sees what Mr. Pettis does not: that these men are lost in a remoter limbo than the nineteenth century, and have no message that is necessary for us (A.D. 1938)."

BG12. Baxter, Robert. "Curtis Alumni Celebrate Samuel Barber." Courier Post (Camden, N.J.), March 10, 1980.
"Never a follower of fads or a seeker of easy success, Barber has, throughout his long career, composed music of quality. Lyrical melodies and traditional forms stand at the core of his fastidiously crafted music. And that music becomes more striking and satisfying as the years pass."

BG13. Berger, Arthur. "Spotlight on the Moderns." Saturday Review 34:62 (May 26, 1951)
"It is inevitable for audiences to take pleasure in the music of Samuel Barber...It is quite as inevitable for the experts, who are interested in the music's relation to the past and its potentials for the future, to view a bit suspiciously its improblematic nature. So polished a technique and such untroubled musicianship, both innate and highly cultivated, cannot fail to elicit the admiration of the expert and the envy of fellow composers. But at the same time there is the factor that these precious assets manifest themselves with such consistency precisely because

he takes so few chances with them...It is as if he felt
that to make a mistake would be to let his audience down
and disturb his well ordered mind. This is a source of
strength at the same time that it leaves us wishing he
would struggle more with the musical medium."

BG14. Briggs, John. "Samuel Barber." International Musician 60:20-21, 33 (December 1961)
Lengthy biographical sketch from the beginnings up to
Barber's then-in-progress Piano Concerto.

BG15. Broder, Nathan. "The Music of Samuel Barber."
Musical Quarterly 34:325-335 (July 1948)
"Barber's feeling for form is very strong, and it is
in this respect that his music shows the closest ties with
the past. The large works are firmly rooted in the principles of sonata construction. Yet even here one seldom
(except perhaps in the earliest pieces) has the impression
of a slavish reliance upon well-tested models; instead, all
sorts of changes are rung on the traditional procedures,
and the resulting structures usually seem the logical ones
for imaginative and well integrated treatment of the material."

BG16. -----. "Samuel Barber." Boston Symphony Orchestra
Program Notes, September 28, 1962, p. 84+.
General article on Barber in program notes to accom-
pany the September 29, 1962 Boston premiere of the Piano
Concerto. "Samuel Barber's life has been principally
eventful in the inward sense of his musical activity. He
has not known want, nor been hampered in his constant
eagerness and enterprise as a composer. His association
with Rosario Scalero at the Curtis Institute of Music in
Philadelphia was enormously helpful to him. Living abroad
and later doing service in the Air Force during the War, he
was enabled to continue composing."

BG17. Carter, Susan Blinderman. The Piano Music of Samuel Barber. Thesis (Ph.D.)--Texas Tech University, Lubbock, 1980. 188 p.
"Related to Barber's traditional formal designs is his
consistent adherence to principles of tonality. Although
music composed after 1969 displays a more dissonant and
chromatic harmonic style, all of his works are based on
well-defined tonal centers [p. 28]...Barber's rhythmic
style ranges from smooth, flowing patterns to the most
powerful, often complex, driving figures. The vocal music
is carefully suited to the rhythm of the text, often marked
by necessary changes of meter. The instrumental music,
particularly in the later works, usually avoids obvious or
regular patterns; hemiolas, syncopations, cross rhythms and
irregular groupings are frequent." [p. 30]

BG18. "The Case of Samuel Barber." Newsweek 23:94+
(March 13, 1944)

"Since Barber is probably the most outstanding American serious composer in uniform, the question of how best
to use his talent has been controversial ever since he was
inducted in September of 1942. At a Town Hall symposium on
music for the armed forces in January last year an unnamed
'distinguished young composer' became a mild cause célèbre
when Lawrence Tibbett stated that the Army had refused the
composer permission to write a special American musical
greeting to the Russian people and, because of his limited-
service classification, had kept him doing a clerk's work
instead...Barber was never named as the composer in question, but the facts fitted him because of his own limited
service and because his music is extremely popular in
Russia. Some time thereafter Barber was transferred to the
Air Force and was assigned to write the new symphony [his
Symphony No. 2, op. 19]. He now says that he is 'very
happy that America is beginning to use composers in the
same way Russia uses Shostakovich.'"

BG19. Coke, Austin Neil. _An Analysis of Some of the
Purely Instrumental Works of Samuel Barber_. Thesis (M.A.)--
California State College at Long Beach, 1968. 82 p.
        A study of the orchestral music of Samuel Barber from
1930-1950. An attempt was made in the study to discover
"how much Barber absorbed of the current trends in musical
composition and to discover if he was ever an innovator of
any new techniques or principles of composition."

BG20. "Composer Wins Again." _New York Times_, April 12,
1933, p. 24.
        News article indicating that Barber "had received the
Joseph H. Bearns Music Prize for $1200 for the second time
in five years."

BG21. Conly, John N. "Record Reviews." _Atlantic_ 201:113
(March 1958)
        "Mercury here has compressed on two sides what used to
occupy three, managed...to _improve_ the fidelity substantially, and given us a treasury of Barber's sanely modern
and eloquent music." [Mercury MG-50148]

BG22. Cooper, David. "American Music in Europe." _Mu-
sical Courier_ 155:10 (June 1957)
        "Works of such composers as Copland and Barber are now
almost staple items in the repertoires of many European
orchestras, with Gershwin best known."

BG23. Copland, Aaron. "Our Younger Generation: Ten
Years Later." _Modern Music_ 13:11 (May-June 1936)
        "Barber writes in a somewhat out-moded fashion, making
up in technical finish what he lacks in musical substance.
So excellent a craftsman should not content himself forever
with the emotionally conventional context of his present
manner."

BG24. "Craftsman Above All." New York Times, September 17, 1966, p. 18.
Feature biographical article on Barber at the time of the opening of his Antony and Cleopatra.

BG25. D'Amico, Fedele. "Notiziario." Nuova rivista musicale italiana 15:165-166 (January-March 1981)
Obituary.

BG26. Davis, Peter G. "America's Senior Composers--Why Was Their Impact Profound?" New York Times, September 28, 1980, sect. 2, p. 25, 31.
Discussion of the influence on Barber of such composers as Copland, Carter, Thomson, Hanson, Piston, Thompson, and Harris.

BG27. -----. "Repeat Performance." High Fidelity 21:106 (February 1971)
"Samuel Barber has been an infrequent performer of his own works, but unlike many composers he has proven to be a proficient professional in several executive capacities: as a pianist (the sonata), singer (Dover Beach), and on this disc, conductor." [Everest 3282]

BG28. "Dear Mother..." Newsweek 51:62-63 (January 27, 1958)
"His always tasteful, extremely personalized music has been called neo-romantic and has been sometimes damned by the avant-garde as too conservative. Nonetheless, he is one of the few composers active today who lives comfortably on his royalties and does not have to teach to supplement his income."

BG29. Demuth, Norman. Musical Trends in the 20th Century. London: Rockliff, 1952. 359 p.
"Barber is drawn to the romantic virtuosity of Strauss as viewed through late twentieth-century eyes. His music is not only emotionally charged, but picturesquely coloured. It might be said that he is a reactionary, until it is realized that he deliberately withholds himself from the trend to neo-classicism...It is refreshing to meet this unashamed romanticism to-day, and one hopes that Barber will have a little influence upon the young idea in this regard. If he can supply a leaven of softening to the hard American outlook and personality, he will achieve much." [p. 317-318]

BG30. Dexter, Harry. "Samuel Barber and His Music." Musical Opinion 72:285-286 (March 1949) and 72:343-344 (April 1949)
Lengthy biographical and critical article. "Samuel Barber, of all American composers, is the one most likely to appeal to English ears. His work is remarkable chiefly for its design, for its emotional stability, its controlled enthusiasm, its depth of feeling, which scorns obvious

expression or over-elaborated detail...His serious approach
to the art of music, his prodigious technique, his record
of work and achievement, not only command our profound
respect but lead us to expect even greater things."

BG31. Dickinson, Peter. "Music Reviews: Americans."
Musical Times 122:834 (December 1981)
      With regard to Schirmer's edition of the Complete
Choral Music: "His publishers have served him handsomely by
following the complete songs with the complete choral
music. The 122-page volume, cheap at the price, does
manage to include the inevitable Adagio for strings (he
transcribed it as an Agnus Dei for chorus in 1967) as well
as other numbers out of Vanessa and Antony and Cleopatra,
and choral versions of the familiar songs Sure on This
Shining Night and The Monk and His Cat. Twelfth Night, a
late setting of Laurie Lee, is rewarding, and so is the
earlier Spender setting, A Stopwatch and an Ordnance Map
for male voices and timpani. The Adagio/Agnus Dei would
still be an emotional knock-out in a fine performance, but
the two funeral numbers from Antony and Cleopatra would
suffer without the orchestra. Altogether, Barber's solo
songs reach a higher level."

BG32. ------. "Obituary." Musical Times 122:193 (March
1981)
      Brief obituary. "...he was one of the most widely
performed American composers of this century, possibly
because his music fits easily into the international mainstream of the early 20ᵗʰ century. Nevertheless, some of his
fastidious songs, piano and chamber music, and orchestral
works have become modern classics. Barber achieved this
status in an environment which has been increasingly un-
favourable to expressive romanticism, and he consistently
held to his own path."

BG33. Dommett, Kenneth. "The Piano Music of Samuel
Barber" [album notes for Hyperion A66016 disc]
      "Barber's harmony is basically tonal though it is
rarely uncomplicated and nearly always very fluid. His
sense of form, on the other hand, is very strong. The
loose structures of the Romantics have no place in his
music which is always written with great economy and an
absence of rhetoric. In short, it is always perfectly
measured to meet the demands of what needs to be said. It
is not 'paper music,' to be probed analytically, though it
can be; rather it is emotional, full-blooded music, often
witty but always aimed directly at the heart."

BG34. Drew, David. "American Chamber Music." In:
Chamber Music, edited by Alec Robertson. Baltimore: Penguin Books, 1957. 427 p.
      "Barber's lyrical talent is at its best when inspired
by poetry. He is perhaps a trifle self-conscious about his
traditionalism, and purely instrumental forms seem to en-

courage in him extravagances which he may regard as camou-
flage. The flashy rodomontade of the piano sonata and the
unconvincing neo-classicism of the Capricorn Concerto for
chamber orchestra do no credit to the composer of Dover
Beach (for baritone and string quartet), Knoxville: Summer
of 1915, and the String Quartet, op. 11, from which the
celebrated Adagio is taken." [p. 327]

BG35. Ellsworth, Ray. "Americans on Microgroove: Part
II." High Fidelity 6:61-62 (August 1956)
    "Samuel Barber, perhaps the most frequently performed
American composer of stature living today, possesses the
rare faculty of being able to touch greatness and the heart
of the listener at the same time."

BG36. Elson, James. "The Songs of Samuel Barber." NATS
(National Association of Teachers of Singing) Bulletin
34:18-19 (October 1977)
    The article concludes: "Considering his musical gifts
and affinity for vocal music, we can only regret that
Barber has not written more songs during his career. Because of the high standards reached and maintained from the
first, however, it would appear that most of Barber's songs
will be performed for some years to come."

BG37. Ericson, Raymond. "Mehta Plans Barber Premiere
to Open Philharmonic Season." New York Times, March 14,
1978, p. 30.
    News article announcing the Fall 1978 plans for the
New York Philharmonic Orchestra, including the world premiere of a new work by Samuel Barber, 'The Ambiguities
(After Melville).' [Note: No trace of this work could be
found as the three major New York City newspapers were on
strike during the period.]

BG38. -----. "Notes: Reviving the L.A. Chamber Orchestra." New York Times, February 24, 1980, sect. 2, p.
19, 25.
    Concerns programs honoring Barber's 70ᵗʰ birthday. The
Curtis Institute of Music in Philadelphia will present two
programs: on the afternoon of May 9, Rose Bampton will sing
Dover Beach and Ruth Laredo will perform the Piano Sonata,
and during that same evening, Calvin Simmons will conduct
the Curtis Symphony in an all-Barber program, including the
Violin Concerto (Jaime Laredo, soloist). Efrem Zimbalist,
Jr., will deliver a tribute and the program will be broadcast on National Public Radio. On March 11, Barber will be
in Washington to receive the Wolf Trap Award, to be presented at the White House by Rosalyn Carter. In the
evening, James Tocco will be the soloist in the Piano
Concerto, with Antal Dorati conducting the National Symphony. In July, there will be an all-Barber chamber music
concert in London and a tribute is scheduled late in the
summer at the Festival of Naples.

BG39. Eschelman, Jeffery. "Leon Bates Explores Music
of the the New World" [album notes for Orion ORS 76237
disc]
    "Samuel Barber is one of the best examples of the
American-trained cosmopolitan composer...He has developed a
style at once 'conventional' (meaning, today, tonal and
expressive) and highly personal, with one of his era's
purest melodic gifts."

BG40. Evett, Robert. "How Right Is Right?" The Score
12:33-37 (June 1955)
    "Samuel Barber has always been a right wing composer;
ten years ago, his music, with its key-signatures and
unaltered dominant cadences, was considered awfully soft by
composers like those mentioned here [William Schuman, Peter
Mennin, and Vincent Persichetti]. It is still difficult to
think of most of his writing as 'modern,' and to list him
here is only to show what strange bedfellows adversity can
make. Actually, adversity has never come too close to
Barber. From the outset, he was a composer after Toscanini's own heart, with a wonderful sense of the orchestra and
a knack for writing attractive music that would still bear
considerable scrutiny. Barber's own stylistic evolution
was certainly affected by the vogue for austere music; his
employment of twelve-note devices, as in the Piano Sonata,
has helped to relax the melodic substance of his work, and
his gradual adoption of a more astringent harmonic idiom
has brought with it an intensity which his earlier music
lacks."

BG41. Ewen, David. Composers Since 1900: a Biographical and Critical Guide. New York: H.W. Wilson, 1969, pp.
28-32.
    General article of moderate length written before
Barber had died. Appended are a list of works and a brief
bibliography.

BG42. -----. -------. First Supplement. New York:
H.W. Wilson, 1981, pp. 24-26.
    Supplementing BG41 above, this article covers from
1971 (Fadograph of a Yestern Scene) to Barber's death in
1981; the list of works and bibliography cover the same
ten-year period.

BG43. -----. "Modern American Composers." Musical
Times 80:415-416 (June 1939)
    Six American composers are discussed. Concerning
Barber, Mr. Ewen notes: "I know of no other American composer who has written so fluently and professionally at the
age of twenty-six. Samuel Barber is already a fine and
original composer; there is every reason to believe that he
may ultimately develop into a great one."

BG44. F., H. "Orchestral." Gramophone 29:4-5 (June
1951)

"He is not one of the most exciting, startling, rugged, nationalistic, far-seeing, or anything else in the way of alluring adjectives. But he has a real musical quality, which perhaps comes from his having been brought up as a singer himself...He is a cultured man of literary as well as musical interest."

BG45. Fairleigh, James P. "Serialism in Barber's Solo Piano Works." Piano Quarterly no. 72:13-17 (Summer 1970)
Analytical article with musical examples, with emphasis on the Piano Sonata and Nocturne. "The twentieth century has witnessed in serialism a rejection of orthodox tonality, but this does not mean, as some of Schoenberg's more radical disciples have maintained, that tonality and serialism are totally irreconcilable. Barber's successful fusion of tonal and serial procedures provides ample refutation of this contention, and it is entirely possible that such a fusion might foreshadow future trends."

BG46. Fegley, Brent. "Samuel Barber: the Formative Years" [paper presented at the Sonneck Society Conference, Philadelphia, March 4-6, 1983]
Discusses Three Sketches for Pianoforte and compares thematic transformations of "Minuetto."

BG47. Felton, James. "Mother, 'Don't Cry,' I Was Always Meant to be a Composer." Bulletin (Philadelphia), March 9, 1980.
"The theme of Barber's music, whatever form it takes, is an appeal to romantic feeling and nostalgia. As such it has survived the landslides of passing style and modishness. Barber's appeal to the heart is his message."

BG48. -----. "A Moving Tribute to Barber." Bulletin (Philadelphia), March 10, 1980.
On the occasion of the March 9, 1980 evening Barber tribute, Efrem Zimbalist, Jr., noted that, "Sam was born with a song in his heart. We live by change, yet some things endure. Samuel Barber is acclaimed throughout the world today. We look forward to more to come from him. With lifted glass let us proclaim, Happy birthday, Sam!"

BG49. Fenton, John H. "Dillon Urges Aid to Needy Nations." New York Times, June 12, 1959, p. 3.
At the annual alumni meeting at Harvard University, Samuel Barber received an Honorary Doctor of Music degree. The citation read: "Samuel Barber, composer of orchestral and choral music. His music lends strength and grace to the culture of our time."

BG50. "Final Bar." Downbeat 48:13 (May 1981)
Written shortly after Barber's death. "Throughout his career, Barber's music was known for its careful craftsmanship and long-limbed, neo-Romantic melodies."

BG51. Flagler, Eleanor. "Toscanini Visit Started Him Off." News and Courier (Charleston, S.C.), May 28, 1978.
News article which summarizes Barber's accomplishments and lends some insight to his personality, his likes and dislikes.

BG52. Frankenstein, Alfred. "Review of Books: Samuel Barber by Nathan Broder. New York: G. Schirmer, 1954. 111 p." Musical Quarterly 41:105-106 (January 1955)
"The biographical story as Broder tells it is simple. Barber was the fair-haired boy at the Curtis Institute. He has gone to Europe and he has come back again, and he has won many prizes and awards. He is one of the few serious composers in America who has been able to make a living out of composition; he has never had to teach or edit or do any of the other chores to which most contemporary composers are driven by economic necessity...Broder's biography draws heavily upon Barber's letters, for Barber writes the best letters of any American composer. His literary style is absolutely brilliant."

BG53. Friedewald, Russell Edward. A Formal and Stylistic Analysis of the Published Music of Samuel Barber. Thesis (Ph.D.)--Iowa State University, 1957. 357 p.
"It has been found that traditional procedures are characteristic of nearly all of Barber's music up to about 1939. After this time these procedures begin to be mingled with or replaced by, a technical enrichment. Although foreshadowed here and there in earlier works, the first extensive evidence of the change of style and the musical growth that results from this fusion of the old and new elements, is found in the Concerto for Violin and Orchestra, Opus 14, written in 1939. The musical growth reveals itself in the technical aspects of melody, harmonic and contrapuntal texture and rhythm, as well as in alterations of structural design [p. 335-336]...Barber's rhythms are varied and free from mannerisms. In the song literature the vocal lines are carefully suited to the rhythm of the words, frequent meter changes being employed when necessary. In the instrumental music the rhythms range from the even stride of quarter notes in the Adagio for Strings to the more irregular and unusual organizations used in the third movement of Excursions [p. 338]...It would appear that the composer's choice of a text for his solo songs and choral pieces is often determined by the formal possibilities it offers. The larger compositions are firmly rooted in the principles of sonata construction [p. 339]...Most of Barber's large works are scored for the usual woodwind, brass, percussion, and string groups that make up the twentieth-century orchestra. Even in his earliest works, in which he tends to rely upon well-tested instrumental combinations and doublings, his orchestration is tasteful and varied and his sense of instrumental colors is in keeping with the fundamentally lyric character of his music. In the later music Barber shows his ability to

exploit the idiomatic capacities of the individual instruments; his use of the English horn, bass clarinet, and especially the piano is noteworthy." [p. 340]

BG54. Goodfriend, James. "Anglophilia." _Stereo Review_ 46:60 (March 1981)
"Entirely cognizant that music is made of notes, not feelings, they [composers] often forget that poetry is made of words...Our most splendid twentieth-century American exception to this has been Samuel Barber, whose many vocal works exhibit both the taste for the text and the willingness to serve it while still creating wonderful _and_ personal music (at least they did until the Menotti influence showed up)."

BG55. Goodwin, Noël. "Samuel Barber." _Times_ (London), July 7, 1980, p. 13.
"Samuel Barber was unfortunately prevented by ill health from coming to London on Friday, when he had planned to attend a concert at Christ Church, Spitalfields, celebrating his seventieth birthday earlier this year. He would have heard performances of musical distinction by members of the London Sinfonietta, who divided themselves into separate ensembles of wind and strings in the course of the six chamber works by him that made up the program." [Note: the works were _Summer Music_, _Serenade For Strings_, _Dover Beach_, _Hermit Songs_, _Knoxville: Summer of 1915_, and the _String Quartet_]

BG56. Gräter, Manfred. "Der Sänger von Capricorn." _Melos_ 21:247-250 (September 1954)
Biographical article with general discussion of works and a list of compositions through op. 27.

BG57. Greenfield, Edward. "Philadelphia Romanticist." _Guardian_ (Manchester), March 16, 1980. [Note: The same article appeared in the _Guardian_ for March 4, 1980, p. 9]
While riding in a Cadillac with Barber from the airport to the Van Cliburn Piano Competition in Fort Worth, Texas, Mr. Greenfield discusses the writing of the _Second Symphony_ and then expresses his own feelings about Barber's works.

BG58. Gruen, John. "And Where Has Samuel Barber Been...?" _New York Times_, October 3, 1971, sect. 2, p. 15, 21, 30.
"Samuel Barber is not given to rhapsodizing over his music. If anything, he tends to minimize its importance or place in American musical history. This is not a matter of modesty, but more a matter of personality which in Barber's case is one totally devoid of flamboyance. A soft-spoken, cultivated man of aristocratic bearing, Barber never suggests the impassioned, idiosyncratic composer of this or any other age. No brooding, temperamental or electrifying qualities hover about him. A calm exterior, an understated

wit, present the image of a man who knows what he's about
and who, during the course of most of his life, has composed a body of work that has earned him substantial rewards and considerable admiration." Samuel Barber says:
"'I guess for better or for worse, I am an American composer, and I've had little success in intellectual circles.
I'm not talked about in the New York Review of Books, and I
was never part of the Stravinsky 'inner circle.' In Aaron
Copland's book, Our American Music, my name appears in a
footnote.' [There is a bit of confusion here, for Copland
did not write a book entitled Our American Music. John
Tasker Howard did, however, and Barber is afforded numerous
pages in each of the several editions. Copland did write
Our New Music, and in that book Barber is not mentioned,
even in a footnote!] Samuel Barber smiles, sips some wine,
then begins to chuckle. 'You know,' he says, 'years ago
someone wrote a book about me, and when it was done, the
proofs were sent to my sister. She sent me a telegram,
saying 'Have this book stopped. You're dull but not that
dull!'"

BG59. Gruen, John. "When the New York Critics Damn
You..." New York Times, April 14, 1974, sect. 2, p. 1, 17.
Lengthy interview with Menotti in which he discusses
his own career and also discusses his long-standing friendship with Barber.

BG60. Hall, David. "Classics." HIFI/Stereo Review 6:61
(June 1961)
"The thirty-year span between the dewy-eyed lyricism
of the Serenade for Strings...to the bitterness of A Hand
of Bridge...has seen a transformation in Barber's creative
orientation from a spring-like melodic impulsiveness to a
maturely melancholy worldliness.

BG61. -----. The Record Book. New York: Oliver Dur-
rell, 1948. 1063 p.
"Samuel Barber has been frowned upon in certain 'advance guard' circles as an old-fashioned romantic, and it
is perfectly true that until the forties he avoided most of
the more radical musical procedures...During the forties
Barber has attempted to streamline his style via some
experiments with the Stravinskian neo-classic idiom; but
whether this excursion will contribute anything positive to
his development as a composer is yet to be determined."
[p. 117]

BG62. Hartshorn, William C. "Music in Our Public
Schools: American Composers--Samuel Barber." Musical Courier 159:41 (February 1959)
Biographical article with emphasis on the early years
and schooling.

BG63. Harvey, Trevor. "Opera." Gramophone 46:272 (August 1968)

"...Barber is a composer who evidently feels free to express himself as he wants. He is a romantic whose music yet has strength and--unlike many romantics--concision...If you enjoy Britten, who also writes music that he wants to write and doesn't bother about what some people think a contemporary composer ought to write, then you will enjoy Barber."

BG64. Heinsheimer, Hans. "Adagio For Sam." Opera News 45:30-31 (March 4, 1981)
"The day after Samuel Barber died, the New York Times carried the news on its front page, where international events compete for space. There were two columns on the passing of Barber with two imposing headlines over an article by chief music critic Donal Henahan. That a composer who had written no film scores, no TV shows, no Broadway musicals, nothing to bring him popularity with the general reader, who had rarely appeared in public and had led through his seventy years of his life a secluded existence that allowed no other activity but the painstaking composing of art songs, orchestral works, choral, chamber music and operas, should be given such editorial prominence speaks for the depth of his work and for the dominant position he carved out for himself in American arts and letters." So begins this moving tribute written immediately after the death of Samuel Barber.

BG65. -----. "The Composing Composer: Samuel Barber." ASCAP Today 2:4-7 (Autumn 1968)
Long, well-illustrated general article on Barber.

BG66. Henahan, Donal. "American Composer Samuel Barber, 70, Dies." Herald Examiner (Los Angeles), January 24, 1981. (Located in NewsBank, Review of the Arts [Microform], Performing Arts, 1980/81, 95:A4, fiche)
"Throughout his career, Samuel Barber was hounded by success. Probably no other American composer has ever enjoyed such early, such persistent and such long lasting acclaim."

BG67. -----. "Birthday Concert (Not Beethoven). New York Times, December 19, 1970, p. 18.
Article about a New York Philharmonic concert honoring the 60th birthday of both Barber and William Schuman. The orchestra performed Medea's Dance of Vengeance, op. 23a, with the orchestra conducted by Stanislaw Skrowaczewski.

BG68. -----. "I've Been Composing All My Life, Off and On." New York Times, January 28, 1979, sect. 2, p. 19, 24.
Interview with Barber prior to his Vanessa being telecast. The production is a tape of a performance at the Spoleto USA Festival in Charleston, S.C.

BG69. -----. "Samuel Barber, Composer, Dead; Twice Winner of Pulitzer Prize." New York Times, January 24,

1981, p. 1, 16.
     News article announcing Barber's death. "One reason
for the acceptance won by Mr. Barber's music--apart from
its undeniable craft and thorough professionalism--was its
deep-seated conservatism, which audiences could find congenial even at first hearing. Although he often dealt with
pungent dissonances and complex rhythms, like most of his
20th-century contemporaries, there was a lyrical quality
even to his strictly instrumental pieces that from the
first established him as a neo-Romantic. That earned his
music some disdain in avant-garde circles, but Mr. Barber
went his own way, nonetheless. Most of the century's
composing fashions passed him by. He did not adapt 12-tone
music or its serial refinements, he did not dabble n chance
or electronics. He wrote nothing that required consulting
I Ching."

     BG70. Horan, Robert. "American Composers, XIX: Samuel
Barber." Modern Music 20:161-169 (March-April 1943)
     "What has designated as conservative in Barber's work
is partially due to this emphasis on the larger aspects of
architecture. Instead of cohering small units, he cohers
large ones; instead of designing for textural pieces, ex-
plosions, surprises, unusual sound combinations in small
relationships, he regards these as a matter of texture, and
texture as the surface of his fabric. His orchestration is
simple and aristocratic. His movement uses little static
development and the inventions seem to move underneath
rather than on top of the music. It is essentially non-
eclectic and non-urban and often romantic in character...He
makes concessions to simplicity but none to pedestrianism,
although his work suffers occasionally from a false sense
of security...It is unfortunate that Barber's songs...are
not better known to serious musicians. They reveal an
intimate, sensuous quality not always to be found in the
larger works. Virgil Thomson referred on one occasion to
Barber as 'pure in heart.' The songs would seem to profess
less purity and more heart. It must be remembered that
Barber himself sings. Anyone who has heard him sing Monte-
verdi or Cavalli can realize that he has given close attention to a study of the 'declamazione lirica' of the Renaissance. Due to his intimacy with the actual possibilities
of the voice, he is not limited to the rules and regula-
tions of the current cult of prosody, the literal imitation
of spoken diction."

     BG71. -----. "And 3 Modern Young Men Lead a Modern Life
in This 'Swiss Chalet.'" American Home 36:36-38 (July
1946)
     Informal description of the home, built by William
Lescaze at Mount Kisco, New York, where the author, Barber,
and Gian-Carlo Menotti, lived and worked. Includes photo-
graphs of Barber and the home.

     BG72. Horowitz, Linda. "Literature Forum." Choral Jour-

nal 21:26-29 (December 1980)
"If Barber's appreciation for and understanding of the
singing voice has aided his ability to create lyrical
melodies, then similarly, it is Barber's familiarity with
great literature that has helped him to carefully choose
and set texts to music. Barber's interest in this field
has greatly developed his sensitivity to the natural rhythm
of poetry and as a result Barber frequently uses complex
musical rhythms to preserve the original intent of the
poet."

BG73. Hume, Paul. "Honored American Composer Samuel
Barber, 70, Dies In New York." Washington Post, January
25, 1981, sect. B, p. 6.
In this lengthy article, the author remarks, "Mr.
Barber was one of the few American composers of his generation who was as completely comfortable writing for large
and small instrumental combinations as for voices in various idioms...Because of the inescapable sense of beauty
that informs Mr. Barber's music and in the light of the
current powerful wave of interest in music that speaks
expressively to audiences on first hearing, it is likely
Mr. Barber's music, which exists in every idiom, will
continue to win enthusiastic admirers for years to come,
and that it will find permanent place among the finest
music of this century."

BG74. -----. "The Musical Legacy of Samuel Barber."
Washington Post, February 1, 1981, sect. K, p. 1.
"Barber was not a composer driven to write unceasingly
or on any set schedule. He did not turn out numbers of
quartets or concertos or symphonies...One of the remarkable
aspects of Barber's music is his equal mastery of both
vocal and instrumental writing, a dual gift not common to
his other American colleagues..."

BG75. "In 1980-81 Opera/Music Theatre Lost..." Central Opera Service Bulletin 23:21-22 (Summer 1981)
"This world-renowned musician was celebrated as one of
America's leading composers during his lifetime, and received among many honors, two Pulitzer Prizes, one in 1958
and one in 1963. His orchestral compositions became part
of the standard repertoire, and were played by all international orchestras."

BG76. Jackson, Richard. "Samuel Barber." Vol. 2 of
The New Grove Dictionary of Music and Musicians. Ed.
Stanley Sadie. London: Macmillan, 1980, pp. 133-136.
General article of moderate length with list of
compositions and selected bibliography.

BG77. "John Browning Plays" [album notes for Desto
DC7120 disc]
Barber "...has been a prolific composer working in all
forms and, whether in the briefest song or chamber piece to

a grand opera or symphony, he has always maintained his
'integrity of craftsmanship, expressive intensity and
stylistic development.' Even when he used neo-classicism
or post-Webern serialism he has never allowed mere technical devices to become ends in themselves. He has always
been able to integrate these modern techniques with his own
romantic aesthetic."

BG78. Jones, R. E. "Orchestra." New Records 29:4 (May
1961)
    "The Barber disc presents another chapter of the
Philadelphia story with a slightly happier ending. Barber's works always seem to convey meaning, and the present
collection supplies varied evidence of this. Chief interest lies in the chamber opera A Hand of Bridge, and the
brief A Stopwatch and an Ordnance Map, for male chorus,
brass, and percussion. The former is fascinating for its
interesting exposition of the subconscious thoughts of the
players of the hand. The latter work is a moving atmospheric setting of a poem by Stephen Spender, inspired by
the Spanish Civil War." [Vanguard VRS 1065]

BG79. Kelberine, Alexander. "Drawn From the Mail
Pouch: What is 'Contemporary Idiom.'" New York Times, November 20, 1938, sect. 9, p. 8.
    In reply to Ashley Pettis' letter, "Important American
Music" in the New York Times for November 13, 1938: "A
choice of American music by the maestro should at the very
outset serve as encouragement and be welcomed by all his
colleagues. But it does not necessarily follow that unless
a work by an American composer is featured by Arturo Toscanini the creative force of the said composer should suffer
a relapse...Whether Samuel Barber's music will meet this
test of time is as good a guess for Arturo Toscanini as for
Mr. Pettis..."

BG80. Kolodin, Irving. "Farewell to Capricorn." Saturday Review/World 1:44-45 (June 1, 1974)
    Beautiful and touching article written soon after the
sale of Capricorn, the home at Mt. Kisco, New York, which
Barber and Gian-Carlo Menotti shared for several decades.
Mr. Kolodin traces their friendship over the period from
1927, and concludes, "If Capricorn finally commemorates the
best of Barber, or Menotti's The Medium, The Telephone,
Amahl, and other things that prompted Virgil Thomson to
extol him as 'The Count of Mt. Kisco," it will remain a
unique symbol of a dual occupancy that endured over thirty
years. It was a span of time in which the campaign to
create an American audience for American composition was
being waged and won and what was done at Capricorn helped
mightily."

BG81. Kozinn, Allan. "Samuel Barber" [album notes for
Nonesuch Digital D-79032 disc]
    "Samuel Barber was concerned primarily with writing

146

music that expressed his own basically Romantic impulse, with concession to neither the experimentalist nor the populist trends of his day. Even so, the widespread impression that all of Barber's music aspires to the simplicity of his most famous work, the Adagio for Strings, is quite mistaken: For while Barber never attempted to be a trailblazer, he did endow each of his works with a distinct character--an exercise that took him through a broad range of harmonic ideas, some dense and complex, others comparatively simple."

BG82. Kozinn, Allan. "Samuel Barber: the Last Interview and the Legacy." High Fidelity 31:44-6+ (June 1981)
"In the 1940's, when the predominant American style emphasized the rediscovery of nationalistic musical roots, Barber's major works--the Violin Concerto (1939-40), the Second Essay (1942), the Capricorn Concerto (1944), and the Cello Concerto (1946)--reflected an impulse to continue developing in his own direction rather than turn to folk tunes for raw material. When the compositional world dove headlong into atonality, serialism, and a host of experimental, intellectual forms in the 1950's and 1960's, he proceeded along his own lyrical and often intensely subjective path, veering moderately towards a more chromatic, angular, and dramatic language."

BG83. Kresh, Paul. "Classical Discs and Tapes." Stereo Review 41:105 (September 1978)
"Barber, at his best matched by few contemporaries in writing for the voice, is represented in top form with a wistful treatment of A.E. Housman's With Rue My Heart Is Laden and an ode to the beauties of a summer night by James Agee [Knoxville: Summer of 1915]...Most absorbing of all of are Barber's moving miniatures inspired by lines from the works of James Joyce...and I Hear an Army, a poem of such surging power that it is remarkable how well the composer has matched its flashing imagery with his music." [Musical Heritage Society MHS 3770]

BG84. La Grange, Henri-Louis de. "D'Amérique: Un compositeur américain indépendent." Contrepoints no. 4:63-67+ (May-June 1946)
"Nous trouvons aussi chez lui une sincérité parfaite autant qu'attachante. Ses premières œuvres nous convainquent qu'avec les qualités dont nous avons parlé, une musique moderne peut être très belle sans frottements de sonorités constants. Il est vrai, d'ailleurs, que si l'on n'y trouve pas non plus d'archaïsme: la langue musicale y est bien celle du xxe siècle, et aucune des incontestables trouvailles de l'époque moderne n'est oubliée. Mais le compositeur reste fidèle à son inspiration et son évolution n'a eu pour lois que les lois internes qui ont régi le développement de sa personnalité musicale." ["We also find in him an incomparable as well as engaging sincerity. His first works convince us that with the qualities we have

already talked about modern music can be very beautiful
without the friction of constant sonorities. Furthermore,
it is true that if one doesn't find a systematic modernism
here, neither does one find any archaism: the musical
language is certainly that of the 20th century, and none of
the incontestable finds of the modern period is left out.
But the composer remains faithful to his inspiration and
his evolution has had for laws only the internal laws which
have governed the development of his musical personality."--L.M.]

BG85. Lieberson, Goddard. "Over the Air." Modern
Music 16:65-69 (November-December 1938)
     In discussing the broadcast by the NBC Symphony
Orchestra under Arturo Toscanini, Mr. Lieberson remarks:
"These pieces of Samuel Barber [Adagio For Strings and
Essay For Orchestra] fall neatly into line with the other
American music which Toscanini has chosen in the past. It
is contemporary only in the sense that the composer is
still alive. There is but a fraction of the whole which
even suggests an individual technic; and instead of melodic
creativeness and harmonic invention, Mr. Barber has substituted his wealth of experience in listening to the works of
other composers. Expert orchestration need not concern us
in this case and cannot be considered as sufficient recom-
mendation for performance, indeed, a clear orchestration
sometimes serves to further emphasize the thinness of content."

BG86. Lipman, Samuel. "American Music: The Years of
Hope." Commentary 71:56-61 (March 1981)
     In an article discussing many twentieth-century com-
posers, Mr. Lipman remarks about Samuel Barber: "As an
orchestral composer he possessed the grand line, as his
works demonstrate from the 1936 First Symphony on. His
melodies and harmonies linger in the ear; once heard, the
famous Adagio For Strings, also written in 1936, can never
be forgotten. His vocal music, too, has a special prominence...Antony and Cleopatra (1966), written for the opening of the new Metropolitan Opera House at Lincoln Center,
proved an initial disappointment. Still, listening to a
tape of the original performance strongly suggests that
here, too, Barber's music will last, and that his vocal
music may well represent his finest achievement."

BG87. Lybeer, E. J. "Jo Alfidi: Samuel Barber" [album
notes for Queen Elizabeth International Competition 1980-
081 disc]
     "Samuel Barber rose to fame because he found the rare
and desirable balance between music made for an especially
perceptive elitist audience and the amateur concert-goer.
He may not be an indispensable composer but some of his
works rank among the outstanding achievements of the American mainstream composers...No concepts of chance; no super-
serialism, no talismanic scores resembling city-planners

visions, not a music as thought or philosophy, but a music of sounds and flesh. Barber was never the newest of the new, but the oldest of the old: a highly sensuous musical experience in technicolor, rooted in the best tradition of late European romantic expressivity."

BG88. McCandless, William Edgar. Cantus Firmus Techniques in Selected Instrumental Compositions, 1910-1960. Thesis (Ph.D.)--Indiana University, 1974. 309 p.
"Probably as a result of his interest in singing, Barber's style is essentially lyric, and as a result of his study with Scalero, his texture is basically contrapuntal. In most of his works he maintains a tonal center, and he adheres closely to traditional principles of musical form. His rhythms are varied and flexible with frequent changes of meter in some pieces. His melodies are sometimes characterized by wide leaps and, in his mature style, often colored with chromaticism." [p. 68-69]

BG89. Mead, Rita H. "Samuel Barber Summer Music" [album notes for Musical Heritage Society MHS 4782 disc]
"Barber's music, from his early years as a student at the Curtis Institute of Music to the present, has remained in the mainstream of musical tradition. While at times incorporating contemporary elements--dissonance, atonality, 12-tone writing--Barber's harmonic language, formal structures, and orchestral textures marked him as a past romantic. A further anachronism in Barber's music is its dramatic quality. Eschewing the cool neoclassicism of the early part of the century, as well as the depersonalized avant-guardism of later years, Barber produced expressive music, rich in emotional content. His lyricism is unsurpassed; examples can be found in works from both early and late periods."

BG90. Menen, Aubrey. "Opinion: An American Renaissance: the Impossible Dream?" Vogue 171:315-316+ (November 1981)
Lengthy article in which the author attempts to show that there is no American Renaissance. Unfortunately, the article sheds little light on Barber, his music, or an "American Renaissance."

BG91. Menotti, Gian-Carlo. "Drawn From the Mail Pouch: Which is 'Modern Music.'" New York Times, November 20, 1938, sect. 10, p. 8.
In a reply written November 16, 1938 to Ashley Pettis' letter, "Important American Music" in the New York Times for November 13, 1938, Menotti notes: "I am afraid Mr. Pettis is very passé and still accepts as the modern idiom the Parisian style of twenty years ago. If Mr. Barber dares to defy the servile imitation of that style (which has been called American music) and experiments successfully with melodic line and new form, is he not to be praised for his courage?...isn't it high time that a young David appeared

and struck on the forehead that inflated monster which still parades under the anachronistic name of modern music?"

BG92. "Milestones." Time 117:81 (February 2, 1981)
Brief obituary noting that "His grand effort, 'Antony and Cleopatra,' was a rare failure for a composer who loved and understood the human voice and stood apart from avant-garde trends."

BG93. Mitchell, Donald. "London Music." Musical Times 96:433-434 (August 1955)
"If Barber has a style at all, it belongs to the category of contemporary academicism, a kind of tasteful middle-brow modernity that may have a topical function but will not prove of much interest to the future."

BG94. Moore, Dale. "Favorite American Concert Songs by Samuel Barber and Others" [album notes for Cambridge CRS 2715 disc]
"It is unnecessary to write of Samuel Barber's stature as a composer. It does not hurt to state, however, that he is a member of a sadly small group of 20th-century composers of whatever nationality who know the human voice and write for it sensitively, idiomatically and gratefully."

BG95. "Music Fame at 28: Samuel Barber's Compositions Played by Symphonies." Newsweek 11:24 (April 11, 1938)
"Young composers often complain they can't persuade orchestras to perform their works. Samuel Barber, 28-year-old nephew of the contralto Louise Homer, last week was not bothered by any such troubles. Within four days the nation's oldest [New York Philharmonic-Symphony] and youngest [NBC Symphony Orchestra] symphonies played Barber compositions."

BG96. "Names, Dates and Places." Opera News 30:5 (February 19, 1966)
Short paragraph mentioning the surprise appearance of Samuel Barber at the Opera Guild Lecture-Tea on January 17, 1966 at the Colony Club. He spoke "humorously on the problems of writing an opera and finding a good libretto."

BG97. "Names, Dates and Places." Opera News 45:4 (March 14, 1981)
Brief news item stating that "in addition to approximately 35 percent of his $1 million estate, the late Samuel Barber left fellow composer Gian Carlo Menotti his books, tapes, memorabilia and the lifetime use of his home in Santa Cristina, Italy."

BG98. "Nunc Dimittis." Diapason 72:3 (April 1981)
A summary of the life and works of Samuel Barber.

BG99. "Obituary." Strad 91:895 (April 1981)

"His music held a firm place in the lyrical and Romantic tradition and remained unaffected by contemporary developments and the avant garde. Although conservative, his compositions display a highly individual style based on Barber's melodic gifts combined with a most expressive and evocative lyrical idiom."

BG100. "Obituary: Mr. Samuel Barber." The Times (London) January 26, 1981, p. 14.
    In a lengthy obituary, The Times discusses the career and compositions of Samuel Barber. Of him and his compositional skill, The Times remarks, "His temperament tended towards the Romantic and the lyrical rather than the Neo-classical and the many experimental trends in modern composition largely passed him by. His early works, indeed, tended to sound conservative but he was always an expressive composer who developed a highly individual style; and his reputation held steady, even tended to increase as the years went by."

BG101. "Obituaries." Gramophone 58:1148 (March 1981)
    "His works are more European in character than specialy American, essentially elegant and conservatively melodic."

BG102. "Operatic Newcomer: Samuel Barber." New York Times, January 16, 1958, p. 33.
    News article, mainly biographical, presented alongside the review of his first opera, Vanessa..."His composition teacher was Rosario Scalero, a strict master who was also a conscious repository of the Great Tradition...Although Mr. Barber's music has come a long way from the Scalero influence, and is unmistakably contemporary in idiom, its formal structure and its tendency toward lyricism shows the influence of his early training...Mr. Barber as a young man, the photographs show, was almost unbelievably handsome, and he remains one of the most photogenic of today's composers. He is of medium stature, with deep brown eyes and brown hair. He talks rapidly in a low voice. He is fond of travel and is facile in all the operatic languages--French, German and Italian."

BG103. Parmenter, Ross. "Music: Orchestra of America Opens 2d Season." New York Times, November 17, 1960, p. 45.
    News article announcing the honoring of Samuel Barber along with Wallingford Riegger and Aaron Copland on their respective birthdays. In Mr. Barber's honor, the orchestra played on November 16, 1960, at Carnegie Hall, his Second Essay for Orchestra, op. 17.

BG104. -----. "Music World: Barber Sitting In." New York Times, March 25, 1962, sect. 2, p. 13.
    The Third Biennial Congress of Soviet Composers had Samuel Barber as a guest observer. Mr. Barber interrupted

his work on the piano concerto, to be played at the opening
of Lincoln Center, to attend.

BG105. Parmenter, Ross. "The World of Music: Two New
Operas on Way." New York Times, December 29, 1946, sect.
2, p. 7.
     News article indicating that Samuel Barber and Marc
Blitzstein are the recipients of commissions from the Koussevitzky Foundation to each write an opera. Mr. Barber had
accepted the commission in 1942, but military service delayed implementation.

BG106. Penchansky, Alan. "Classical." Billboard 91:82
(October 27, 1979)
     Report of a Billboard survey of major American or-
chestras indicating that Samuel Barber, Aaron Copland, and
Sir William Walton are most frequently performed of more
than fifty living composers. The Chicago Symphony and the
New York Philharmonic ranked first and second in the number
of works performed; the Los Angeles Philharmonic ranked
last. The single work by a living composer most performed
during the 1979-80 season was Barber's Third Essay.

BG107. Pettis, Ashley. "From the Mail Pouch: Important
American Music." New York Times, November 13, 1938, sect.
9, p. 8.
     Remarks contained in a letter to the New York Times by
pianist, teacher, lecturer, and writer Ashley Pettis:
"There are important American composers and important American compositions of every type of thought and tendency.
But from 'at least one listener's point of view' neither
Mr. Barber nor his works may be termed so. One listened
in vain for evidences of youthful vigor, freshness, or
fire, for use of a contemporary idiom (which was characteristic of every composer whose works have withstood the
vicissitudes of time). Mr. Barber's was 'authentic,' dull,
'serious' music--utterly anachronistic as the utterance of
a young man of 28, A. D. 1938! Such a choice by the great
musical Messiah [Arturo Toscanini] in our midst can only
have a retarding influence on the advance of our creative
musicians."

BG108. Pisciotta, Louis Vincent. Texture in the Choral
Works of Selected Contemporary American Composers. Thesis
(Ph.D.)--Indiana University, Bloomington, 1967. 416 p.
     "The choral works of Samuel Barber abound in contra-
puntal and homophonic textures. The early works tend toward a predominance or even exclusive use of one or the
other kind of texture [p. 36]...The later works, however,
utilize both textual categories in a way that lets them
participate more actively in the formal design. Within
this group the composer favors a homophonic texture for
strong opening statements followed by contrapuntal material
developmental or otherwise [p. 36]...In his accompanied
works the composer interlaces the choral writing with in-

strumental color and sonority. He also obtains rich sonorities from the male voices alone (<u>Stopwatch</u>) through interlocking octaves and a solo embellishment of the ensemble in
a high register. As a rule solo voices are used sparingly
and mostly in relation to a choral background." [p. 37]

BG109. Rands, Bernard. "Samuel Barber--A Belief in
Tradition." <u>Musical Opinion</u> 84:353 (March 1961)
    Critical article on Barber's music. "Those concerned
with future developments in composition techniques may
afford no more than a mere glance at Samuel Barber's music,
but those who examine more closely, will be well rewarded."

BG110. Rawlinson, Harold. "Famous Works for String Orchestra. No. 20: Adagio for Strings." <u>Strad</u> 60:372+
(April 1950)
    Barber's works have "...not divided his critics into
opposed camps because it is not outrageously modern. It is
forceful, and holds our interest, but as a whole lacks
vivid personality. It reflects modern Europe more than it
does modern America."

BG111. Raynor, Henry. "Samuel Barber by Nathan Broder.
Pp. 111 (Schirmer: Chappell) 1954." <u>Music Review</u> 17:164
(May 1956)
    "...his enthusiasm is more convincing than his techni-
cal studies of music and the book demonstrates that a study
of an important and conscientious artist does well to
eschew biography in favor of a detailed study of his work.
The book is, I feel, of limited usefulness."

BG112. "Reviews of New Music." <u>Musical Opinion</u> 79:157
(December 1955)
    Review of the G. Schirmer/Chappell edition of the
collected songs written and published up to 1955.
"...where his superb artistry and glowing imagination meet
responsive interpreters, audiences will be brought to
realise that his songs are among the finest of our generation."

BG113. Rich, Alan. "Khrushchev Talks of Modern Music."
<u>New York Times</u>, April 14, 1962, p. 14.
    Mr. Barber, as the first American to attend the Bien-
nial Congress of Soviet Composers (in Moscow March 26
through March 31, 1962) at which a thousand composers were
present, had an opportunity to meet and talk with Premier
Khrushchev. Mr. Barber also spoke to the congress and
"...warned that there could never be a five-year plan for
talent, and that too much interference with a composer
was as unwise as too much encouragement." He also reports
that "I even made a plea for experimentation. They seemed
to like what I said, although much of it was at variance
with policies and thoughts outlined at the conference." He
reported that Mr. Khrushchev remarked that "Any statesman
who doesn't like music is an abnormal person."

BG114. Sabin, Robert. "Nathan Broder Writes Study of Samuel Barber." Musical America 76:46 (January 1, 1956)
"Nathan Broder, in this study of the man and his music, has avoided the tone of tedious panegyric which is the curse of most biographies of living people and given us a sympathetic but realistic portrait."

BG115. Salzman, Eric. "Samuel Barber." HIFI/Stereo Review 17:77-89 (October 1966)
The sixth article in a continuing series on "The Great American Composers." A general article including much biographical information and many illustrations. A discography of recorded works is included. "...he is a cosmopolitan and, with the exception of a single work, there is almost no perceptible trace of an American musical accent in it--unlike his conservative-tonal colleagues and contemporaries who exhibit distinctly American traits. His music has been generally classified as avowedly Romantic, quiet, elegant, and wholeheartedly traditionalist...While he has, on occasion, written quickly, he is basically a slow-and-steady. His friends say that he can be moody and bad-tempered when a composition is giving him trouble, light-hearted and exhilarated when in the vein. Ideas may come to him anywhere--since his childhood he has been fond of long walks in the country...but generally he works things out at the piano. He likes to orchestrate standing up at a high table."

BG116. Salzman, Eric and James Goodfriend. "Samuel Barber: a Selective Discography." HIFI/Stereo Review 17:88 (October 1966)
A two-page discography appended to "Samuel Barber," by Eric Salzman, the sixth article in a continuing series entitled "The Great American Composers."

BG117. "Samuel Barber." Variety 301:94 (January 28, 1981).
Brief obituary in which it is remarked that "Almost every piece of music by Barber was introduced by an internationally known orchestra or artist."

BG118. "Samuel Barber Back From Rome Sojourn." New York Times, December 15, 1949, p. 46.
News article announcing the return to the United States of Samuel Barber from Rome. While there he served as musical advisor to the American Academy in Rome.

BG119. "Samuel Barber Cited." New York Times, May 21, 1958, p.40.
News article noting that Samuel Barber has been awarded the Henry Hadley Medal for American Composers and Conductors.

BG120. "Samuel Barber Cited." New York Times, March 10, 1950, p. 37.

News article concerning an all-Barber concert in Philadelphia concert honoring the composer on his fiftieth birthday.

BG121. "Samuel Barber gestorben." Opern Welt 22:6 (March 1981)
Very brief obituary with portrait.

BG122. "Samuel Barber Wins Another Prize." New York Times, May 10, 1935, p. 24.
News report that Samuel Barber had received the Prix de Rome. The compositions he submitted were Sonata for Cello and Piano, op. 6 and Music for a Scene From Shelley, op. 7. The jury making the award was composed of Deems Taylor, Carl Engel, Leo Sowerby and Walter Damrosch.

BG123. Sargeant, Winthrop. "Musical Events." New Yorker 36:106 (January 14, 1961)
"Mr. Barber, I think, may someday be regarded as the outstanding composer of his period. He has a style that is both individual and communicative. He has a sure sense of his own limitations and of what sort of music is appropriate to his talents. His departures from tradition are made not through ignorance but by virtue of a firm knowledge of just what tradition is and of just how far it can by meaningfully stretched to accommodate personal impulses and whims. He is no academician, and yet his music is generally cast in a frame that is accessible to the average educated listener. He is not afraid of 'charm,' a word that is mistakenly regarded as a devilish one by many of his contemporaries."

BG124. -----. "Musical Events." New Yorker 39:127-8 (November 16, 1963)
"In my opinion, it cannot be too often reiterated that Samuel Barber stands head and shoulders above all the other American composers whose works one is likely to encounter on current symphonic programs. This is not a snap judgement but one founded on twenty-five years of familiarity with his music. He is not a follower of any technical system of composition. He has avoided both the fashionable tricks of the disciples of Nadia Boulanger and the meaningless mathematical intricacies of the serialists. He does not indulge in any of those unsuccessful experiments that congest the present musical scene like automotive hulks in a junk yard. He knows exactly where he is going, and has personal style that gets him there...The important thing is that it [his music] moves, that it conveys emotions and states of mind, that it entails an ingredient of suspense, and that the listener is drawn into its insistent dramatic flow."

BG125. -----. "Musical Events." New Yorker 39:153-4 (April 13, 1963)
"His writing for orchestra is never either cheap or

arcane. Although it has its own recognizable style, it
never pursues style as an end in itself...In an age when
revolution is all the rage, and nearly every tyro is busy
thumbing his nose at the accepted masterpieces of the past,
Mr. Barber has distinguished himself by not being a revolu-
tionary."

BG126. Sargent, David. "Music: Celebration! An American Tradition is Reborn." Vogue 170:53-54 (October 1980)
    A general article which points to a revival of in-
terest in composers such as Barber, Schuman and Copland.

BG127. Schillaci, Daniel. "For the Record. New West
6:118 (April 1981)
    "A few days after Barber's death in January, 1981, an
obituary appeared in the Los Angeles Times, a scant few
inches in length at the bottom of the page, ludicrously
upstaged by a full-scale reportage of the death of Maria
Callas's former husband, Giovanni Meneghini. Is this, one
had to ask, all the recognition a fine American musician
had earned? Barber was not a great composer. He probably
never realized his full potential: while romanticism remains a viable style, it still requires the composer who
constantly seeks out new ways of saying things. Yet Barber's work represents a historically important generation
of American music, and much of it is far too attractive,
one suspects, to become insignificant. Certainly no one
who is touched by it need worry about the precious few who
will no doubt always scoff."

BG128. Schonberg, Harold. "Book Reviews." Musical
Courier 150:43 (November 1, 1954)
    "Mr. Broder's enthusiastic comments on the music are
buttressed by a solid quality of musicianship. Whether or
not you may agree with them, they are pertinent and
thoughtful."

BG129. Shawe-Taylor, Desmond. "Music." Times (London)
January 25, 1981 p. 40.
    News article reporting the death of Samuel Barber. A
brief summary of his life and works is given.

BG130. Shenk, Mary Nic. "Sarasota." Opera News 45:40
(April 11, 1981)
    "Quintet, five Samuel Barber works staged together,
became an unexpected memorial to its composer, who died
January 29. Despite creative combination of voice, dance,
mime and instrumental music to interpret The Hermit Songs,
Dover Beach, Autumn Dialogues [unable to identify], A Hand
of Bridge and Knoxville: Summer of 1915, the production was
not fulfilling as an operatic concept."

BG131. Simmons, Walter. "Classical Recordings." Fanfare 2:22, 24 (March/April 1979)
    "Despite frequent comments praising its [his music's]

'superb craftsmanship,' Barber's sense of form and development are weak, just barely adequate to convey the essence
of his distinguished thematic ideas and his effects of mood
and emotion. This shortcoming is not devastating to his
stature as a composer; a melodic gift as distinctive as
Barbers is a fare rarer commodity than the ability to build
a tight musical structure, contrary perhaps to common belief."

BG132. Simmons, Walter. "Classical Recordings." Fanfare 7:134-35 (September/October 1983)
        "Barber's spontaneous lyricism has often been charac-
terized as Italianate, but it is far more refined and
elegant than Italian melody. Probably the composer to whom
he seems closest is Elgar, but the Englishman's imperial
grandeur was foreign to Barber's more modest nature. His
orientation was thoroughly European, however, until the
1940's, when he seemed somehow pressured to broaded his
style--perhaps artificially."

BG133. "Sketches of the Pulitzer Prize Winners for 1958
in Letters, Music and Journalism." New York Times, May 6,
1958, p. 38
        An appraisal of Mr. Barber in which his career "has
almost reversed the familiar pattern of the young revo-
lutionary who grows more conservative with the years. Mr.
Barber began as a conservative, whose tuneful music made
decidedly easy listening. Only gradually did he add some
of the tense harmonics and other complications associated
with much contemporary music. In externals, at least, he
grew more radical as he approached middle age. Through his
career he has kept two things: his strong melodic gift and
an aptitude for successful 'firsts.'"

BG134. Slonimsky, Nicolas. "Four Melodic Masterpieces
of Samuel Barber" [album notes for CBS 32 11 0006; 32 11
0005 disc]
        "In the artificial, though convenient, categories of
music criticism, Samuel Barber is classified as an American
Romanticist...He is a Romanticist in his attitude toward
the function of music. His melodies are broadly songful;
his harmonies are opulent; his orchestration is resplendent
with color. His technical idiom is however, decidedly modern. He possesses the intellectual curiosity of a progressive artist, and no effective method of composition is
alien to his absorptive mind. Thus he makes use of twelve-
tone configurations in several works, but applies these
devices in his own way, without doctrinaire subservience."

BG135. Soria, Dorle J. "Artist Life." High Fidelity/Mu-
sical America 24:MA 5-6 (September 1974)
        "On the night of last November 7, a fire swept the
Metropolitan Opera warehouse on Third Avenue and 186th
Street. The loss was estimated at three million dollars.
Costumes for forty-one productions were destroyed. Among

them were <u>Vanessa</u> and <u>Antony and Cleopatra</u>." With this beginning we go on to an interview with Samuel Barber in which he discusses his feelings about the losses and then talks about the causes of the failure of <u>Antony and Cleopatra</u> and the fact that he and Gian Carlo Menotti are working on a revised version to be presented later.

BG136. Soria, Dorle J. "Young Concert Artists: Twenty and Triumphant." <u>High Fidelity/Musical America</u> 31:MA 4-5+ (November 1981)
      Charles Turner, friend and student of Samuel Barber, discusses Barber's love of good food and relates an incident concerning the composer and Maria Callas. A very general, anecdotal article.

BG137. "Spoleto Salute." <u>Times</u> (London) June 18, 1975, p. 11
      Short news article announcing that "a highlight of the Spoleto Festival of Two Worlds this summer [1975] will be a 'Salute to Samuel Barber.'" The Festival will, on June 28 and 29, honor Barber with a dance presentation, and an orchestral and operatic recital.

BG138. Talley, V. Howard. "Samuel Barber by Nathan Broder." <u>Journal of Research in Music Education</u> 3:65-6 (Spring 1955)
      "Though Barber is undisputedly American, his art is deeply rooted in that of Europe. That is why, perhaps, such works as the first Essay for Orchestra and the Adagio for Strings, both performed for the first time with Toscanini conducting, caught on and have had many performances since. The outstanding quality of Barber's music is its musicality, its deep seriousness, even in his lighter works."

BG139. Tircuit, Heuwell. "Stunning Barber Masterpiece." <u>San Francisco Chronicle</u>, January 21, 1979, World Section, p. 53.
      "What is remarkable about this disc [UNI-72016] is the idiomatic propriety of the whole. Ronald Thomas is the violin soloist in the Concerto and Molly McGurk the soprano in 'Knoxville.' They perform with flawless style, sound more like American musicians than most Americans do. Everything about this disc is first rate, and that goes for sound and pressing too."

BG140. Turner, Charles. "The Music of Samuel Barber." <u>Metropolitan Opera Program</u> (January 15, 1958)
      "From the beginning it is difficult to categorize him, although dictionaries call him neo-romantic. Like Picasso, he has tried many different things, always with distinction. Unlike Picasso, he studies for months or years before each new work, travels in search of a sympathetic atmosphere that will stimulate the new composition, polishes with infinite pains...He has never felt the ne-

cessity of being shocking, experimental or rebellious a-
gainst the strict classic training he had as a boy from his
composition teacher, Scalero, at the Curtis Institute of
Music in Philadelphia. He has added to his early schooling
enormously but never rejected it, and usually he has preferred to work within the framework of traditional forms
and techniques, adapting them to his personal utterance,
rather than invent new ones. In this, he somewhat resembles Bach and Mozart."

BG141. Turner, Charles. "The Music of Samuel Barber."
Opera News 22:7+ (January 27, 1958)
A discussion of the music of Samuel Barber in some
detail. While not actually related to the writing of
Vanessa, the author, in discussing Barber's style in
various works, prepares the listener for what may be expected in Vanessa.

BG142. Turner, Robert. "Five American Operas." Canadian Music Journal 4:44+ (Winter 1960)
"Since the war Barber has shown in increasing interest
in more dissonant, chromatic sonorities, contrapuntal
devices like the fugue and canon, and even a little free
twelve-tone writing. His melodic line makes frequent use
of the interval of a fourth (curiously Russian), and often
more chromatically, within a restricted range. His rhythmic and metrical patterns, too, are more varied. These new
influences would appear to come mainly from Bach and Bartok, and possibly Berg. But it should be noted that these
technical and formal additions have not been wholly integrated into the over-all texture. Mostly, they are reserved
for moments of irony or ugliness, or for neutral and descriptive backgrounds. When Barber has more personal and
profound things to say he reverts to his earlier diatonic
and romantic idiom."

BG143. "U. S. Composer in Soviet." New York Times,
March 30, 1962, p. 27
Barber addressed the Third Biennial Soviet Congress of
Composers in Moscow, March 26-31, 1962. He remarked that
Soviet and American composers have many of the same problems. "For instance, we also now search for a contemporary
style. In the same way as mutual enrichment of national
cultures is necessary in the Soviet Union, it is also
necessary to expand the sphere of mutual influence between
the music of the U.S.S.R. and the United States. Our youth
is eager to establish contacts with Soviet musicians and I
am sure that such contacts are fruitful."

BG144. "U. S. Musicians Honored." New York Times, June
26, 1935, p. 19
A short news article announced that Viscountess Astor
gave a reception which honored three American composers.
"The program was featured principally by the music of
Samuel Barber."

Bibliography

BG145. Waters, Edward N. "Harvest of the Year: Selected Acquisitions of the Music Division: Holographs of
Living Composers." Quarterly Journal of the Library of
Congress 24:54-55 (January 1967)
    Description of six manuscripts from Barber received by
the Library in 1966: (1) Adventure, for flute, clarinet,
horn, harp, and a number of exotic "instruments from the
Museum of Natural History" (completed November 25, 1954);
(2) reproduction of a copyist's manuscript of Hermit Songs,
op. 29, including many holograph corrections and performance indications (world premiere was at the Library of
Congress, October 30, 1953, with Barber accompanying Leontyne Price); (3) Monks and Raisins, for voice and orchestra
[originally op. 18, no. 2, for voice and piano], the ex-
panded present version becoming the second of Barber's Four
Songs for Voice and Orchestra; (4) Sonata, op. 26, including a single leaf of holograph corrections and two
reproductions of a copyist's manuscript showing further
corrections; (5) Souvenirs, op. 28, in two holographs; one
for piano duet (undated but performed July, 1952 by Robert
Fizdale and Arthur Gold on NBC-TV) and one for full orchestra (published by G. Schirmer in 1954, first performance by
the Chicago Symphony Orchestra, Fritz Reiner, conductor,
November 12, 1953), the second conceived as a ballet; (6) A
Stopwatch and an Ordnance Map in two versions: four-part
male chorus and three tympani (published in 1942 by G.
Schirmer with first performance in New York City on December 16, 1945 by the Collegiate Chorale, Robert Shaw, conducting), having neither date nor title, and a version for
four horns, three trombones, & tuba (published 1954 by G.
Schirmer).

BG146. -----. "Music." Quarterly Journal of Current
Acquisitions [of the Library of Congress] 14:10 (November
1956)
    An announcement that "Samuel Barber (b.1910), in the
forefront of American composers, presented five of his
holographs to the library: the score of Capricorn Concerto
[op. 21] and four songs with accompaniment (A Nun Takes the
Veil [op. 13, no. 1], The Secrets of the Old [op. 13, no.
2], Sure on This Shining Night [op. 13, no. 3], With Rue
My Heart Is Laden [op. 2, no. 2]. These are highly significant additions to the collection of manuscripts of
American composers."

BG147. -----. "Music." Quarterly Journal of Current
Acquisitions [of the Library of Congress] 16:9 (November
1958)
    "Pursuing a practice initiated some years ago, Samuel
Barber...gave the Library four of his autographs: the penciled orchestra score of the ballet suite, Medea (1946)
[op. 23], his song Nuvoletta [op. 25], pen-and-ink versions
of another song, Nocturne [op. 13, no. 4], and pen-and-ink
versions of still a third song, The Queen's Face on the
Summery Coin [op. 18, no. 1]."

BG148. Waters, Edward N. "Music." Quarterly Journal of Current Acquisitions [of the Library of Congress] 17:19 (November 1959)
"As gifts from Samuel Barber...came two autograph songs, Rain Has Fallen [op. 10, no. 1] (two versions) and Sleep Now [op. 10, no. 2], both composed to words by James Joyce. Written in Rome in November, 1955, they are welcome additions to a growing collection of this composer's holographs."

BG149. Wathen, Lawrence Samuel. Dissonance Treatment in the Instrumental Music of Samuel Barber. Thesis (Ph.D.)--Northwestern University, 1960. 141 p.
"This study...is an attempt to determine the circumstances under which dissonance occurs in his music. The selected music includes all of Barber's published instrumental music from Opus 1 through Opus 31 (dated 1957). The problem of this survey is to define the composer's employment of dissonance as a characteristic of his style or technique, and to present this treatment in a comprehensive way in order that inferences and conclusions can be plausibly drawn." [p. 1]

BG150. Webster, Daniel. "Curtis Institute Concerts Salute Barber's 70th Birthday." Philadelphia Inquirer, March 10, 1980.
"Barber has done what composers must: written prolifically and in various forms, not to establish an orthodoxy or a pattern, but to clarify his own artistic voice. His music avoided the currents of fashion and remained his own from the earliest examples to the songs from 1974. The music did not open the door on the 21st century any more than it closed the door on all that had happened before he wrote his Opus 1. It expressed the vision of a composer wholly in command of his craft, a man with special gifts for melody and song for whom all of his music echoes with the eloquence of the human voice."

BG151. -----. "Debuts & Reappearances." High Fidelity 30:MA36 (July 1980)
Concerns the Curtis Institute of Music's tribute to Barber on his 70th birthday. "This birthday observance suggested that Barber's breadth is based on familiarity with all forms. None of these pointed to a future transfiguration, but to a present fulfillment. Each is a model of urbane expression of a personal eclecticism. The choices stressed that Barber created a repertoire with a style and outlook he found early in his life."

BG152. Yarustovsky, Boris. "Journey to America." Journal of Research in Music Education 10:121-28 (Fall 1962)
In November, 1959 musicologist Yarustovsky and a group of Soviet composers visited the United States, Mr. Yarustovsky in commenting on Barber said "Samuel Barber, whose

Adagio for Strings and Dance of Medea have already received recognition in the U.S.S.R., possesses a brilliant gift. We heard the last scene of his opera Vanessa, a work which bears witness to his great talent, especially manifest in the vocal ensembles. Unfortunately, we were not able to hear the work in the theatre (it had been presented at the Metropolitan), because after a few performances it was removed from the repertory, not having survived the 'competition' with the classical Italian masterpieces."

REFERENCES RELATING TO INDIVIDUAL WORKS

OPERAS

B1. ANTONY AND CLEOPATRA, OP. 40.

   B1a. Alexander, Shana. "Culture's Big Super-Event." Life 61:30B (September 30, 1966)
   A 'feminine eye' point of view of the opening night. "Poor Miss Price, imprisoned in her ponderous hairdo, looked alarmingly like an old photograph of Sitting Bull...I agree that the Met should have commissioned an American opera for the great occasion, even if its reasons were political, not artistic. But maybe that was the basic mistake. Another mistake was Barber's choice of a dramatic subject so at odds with his own musical style. In any case Barber's music was monotonous. Miss Price's costumes were ridiculous..." See: W1a

   B1b. Anderson, William. "Editorially Speaking." HIFI/Stereo Review 17:4 (November, 1966)
   Sampling of critical response to the Met premiere. "What we optimistically and perhaps unwisely hoped for was a miracle, a succes fou; what we got fell somewhere between estime and fiasco." See: W1a

   B1c. "Antony and Cleopatra." Opera News 31:36-7 (September 17, 1966)
   A two page summary of Antony and Cleopatra. See: W1

   B1d. Ardoin, John. "Menotti at Work." Dallas (Texas) Morning News, May 31, 1983 (Located in NewsBank, Review of the Arts [Microform], Performing Arts, 1983 98:C8, fiche)
   The premiere of Antony and Cleopatra was a defeat from which Barber never recovered. With Menotti's help, he "pared down the libretto...and began adjusting his score to a more intimate plane...This entire production will now move en masse to the Italian Spoleto Festival, but what the ultimate fate of Antony may be is a matter of conjecture. One thing is abundantly clear, however: the opera now has a

fighting chance and beyond question a new lease on life."
See: W1

B1e. Barnes, Clive. "Ballet's Modest but Hectic Contribution." New York Times, September 17, 1966. p. 16.
"Alvin Ailey, making his debut as a Metropolitan choreographer in Antony and Cleopatra, has been given comparatively little opportunity by Samuel Barber and his librettist to display his wares." See: W1a

B1f. Bernheimer, Martin. "New Met Splendid, But New
Opera Isn't." Los Angeles Times, September 17, 1966, pt.
3, p. 1.
"The opera is well constructed, eminently palatable,
theatrically valid, and a bore...It is unlikely that, even
under the best conditions, Barber's score (or for that
matter, Franco Zeffirelli's Shakespeare adaptation) could
seem really stimulating. But the Met did not give it a
chance. Instead, it allowed Zeffirelli to overpower the
work visually to the point of distraction...The characters,
the drama, and, yes, the music too are thus obscured by the
spectacle...Zeffirelli permitted Leontyne Price as Cleopatra to be more vulgar than seductive, more awkward than
dignified. And in writing so much of the part for the low
voice, Barber exposed the soprano's greatest weakness.
There were, however, enough of her glorious arching phrases
at the top to justify the apparent happiness of the prima
donna's fans." See: W1a

B1g. Breuer, Robert. "Barbers Monsteroper in Zeffirel-
lis Leichtmetallverpackung." Melos 33:333-335 (October
1966)
Review of the New York Metropolitan Opera production.
"...Schliesslich: war man doch eher zu einem historischen
Ereignis denn aus künstlerischer Neugier gekommen--und soll
man Barber ernsthaft vorwerfen, den Schaulustigen nicht die
geringsten Hörrätsel vorgesetzt zu haben?" ["To sum up:
didn't we come to an historical event rather than to a
musical creation? Should one really criticize Barber because he knew his audience had come for a show and therefore he presented not the slightest musical challenge?"--
R.F.] See: W1a

B1h. -----. "New Yorks neue Opernhaus." Österreichische
Musikzeitschrift 21:571-573 (October 1966)
Review of the Metropolitan premiere performance. "Dem
Jahrmarktcharakter dieser schwülustigen Inszenierung setzte
eine graziös sich um die eigene Achse drehende Riesensphinx
die Krone auf." ["The carnival atmosphere of this pretentious production provided a fitting inauguration. The high
point was provided by a gigantic sphinx which gradually
rotated on the stage."--R.F.] See: W1a

B1i. Browning, James. "Juilliard." Music Journal
33:38 (April, 1975)

"The work obviously needed editing and rewriting; in its present form it holds audience interest with many moments of sweep and power. The libretto has been 'completely transformed' by Menotti who also staged the new production. Sets are now tastefully simple and costumes are grand, but without excess. With at least an hour cut from the original and some new music furnished, the plot moves forward with more propulsion and a greater degree of clarity." See: W1b

B1j. Coleman, Emily. "Leontyne Makes a Date With History." New York Times, September 11, 1966, sect. 1, p. 21.
        Interview with Miss Price in which she discusses her role in Antony and Cleopatra, to premiere at the opening of the new Metropolitan September, 16th. "As the date of the opening approached, Miss Price confessed that I wish I could sleep a little more. Right now, I am singing the music all right, and I am trying very hard not to feel that I'm walking on a tightrope, for this is the time when no slips are allowed. To find a quietness within myself may require a number of qualities I may or may not have. As my teacher says: 'A talent is formed in silence, and a character in the stream of life.'" See: W1a

B1k. "Diva Sang for the Old Met Ghosts." Life 61:36 (September 30, 1966)
        Pictorial story of the opening of the new Metropolitan Opera House, emphasizing the part Miss Price had. "When she made her New York debut 12 years ago, she sang some of Barber's songs--lovely, melodic ones. But Cleopatra's music was vastly different. Price had to find strange minor keys, push her voice with gutteral outcries. Only on rare moments could the shimmering gold of her voice shine through." See: W1a

B1l. Edwards, Sydney. "Paste Amid the Diamonds." Music and Musicians 15:20-21 (November 1966)
        "What went wrong? Everything about Antony and Cleopatra...seemed right until the curtain went up...In the event, the opera was tragically overshadowed by almost everything else. A New York show-off night of a magnificence that only the richest city in the world could provide, the TV cameras and radio reporters, the huge crowds lining the roads outside, diamonds enough to rescue Britain from debt forever, plus the glamour of the £16 million opera house. ...The music, also was like a chic Aida. What was mainly missing was definite characterisation. The opera failed to concentrate on the essential relationships between 'the characters.' What was also obvious was the fact that Barber writes more skilfully for an orchestra than for voices. There were some fine lyrical moments, but they were given to the orchestra. The singers' roles were often declamatory, but Barber only struck gold once or twice in arias for Cleopatra, particularly the closing I have Immortal longings in me. Lovely soaring phrases which Leontyne

Price sang most beautifully. Thomas Schippers conducted with immense care, and held the whole thing together remarkably well." See: W1a

B1m. Freeman, John W. and William Mayer. "The Met's Double Christening." Music Journal 24:23-35, 46 (October 1966)
"Antony and Cleopatra was conceived for the Metropolitan Opera House, which explains the many quick changes of scene. Technical facilities of the new stage here receive a fuller test than standard operas can give. The sequence of scenes in the opera could have been simplified for conventional staging, but to do so would have eliminated much of the play's uneasy validity. Thus Barber's opera is not a trick piece to show off a new theater, but an adaptation kept closer to Shakespeare by production techniques newlyplaced at the command of composers." See: W1a

B1n. Freeman, John W. "In the Grand Tradition." Opera News 31:40-41 (September 17, 1966)
Discussion of the music for Antony and Cleopatra, with brief examples given. See: W1

B1o. Fuchs, Harry. "At the Metropolitan." Musical Leader 98:3, 11 (December 1966)
Review of the November 16, 1966 Met performance. "Mr. Zeffirelli...used all of the most uncontemporary and archaically Shakespearean lines from the original; Mr. Barber and Mr. Schippers covered good many of them with too heavy scoring and playing; and, most grievously, the cast for the most part seemed totally unconcerned with clearly projected English enunciation. Opera in English? By all means, but let us understand the English!" See: W1a

B1p. Gelatt, Roland. "New Wine in New Bottles." Reporter 35:57 (November 17, 1966)
"...it is full of well-calculated effects and skillful instrumentation, and it has fitful moments of real melodic beauty--chiefly in the last act, when the music finally begins to gain some altitude. But it is all synthetic stuff, a piece of expert musical manufacture that proceeds in jerks from scene to scene, as if the composer were dutifully meeting deadlines rather than responding to a genuine creative impulse...in his zeal to show off the spectacular capabilities of the Met's backstage machinery, Zeffirelli lost his head. Sets were kept in almost constant motion--careening up and down, to and fro, back and forth, around in circles--and the maladroit herding of supernumeraries and choristers, the chaotic agglomeration off visual styles (Egyptian, Roman, Elizabethan, Cecil B. DeMille, Bauhaus), the unlovely costuming of the leading lady, all seemed like something out of a bad dream....The trouble with Antony and Cleopatra was that it was all husk and no heart, a ritual rather than a creation." See: W1a

B1q. Gelatt, Roland. "Opening Night at the New Met." HiFi/Musical America 16:MA8-10 (November 1966)
"Before we begin laying into Samuel Barber too heavily for his failings we should pity the plight of the composer whose task it is to find a musical setting for lines as freighted with their own music as these...His Antony and Cleopatra is a prosaic and spiritless exercise--its pre-dominantly flat and barren musical landscape relieved only occasionally by a rare oasis. But the work is not an utter fiasco. It should be given its due as a well-orchestrated, carefully executed hybrid...The end impression, neverthe-less is of a passionless, uncommitted Meyerbeerian spec-tacle--a piece of manufacture more than a creation. This at least is my first reaction." See: W1a

B1r. Gruen, John. "And Where Has Samuel Barber Been...?" New York Times, October 3, 1971, sect. 2, p. 15, 21, 30.
In a long general article Barber remarks: "As far as I am concerned, the production had absolutely nothing to do with what I had imagined...The Met overproduced it. The opera didn't call for it. I mean, the Shakespeare play is rather intellectual--it's one of his problem plays. Cleo-patra is an older woman and Antony is going downhill. What I wrote and envisioned had nothing, but nothing to do with what one saw on the stage. Zeffirelli wanted horses and goats and 200 soldiers, which he got, and he wanted ele-phants which he fortunately didn't get. The point is, I had very little control--practically none. I was not sup-ported by the management. On the other hand management supported every idea of Zeffirelli's. Then, of course, there were all those mishaps of a first night in a new house. I was simply the major victim of all that." See: W1a

B1s. "Hands That Made Met Applaud In It." New York Times, September 12, 1966, p. 54
News article detailing the dress rehearsal of Antony and Cleopatra before an invited audience consisting chiefly of workmen who had helped build the opera house and their families. The entire opera was not performed; only Act I. See: W1a

B1t. "Happiest People Sat 4th Row Center." New York Times, September 17, 1966, p. 17
Feature article on James and Katharene Price, parents of Leontyne, and about their attending the premiere of Antony and Cleopatra. See: W1a

B1u. Harewood, Lord. "The New Metropolitan." Opera 17:841-845 (November 1966)
"At all events, Antony and Cleopatra got off to a bad start, and all its skill and craftsmanship and middle-of-the-road approach to the problem did not save its first two acts for most of the listeners on September 16,[1966] until

perhaps the moment of Antony's suicide at the end of Act 2,
with its flute and tympani accompaniment. Here, as in
little that had gone before was a truly operatic moment.
Some of Cleopatra's music in the last act took wing, but
until Antony was dying, none of the passion of the words
Shakespeare wrote for his lovers had been successfully
transmuted into music. In fact, the great moments made a
curiously subdued effect for a work presumably planned for
a great occasion, even the choruses of the big public
scenes coming over with little impact. Granted that much
of the music was obscured by the relentless fluidity of the
production, apparently determined at all costs to keep
something moving at all time, it is still hard to persuade
oneself that the eclectic score will outlast its rather
unfortunate christening and join the repertory."
See: W1a

   B1v. Harris, Dale. "Opera: New York." Music and Musicians 23:43-5 (June 1975)
   "Barber's recent cuts, changes and additions to the
score have made very clear the intimate nature of his
original conception. With the aid of Gian-Carlo Menotti,
who has re-worked Zeffirelli's libretto, he has thrown the
lovers into sharper focus and diminished the importance of
the world at large. There is now more Egypt and Rome and
few indications of Shakespeare's epic scale...One could not
help feeling that Barber would have been more comfortable
with the cooler style of Shaw's Caesar and Cleopatra, for
he showed no gift for depicting passion and its consuming
energies." See: W1b

   B1w. Heinsheimer, Hans. "Birth of an Opera." Saturday
Review 49:49-50+ (September 17, 1966)
   An excellent article which presents the background for
Antony and Cleopatra. The difficulties in getting a libretto were almost as trying as getting one for Vanessa.
Barber finally went to Zeffirelli's villa in Italy and
there the two completed the libretto. "The draft that
Barber brought back from Italy is almost line by line
identical with the final version which he set to music.
This was a wonderful point of departure for so painstaking
and dedicated a composer. He began writing the first scene
with its great choruses, thus setting for himself the mood
and style of the whole work. From then on he jumped once
in a while, completing scenes that appealed to him at one
particular moment before going back to earlier ones."
See: W1

   B1x. Henahan, Donal. "Juilliard Rehabilitates Barber's
Antony and Cleopatra." New York Times, February 7, 1975,
p. 13.
   "And last night at the Juilliard Theater, the composer's extensively rewritten work went a long way toward
escaping entirely from the shadow of its dismal premiere...In revising the score, Mr. Barber says he tried to

tighten the two basic elements of the opera, the political
and the amorous, combining them into one and, in general,
giving more space to the lovers...Since the premiere he has
added some music even though he cut at least an hour from
the original. Ten characters, all minor, have been eliminated, so that the work now moves with a greater sense of
purpose and more clearly. In one notable change, Cleopatra
no longer dies melodramatically in mid-phrase, but is given
a short but poignant coda full of sensuous longing and
possibly remorse." See: W1b

B1y. Hering, Doris. "I Have a Turntable." Dance Magazine 40:29 (December 1966)
A review of the first three productions of the new
Metropolitan Opera House. "His Antony and Cleopatra score
was, for example, at its most expressive in the final act
duet for Antony and his shield bearer and in a subsequent
trio for Cleopatra and her handmaidens. Perhaps significantly, the first of these was for men alone; the second
for women. And this points up a fundamental dramatic
weakness in the opera. The Shakespeare play, upon which
Franco Zeffirelli based his libretto is concerned with the
conflict between love and duty. But Barber and Zeffirelli
made the relationship between Antony and Cleopatra strangely objective. The conflict was thus never ignited." See:
W1a

B1z. Hughes, Allen. "Radio U. S. Hears Premiere of
Met." New York Times September 17, 1966, p 58.
News article concerning the broadcasting of the opening of Antony and Cleopatra. 130 AM and FM stations carried the premiere from coast to coast. Milton Cross,
familiar to millions for his Saturday afternoon Texaco
broadcasts from the Met was the announcer. See: W1a

B1aa. Jacobson, Robert. "New York." Opera News 39:36-
37 (April 5, 1977)
"Barber has lightened his orchestral score and added a
necessary ingredient--a love duet for the Roman general and
Egyptian princess in scene four of Act III, an unabashedly
romantic rhapsody...How did it stack up this time? What
excelled at the world premiere still does so...and these
are the two eloquent scenes for Cleopatra...which soar in
their golden outpouring...But when all is said and done,
Antony remains a non-opera, possibly able to make equal
impact in concert. The characters seem to pass by without
engaging us. Their lyrical scenes are lovely, giant orchestral songs, yet Barber does not work them into a consistently dramatic fabric. For his drama he turns to the
orchestra and then the music sounds as if it might be
suited to an epic film." See: W1b

B1bb. Kauffmann, Stanley. "Tenor on Horseback." New
Republic 155:23+ (October 22, 1966)
"I have been feeling a bit depressed for the past few

days, and I know why. It was that tenor on the horse. He appears in Samuel Barber's new opera, Antony and Cleopatra...If the opening had been planned to aid those who criticize Lincoln Center and the cultural explosion, it could hardly have been better designed. Around Barber's opera, clouds of oblivion have already begun to gather." See: W1a

B1cc. Klein, Howard. "The Birth of an Opera." New York Times, August 28, 1966, sect. 6, p. 32.
"The overture began on a liner somewhere in the Atlantic Ocean three years ago. Rudolf Bing conducted, and Samuel Barber listened." So begins a feature article on the birth of the idea for Antony and Cleopatra. Later in the article: "The first person to be involved was Leontyne Price. Bing and Barber agreed on that ship in the Atlantic that the opera--whatever it was--should be for her. Barber had played piano for her debut recital here in 1954; he knew the voice intimately--the husky voice, the sultry middle and the sensuous high. Writing for her would be like writing for a Stradivarius violin." See: W1

B1dd. Kolodin, Irving. "Music to My Ears: Barber's Antony, After Zeffirelli." Saturday Review 49:35-36 (October 1, 1966)
"As was almost predictable, the new work was all but overshadowed by the pomp and the panoply of the evening. But taken as a whole, in his elaboration of the libretto evolved by Zeffirelli from the lengthy text of Shakespeare, Barber has produced an occasional work of more than occasional quality...it repeatedly encounters obstacles erected by a collaborator who is eye minded rather than ear minded...A 'cast of thousands' may be suitable billing for a film, but it does not match the needs of the musical theater. It is only in the third act, when Cleopatra has retired to the monument and Zeffirelli has run out of opportunity to ring changes on the scenic side, that Barber rises to a surge of music that represents him at his best. Here, finally, the composer is no longer fighting the librettist-stage designer-costume conceiver-action supervisor for supremacy. It is still no inconsiderable problem, for the final setting, with its rising tiers of pyramidical steps...crowned by the throne on which Cleopatra awaits her lover, and her end, is a stunner. Here too Miss Price is finally triumphant through the beauty of her vocal art and by release from the need to suggest something she is not, a hot-blooded siren, all movement and allure. She is rather a woman(or all women) lamenting a lost lover--Iseult over Tristan, Brunnhilde over Siegfried, agony over agony. In the spirit of the poet he essentially is, Barber has embalmed this emotion in a pensive essence of elegy, with a rich intersticing of instrumental silver among the vocal gold. It is...instructive to hear a tape derived from the broadcast, and perceive how much the musical proceedings gain in interest without the distrac-

tion of the scenery and staging." See: W1a

B1ee. Kolodin, Irving. "Music to My Ears: Evenings With Carter, Rubinstein and Barber." Saturday Review 2:34 (March 22, 1975)
"Samuel Barber has taken the time and thought to separate the best of the Antony and Cleopatra...and amend it for presentation by the American Opera Center in the Juilliard Theater. Reduced in scale from a spectacular to a mini-music drama, it profited greatly from the participation of a mostly youthful cast, well directed by Gian-Carlo Menotti, and inspired by the flaming spirit of its young conductor, James Conlon...The revision does not make a new opera of Antony and Cleopatra: it puts the old one in better perspective of Barber's gifts and makes it far more accessible to theaters of modest means. It does, appealingly and often compellingly, plead the case of love fettered by fate to an unhappy outcome. There is, however, much more to Shakespeare's Antony and Cleopatra than this: a panorama of war, of politics, of a power struggle pitting Roman against Roman. In this version they are either backed off center stage or inadequately served by Barber's music to convey the place in literature occupied by these lovers." See: W1b

B1ff. Kupferberg, Herbert. "Barber, The Bard, and the Barge." Atlantic 218:126-129 (September 1966)
Written before the initial performance of Antony and Cleopatra the author discusses, with Barber, the composition of opera and some of the problems encountered. "When I remember that Debussy spent ten years writing Pelleas et Melisande, I feel better," said Mr. Barber. "But when I think that Verdi wrote Aida in six months...how was that possible? Again quoting Barber, "Actually Shakespeare's Antony and Cleopatra is a very sophisticated play and by no means spectacular. There's a dichotomy between the struggle for political power and the great passion which blazes through to sheer poetry at the end. What I'm trying to say is that for this occasion, the opening of a new opera house, the spectacular side is being emphasized more than it has to be. This opera is suitable for smaller productions too." See: W1b

B1gg. Landry, Robert J. "Tres Chi Chi Bow of $45 Million Metop Faces Very Chilly Antony and Cleopatra." Variety 244:1 (September 21, 1966)
"It proved an almost uninterrupted bore of little music and no sexual conviction...Zeffirelli has to bear a major burden of responsibility for what was wrong with Antony and Cleopatra!...Samuel Barber's score is not, of course, dramatic, but it is often skilled, occasionally interesting (Thomas Schippers conducted). Understandably the Met sought an American composer for the premiere of the new house, and Barber's Vanessa some years ago had shown melodic and compassionate passages. As the production

turned out, the music was subordinate to the breakaway pyramid, the stage-wandering sphinx which at one point turned full-face to the audience, showing sparkling eyes which seemed about to blink, but thankfully did not." See: W1a

B1hh. "Make Mingle With Our Tambourines That Heaven and Earth May Strike Their Sounds Together." Opera News 31:32-35 (September 17, 1966)
Interview with Barber, Zeffirelli and Schippers concerning the upcoming premiere of Antony and Cleopatra as the opening production of the new Metropolitan Opera House. Barber admits, "that the music of Antony and Cleopatra is more difficult than Vanessa because the story is." See: W1a

B1ii. Mercer, Ruby. "The New Metropolitan. A Gala Opening." Opera Canada 7:16-19 (December 1966)
"The opera itself, Antony and Cleopatra impressed more as a vehicle for exploiting the advantages of the new house plus, perhaps, the vocal resources of Leontyne Price as Cleopatra, than as an opera for posterity. The music, brilliantly conducted by Thomas Schippers, abounded neither in memorable melodies nor the familiar idiom of the modern music drama, but seemed more a score for a great dramatic pageant." See: W1a

B1jj. Meyerowitz, Jan. "Aus dem Musikleben." Musica 21:176 (July-August 1967)
"Es ist in der ganzen Welt berichtet worden, dass die Oper kein Erfolg war. So wollen wir denn berichten, was der Komponist selbst zu sagen hat. Er denkt, dass sein Werk von der kostspieligen, verwirrenden, überladenen Inszenierung, die nicht einmal funktionierte, erdrückt worden sei. Daran mag viel Wahres sein; eine einfache stilisierte Aufführung würde vielleicht einen wesentlich anderen Eindruck vermitteln. Hoffen wir, dass das Experiment bald gemacht wird." ["Everyone in the world has heard that this opera was not a success. Now, however, we want to report what the composer himself has said. He thinks that his work was strangled by the costly, confusing, overloaded production which did not even function. There may be lots of truth in this; a simple, stylistic production may possibly give a completely different impression. We hope that this experiment is being put into action soon."--R.F.] See: W1a

B1kk. "The New Met and the Old." Musical America 84:18 (July 1964)
Written in anticipation of the September 16, 1966 Lincoln Center production. "The opera is still very much in the formative stages. 'Not one note, not one line of the opera has been written,' said John Gutman, assistant general manager of the Met." See: W1a

B1ll. "N. Y. Times' Critics Equal 4 Pans." _Variety_ 244:66 (September 21, 1966)
An article which summarizes the reviews of four _New York Times_ critics. _See_: W1a

B1mm. Mordden, Ethan C. "The Once and Future American Opera." _Opera News_ 40:16-21 (August 1975)
General comments about American Opera in a long article. _Antony and Cleopatra_ is mentioned briefly.

B1nn. "Opening Night." _Opera News_ 31:12-17 (October 15, 1966)
A profusely illustrated article which conveys some of the glamour and expectancy of opening night of the new Metropolitan Opera House, with the world premiere of Samuel Barber's _Antony and Cleopatra_. _See_: W1a

B1oo. Oppens, Kurt. "Opern Brief aus New York." _Opern Welt_ 16:49-51 (May 1975)
Review of the Juilliard School performance, February 6, 1975. "Die Oper verdient weitere Aufführungen und könnte sehr wohl, unter günstigen Bedingungen herausgebracht, ein Zugstück werden." ["The opera deserves to be performed more often, and quite possibly could become a popular success, if staged under favorable conditions."--H.L.] _See_: W1b

B1pp. Porter, Andrew. "Musical Events: _Antony_'s Second Chance."_New Yorker_ 51:123-144 (February 24, 1975)
"The music, while containing several most agreeable lyrical passages--mellifluous, fluent, and romantic in a general way--and much able invention, simply did not rise to the size of the subject. Maybe, at the Met, it has been treated as 'music to move scenery to,' but then much of it seemed to do little more than go through the familiar gestures of late-Romantic grand opera." After a lengthy discussion of both versions, Mr. Porter suggests, "that _Antony_ (even though it may not show 'a grandeur of characterization...that only the greatest opera composers have possessed') deserves a third chance: a large-scale production given preferably in France, Italy, or Germany, where the first hurdle--the dependence on Shakespeare's verbal poetry--could also be removed; and in a house the size of Hamburg's or West Berlin's, where the stage can hold big spectacle and the auditorium is small enough for the voices to tell strongly." [reprinted in Porter's _Music of Three Seasons, 1974-77_. New York: Farrar, Straus, Giroux, 1978, p. 97-102] _See_: W1b

B1qq. Price, Leontyne. "What Opera Would I Like Revived?" _New York Times_, February 11, 1973, sect. 2, p. 17.
"Hold on to your hat, but under the proper circumstances, I'd love to see a revival of _Antony and Cleopatra_. The music is glorious. Redirected and quieted down, with the proper respect for the music--which is what opera is

all about--it could be given a fair chance. When it was
first done the direction was overwhelmingly heavy...Al-
though it's not an ensemble opera, other singers, like the
tenor and bass-baritone, have their share of vocal privi-
leges, too. It's also one of the few contemporary operas
that employs the chorus and dancers. The third act has
some of the most beautiful music ever written. I've pro-
grammed two scenes from it with major orchestras here and
in Europe, with great success." See: W1

    B1rr. Ringo, James. "From Schirmer, Barber's _Antony_
and Cleopatra." _American_ _Record_ _Guide_ 33:871-872+ (May
1967)
    Review of the G. Schirmer vocal score. "It is not a
masterpiece, not even a sturdy minor masterpiece, but neither is it as bad as its press almost uniformly indicated...There are highly successful things in _Antony_ _and_
Cleopatra: a vigorous Stick-dance aboard Antony's galley,
with the alternating moments of vigor and languor...the
strange eerily effective 'Music I' th' air' episode, featuring the Ondes Martenot;...the superb scene in Barber's
best wintry mood in which Antony spent, experiencing the
bitter aftertaste of defeat, falls on his sword (Act II,
Scene 8); with an accompaniment except for the last few
measures of kettledrums and flute, achieving an almost
oriental majesty through economy of means; and the whole of
Act III, the only fully-articulated scene in the opera, in
which the composer, relaxing for the first time, comes to
grips with his subject and writes opera-to-be-sung instead
of arioso-to-be-declaimed." See: W1a

    B1ss. Rizzo, Eugene. "Smash Late Events Put Over Click
of Italy's Spoleto Fest." _Variety_ 311:119, 122 (July 20,
1983)
    "The other main opera at Spoleto this year was Samuel
Barber's _Antony_ _and_ _Cleopatra_...Received politely if not
exactly enthusiastically by critics and public alike, the
production subsequently netted lead singer Esther Hinds the
Golden Pegasus Award as the outstanding artist of this
year's festival." See: W1f

    B1tt. "Sam Barber Rep As Composer Back After Zeffirel-
li." _Variety_ 278:81 (February 12, 1975)
    News article concerning the production of the revised
version of _Antony_ _and_ _Cleopatra_. The _Variety_ reporter
comments on the 1966 production, "In the process Zeffirelli
succeeded in generating the embarrassment of the century
for the Met and Sir Rudolf Bing, wrecking the turntable,
drawing universally adverse reviews and angering the composer who felt he was the victim of the Italian director's
'Renaissance man' vanity." See: W1a

    B1uu. Sans, Jeremy. "In Concert." _Opera_ (Eng.) 33:658
(June 1982)
    Review of the March 27, 1982 Camden Festival concert

performance. "A couple of bars of <u>Carmina Burana</u> and a few MGM fanfares and we launched straight into one of the strangest operatic mismatches of recent decades: Samuel Barber meets William Shakespeare...there was some fine music and on occasion there was some fine singing. David Wilson-Johnson was in glorious full voice and elevated his suicide scene to something quite substantial. Similarly Donald Stephenson...coped successfully with the fiendishly hard role of Caesar. Susan Bingemann sang Cleopatra, a role which has so many <u>pianissimo</u> floats in it that I gave up counting them. She manages them all very prettily, but this sort of vocal writing is hardly conducive to any great depth of characterization." <u>See</u>: W1d

B1vv. Sargeant, Winthrop. "Musical Events." <u>New Yorker</u> 42:114 (September 24, 1966)
A long article on both the opening night celebration of the new Metropolitan Opera House at Lincoln Center and a review of the opera. Of the opera he comments, "If any contemporary composer <u>should</u> be capable of infusing melody into a new opera, it is Mr. Barber, whom I have long regarded as one of America's truly professional composers of serious music, and whose compositions I have frequently admired. But I am afraid that <u>Antony</u> <u>and</u> <u>Cleopatra</u> is not entirely successful." Mr. Barber's sensitive, retiring temperament seems out of its elements in a spectacle of such grandiose proportions...The music of the last act is superior to the rest of the score. During the first two acts, there is no music of passionate, lyric quality to express the great love that is supposed to be going on between the two protagonists...the truth is that his previous opera, <u>Vanessa</u> is superior to <u>Antony</u> <u>and</u> <u>Cleopatra</u> in almost every way. But even if <u>Antony</u> <u>and</u> <u>Cleopatra</u> had been a masterpiece, the production given it by Franco Zeffirelli would have killed it. His staging of it was, I thought, appallingly pretentious, appallingly arty, and, in most respects, destructive." <u>See</u>: W1a

B1ww. Schillaci, Daniel. "For the Record." <u>New West</u> 6:118 (April 1981)
"The opera...failed when it was premiered for the opening of the new Metropolitan Opera House in 1966, and although it has since been revived by the Juilliard School in a slightly revised version, it has never really caught on; its exoticism is rather too much like calendar art." <u>See</u>: W1b

B1xx. Schonberg, Harold C. "Onstage, It Was 'Antony and Cleopatra.'" <u>New York Times</u>, September 17, 1966, p. 16.
"And so, last night, it finally came to pass: the grand, grand opening of the grand, grand Metropolitan Opera. It was quite a spectacle, situated on the cosmic scale somewhere above the primeval atom, the original Big Bang, and somewhere below the creation of the Milky Way it

was a spectacle that connoisseurs will put in their memory box and treasure forever. It was a big, complicated package: big, grand, impressive and vulgar; a Swinburnian mélange of sad, bad, mad, glad; rich and also nouveau-riche; desperately aiming for the bigger and the better. Not many will deny that the Metropolitan came up with the bigger...The emphasis, quite understandably from the point of view of the Metropolitan Opera, was to show the public what nearly $50-million worth of opera house could do...But the singing was good. Miss [Leontyne] Price was in superb voice, and she was backed up by some of the best singers currently on the Metropolitan roster." See: W1a

B1yy. Schwinger, Wolfram. "Der gute alte Staub: Bar-bers 'Antony and Cleopatra' in der neuen Met und andere Opernpremieren." NZ: Neue Zeitschrift für Musik 127:447-448 (November 1966)
    Review of the September 16, 1966 New York City pre-miere. "Konnte man bei der Eröffnungspremiere der neuen Met den konventionell aufgeplusterten musikalischen Stil von Barbers 'Antony and Cleopatra' und den hektischen Pomp von Zeffirellis Inszenierung immerhin als den Versuch gel-ten lassen, alles zu zeigen, was man aufzubieten hat: grosse Stimmen, eine Riesenbühne, enorme technische Möglichkeiten--so stimmt es schon weit bedenklicher, wenn auch mit den zweiten Premiere wieder nur ausserlicher, spektakulärer Aufwand getrieben wird, der von einem neuen Geist im neuen Hause nicht das mindeste spüren lässt." ["If one could account for the conventional puffed up musical style of Barber's 'Antony and Cleopatra,' and the hectic plush of Zeffirelli's production at the opening night of the new Met as an experiment to show everything there is available: great voices, a giant stage, vast technical possibilities--then it is even more disturbing that at the second premiere as well there was only the same spectacular, superficial effects, untouched by any hint of a new spirit in the new opera house."--R.F.] See: W1a

B1zz. Smith, Patrick J. "Debuts & Reappearances." High Fidelity/Musical America 25:MA25-26 (May 1975)
    Review of the February 6, 1975 Juilliard American Opera Center's production of the revised opera. "Barber was correct in shearing away a good deal of the epic, since the grand gesture is not his musical forte...Barber is a thoroughly competent, often interesting composer of the old school, but the one thing he does not have in his make-up is a knack for the dramatic stage. The quick of opera life is not in him, and thus his personages move about in the well-made music without a real feeling that they belong there. The Juilliard production was carefully directed by Menotti, who drew the most from the score with a striking series of stage pictures." See: W1b

B1aaa. Strongin, Theodore. "American Opera to Open New Met." New York Times, May 7, 1964, p. 39.

175

Bibliography

Note that <u>Antony and Cleopatra</u> will be the opening
work when the new Metropolitan Opera opens at Lincoln
Center in the fall of 1966. Leontyne Price is scheduled to
sing the role of Cleopatra and Franco Zeffirelli has agreed
to stage and design the production. <u>See</u>: W1a

B1bbb. "Tony and Cleo." <u>Newsweek</u> 68:98 (September 26,
1966)
"Music must furnish the poetry of the opera, the
thrust of the dialogue. In Barber's labored, uninventive
score, chromatic and unmelodic, it is hard to find any
connection between the vocal and orchestral line. The
opera is unrelentingly funereal, static, pompously solemn
in tone and emotionally elementary. Still there are saving
moments when the tone and pace suit the action: in Enobarbus's remorseful aria after he betrays Antony, in Antony's
Roman suicide, and in the touching trio as Cleopatra and
her handmaidens prepare their ritual deaths." <u>See</u>: W1a

B4. ANTONY AND CLEOPATRA. TWO SCENES.

B4a. Ericson, Raymond. "Old Fashioned But Not Sac-
charine." <u>New York Times</u>, March 30, 1969, sect. 2, p. 30.
"Samuel Barber has taken two of the best scenes from
his opera <u>Antony and Cleopatra</u> and turned them into a kind
of concert suite for soprano and orchestra...It is sung by
Leontyne Price, as it should be since she created the role
for the work's premiere at the new Metropolitan Opera House
in 1966...Barber has provided an introduction and an inter-
lude that binds the arias together. The results is eloquent and beautiful, particularly in the quite gorgeous
singing of Miss Price. It makes one hope that the composer
can salvage the opera someday, for it was a work that was
crippled at its premiere more by a vulgar and distracting
production than by the admitted inadequacies of the music."
[RCA LSC 3062] <u>See</u>: D4a

B4b. Fogel, Henry. "Collections." <u>Fanfare</u> 7:293 (Jan-
uary/February 1984)
"For me the highlight is Price's recording of 'Give Me
My Robe' from Samuel Barber's <u>Antony and Cleopatra</u>; the
more I hear the music from this opera, the more I am con-
vinced it has been severely underrated." [RCA Red Seal ARL
1 4856] <u>See</u>: D4b

B4c. Henahan, Donal. "<u>Antony and Cleopatra</u> Scenes
Please Philharmonic Audience." <u>New York Times</u>, December
11, 1971, p. 22
"Of course, two scenes do not an opera make, but there
is obviously more quality in this score than the Metropolitan premiere discovered, and no doubt another try here-
abouts is indicated, perhaps in a revised, smaller-scale,
more musically centered version. Miss Arroyo's performance
expertly caught the life-and-death contrast in the two

scenes, and except for a few measures when the music dropped to gruffness she spun out Mr. Barber's difficult vocal
line with disarming ease." See: W4d

B4d. Kolodin, Irving. "Recordings in Review: The Best
of Barber and of Price." Saturday Review 52:52 (March 29,
1969)
"It will confirm, for those who have not had the
opportunity to check back on their initial impressions, or
were denied such impressions altogether, that there is much
music in the score of higher quality than was generally
acknowledged at the time." [RCA LSC 3062] See: D4a

B4e. Lowens, Irving. "Pianos and Ping-Pong Balls."
Inter-American Music Bulletin no. 66:3 (July 1968)
"Samuel Barber's synthesis and adaptation of two
scenes from his ill-fated Antony and Cleopatra, introduced
last season by Leontyne Price and the National Symphony,
playing under Howard Mitchell, is so thorough a reworking
that the composer gave the scena an entirely new opus
number [present author unable to verify]. It is convincing
as a concert-piece, as the June 23 performance once again
demonstrated and may well survive the opera." [Fourth
Inter-American Musical Festival, Washington, June 20-30,
1968] See: W4a

B4f. Osborne, Conrad L. "Classical." High Fidelity
19:82 (June 1969)
"That Barber operas have somehow missed the boat con-
stitutes, to my mind, a miscarriage of a very real operatic
talent. Neither Vanessa nor Antony works, yet there is a
fair amount of interesting and effective writing in the
former, and some in the latter. There can be no doubt of
the composer's gift or of his love for the voice and for
the lyric stage. He has not been fortunate in his collab-
orators (or at least in what they have produced for him),
in the matching of his style to his subjects, or in the
milieu for which he has written. One can't help wondering
what might have emerged had he been tendered a subtle,
poetic libretto on an essentially lyrical subject for an
ensemble company of singing actors with no epic preten-
tions." [RCA LSC 3062] See: D4a

B4g. Porter, Andrew. "Opera." Gramophone 47:302 (August 1969)
"Barber's musical idiom is late-Romantic. The easiest
point of reference is Richard Strauss. And people who enjoy
late Strauss(as I do) should also enjoy, specially, the
second Antony excerpt, the death scene." [RCA SB 6799
(same as LSC 3062)] See: D4a

B4h. Sagmaster, Joseph. Cincinnati Symphony Orchestra
Program Notes, April 17-18, 1971, p. 717.
"Indeed, some critics complained that more attention

was paid to production than to the music. There was general agreement, however, on the beauty and dramatic power of the suicide of Cleopatra." [Beverly Wolff, soprano, singing "Give Me My Robe"] See: W4c

B4i. Sagmaster, Joseph. "Musical Events: Hearing Barber Plain." New Yorker 47:116 (December 18, 1971)
"His music stems from a much more vigorous tradition, grounded in Strauss and Mahler." Martina Arroyo sang the soprano role. See: W4d

B5. A HAND OF BRIDGE, OP. 35.

B5a. Ardoin, John. "Opera in New York: Mannes College Presents Premiere of Barber Work." Musical America 80:39-40 (May 1960)
"The joint result is a charmer, a vignette of sophistication, which never becomes pretentious." See: W5b

B5b. Finkelstein, Sidney. "Samuel Barber" [album notes for Vanguard VRS 1065]
"The opera is a little masterpiece in depth, unfolding within its light comedy framework of two couples playing bridge, an acute and sad portrayal of four people alienated from one another, each living in his or her own private world." See: D5a

B5c. Frankenstein, Alfred. "Classical." High Fidelity 11:49 (July 1969)
"A Hand of Bridge is a short chamber opera with text by Gian-Carlo Menotti. The music, too, sounds as if Menotti had written it--which in my opinion means sleazy and slovenly." [Vanguard VSD 2083, VRS 1065] See: D5a

B5d. Goldberg, Albert. "Samuel Barber Opera At Immaculate Heart." Los Angeles Times, April 7, 1970, pt. 4, p. 10.
"For this nonsense--or maybe it isn't such nonsense--Barber has written a pert and jazzy little score. No one has much to sing, but...[the soloists] made it rather amusing." See: W5c

B5e. Hall, David. "Classics." HiFi/Stereo Review 6:61 (June 1961)
The work "...hardly counts as a major addition to Barber's output, but it has a curious bitter poignancy, like that of one of the better short stories in The New Yorker." See: W5

B5f. Hughes, Allen. "Landmarks." New York Times April 30, 1961, sect. 2, p. 21.
"Patricia Neway, Eunice Alberts, William Lewis and Philip Maero are the vocalists at bridge, but even their expertise cannot make one think that the trifling game in

which they are caught really belongs with the more thoughtful Barberiana on this disk." [Vanguard VRS 1065] See: D5a

B5g. Salzman, Eric. "Samuel Barber." HIFI/Stereo
Review 17:77-89 (October 1966)
    "A second Barber-Menotti collaboration, the one-act
opera...is a very different sort of show; four people
playing a game of bridge reveal, in a series of asides,
their true, despicable characters and the real, grasping,
brutal nature of the relationships between them. The piece
is short, biting, and bitter." [Vanguard VSD 2083, VRS
1065] See: D5a

B5h. Taubman, Howard. "Opera:A Hand of Bridge." New
York Times, April 7, 1960, p. 45.
    Review of the Mannes College of Music production. The
work is "...one of the shortest operas ever written. Its
nine minutes of music were surrounded by about an hour of
intermission last night. Seldom in operatic history have
so many waited so long for so little...The new Barber-
Menotti collaboration is an amusing little jeu d'esprit,
but its wispy humors were almost crushed by the longueurs
in which it was framed...Neither Mr. Menotti nor Mr. Barber
have taken themselves seriously. The latter has written
music in an agreeable old-fashioned vein. The very pre-
dictability of the idiom adds to the flavor of the piece."
See: W5b

B5i. Yellin, Victor. "Samuel Barber." Notes 18:641
(September 1961)
    In the score, "...the touch of a master theatrical
craftsman is evident...Barber's music is, as the nine-
minute drama requires, jazzy, funny, sensual, psychoanalyt-
ical, and vulgar; always on a firm harmonic base, propelled
by appropriate rhythms." See: W5

B7. VANESSA, OP. 32.

B7a. Abbiati, Franco. "Teatri e concerti." Musica d'Oggi (nuova series) 4:177-179 (July-August 1961)
    Review of the June 15, 1961 Spoleto performance. "La
misura del successo e risultata da una trentina di vibranti
chiamate complessive agli interpreti dopo i cinque quadri
e dulla intensita di alcuni applausi a scena aperta. Anche
gli autori sono stati lungamente applauditi alla fine dell'
esecuzione." ["The measure of the production's success was
indicated by the thirty or so curtain calls for the singers
after the five acts were over, and by the intensity of
applause during the course of the performance."--R.F.]
See: W7e

B7b. "American Masterpiece." Newsweek 51:62-63 (January 27, 1958)
    "Shortly after the start of the second act the house

[Metropolitan Opera] broke into spontaneous applause after a delightful waltz song called Under the Willow Tree. A passionate love duet in the third act stopped the show, and a hauntingly beautiful farewell quartet [sic, quintet] in the fourth and last act brought the final curtain down to cheers and bravos. When Barber was finally brought out for a solo curtain call, the audience broke out with the full-throated roar usually reserved for prima donnas and seldom heard by the composers." See: W7a

B7c. B., R. "New York." Schweizerische Musikzeitung 98:133-135 (March 1958)
Review of the New York premiere. "Das Werk verrät deutlich sichtbare Zeichen könnerischen Gesamtführung, es ist als abendfüllende Theateroper (Dies im Gegensatz zu der beliebten Neuform der Fernseh-Oper gesagt) zumindest ein Beweis der Lebensfähigkeit des Opern-Genres, das man in den letzten Jahrzehnten wiederholt totgesagt hatte." ["The work shows clearly visible signs of skillful execution; as an opera for a full evening performance (in contrast to the newly popular form of television opera) it is at least proof for the continued vitality of the genre of opera which had been called dead repeatedly during the last decades."--H.L.] See: W7a

B7d. Banfield, Stephen. "Records: Barber's Vanessa." Music and Musicians 27:39-40 (October 1978)
"Barber's Vanessa is a work, like Walton's almost contemporary and very similar-sounding Troilus and Cressida and Bliss's The Olympians, where a dramatically gifted composer failed to find the subject matter and to grasp the terrific opportunities for doing something personal in what was still in the 1950's an almost virgin field: opera written in the English language. Instead they all took subjects set in countries other than their own, and composed them in a cosmopolitan style full of Puccinian cliches. Had Barber looked for a genuinely American subject, he might have regained the idiomatic freshness of Knoxville: Summer of 1915. It is significant that he nearly does in the scene with a country dance going on in the background, where his style takes a welcome breath of wit and detachment similar to that of Britten...However, the music is mellifluous and at times gripping, the performances and sound quality exemplary, the singing excellent and the words remarkably clear." [RCA RL 020914] See: D7a

B7e. Barber, Samuel. "Birth Pangs of a First Opera." New York Times, January 12, 1957, sect. 2, p. 9.
Mr. Barber gives a personal account of the writing of Vanessa. "As were not bound by the conditions of a commission, we were utterly free in choice of time and place...Waiting for the finished libretto required the patience of Job." Due to outside commitments Mr. Menotti was unable to continue on Vanessa after a part of the first

act. Four months later Mr. Barber reports, "When, the next
spring, Menotti was at last free, I refused to write a note
until the complete libretto was finished. My tactic succeeded brilliantly. It made him so nervous he sat on a
rock by another sea--the Mediterranean this time--every
morning until by summer's end, what I think is perhaps the
finest and most chiseled of his libretti was finished.
Although Menotti and I often discussed twists and turns of
plot and character, I had to change very few words." See:
W7

   B7f. Barber, Samuel. "On Waiting for a Libretto."
Opera News 22:4-6 (January 27, 1958) [also reprinted in:
Contemporary Composers on Contemporary Music, edited by
Elliott Schwartz and Barney Childs. New York: Holt, Rine-
hart & Winston, 1967. p. 165-169]
   In his own words Samuel Barber tells about his life
before thinking about an opera, his working relationship
during the writing of the libretto, by his good friend,
Gian-Carlo Menotti, and of the ease with which he found he
could fit Menotti's words to his music. "...I could immediately understand and appreciate the economy of Menotti's use of words, so necessary for the singing stage;
their utter simplicity (how wonderful to set!) and his
sense of theatrical timing, which seems to me indeed unique." See: W7

   B7g. "Barber at the Met." Time 71:59-60 (January 27,
1958)
   "With last week's opening-night audience, at least, it
was a direct hit. Composer Barber's Vanessa failed to be
intensely moving or to spring any musical or dramatic
surprises; but it could lay claim to being the best U.S.
opera yet staged at the Metropolitan...Its chief merits are
showy orchestration and dazzling vocal writing owing much
to the knowledge of singing that Barber picked up as a
onetime vocal student..." See: W7a

   B7h. Beatie, Bruce A. and Rita V. Beatie. "Samuel Barber's Vanessa: The Sounds of Silence." NATS [National
Association of Teachers of Singing] Bulletin 36:16-21
(September/October 1979)
   A lengthy discussion of Vanessa in which the authors
conclude, "But the central symbol of the opera is the
'awful silence' of the Old Baroness, a rock against which
the flowing speech of Anatol and the Doctor break and
dissipates into timelessness. She is the eternal balance
to Anatol's cyclic return--and because eternal, immeasur-
able. Here is the ultimate silence that breaks our every
attempt to give voice to the opera's lesser silences. As
in a Dinessen tale we can peel off layer after layer of
meaning, but the mysterious core remains untouched, in the
silences beyond melody and words." See: W7

B7i. Blanks, Henry. "_Vanessa_ by Samuel Barber." _Canon:_
Australian Music Journal 11:284-285 (March-April 1958)
"It is contemporary but not radical, it has arias and
it has a quintet, its overture in the first instance reminds one of Puccini in its dramatic intent. But if these
are recognisable and memorisable, tunes and cadences, then
their treatment is still original and individual. A climax
is the quintet toward the end--it starts as a sort of
fugue, becomes quintet and then great chorus with each
character singing one line and the others then responding
with their secret knowledge about the future's probabil-
ity." _See_: W7

B7j. Bourke, Gerard. "European Chronicle." _Musical_
Opinion 82:103 (November 1958)
Review of the Salzburg performance. "The Austrian and
German critics and musicians with whom I discussed the
opera at Salzburg seem to have considered the subject...and
its treatment...to be unacceptable at a modern festival...Frankly I was surprised at the unanimity of the
verdict since I found merit in the work if one is prepared
to agree that an opera written entirely within this period
may still be presented." _See_: W7c

B7k. Breuer, Robert. "Samuel Barbers _Vanessa_ in New
York." _Österreichische Musikzeitschrift_ 13:70-72 (February
1958)
Review of the Metropolitan premiere. "Erika, der
sämtliche Aktschlüsse zufallen und die zweifellos die
lohnendste Rolle innehat, wurde von Rosalind Elias in
unüberriebener Weise verkörpert; dass ihr der Haupanteil
des Erfolges zufiel, schien ein gerechtes Dankeszeugnis der
Zuhörer gewesen zu sein, die ausserdem intuitiv gefühlt
haben mussten, dass diese Oper eigentlich den Titel 'Erika'
tragen sollte." ["Erika, who dominates all the final
scenes and is without doubt the most rewarding role, was
sung by Rosalind Elias in an unexaggerated manner. It
seemed to be a just testimony by the audience that she
earned the main share of the success. Intuitively the
audience must have felt that this opera should have been
called 'Erika.'"--H.L.] _See_: W7a

B7l. Briggs, John. "Liturgical Music." _New York_
Times, October 5, 1958, sect. 2, p. 21.
"Hearing the work on records reinforces the impression
made by its Metropolitan premiere, that it was a stout try.
Mr. Barber knows how to write for voices, being himself a
singer...He writes considerately for his vocalists, and his
orchestra does not annihilate them. The music has a pleasant Straussian flavor, and there are passages of great
beauty throughout. On records, however, as in the theatre,
the work just misses that indefinable element of vitality
that brings a theatre piece to life. Although _Vanessa_
gains momentum as it goes along, its total impact is that
of a somewhat static theatre work. But it is a composition

of such elegance and distinction that one hopes the composer will soon try his hand again at this demanding musical form." [RCA LM 6138] See: D7a

B7m. Broder, Nathan. "Current Chronicle: New York."
Musical Quarterly 44:235-237 (April 1958)
     "For this romantic story Barber has written rich and
poetic music, including some in the neo-Romantic style of
his early works. The singers usually express themselves in
a kind of arioso, which leads smoothly into set numbers.
The general technique is that which was perfected by the
aging Verdi and carried on by Puccini. Much of the thematic material is moving and trenchant. It is usually
either open and diatonic or constricted in range and highly
chromatic...The workmanship throughout is of Barber's usual
excellence, and the orchestration is superb...What is unusual in this first opera is not that some of it is not
effective, but that so much of it is strong and beautiful." See: W7

B7n. Brunner, Gerhard. "The International Scene."
Musical Courier 158:33-34 (October 1958)
     "Vanessa left varied impressions here [Salzburg Festi-
val], with the negative points dominant...A special characteristic is a genuine, deeply rooted romantic and strongly Pucciniesque sentiment, which in Barber's score shows
itself in beautiful oboe and English horn passages, magnificent vocal lines, and a masterly orchestration...Bar-
ber's strong expressive score, most convincing in the beautiful closing quintet, could not be a complete success in
surroundings and in an adaptation that had so little of the
contemporary about them." See: W7c

B7o. Calta, Louis. "Menotti writes a 4-act libretto."
New York Times, January 7, 1956, p. 21.
     News article announcing that Mr. Menotti has completed
the libretto for Vanessa. It is estimated that it will take
Mr. Barber a year to complete the score. See: W7

B7p. Coleman, Emily. "Samuel Barber and Vanessa. Theatre Arts 42:68-69 (January 1958)
     Interview with Samuel Barber before the premiere of
Vanessa. On the question of doing his own orchestration
Mr. Barber remarks, "Of course I do my own. Only in this
country do people allot their work to others for orchestration. Every composer worth his salt does his own orchestration, from Mozart through Stravinsky. It is a great joy
for the composer himself to decide which of the ten thousand possibilities he might chose for the color of one
chord. How can one hire someone else to do this? It is a
Broadway musical technique." See: W7

B7q. -----. "A New and True...Grand Opera." Theatre
Arts 42:66-68 (March 1958)
     A lengthy review of the premiere of Vanessa. "Vanessa,

in short is a true grand opera. For an American work, it
is the best yet heard at the Metropolitan.   Unclassified
nationally, it ranks with the four or five finest written
anywhere in the last quarter century." <u>See</u>: W7a

B7r. Confalonieri, Giulio. "La vita musicale all'estero: Stati Uniti." <u>Musica d'Oggi</u>, nuova serie, 1:179-182
(March 1958)
     Discussion of <u>Vanessa</u> within the general framework of
American opera, with particular reference to the January
15, 1958 Metropolitan Opera production. <u>See</u>: W7a

B7s. Craig, Mary. "New York Concert and Opera Beat."
<u>Musical Courier</u> 159:8-9 (February 1959)
     "Mr. Barber's opera starts slowly, a fact that is more
apparent on a second hearing; but it moves steadily and
strongly toward a climactic peak in its action and in its
music." <u>See</u>: W7

B7t. D., E. "Harvuot Sings Role in <u>Vanessa</u> at 'Met.'"
<u>New York Times</u>, February 22, 1958, p.8.
     "Clifford Harvuot made his first appearance in the
role of the old doctor last night at the Metropolitan Opera
House in the fifth performance of Samuel Barber's <u>Vanessa</u>
Mr. Harvuot not only sang well, but also proved an effective character actor, too. He handled himself with ease
on the stage and sprang about quite briskly for an old
doctor, yet not too briskly in his second act dancing
demonstration. In what might be called his 'champagne
monologue' of the third act he reeled about the stage with
comic grace and sang the humorous lines of Gian-Carlo
Menotti's text with the greatest of tipsy ease. It was a
more than professionally smooth performance."

B7u. Dickinson, Peter. "Record Reviews." <u>Musical
Times</u> 119:864 (October 1978)
     "Such latterday Straussian sumptuous music needs a
better recorded sound to emerge with any satisfaction."
[RCA RL 02094] <u>See</u>: D7a

B7v. "8th Opera Season Opens in Capital [<u>sic</u>]." <u>New
York Times</u>, November 9, 1963, p. 14.
     The Opera Society of Washington opened its season with
a performance of Samuel Barber's <u>Vanessa</u>. <u>See</u>: W7f

B7w. Ericson, Raymond. "Salzburg Stages American Opera
for First Time." <u>Musical America</u> 76:6 (September 1958)
     Review of the August 16, 1958 Salzburg performance
"Cordially greeted by the public, it was condemned by the
Austrian and German critics in almost brutal terms...Un-
fortunately, all the best efforts of these distinguished
artists could not persuade the critics that Menotti's
libretto was not foolishness and that Barber's music was
not a pastiche of ideas borrowed from Puccini and Strauss."
<u>See</u>: W7c

B7x.   Ericson, Raymond.   "Vanessa Revived by Metropolitan." New York Times, March 15, 1965, p. 38.
     "In the final analysis it establishes a character of its own by the nature of Barber's style and the atmosphere of the story, best exemplified in the beautiful last-act quintet. The three women with the two leading men...provide people to whom Barber has given full-blooded music. They also provide solid parts for opera singers who can act, and the Metropolitan had such singers for the revival." See: W7g

B7y.   Evett, Robert. "Yankee Doodling at the Met." New Republic 138:18-19 (January 27, 1958)
     "The work suffers from the weak libretto of Gian-Carlo Menotti, and suffered at its premiere from a seedy performance. "But the fatal weakness is in the score itself. Barber has repressed his own stylistic individuality and instead favored an imitation of Menotti's musical mannerisms. There are surely few composers who could sustain a borrowed style as efficiently as Barber does here. But, efficient or not, his piece has a spurious ring...in the main, the piece's only real distinction is technical; the orchestration is always good, the balance is always right, etc. But we are all so used to technical perfection that mere virtuosity is no longer an adequate mask for poverty of materials and design." See: W7a

B7z.   Eyer,   Ronald.   "America" Opera (London) 9:165 (March 1958)
     "This is opera in the grand manner stemming from the romantic traditions of Central Europe and Italy.   It is American only in so far as its composer was born in this country...The music, couched in the lyrical language which is characteristic of Barber and revealing all the expertness of a versatile, seasoned composer, is quite frankly derivative in the best sense of the word. One has no trouble identifying moods, types of development and treatment, bits of orchestration, and so on...Everything is distilled through Mr. Barber's own highly individual viewpoint and imagination, and he has dared to use what he considered the best of many operatic styles at the risk of being accused of a want of originality. It takes courage to eschew being 'different' simply for difference's sake." See: W7a

B7aa.   -----. "Premiere of Barber's Vanessa. Musical America 78:5+ (February 1958)
     "This was not just the succes d'estime commonly allotted to composers of Mr. Barber's reputation, but an expression of enthusiasm for an exciting, moving experience in theatre for which the far from naive spectators were genuinely grateful. The Metropolitan has not produced a new American opera in ten years, but when it got around to one again, at long last, it came up with a winner. Sensing a hit, apparently, the management left nothing undone--from

the elegant Edwardian sets of Cecil Beaton to the deport-
ment of the lowliest walk-on--to insure a worthy mounting."
See: W7a

B7bb. F., G. "Washington Vanessa." Opera News 28:34
(December 28, 1963)
Brief review of the November 9, 1963 Washington Opera
Society production. See: W7f

B7cc. Fleming, Shirley. "A Janacek Celebration at
Spoleto USA." High Fidelity/Musical America 28:MA43+ (October 1978)
"It seems incomprehensible...that...[Vanessa] should
have been performed so sporadically since its premiere at
the Metropolitan in 1958. It has all the characteristics
that opera goers profess to yearn for today--abundant melody, luxuriant orchestration, an integrated thematic structure and above all an utterly idiomatic approach to vocal
writing; every singer in the compact cast has the sort of
soaring line that is tailormade for the voice...[it]...
should come out of retirement." See: W7i

B7dd. Freeman, John W. "Barber's Vanessa. Opera News
29:34 (April 3, 1965)
Brief review of the recording of the Metropolitan
production. [RCA LM 6138, LSC 6138] See: D7a

B7ee. -----. "To Weep and Remember." Opera News 29:24-
26 (April 3, 1965)
A short analysis of the music of Vanessa with some
musical examples. See: W7

B7ff. Gatti, Guido M. "Spoleto." La rassegna musicale
31 no. 2:131-132 (1961)
Review of the Spoleto performance. "Quanto ad aver
creato una opera americana, grande o piccina, saremmo piut-
tosto perplessi nell'affermarlo: da mezzo secolo studiosi e
musicisti statunitensi attendono di annunziarne la nascita,
ma I tentativi fatti sinora, da Taylor a Hanson, da Cadman
a Gruenberg, da Virgil Thomson ad Antheil, tutti più o meno
legati a moduli stilistici e sintattici europei, non hanno
permesso di farlo." ["As to the question of whether an
American opera has been created--whether grand opera or
light--we are perplexed as to what to say. For 50 years
American musicologists and musicians have been waiting to
announce its birth, but the attempts made so far--from
Taylor to Hanson, from Cadman to Gruenberg, from Virgil
Thomson to Antheil--all have been more or less shaped by
European styles and syntax, and all have failed to produce
an American opera."--R.F.] See: W7e

B7gg. Gradenwitz, Peter. "New Music at the European
Festivals, Summer, 1958." Chesterian 32:52-53 (Autumn
1958)
"Salzburg has recently made it a matter of artistic

policy to include one contemporary opera (possibly a world premiere) in its programmes, but the inclusion of <u>Vanessa</u>...must have been motivated by other than artistic policy proper. The work was hailed by American critics, after its first performance, as a great new American opera; but public and critics on this side of the ocean could detect neither greatness nor novelty in the opera, and certainly no musical elements of distinct American character. There is hardly anything in this music that has not been said in a better, and more modern, way by Leoncavallo, Puccini, d'Albert, and Richard Strauss." <u>See</u>: W7c

B7hh. Guentner, Francis J. "Music." <u>America</u> 99:629-631 (September 13, 1958)
The title characters of <u>Vanessa</u>, Cherubini's <u>Medea</u> and Puccini's <u>Suor Angelica</u> are briefly compared and the story line of <u>Vanessa</u> is summarized. <u>See</u>: W7

B7ii. Haskell, Harry. "Conviction Lacking in Lyric's <u>Vanessa</u>." <u>Star</u> (Kansas City, Missouri) October 17, 1979 (Located in NewsBank, Review of the Arts [Microform], Performing Arts, 1979, 35:E7, fiche)
General review of the Kansas City Lyric Opera's production of <u>Vanessa</u>. <u>See</u>: W7k

B7jj. -----. "Reports: U.S.: Kansas City." <u>Opera News</u> 44:26 (February 2, 1980)
Review of the Kansas City Lyric Opera production. <u>See</u>: W7k

B7kk. Hausswald, Gunter. "Ausklang der Musikfestes: Enttauschung und Erfullung." <u>Musica</u> 12:598 (October 1958)
Review of the Salzburg production. "Dass der Komponist ein versierter, hier meist eklektischer Musiker ist, wurde offenkundig. Streckenweise weiss er zwar sprach-melodische Wendungen geschickt zu deklamieren und zu illustrieren; dennoch bleibt dar Ganze ein stilistisches Konglomerat, das für europäische Ohren nicht zu geniessen ist." ["It becomes obvious that the composer is a versatile, here mostly eclectic musician. At times he knows very well how to recite and illustrate speech-melodic turns skillfully; however, the whole thing remains a stylistic conglomerate which is not pleasant to the European ear."--H.B.] <u>See</u>: W7c

B7ll. Heinsheimer, Hans. "<u>Vanessa</u> Revisited." <u>Opera News</u> 42:22-25 (May 1978)
On the eve of the revival of <u>Vanessa</u> at the Spoleto USA, at Charleston, South Carolina, Samuel Barber talks with Hans Heinsheimer about the writing of the opera. <u>See</u>: W7i

B7mm. Helm, Everett. "Concerts and Opera: Munich and Salzburg Festivals." <u>Music Review</u> 19:323-327 (November 1958)
At Salzburg the European premiere of <u>Vanessa</u> was given

by the same group who presented it at the Metropolitan a few months earlier. Concerning <u>Vanessa</u> Mr. Helm remarks, "Barber's score carries out the implications inherent in the libretto. It is realistically conceived as a companion to the dramatic developments, which it underlines in its free arioso passages and in its set pieces, notable among which is the canonic quintet of the final scene. Barber's style might be described as neo-romantic in its aesthetics and technique. The composer is not an adherent of any musical school or direction but feels free, according to his own statements, to avail himself of whatever musical material suits his purpose. This <u>Vanessa</u> gives the impression of eclecticism, containing reminiscences of Puccini, Wagner, Strauss and the like. Typically Barber, however, is a certain lyric vein which sometimes has an almost folklike quality. His melodic gifts are considerable, as is evidenced in the highly singable lines, and the orchestration is effective without ever being obtrusive." <u>See</u>: W7a, W7c

B7nn. Helm, Everett. "<u>Vanessa</u> in Salzburg." <u>Saturday Review</u> 41:65-66 (September 13, 1958)
A lengthy appraisal of the whole aspect of the production of <u>Vanessa</u> at the Salzburg Festival. It was the first American opera, the first to be sung in English, the first time for a 'guest' appearance by an outside company...it was not a world premiere, but simply a European one. "<u>Vanessa</u> was judged by the European press not only for what it is but, indirectly, for what the critics thought it <u>ought to have been</u> in the light of their ideas about modern opera. This approach led the majority of them to concentrate on what they felt were negative features and to overlook the positive aspects of the work, which might have been given more consideration." <u>See</u>: W7c

B7oo. Hoelterhoff, Manuela. "Charleston Is Living Up to Its Billing." <u>Wall Street Journal</u>, May 31, 1978, p. 20.
General article on the Spoleto Festival USA. "Time more often than critics, separates the chaff from the good stuff, and Barber's <u>Vanessa</u> now 20 years old, came across as a superlative work." <u>See</u>: W7i

B7pp. Holde, Artur. "Grosse Premiere in der Met." <u>NZ</u>: <u>Neue Zeitschrift für Musik</u> 119:151-152 (March 1958)
"Chor und Orchester hatten das hohe Niveau, das jetzt die Regel an der Met ist. Samuel Barber hat die grosse Genugtuung, dass sein Werk nicht nur die Feuerprobe in New York bestanden hat, sondern auch für die Salzburger Festspiele...angenommen ist." ["Chorus and orchestra had the same high level as is now the rule at the Met. Samuel Barber received the great satisfaction that his work has not only passed the acid test in New York, but was also accepted for the Salzburg Festival..."--H.B.] <u>See</u>: W7a

B7qq. Hope-Wallace, Philip. "Opera." <u>Gramophone</u>

44:601 (May 1967)
   "<u>Vanessa</u>? Well, I daresay it will catch me, at a few
further hearings, though 'cold' it seemed the odd man out."
[RCA Victor SB 6700 (Great Britain)] <u>See</u>: D7c

   B7rr. Horowitz, Linda. "Literature Forum." <u>Choral</u>
<u>Journal</u> 21:26-29. (December 1980)
   "There can be no question that Barber has a way with
music and words. He has a gift for choosing exquisite
poetry and composing music that only further enhances it."
<u>See</u>: W7

   B7ss. Hull, Robin. "Broadcast Music." <u>Musical Times</u>
99:546 (October 1958)
   Broadcast of the Salzburg Festival (3d Programme),
with Mitropoulos conducting the Vienna Philharmonic. "The
irony of this misadventure lay in the fact that Barber
showed an extraordinary technical skill in his handling of
words, but this very merit merely gave an embarrassing
clarity to the deplorably banal text." <u>See</u>: W7c

   B7tt. "I. U. Opera Cast Sings <u>Vanessa</u> In Towering Set."
<u>Indianapolis Star</u>, March 3, 1975 (Located in NewsBank,
Review of the Arts [Microform], Performing Arts, 1975,
27:B7, fiche)
   Review of a performance on Saturday, March 1, 1975.
"It's a work of subtle changing moods, with stylistic
variations ranging from romantic arias Puccini might have
composed to a contemporary use of dissonance to increase
dramatic stress and effect. Undaunted by a towering monu-
mental 2-level set like the lobby of Grand Hotel, but
representing a baronial castle in Scandinavia, circa 1905,
the performance of the young artists, conducted by Tibor
Kozma was vivid and moving." <u>See</u>: W7h

   B7uu. Jacobson, Robert. "Reports" U. S.: Charleston,
S. C." <u>Opera News</u> 43:44 (August 1978)
   "...Barber's music sweeps all before it, obviating the
vagaries and making it all work with a treasure trove of
melody, deep feeling and nostalgia as he etches the characters with skill and makes the drama surge with incident and
climax. Barber's glorious orchestration, expressive and
filled with changing colors, was beautifully mirrored in
the conducting of Christopher Keene..." <u>See</u>: W7i

   B7vv. Johnson, David. "Classical." <u>High Fidelity</u> 8:55
(November 1958)
   <u>Vanessa</u> seems to me a failure--a heartbreaking
failure. I add 'heartbreaking' because Samuel Barber is a
composer of genius, because he brings to the score an
integrity that glows in every page, and because so many
have been yearning for a great American music drama...The
libretto accounts for a good deal of what is wrong with
this work, from the double standpoint of literary and
dramatic craftsmanship...Some of the vocal set pieces are

certainly impressive; the ensemble writing in the much praised quintet is too thick and shapeless for my taste, but the arias 'Must the Winter Come?' and 'For Every Love' are first-rate. It is the web of orchestral sound, however, that is most impressive of all. Barber is in complete command here, whether in unifying the tone of a whole scene or in brilliant bits of illustrative instrumentation...All this is so good that it makes the tentative and often downright amateurish handling of much of the 'recitative' the more painful. But the singing per se is far too good to be ignored, even in the most arid patches of vocal writing. Mitropoulos elicits from the Metropolitan Orchestra what is perhaps their most distinguished playing on records." [RCA Victor LM 6138]   See: D7a

B7ww. Johnson, David. "Classical." High Fidelity 8:51 (December 1958)
"The singing per se was one of the unequivocally good qualities of the opera, reviewed in its monophonic edition in these pages last month, although the vocal writing itself is sometimes open to question...The voices are not exactly bunched together but they do hover in a rather constricted area about the right channel. Not once in the recording did I detect a clear-cut instance of left-channel vocal activity...Actually Barber's best is to be found in his orchestral textures, and here a great deal of imagination has gone into the recording. A rich, spread-out effect is achieved, and the incisive sound Victor engineers have drawn from the oboes and clarinets is particularly admirable." [RCA Victor LSC 6138]   See: D7a

B7xx. Kolodin, Irving. "Barber, Menotti, and Vanessa." Saturday Review 41:41+ (January 25, 1958)
"But it is also pertinent to observe that the high point of the fourth act, and the score, is the quintet on the words, 'To leave, to break, to find, to keep,' which, in addition to being the best realized episode I know of in native opera lore, is also a skillful canon. The composer who wrote it should be proud of the accomplishment and heartened to go on from there." Kolodin concludes this long review of the premiere performance, "Taken together Vanessa moves the course of American opera ahead more than a little by showing us a composer with the skill and fantasy to absorb the attention through a full-length work in a frankly romantic tradition. It is no favor, of course, for it to be framed by the huge proscenium of the Metropolitan, which has a leveling effect on the best-founded ambitions. Let us hope that Barber begins his next opera on the peak of quality with which Vanessa ends, and goes on to sustain it throughout." See: W7a

B7yy. -----. "Barber's Vanessa and Menotti's." Saturday Review 41:53 (September 27, 1958)
"The distinction of musical levels in Vanessa is a special case for several reasons: the appalling banality of

some situations and scenes (which Menotti might have carried off blandly, but to which Barber succumbs blindly)
taxing to the composer's basic sincerity, and the eloquence
with which he touches the true individuals of the play...
Vanessa as sung by Eleanor Steber never sounds convincing
for the basic reason that Barber's music leaves her shadowy, unreal and--what is perhaps the worst of operatic
failings for a soprano--something of a shrew." [RCA Victor
LM 6138] See: D7a

B7zz. Kolodin, Irving. "Music to My Ears: Another View
of Vanessa. Saturday Review 48:22 (May 27, 1965)
    Concerning the revival of Vanessa, Kolodin presents
the problems and solutions of a new Vanessa and Anatol as
portrayed by Mary Costa and John Alexander. See: W7g

B7aaa. Kralik, Heinrich. "L'estate musicale all'estero:
Salisburgo." Musica d'Oggi, nuova serie, 1:505-506 (October 1958)
    Review of the August 16, 1958 Salzburg European pre-
miere. "Forse si tratta dell'istintiva avversione contro
il beato ottimismo e contro la cosciente ingenuità americana, manifeste in quest'opera, quell'istintiva avversione
contro un atteggiamento spirituale che cerca di rappresen-
tare anche le cose dell'arte come quelle della vita, con
praticità, communicativa, senso comune, comfort e spirito
borghese." ["What we are dealing with here is probably the
instinctive aversion against that happy optimism and ingenuity of Americans which are manifested in this work, and
also that instinctive aversion against a spiritual attitude
which aims to represent even artistic matters as if they
were part of life and that too with a colloquial and practical manner along with 'comfort' and the ethos of the
middle classes."--R.F.] See: W7c

B7bbb. Kullberg, Barbara L. "De Salzburger Festspiele
1958." Mens en melodie 13:309-312 (1958)
    Review of the Salzburg performance; text in Dutch.
See: W7c

B7ccc. Landry, Robert J. "Met Opera With Vanessa Makes
It Big Except In Diction Department." Variety 209:2
(January 22, 1958)
    "Sputnik fired by Russian rasputniks recently made
Americans look like nudniks but the latest question is
this: can the Russians get it up operatically? Can they
launch a new opera as good as Samuel Barber's Vanessa?
patriotic glow, but it was downright entertaining...Bar-
ber's symphonic musicianship is apparent in the score, his
maiden opera at age 47, and appreciation of his vocal
writing grows act by act. The musical climax comes in the
final act, a superbly beautiful, emotionally moving and
indeed quite glorious fine-voiced fugue. Seldom indeed
does an opera scene 'build and play' and crest inter-
personal feelings as does this 'farewell.'" See: W7a

B7ddd.   Landry,   Robert   J.   "Second-Guessing   Vanessa,
Can't Explain Menotti's Silence in Grand Opera."   Variety
213:2 (January 14, 1959)
     "Yet, Vanessa does not pall for all the dangling
details of its book. The score suggests durability. Nor
is melody lacking, overtures possibly excepted.   The work's
ultimate fate is going to be an interesting study. Since
the chi-chi fans that rallied to see and be seen at the
premiere a year ago were not in evidence last week, the
support must come from more sober-sided lovers of the muse.
One final thought: is there any law to prevent Menotti
taking back the book so that he can give the grandmother
back her tongue?   So many operas fall by the wayside,
forever blamed on the libretto! A little fixing might make
a whale of a difference."   See: W7

     B7eee.   Lang, Paul Henry.   "New American Opera Is Hailed
at the Met."   New York Herald Tribune, January 16, 1958.
     "Vanessa is a major contribution to the international
operatic repertory, even though as contributions to contemporary thought, Mr. Barbers musical ideas are less impressive.   They are varied, exceedingly skillful, and superbly
executed forms of what we have been hearing from Puccini
and Strauss to Sir William Walton, but always on Mr. Barber's own terms; he may be inspired by good examples but he
never borrows...Mr. Barber's mastery of the operatic language is remarkable and second to none now active on the
Salzburg-Milan axis.   This will be an eye-opener for Europeans reared on a diet of School for Wives, or The Moon.
His vocal writing is impeccable and his handling of the
orchestra virtuoso to a Straussian degree.   While the music
is at times a little eclectic, it is always interesting,
well made, beautifully polished, and effective, and there
are some very good tunes."   See: W7a

     B7fff.   Lanier, Thomas P.   "TV."   Opera News 43:8 (April
7, 1979)
     Review of the TV showing on PBS of the final perfor-
mance at the Spoleto USA Festival. "A one-to-one drama,
Vanessa seems made for the screen, and proved a beautifully
documented film of a glowing performance, with the characters' inner feelings superbly externalized and communi-
cated.   If there is any justice, this haunting, loving
performance should spur the major companies into restoring
Vanessa to its rightful place in the permanent repertory.
Barber's music provides an unleashing of lush, rich, varied
melody, which simultaneously conveys inner stirrings and
the outward expression that either embellishes them or
masks them behind a facade."   See: W7j

     B7ggg.   Lawrence, Robert.   "A Tosca at Last."   High
Fidelity/Musical America 15:113-114 (June 1965)
     "...one can find much to praise in Samuel Barber's
Vanessa...the ability to strike an atmospheric mood, the
perceptive setting of the words, and--as a signal achieve-

ment--the whole last scene of the opera, preceded by an intermezzo that has already made a place for itself in the concert hall. The disadvantages of <u>Vanessa</u> lie in its unremitting conservatism (much of the music in the first two acts suggests <u>Adriana Lecouvreur</u> without the tunes), its literal treatment of a libretto by Gian-Carlo Menotti out of the age of <u>Buddenbrooks</u>, and its preoccupation in general with the idea of the well-tailored opera. Only by the time he has reached the climactic quintet does the composer reveal a thoughtfulness, sinew, and flexibility that bode well for things to come..." <u>See</u>: W7

B7hhh. M., F. "Miracle on 39th Street." <u>Opera News</u> 22:15 (January 27, 1958)
A short article in which Dimitri Mitropolous discusses the music of <u>Vanessa</u>. <u>See</u>: W7

B7iii. McConnell, Hughes. "Spotlight on Spoleto." <u>Opera News</u> 26:29 (September 30, 1961)
Short discussion of the production at the Festival of Two Worlds, Spoleto, Italy, on June 15, 1961. <u>See</u>: W7e

B7jjj. Mann, William "Opera." <u>Gramophone</u> 55:1456 (February 1978)
"It was, quite shamelessly, calculated to appeal to an American audience that loved Grand Opera and hated modern music..." [RCA Red Seal RL 02094] <u>See</u>: D7a

B7kkk. Menotti, Gian-Carlo. "Mail Pouch: <u>Vanessa</u>." <u>New York Times</u>, February 15, 1959, sect. 2, p. 9.
In a letter to the <u>Times</u> Mr. Menotti notes: "It seems to me that the time has come to correct the erroneous impression given by many American reports on <u>Vanessa</u>'s debut in Europe that the opera was received adversely by <u>all</u> European critics...<u>Vanessa</u> was reviewed favorably-- often glowingly. Even when reserved, as some English critics were, no critic displayed the outrageous hostility of the Germans. Nevertheless the success of <u>Vanessa</u> with the international audience of Salzburg was as uncontested as with the American public in New York." <u>See</u>: W7

B7lll. Mercer, Ruby. "U.S.A." <u>Opera Canada</u> 19:28 (Fall 1978)
"<u>Vanessa</u>...was given a most sumptuous and impressive new production in Charleston...the production was fully worthy of the young and all-embracing international festival." <u>See</u>: W7i

B7mmm. "Met Star to Create Title Role in <u>Vanessa</u>." <u>New York Times</u>, December 6, 1957, p. 38.
News article announcing that Eleanor Steber will replace Sena Jurinac as the lead soprano in the world premiere of Samuel Barber's <u>Vanessa</u> at the Metropolitan on January 15, 1958. <u>See</u>: W7a

B7nnn. "'Met' to Visit Salzburg." New York Times, April 26, 1958, p. 14.
News article announcing that the Metropolitan production of Vanessa will be presented at the Salzburg Festival during the summer of 1958. "This is the first time since the Met visited Paris in 1910 that one of its productions has been given outside of North America." See: W7c

B7ooo. "Mr. S. Barber's Vanessa." Times (London), January 18, 1958, p. 36.
Short review by 'Our Special Correspondent' of the opening performance in New York City, who noted that "...Mr. Barber's musical ideas are varied and exceedingly skillful. If the music is at times a little eclectic, it is always interesting and well made and there are many good tunes...There is a magnificent quintet in the fourth act." See: W7a

B7ppp. Noble, Jeremy. "An English Critic in America." Opera (London) 10:214 (April 1959)
"Both the music and the libretto of Vanessa hark back wistfully, almost petulantly, to the years just before the First World War, and the immense skill of all concerned fails ultimately to conceal that it is a very good imitation of a romantic opera rather than the real thing. The plot seems to me to be a slightly off-beat women's-magazine story. Its exclusive concentration on romantic love (or is it merely sexual obsession?) gives it a curiously two-dimensional flatness compared with the genuine, if crude, depth of an opera like Ballo, and the music, for all that it contains nothing that would have shocked Strauss in 1912, only once or twice comes up with the tune, that it seems continually to promise." See: W7

B7qqq. O'Connor, John J. "WNET Gets Vanessa, 1958 Pulitzer Prize Opera." New York Times, January 31, 1979, sect. 3, p. 22.
"Vanessa is hardly 'grand opera,' but it has the stature of modern tragedy, somewhat in the manner of Eugene O'Neill or, perhaps more accurately, August Strindberg. And that stature is realized powerfully in this version. Mr. Barber's score has survived its first couple of decades with vigor. Ranging from lovely melodies ('Must the Winter Come So Soon') to charming dances ('Under the Willow Tree') to profoundly moving ensembles (the final scene), the music is alive and well and should be living in repertories in years to come." See: W7j

B7rrr. Olsen, William A. "Opera." New Records 26:10 (October 1958)
"Never does Barber fail in the climaxes and seldom in the interim. The almost 'leitmotif' approach to Act I grows in stature in each act until it shreds the emotions in the Quintet of Act IV, which can be referred to as nothing short of a work of genius. The English language

text has its awkward moments as has the English language
text for any piece of music including the National Anthem.
But the composer has held 'barbarity' to a minimum.   The
stage trappings are almost unnecessary because in the work
for the lyric theatre the librettist and the composer have
managed to paint the characters of people who are contemporary with any age!" [Victor LM 6138, LSC 6138] See: D7a

   B7sss. "Opera Reviews." Variety 291:90 (June 21, 1978)
   A short review of the revival production at Charleston, South Carolina as part of the Festival of Two Worlds--
U.S.A. The reviewer comments, "Restaged for this revival it
was an audience pleaser and as such may prompt other re-
vivals...Vanessa is a creditable production of one of the
best and melodious of contemporary operas." See: W7i

   B7ttt. Parmenter, Ross. "Horn Mute to go on Musical
Trip." New York Times, August 13, 1958, p. 24.
   "When Samuel Barber's Vanessa has its European
premiere...A Viennese trumpeter will use a mute that an
American trumpeter evolved after having heard a similar
mute employed by a folk trumpeter in Puerto Rico.   The
American responsible is Isidor Blank. See: W7c

   B7uuu. -----. "'Met' to present American Opera." New
York Times, November 6, 1956, p. 31.
   News article announcing that during the 1957-58 season
the Metropolitan Opera will present the first full length
opera by an American composer since Howard Hansen's Merry
Mount was presented in February, 1934. It was also announced that negotiations are under way to secure Maria Callas
for the title role." See: W7a

   B7vvv. Porter, Andrew. "Musical Events: Spoleto of the
South." New Yorker 54:66-68 (June 19, 1978)
   "The star of the evening was Katherine Ciesinski, as
Erika. Wide-eyed, with a clear, open brow and a clear,
firm voice. Miss Ciesinski is the latest in the line of
admirable young mezzos from whom much can be expected. She
was both an eloquent, touching, credible actress and an
excellent singer. Barber's music is a weak syrup apparently
brewed from Cilea, Giordano, Tchaikovsky, and Richard
Strauss. It flows along agreeably enough, pausing now and
again to crystallize around an aria, a duet, or an ensemble. Menotti staged the opera as if he had lost any
confidence in his collaborator's ability." [Also reprinted
in: Music of Three More Seasons, 1977-1980. New York:
Knopf, 1981, p. 195-200] See: W7i

   B7www. -----. "Summer Festivals: 4." Opera (London)
9:621-3 (October 1958)
   "Vanessa is old-fashioned; it breaks no new ground; it
was roughly handled by the Austrian and German critics. It
does contain, however, many attractive and well-worked
pieces of music that one could grow fond of. Much of it is

built on motive phrases, piled in sequences, and there is a 'hit' quintet at the close." See: W7c

B7xxx. Reisfeld, Bert. "Samuel Barber: _Vanessa_." _Mus-ica_ 12:218-219 (April 1958)
    "Wir atmen befreit auf, denn die Zusammenarbeit Bar-ber-Menotti hat bewiesen, dass es einen modernen Opernstil gibt, dass die Oper nicht, wie in Amerika vielfach be-hauptet, dem Untergang geweiht ist und dass es möglich ist, Werke zu verfassen, die über den sonst üblichen Achtungser-folg hinaus zum Publikumserfolg der Oper 'Vanessa' in der New Yorker 'Met' wird sich wahrscheinlich in Europa wieder-holen." ["We breathe easier now, because the Barber-Menot-ti partnership has proved that there is a modern style of opera, that the opera is not doomed (as is always claimed in the United States), and that it is possible to compose works that win not only critical acclaim as often happens--but also popular success. The success of _Vanessa_ at the New York Met will perhaps be repeated in Europe."--R.F.] See: W7a

B7yyy. Resnik, Regina. "A New Role in a World Pre-miere." _Music and Musicians_ 6:18+ (March 1958)
    "_Vanessa_ really is an opera--both orchestrally and vocally. Although produced today, _Vanessa_ has been done in the 'grand manner' of opera. The sets by Cecil Beaton are a masterpiece, the costumes are magnificent and opulent. There is an open chorus, and a full-scale ball scene, wedding the elements of music and dance in the full tradi-tional pageantry of opera. The demands on the singers are of 'larger-than-life' dimensions, and the acting demands are equal to those in the theatre. Samuel Barber has written the music with emotion, and has not been afraid to write in a romantic vein. Yet the romantic tone expresses itself in a contemporary musical medium--the modern. There is something for every segment of an audience in the work." See: W7a

B7zzz. Rhein, John Von. "Spoleto--the South Has Risen Again." _Chicago Tribune_, May 29, 1978, sect. 5, p. 5.
    Review of the Charleston premiere. "Some may argue that Barber spreads an almost suffocating blanket of dark passion over Menotti's slender melodrama. Others will find its heaviness absolutely appropriate for the subject. In any case, 'Vanessa' is no dumber than a lot of Romantic works that have found their way into the repertory, and its great surges of melody head straight for the emotions of the audience." See: W7i

B7aaaa. "Samuel Barber's First Opera." _Times_ (London), January 15, 1958, p. 3.
    News article with an illustration of the set of _Vanes-sa_ and a portrait of Samuel Barber. The cast of the opera is given and also a brief summary of Mr. Barbers composi-tional career. See: W7a

B7bbbb. Sargeant, Winthrop. "Musical Events." New Yorker 33:100+ (January 25, 1958)

"The groping of the first act could now be seen in retrospect for what it was--a not too successful effort by a highly intelligent composer to cope with the challenge of opera in the grand manner, or, in other words to write music that is at once original, compelling, and intellectually absorbing--and as the opera proceeded it was quite thrilling to find Mr. Barber conquering his initial difficulties and emerging as a real master of the operatic tradition...a deeply moving, magical, and many-sided evocation of human conflicts and emotions that is capable of holding a respectable place beside the great operatic masterpieces of the past." See: W7

B7cccc. -----. "Musical Events." New Yorker 41:174 (March 20, 1965)

"The music, which improves on rehearing, is unlike that of most contemporary American opera based on the great German tradition that reached its peak in Richard Strauss. It is the 'grandest' of all American operas so far, as well as the product of expert and experienced operatic minds." See: W7g

B7dddd. Schloss, Edwin H. "American Opera Is Met Offering: Native Work Has Star Cast." Inquirer (Philadelphia), February 9, 1958, p. 2D+

Feature written in anticipation of the February 11, 1958 Philadelphia premiere, with the original Metropolitan cast. See: W7b

B7eeee. Schonberg, Harold C. "New Vanessa Heard." New York Times, February 17, 1958, sect. 2, p. 19."

"A new Vanessa was seen in the opera of the same name Saturday evening at the Metropolitan Opera. She was Brenda Lewis, who had sung the role in Philadelphia but never in New York. A fine actress, Miss Lewis moved gracefully through the part. Vocally her work was variable...In the third act, where she was at her best in the duet with Anatol, her singing was sensitive, and sometimes the words of the music could almost be understood."

B7ffff. Simek, Julius Frank. "Opera at the Metropolitan: Vanessa." Musical America 79:22 (January 15, 1959)

"Although, during four long acts one was often tempted to lose complete interest in the characters and their utterances, one had ample opportunity to observe, and occasionally admire, the vocal and histrionic skills with which the singers take care of their parts." See: W7a

B7gggg. Stoddard, Hope. "Good Opera--Good Theater." International Musician 56:36 (March 1958)

Review of the premiere, "...a splendidly unified work. From the very first outpourings of the orchestra, the mood of the opera was set, and this mood was sustained...The audience tried to respect the request printed in the program notes, not to 'interrupt the music with applause.' However, the 'Willow Tree' was given a deserved tribute and the quintet brought down the curtain with cheers." <u>See</u>: W7a

B7hhhh. Storer, William Allen. "Charleston." <u>Opera</u> (London) 29:116-118 (Autumn 1978) [Festival Issue]
"<u>Vanessa</u> remains a curiosity. At times its mood music is superb, quite haunting. One would have expected its librettist to reveal fully the period drama in all its Victorian glory, but in his other role as producer, Menotti did not correct the error of his authorship, expressed in the opera's title. Vanessa is a subsidiary character. Erica, her niece dominates each act, beginning or ending each scene. Vanessa is merely an intruder in her life, and calling the opera by her name is much like giving <u>Medea</u> the title of <u>Jason</u>. Fortunately for the production, the Erica of Katherine Ciesinski was dignified, and always richly evocative of the character's suppressed emotions. Johanna Meier, in the title role, revealed the doubts, fears and joys of a woman past her prime, yet finding she is loved, with commanding ease. Henry Price was suitably befuddled as a foil for both women. Christopher Keene, music director of the festival, conducted for the television cameras, and was roundly cheered by the audience." <u>See</u>: W7i

B7iiii. Taubman, Howard. "Music: <u>Vanessa</u> Returns." <u>New York Times</u>, January 8, 1959, p. 26.
"Upon reacquaintance this score makes essentially the impression it left last year. The composer takes some time to arrive at an individual stylistic fusion...But the good things begin to appear after the opening act. There are places where the music builds a nostalgic atmosphere with grace and color, and some of the climactic passages have eloquence." <u>See</u>: W7d

B7jjjj. -----. "Opera: World Premiere." <u>New York Times</u>, January 16, 1958, p. 33.
"...<u>Vanessa</u>, which had its premiere last night, turns out to be the best American opera ever presented at the stately theatre on Broadway and Thirty-Ninth Street. It need not be claimed that <u>Vanessa</u> is a masterpiece...But the new piece is a collaboration of two gifted men--Samuel Barber, who wrote the music, and his close friend, Gian-Carlo Menotti, who provided the libretto. It is professional; it has atmosphere; it builds to a moving climax...Mr. Barber's musical style began years ago with a commitment to romanticism but has shifted under the impact of contemporary trends. In <u>Vanessa</u> there is considerable eclecticism. Diverse influences from Wagner to Puccini to Strauss are reflected, but the music takes on firmer individuality as it proceeds until at least it generates a touching and brooding power...The gala audience behaved as if it found <u>Vanessa</u> not only an event but a pleasure." <u>See</u>: W7a

B7kkkk. Taubman, Howard. "Vanessa Again." New York Times, January 18, 1959, sect. 2, p. 9.

"Upon reseeing Vanessa this column feels that American praise for the opera was not out of balance. It believes strongly that the violence of the European reaction was excessive. Can it be that criticism abroad did not mete out to Vanessa the even-handed justice it would bring to opera by contemporary Europeans? It can be. You have but to consider the quality of some of the European pieces that are hailed with pleasure to realize that a severer standard is brought to bear on the judgement of an American opera. It is as if some Europeans resented our achievement in a area that has been a European province." See: W7d

B7llll. -----. "Vanessa at 'Met'." New York Times, January 26, 1958, sect. 2, p. 9.

"In essence Vanessa is a late nineteenth century work...There is nothing wrong with old-fashioned orientations. An opera of this nature is particularly fitting in the subdued Victorian splendor of the Metropolitan...At the outset Mr. Barber's musical texture has inconsistency. He writes as if his instincts and intellect were at odds. The orchestra is always effective but the vocal line fails to express character. Slowly and surely he finds unity of style. He still miscalculates. Musical ingenuity takes the place of honest feeling...In the third-act duet between Vanessa and her fortune-hunting young admirer, Anatol, the soprano and tenor have some rousing high notes. But the effect is cold. The fourth and final act is a moving achievement. It sings without self-consciousness...and the concluding scene contains a deeply touching quintet expressing the sorrow of parting which shows Mr. Barber at the height of his powers and which would adorn any opera...You may have heard a lot of nonsense about the inadequacy of English for opera. Where Mr. Barber's musical line gives the singer a chance, they enunciate clearly, and where his music reaches deeply, English is a fine and satisfying vehicle for opera...Go see and hear it--it will not bore you and will end by moving you." See: W7a

B7mmmm. "The Test of Vanessa. New York Times, May 21, 1958, p. 32 [editorial]

"And of most interest will be the European reception of the Barber score. Will the audiences hold still, as New York audiences learned to do, while(as critics here observed) the composer began to write operatically, rather than symphonically; until, with the quintet in the last act, he has mastered the, to him, novel craft? This summer will give the answers." See: W7a

B7nnnn. Thomas, Ernst. "Salzburg--italienisch und amerikanisch." NZ: Neue Zeitschrift fur Musik 119:589-591 (October 1958)

Review of the Salzburg performance, "Man wiederholt quasi die Uraufführung für Europa, was insofern seinen Reiz

haben mag, als mehr als ein Jahrzehnt vergangen war, bevor
die Metropolitan Opera wieder eine amerikanische Oper ange-
nommen hatte. Denn amerikanisch ist dieses Werk trotz
seines europäischen Milieus und seiner europäischen Vor-
fahren." ["The premiere was more or less repeated for
Europe, which has a certain interest in that more than a
decade had passed before the Metropolitan Opera accepted
another American opera. For despite its European setting
and its European models, this work is truly American."--
R.F.] See: W7c

B7oooo. Thornton, H. Frank. "Opera." New Records
45:11 (May 1977)
"Certainly it is well crafted by an accomplished composer, and the cast of this recording, the same as at the
premiere, presents it as well as could be imagined." [Vic-
tor ARL 2 2094] See: D7a

B7pppp. Thorpe, Day. "Washington, D. C. Barber and the
Bells." Musical America 83:268-270 (December 1963)
"The great achievement of Barber and Menotti is the
creation of a wildly controversial work that is not the
slightest avant-garde: this is genius." See: W7

B7qqqq. Trimble, Lester. "Music." Nation 186:106
(February 1, 1958)
Review of the premiere performance. "It lives; it
moves; its characters and its scenes are credible, emotionally interesting, and memorable. Dramatically, then,
Vanessa is more than extremely effective: it is engrossing
enough to make the almost three and a half hours of its
progress seem brief--briefer than most repertory operas of
lesser duration. What therefore, are my reservations?
Just these: I regret that Barber, despite the tastefulness
and the meticulous professional polish of his music, was
not able to present it in an individual personality. He
avoided every cliché and vulgarism to which a composer
with a conservative, eclectic idiom is laid open. But, on
the other hand, he did not present recognizable personal
style. Every measure of the music had a smooth, urbane
gloss, but beneath the surface fumed the dynamism of other
composers. Eleanor Steber, as Vanessa, was a veritable,
heaving dynamo, and other members of the cast...were every
inch up to her in quality. Dimitri Mitropoulos conducted
and, as he loves to do with a new score, dug deeply into it
and sent fireworks shooting high." See: W7a

B7rrrr. Turner, Robert. "Five American Operas." Canadian Music Journal 4:44+ (Winter 1960)
"There are not many American works that surpass this
opera in the mastery and luminosity of its orchestration...his artistic creed is aptly summarized at one point
in Vanessa by Anatol and Erika: A: 'What a sentimental
child you are! You belong to another age.' E: 'Has the
human heart so changed.'" See: W7

B7ssss. "2 Noted Singers Signed by 'Met'." New York Times, March 23, 1957, p. 16.
      News article reporting that Sena Jurinac and Nicolai Gedda have been signed for the 1957-58 season at the 'Met' and both will sing in the premiere performance of Samuel Barber's Vanessa in January, 1958. See: W7a

B7tttt. "Vanessa." Opera News 22:16-19 (January 27, 1958.
      Summary of the plot of Vanessa with excellent photographs of the six principal characters. See: W7a

B7uuuu. "Vanessa." Opera News 29:facing 16 (April 3, 1965)
      Insert with a page of the Barber manuscript for Vanessa, followed by the plot summary and three pages of photographs from the current production. See: W7g

B7vvvv. "Vanessa Criticized." New York Times, August 19, 1958, p. 23.
      Short news article reporting criticism of Vanessa by two Vienna newspapers. "The artist involved won praise, particularly Dimitri Mitropoulos, conductor, but as the critic of Neuer Kurier put it: 'We have seldom heard so fine a musician conduct such poor music.' Neuer Kurier's critic described Mr. Barber as a 'collector and publisher of a musical anthology'...The critic of The Express said the opera 'is enough to make one cry...the book is simply disgusting.'" See: W7c

B7wwww. "Vanessa Debut Given in Europe." New York Times, August 17, 1958, sect. 1, p. 71.
      News article concerning the premiere of Vanessa at the Salzburg Festival. "Music critics from all parts of the world were on hand for the opening...Many were surprised that the much advertised 'modern' opera should contain so much conservative music.   Some murmured that there were borrowings from Puccini, Gluck, Richard Strauss and others. But much admiration was expressed at the instrumentation of the modern passages and the use of a variety of rhythms." See: W7c

B7xxxx. "Vanessa Makes Ready." Opera News 22:10-11 (January 27, 1958)
      Two pages of pictures showing Vanessa in preparation. See: W7a

B7yyyy. "Vanessa Sung in Italy." New York Times, June 17, 1961, p. 12.
      News article hailing the Italian premiere of Barber's Vanessa at the fourth Festival of Two Worlds at Spoleto. "The opera was given before an international audience in the Teatro Nuovo of this ancient walled city. It was conducted by Werner Torkanowsky of New York. The opera had a cast of young Italian singers. In the audience were Mr.

Barber and Thomas Schippers, musical director of the festival." See: W7e

B7zzzz. "Violets in the Snow." Opera News 22:20-21
(January 27, 1958)
A description of the sets and costumes used in Vanessa. Included are some comments by Cecil Beaton who designed the production: "I've tried to capture the evanes-
cent elusive atmosphere of the opera...which is mysterious
and non-specific. You might call the period Edwardian
gothic." See: W7a

B7aaaaa. Walldrop, Gid W. "New York Concert and Opera
Beat." Musical Courier 157:10 (February 1958)
We have only praise for Barber's musical content, for
his lyrical vocal writing, and for his brilliant orchestration...All in all, however, Vanessa is one of the best
operas of our century and is certainly superior to most
contemporary European operas of today. In the Grand Opera
tradition, it will no doubt be an eye-opener to European
audiences. The music is not startling, nor is it very
contemporary. In a sense, this is an advantage, for certainly it is singable and can be assimilated immediately."
See: W7a

B7bbbbb. Weaver, William "Spoleto." Opera (London)
12:43 (Autumn 1961) [Special Festival Number]
The Italian public is notoriously inhospitable to
foreign operas, and especially to modern foreign opera, and
Vanessa was given much the same sort of reception that a
few weeks before, Britten's Midsummer Nights' Dream had
received at La Scala: polite audiences, respectable
reviews...It was almost impossible to believe that two
ladies like Vanessa and Erika could have so thoroughly lost
their heads over this clumsy young man [Anatol, sung by
Alvino Misciano]" See: W7e

B7ccccc. Williams, Rodney H. "Your HiFi Concert."
HiFi Review 2:57 (January 1959)
"With repeated hearings the musico-logic becomes more
and more evident, and reveals Mr. Barber's splendidly conceived craftsmanship. The musical form of Vanessa is
four-square, with no unsupported off-shoots left dangling
to weaken its structure. The opening harmonic pattern with
its descending line immediately following is repeated at
the beginning and end of Act IV, and serves as a motive in
much the same manner as the opening chords of Tosca are
always associated with Scarpia...Curious is the opera's
conclusion, with the music's texture thinning, becoming
pallid and at the very end dissipating into--what? It left
this reviewer with a strong impression of emotional irres-
olution in much the same style that Puccini ends Madame
Butterfly with an unresolved harmonic chord suggesting
perhaps an unfinished tale." See: W7

B8. VANESSA. DO NOT UTTER A WORD.

B8a. Osborne, Conrad L. "Recitals and Miscellany." High Fidelity 16:113 (December 1966)
"Detached from its theatrical ambience, Vanessa's monologue [Do Not Utter a Word] can be heard as a rather good piece of craftsmanship, and though it is demanding, Miss Price does better with it than anyone else we've heard in the part." [RCA Victor LM 2898, LSC 2898] See: D8b

B8b. Simmons, Walter. "Collections." Fanfare 7:293-294 (March/April 1984)
"In a sense, Barber is the musical father of the genre, and much of the music on this disc reveals kinship--if not debt--to him, in one way or another. It is appropriate that his characteristic gothic romanticism is represented by an excerpt from Vanessa, a marvelous work that brought the composer a Pulitzer Prize in 1958." [Eb-Sko Production EB-SKO 1007] See: D8a

B8c. Strongin, Theodore. "No Dazzle for Dazzle's Sake." New York Times, December 4, 1966, sect. 2, p. 34.
"The Vanessa excerpt alone is worth the whole album. It also calls for the orchestra (the RCA Italiana Opera Orchestra led by Francesco Molinari-Pradelli) to be busier. The orchestra becomes an equal instead of the obsequious servant it is elsewhere in the album." [RCA Victor LM 2898, LSC 2898] See: D8b

B9. VANESSA. INTERMEZZO.

B9a. Frankenstein, Alfred. "Classical." High Fidelity 9:61 (April 1959)
"The Barber Intermezzo is a pleasant whiff from Vanessa's boudoir." [Columbia ML 5347, MS 6040] See: D9b

B9b. Miller, David H. "Record Reviews." American Record Guide 25:728 (June 1959)
"Most penetrating, both as to performance and as music, is the Barber. This is skillful dramatic writing, and it holds together very well out of context." [Columbia ML 5347] See: D9b

B9c. "Score by Barber Heard." New York Times, March 17, 1958, p. 21.
The Intermezzo had its first New York concert performance on Saturday evening, March 15, 1958 in a Carnegie Hall concert by the New York Philharmonic with André Kostelanetz conducting. See: W9a

CHORAL MUSIC

B14. AGNUS DEI.

B14a. Dickinson, Peter. "Music Reviews: Americans." _Musical Times_ 122:834 (December 1981)
In a brief review of Schirmer's edition of the _Complete Choral Music_, it is noted that it included "...the inevitable _Adagio_ for strings (he transcribed it as an _Agnus Dei_ for chorus in 1967)..." [but cf. transcription date in B14b below] _See_: W14

B14b. Horowitz, Linda. "Literature Forum." _Choral Journal_ 21:26-29 (December 1980)
Agnus Dei is Barber's 1939 transcription for chorus of his successful and lovely _Adagio for Strings_, op. 11. [but cf. transcription date in B14a above] _See_: W14

B15. EASTER CHORALE.

B15a. Horowitz, Linda. "Literature Forum." _Choral Journal_ 21:26-29 (December 1980)
"For this work Barber has chosen a poem by Pack Browning that tells of the rebirth of Spring, a poetic analogy to the resurrection of Jesus Christ." _See_: W15

B18. LET DOWN THE BARS, O DEATH, OP. 8, NO. 2.

B18a. Anderson, W. R. "New Music: Choral." _Musical Times_ 91:31 (January 1950)
"...a very short piece in which Samuel Barber sets a poem by Emily Dickinson, that strange, powerful, tragic character. This _Let Down the Bars, O Death_, contains but thirty bars of unaccompanied S.A.T.B. music, swiftly impressive in the modern way, which is that of the sudden key-lift." _See_: W18

B18b. Horowitz, Linda. "Literature Forum." _Choral Journal_ 21:26-29 (December 1980)
"In Opus 8, No. 2, composed in 1936, Barber used a text by the poet Emily Dickinson...Though the notes and rhythms provide few difficulties, this is not an easy piece. Finding the correct tempos for the various moods, developing superb diction, and creating the intense legato necessary for this work are the tasks facing the conductor and choir." _See_: W18

B18c. Waters, Edward N. "Music." _Quarterly Journal of Current Acquisitions_ [of the Library of Congress] 18:15 (November 1960)
"The second work is the autograph of _Let Down the Bars, O Death_, for mixed voices, unaccompanied, also com-

posed in 1936. The words are taken from Emily Dickinson.
On this manuscript the composer wrote quotations from Rilke
and Melville, and also the sketch of a melody.   As a
matter of fact, there are two musical sketches, the second
being for unaccompanied chorus with these words: "The Sky-
like girl whom we knew." <u>See</u>: W18

B19.   THE LOVERS, OP. 43.

B19a. "Bank Commissions Samuel Barber Work." <u>Bulletin</u>
(Philadelphia), January 18, 1971.
    Note that Philadelphia's Girard Bank commissioned <u>The</u>
<u>Lovers</u>. Barber "...described the Girard commissioning as
one of his most challenging but stimulating undertakings."
<u>See</u>: W19a

B19b.   Derhen, Andrew. "Debuts & Reappearances." <u>High</u>
<u>Fidelity/Musical America</u> 22:MA 23 (January 1972)
    "<u>The Lovers</u> leans on any number of earlier Barber
works without measuring up to its predecessors or achieving
stylistic solidarity. On the other hand; those who admire
such familiar Barber virtues as good taste, considerate
vocal writing, and transparent orchestration (watery is
often a better description) may find <u>The Lovers</u> agreeable
enough. Ormandy [conducting the Philadelphia Orchestra]
led a rather cautious-sounding, if effective, performance;
Tom Krause projected the baritone part sonorously; and the
Temple University Choirs once more demonstrated the ease
with which they can handle difficult modern assignments."
<u>See</u>: W19a

B19c.   Gruen, John.   "And Where Has Samuel Barber
Been...?" <u>New York Times</u>, October 3, 1971, sect. 2, p. 15,
21, 30.
    Barber remarks, "I was fascinated by the <u>Twenty Poems</u>
<u>of Love and a Song of Sadness</u> by Pablo Neruda...I was
inspired by them and wanted to set a number of them to
music...the poems themselves are extremely erotic and some
of the Girard board members [the work was commissioned by
the Girard Bank of Philadelphia] raised their eyebrows.
Finally, I asked the board whether they didn't have love
affairs in Philadelphia, and learned that they did...At any
rate the bank was very nice about it all, and gave me
complete freedom." <u>See</u>: W19a

B19d.   Horowitz, Linda. "Literature Forum." <u>Choral</u>
<u>Journal</u> 21:26-29 (December 1980)
    "More than in any other work up to this point, Barber
has drawn upon the passion within his musical soul to
skillfully wed the text to the musical setting." <u>See</u>: W19

B19e. Kolodin, Irving. "Music to My Ears: Barber's <u>The</u>
<u>Lovers</u>..." <u>Saturday Review</u> 54:14-15 (October 23, 1971)
    "Samuel Barber's <u>The Lovers</u>, an extended setting of

texts by the Chilean poet Pablo Neruda for solo baritone, chorus, and orchestra...left no doubt at all that Barber has retained the impulse, his craftsmanship, and his artistic balance...His involvement with Neruda's celebrations of erotic love...is replete with lovely sounds, artful exploitation of a motival element, and finely shaded orchestral colorations. Where it lacks however, is in the precious category of individuality...the chorus sang its several sections exquisitely, but Tom Krause's dry voice and unengaging manner did not, for my taste, validate his choice for three prominent solos assigned to the baritone." See: W19a

B19f. "Philadelphia: Orchestra and Bank Combine To Make Music." New York Times, January 24, 1971, sect. 3, p. 15.
Announcement that the Girard Bank of Philadelphia was commissioning Samuel Barber to compose a work which would have its world premiere at the opening performance of the 1971-72 season of the Philadelphia Orchestra; Eugene Ormandy, conductor. The work, entitled, The Lovers is based on love poems written by Pablo Neruda, the internationally known Chilean poet, in 1924. See: W19a

B19g. "Philadelphians Hail Return of Ormandy and Premiere." New York Times, September 24, 1971, p. 36.
The 73rd season of the Philadelphia Orchestra opened September 22, 1971 with Eugene Ormandy conducting the world premiere of The Lovers. "Based on the love poems of Chile's laureate, Pablo Neruda, the Barber work won the adulation of a full house at the Academy of Music." See: W19a

B19h. Schonberg, Harold C. "Emphasis is on the Voice in Philadelphia's Concert." New York Times, October 7, 1971, p. 56.
The Lovers "...is a score that will help re-establish Mr. Barber's reputation as America's most important lyricist. As expected, the writing is conservative--conservative even for Mr. Barber. But the idiom is by no means exhausted, and in The Lovers Mr. Barber has composed a work that has a distinctive profile. This composer has always been happy writing introspective music for the voice...The thing that impresses about The Lovers is its naturalness. Here Mr. Barber is not forcing his talent, and he is at his very best. The work was enthusiastically received and the composer was present to take his bows. The performance was elegant. Mr. Krause is a fine artist with a commanding voice, and the Temple University Choirs are one of the country's better-trained, fresh-sounding groups." See: W19c

B19i. Turok, Paul. "The Journal Reviews: Alice Tully Hall" Music Journal 30:75 (January 1972)
"Samuel Barber's suave, sentimental musical style just can't cope with the flaming challenge of Pablo Neruda's

vibrant love poetry...The text, in sheer number of words, is enormous and the work--although elegantly proportioned-- is therefore committed to a somewhat exclamatory style. Barber, within the limits of his own style, is an excellent craftsman, and it seems to me that he relied too heavily on his craft to pull him through this work. Always tasteful, though sometimes painfully obvious and cute, it is not the sort of music one longs to hear again." See: W19c

B20. PRAYERS OF KIERKEGAARD, OP. 30.

B20a. Broder, Nathan. "Current Chronicle: New York." Musical Quarterly 41:227-228 (April 1955)
"The work, which lasts for about 18 minutes, opens with an unaccompanied male chorus singing a Gregorian-like chant in the Dorian mode, and continues with the full chorus and orchestra in writing that is now chordal, now contrapuntal, and a prayer by the soprano solo followed by soft, rich chords in the chorus. Then begins a long development, involving first a solo tenor and alto, and growing in intensity until double chorus and full orchestra unite in a powerful climax. The orchestra carries on alone in more and more frenzied mood, with ejaculations by the chorus, and then dies down. A triple chorus now intones, softly and antiphonally, 'Father in Heaven,' and then all singers and players join in a broad, fervent chorale, which brings the work to an end." See: W20

B20b. Daily, William Albert. Techniques of Composition Used in Contemporary Works for Chorus and Orchestra on Religious Text... Thesis (Ph.D.)--The Catholic University of America, 1965. 334 p. Their Studies in Music, no. 23.
"His flowing lyricism, his ebullient expressiveness, his strong tonal foundation, and his brilliant sense of orchestration are all evident in this work...His harmonics become more dissonant, his lines more chromatic, and he grew toward contact with some of the practices of the twelve-tone school." [p. 310] See: W20

B20c. Downes, Olin. "Munch Conducts Work by Barber." New York Times, December 9, 1954, p. 40.
"The first performance in New York of Samuel Barber's Prayers of Kierkegaard, a work of imposing dimensions and grand and severe line was given last night at Carnegie Hall by the Boston Symphony Orchestra, Charles Munch conducting, with the Schola Cantorum (director Hugh Ross) and Leontyne Price, Mary McMurray and Earl Ringland as solo singers...It is not one to be jauntily commended for its obvious effectiveness and the technical mastery with which it is written, or condescendingly dismissed after a single hearing...The unrhythmical and free-metered recitation in carefully shaped recitative has the flavor of the plain chant, reshaped, freely recast in forms of our own modern con-

sciousness. Sometimes the music becomes nearly barbaric, and intensely dramatic in its effect. Polytonality is used freely, logically, with distinction." See: W20b

B20d. Durgin, Cyrus. "Boston Winter Season Busy for Composers and Artists." Musical America 75:14 (January 1, 1955)
Review of the December 3-4, 1954 Boston performances, Symphony Hall, Boston Symphony Orchestra, Charles Münch, conductor; soloists: Leontyne Price, Jean Kraft, and Edward Munro; Cecilia Society [chorus], prepared by Hugh Ross. "It is...music not alone of structure and logic, but deeply felt and very moving in effect. It is one of the best productions to have come out of a Koussevitsky Music Foundation commission and deserves to be repeated until it is familiar." See: W20a

B20e. Eyer, Ronald. "Prayers of Kierkegaard Set by Samuel Barber." Musical America 75:17 (January 1, 1955)
Review of the December 8, 1954 Carnegie Hall performance. "The writing is free and wide-ranging in style; there is modal and classical harmony as well as atonality; the construction is tight and always meaningful, and there is no want of dynamic coloration, either chorally or orchestrally. As a musical work, it has undeniable power and persuasion, but one may hesitate to espouse it as a true evocation of the thoughts of Kierkegaard." See: W20b

B20f. G.-F., C. "In My Opinion: The London Concert World." Musical Opinion 78:647-648 (August 1955)
Review of the June 10, 1955 London performance. "...the surging sonorities, lavish use of percussion and frequent recourse to aggressive dissonance...are entirely at variance with the spirit of the Prayers and leave an impression of misdirected effort." See: W20c

B20g. H., W. C. "The New York Concert and Opera Beat." Musical Courier 151:13 (January 1, 1955)
"The piece is an extremely interesting example of Barber's music. The chorale writing is finely delineated and the orchestral part is full of climactic effects. The work begins in a rather quiet and reserved manner, but in the middle builds up to some big climaxes, and ends with (of all things!) a concerted chorale à la baroque cantata...Barber has again proven himself one or our ablest composers." See: W20b

B20h. Hall, David. "Classical Discs and Tapes." Stereo Review 42:94 (January 1979)
"At long last we have a recording, and it has been well worth the wait. Kierkegaard's deeply moving text is first heard in a quasi-Gregorian melody intoned by the male choir, and out of this grows a musical structure that is majestic, intensely lyrical, and, at its climactic point, highly dramatic. This is prime Barber at his neo-

Romantic best--not overwhelming, perhaps, on first hearing, but the work will grow in impact upon repetition. The Louisville forces do well by Barber's score, most especially the chorus, whose singing carries enormous conviction and whose diction is decidedly better than average." [Louisville LS 763] See: D20a

B20i. Henahan, Donal. "Concert: Barber's Kierkegaard Offered by Brooklyn Ensemble." New York Times, March 20, 1981, sect. C, p. 18.

"The Prayers of Kierkegaard may at first strike the 1981 listener as somewhat modish Existentialism--or rather, chat about existentialism--was very much in the air back in the 50's when Mr. Barber chose his text. But the music does not suggest anything faddish or superficial. The composer plainly found a great deal with which to connect in Kierkegaard's dour message. But music is music, not philosophy, and the Barber brand of lyricism ends up infecting the whole work. It is hard to remain cheerless when such a master of the vocal craft is blending vagrant strands of tone into mellifluous wholes. Not that this score is essentially one long sweet trip; in fact, the dominant mood is dark, and the sense of individual solitude and struggle that Existentialists believe is at the core of life came through powerfully...The performance...was strong enough to show the work in a good light, despite some roughness of choral tone and raggedness of instrumental ensemble...'The Prayers of Kierkegaard' does not deserve to be left on the shelf when so many far less attractive scores are making the concert rounds every year." [Note: This article later appeared in the American Choral Review 24:15-16 (October 1982] See: W20h

B20j. Horowitz, Linda. "Literature Forum." Choral Journal 21:26-29 (December 1980)

"The text...alternates between two principal ideas; the first thought deals with the infinite, everlasting, and unchangeable mercy of God, while the second idea stresses the desire of people to be forgiven for their sins and redeemed." See: W20

B20k. "Kierkegaard Cantata." Times (London), June 11, 1955, p. 5.

"Barber's cantata is a short work in four sections concerned with immutability, suffering, longing, and salvation. Though the music is continuous, it lacks unity. The choral writing is bold and the orchestral[sic] elaborate. There is a bite in it which accords with the Danish theologian's austere piety, though austerity does not entail economy. It had a certain stark impressiveness and sounds a new note in modern choral music, as might be expected from tapping a new source of religious texts for music." See: W20c

B201. Kolodin, Irving. "Barber on Kierkegaard, Stiedry on Mozart." Saturday Review 37:23 (December 25, 1954)
In his review, Mr. Kolodin remarks, "To be sure, discrimination in the choice of texts is only the beginning of musical virtue, but Barber has validated his choice by laying out a libretto (using the term in its broadest sense) consecutive in mood and cumulative in impact, and providing for it a musical texture of real distinction. He was fortunate in his interpreters, especially in the eloquence and discipline of Leontyne Price's singing of the soprano's music, the excellent work of the Schola Cantorum, trained by Hugh Ross and the impelling direction of Munch." See: W20b

B20m. Mitchell, Donald. "London Music." Musical Times 96:433-434 (August 1955)
Review of the English premiere, June 10, 1955. "The music is always deft and fluent, but lacks pungency and bite; it leaves a final impression of a creatively unmotivated display of excellent craftsmanship." See: W20c

B20n. "Next to Godliness." Time 64:57 (December 20, 1954)
"The great and gloomy Dane, Søren Kierkegaard has turned up in many strange guises...Last week Kierkegaard appeared in music. His musical interpreter: U. S. Composer Samuel Barber, 44, who studied Kierkegaard for a decade and made him the subject of his first major composition in four years." Barber's 20 minute work used as a text none of Kierkegaard's intricate philosophizing, but some simple and often beautiful prayers which Composer Barber culled from the preacher's writing...the overall effect is quiet, without either the sweetness or the grandeur expected of religious music. It is clean rather than austere. But at its best, the music matches the tender earnestness of the prayers' poetry...On one point most of the critics were agreed: they wanted to hear Barber's Prayers of Kierkegaard again." See: W20b

B20o. Pavlakis, Christopher. "The Journal Reviews: New York." Music Journal 35:36-37 (December 1977)
"The Barber work is rated very highly by many admirers of his music. Its choral writing is rich and flowing and there are numerous forceful instrumental moments. But despite the touches of modernity, the work seems as much a painful anachronism in 1977 as it was in 1954 when it was composed; and although both Schermerhorn [conducting the Milwaukee Symphony Orchestra] and the director of the chorus, F. Austin Walter, lavished care on the performance, very little of the sung test [sic] was intelligible, including that delivered by Miss [Evelyn] Lear. The audience seemed to appreciate the work, however, and gave it warm applause." See: W20f

B20p. "Performance Reviews." Choral & Organ Guide 7:29 (January 1955)

Review of the December 8, 1954 Carnegie Hall performance. "Without a doubt Samuel Barber's first venture into the choral idiom places upon his talents the cherished stamp of genius...we await with keen interest the publication of the score for more exacting subsequent coverage...Obviously the choral director did not share the interpretive characterization of the work with the orchestra conductor and the result was regretful." See: W20b

B20q. Redlich, H. F. "Music from the American Continent." Music Review 19:246-253 (August 1958)

"This is a very serious-minded, hymn-like composition, deeply religious, but deliberately eschewing the ties of dogma and liturgy. The composer uses extracts from the religious, speculative and self-analytical writings of the Danish philosopher as a basis for an almost ritualist work, spiritually akin to Delius' Nietzsche-inspired Mass of Life and Kaminski's Introitus und Hymnus. It shares with both works a certain teutonic ponderousness of style amply circumscribed by the 'grave and remote' unaccompanied solo of the tenors and basses with which the Cantata begins, 'plastic, in plainsong style.' The music sounds more often than not as if written by a German sometime between 1910 and 1935; but occasionally it reaches a high level of formal integration as in the beautiful passage at cue 13, where the xylophone re-echoes in diminution the nostalgic eloquence of the tenor solo..." See: W20

B20r. "Reviews of New Music." Musical Opinion 79:157 (December 1955)

Review of the G. Schirmer/Chappell vocal score. "There is no doubt that, heard in the concert-hall this intensely moving work would have a tremendous impact on audiences. It is not easy to sing, but the demands made on the singers are not, as in so many modern works, extreme." See: W20

B20s. Rockwell, John. "Music: Rich Milwaukee Evening." New York Times, October 30, 1977, p. 61.

"...and her [Evelyn Lear] interpretations of the solo part...were most convincing. Sometimes Miss Lear artsily [!] overinterprets; her work on Friday sounded mature and heartfelt, with all the interpretive niceties appropriate. Mr. Barber's piece, from 1954...is a classic example of 1950's highbrow musical Americana. The writing is sensitive and skilled, the effects sensuous and plush, the Neo-Classicism overt but non-academic. It's not a bad work, all in all, and one suspects it will hold up, even if it doesn't seem very probing or, ultimately, very important." See: W20f

B20t. Sargeant, Winthrop. "Musical Events." New Yorker 30:126 (December 18, 1954)

"Its text, very well sung by the soprano Leontyne Price and the chorus of the Schola Cantorum, consisted of short excerpts from various writings of the great Danish mystic, and Mr. Barber's settings of them seemed to me appropriately austere and dignified." <u>See</u>: W20b

B20u. Schmidek, Kurt. "Cincinnati in Vienna." <u>American Musical Digest</u> 1:7 (October 1969) [translated from <u>Volksblatt</u> (Vienna) May 22, 1969]
"Barber's work is not exactly original, but it is effective and accessible to any audience." <u>See</u>: W20d

B20v. Simmons, Walter. "Classical Recordings." <u>Fanfare</u> 2:16 (November/December 1978)
"Samuel Barber is one of the few composers today whose music is concerned with the idea of pure beauty as understood by the mainstream musical culture. Over the years he has been remarkably successful in achieving this ideal and consequently his music has won a wide following among the general public, as well as among specialists in contemporary music. Yet strangely, it has taken almost 25 years for the <u>Prayers of Kierkegaard</u> to find their way onto a recording...[they] are richly varied settings of a selection of the Danish philosopher's extraordinary religious poetry. The music ranges from awesome moments of hushed neo-Gregorian simplicity to dramatic passages of wild frenzy and chorales of solemn nobility...The performance is generally fine, if a bit too restrained during the work's most frenetic moments, and soloist Gloria Capone's soprano is warm, light, and pliant." [Louisville LS 763] <u>See</u>: D20a

B20w. -----. "New York." <u>Music Journal</u> 34:70-71 (July 1976)
Review of the Carnegie Hall concert of April 26, 1976. "Barber has fashioned choral settings of awesome beauty, ranging from passages of hushed reverence to moments of stark and powerful nobility, as well as several vocal solos characterized by the plaintive lyricism for which Barber is justly renowned. It is a tightly knit work, lasting less than twenty minutes. In fact, if the <u>Prayers of Kierkegaard</u> is flawed, it is only by brief moments of great promise that are often dispensed without sufficient elaboration. Unfortunately this tendency was over compounded by Eugene Ormandy's interpretative strategy, which was to underplay the most pregnant moments while belaboring the insignificant ones." <u>See</u>: W20e

B20x. Waters, Edward N. "Music." <u>Quarterly Journal of the Library of Congress</u> 23:21 (January 1966)
"The full score of <u>Prayers of Kierkegaard</u> enriches the collection of holographs of Samuel Barber (b. 1910). The work for orchestra, mixed chorus, and three solo voices was commissioned by the Library's Serge Koussevitzky Music Foundation and is dedicated to the memory of Serge and Natalie Koussevitzky." <u>See</u>: W20

B21. REINCARNATIONS, OP. 16.

B21a. Cohn, Arthur. "Classical." HiFi/Stereo Review 15:122 (November 1965)
"Barber's Reincarnations is highlighted by the central portion (Anthony O'Daly), a lamentation which moves to an ecstatic conclusion. Always traditionalistic and romantic, Barber's music, whatever one may think of it, never slips into dull pedantry" [Everest SDBR 3129, LPBR 6129] See: D21b

B21b. Ericson, Raymond. "Choir of Oberlin Offers Concert." New York Times, April 7, 1963, sect. 1, p. 81.
"For Barber's Anthony O'Daly, Mr. [Robert] Fountain let his group sing out dramatically." See:W21b

B21c. Frankenstein, Alfred. "Classical." High Fidelity 15:99 (November 1965)
"The Barber is, as one might expect, the most entertaining and obviously delightful of the three pieces, but this work, with texts by James Stephens, also rewards repeated hearings" [Everest SDBR 3129, LPBR 6129] See: D21b

B21d. Henahan, Donal. "Concert: Barber's Kierkegaard Offered by Brooklyn Ensemble." New York Times, March 20, 1981, sect. C, p. 18.
"An earlier and more familiar Barber work set the mood nicely for the religious-philosophical contemplations of the Kierkegaard texts [the later Prayers of Kierkegaard]" See: W21d

B21e. Horowitz, Linda. "Literature Forum." Choral Journal 21:26-29 (December 1980)
"For these works, composed for a cappella choir, Barber has chosen three poems by James Stephens, after the Irish of Raftery. In Mary Hynes the poet sings the praises of his love. Though the sunny joyousness of these sentiments is quickly chilled in the death-dirge of Anthony O'Daly, Barber reassuringly reminds us that spring follows winter with the final delicate love poem The Coolin. See: W21

B21f. MacDonald, Calum. "Recordings." Tempo 101:56 (July 1972)
"...there is much to enjoy in Samuel Barber's attractive cycle of James Stephens settings: beautifully-written pieces, informed with the unassuming lyricism associated with this composer" [Everest SDBR 3129, LPBR 6129] See: D21b

B21g. Mann, William. "Choral and Song." Gramophone 50:86 (June 1972)
"Whether the music is about the creation of the world, as described in Genesis, or the daredevil exploits of death

as imagined by Walt Whitman, nothing is calculated to disturb the most conservative ear. Anyone who sings this music, or listens to it, is mercifully unlikely to go out and commit larceny or even murder...unless out of sheer infuriation with the milk-and-honey butter smugness of this record." [Everest SDBR 6129, LPBR 6129] See: D21b

B21h. Miller, Philip. "Other reviews." American Record Guide 32:538 (February 1966)
"Anthony O'Daly is generally considered to be one of the finest of Barber's works" [Everest SDBR 6129, LPBR 6129] See: D21b

B21i. Oliver, Michael. "Choral and Song." Gramophone 59:307 (August 1981)
Barber's Anthony O'Daly is a rewarding piece, too, taking great risks by conveying a climax of grief through obsessive repetitions of a simple phrase, but succeeding with powerful eloquence" [Orion ORS 75205] See: D21d

B21j. Orr, C. W. "Review of Music." Music Review 4 no. 2:120 (1942)
"Quite possibly there will be others besides the reviewer who will feel like applauding Mr. Barber for not attempting to reproduce the Celtic rusticities of James Stephens' verses by writing in a pseudo-Irish folk-song style. As it is, Mr. Barber has succeeded quite well in finding a musical equivalent for the words..." See: W21

B21k. Shupp, Enos E., Jr. "Choral." New Records 44:8-9 (April 1976)
"A choral disc not to be missed by any interested in this phase of music, for it is as nearly perfect an exhibition of the art of choral singing as you will likely encounter, and much of this music is of surpassing beauty, all of it well worth hearing" [Orion ORS 75205] See: D21d

B22. A STOPWATCH AND AN ORDNANCE MAP, OP. 15.

B22a. Anderson, W. R. "New Music." Musical Times 84:83 (February 1943)
"With some well chosen points of rest, the music, rather astringent though not bitter, seems to suit the familiar angularity of unfamiliar angles in much of Mr. Barbers imagery..." See: W22

B22b. Clapham, John. "Reviews of Music." Music Review 16:341-342 (November 1955)
"...Barber develops a skilful form in that his ever-widening rhythmic structures yet obey the demands of a succinct ternary design and its stressed thematic economy." See: W22

B22c. Finkelstein, Sidney. "Samuel Barber" [album notes for Vanguard VSD 2083 disc]
"A Stopwatch and an Ordnance Map, op. 15, for male chorus, with percussion and brass is typical of Barber's moving choral works and settings of poetry...The poem by Stephen Spender was inspired by the Civil War in Spain, and the music has the character of a lament for one of the fallen." See: D22b

B22d. Frankenstein, Alfred. "Classical." High Fidelity 11:49 (July 1961)
"The choral piece...and the Serenade for Strings (Barber's Opus 1) are not of sufficient stature or importance to arouse much interest or comment, one way or another" [Vanguard VRS 1065, VSD 2083] See: D22b

B22e. Hall, David. "Classics." HIFI/Stereo Review 6:61 (June 1961)
It "...is a masterpiece. This is an extraordinarily powerful and poignant setting of a Stephen Spender poem from the Spanish Civil War..." See: W22

B22f. Harrison, Lou. "New Music in Recitals and Symposiums." Modern Music 23:52 (Winter 1946)
"Samuel Barber's A Stop Watch [sic] and an Ordnance Map for men's voices, brass and timpani was presented on the Collegiate Chorale program. This quite moving work is rich in chromatic voice movements, sudden silences, tense timpani solos and a general atmosphere of the terrible." See: W22b

B22g. Harvey, Trevor. "Opera." Gramophone 46:272 (August 1968)
"The Robert De Cormier Chorale is very good. The poem should have been printed, though the choir's words are generally audible" [Philips Vanguard VSL 11019] See: D22b

B22h. Horan, Robert. "American Composers, XIX: Samuel Barber." Modern Music 20:168 (March-April 1943)
"In A Stopwatch and an Ordnance Map (Stephen Spender), for unaccompanied men's chorus and kettledrums, the ominous and haunting quality of the chorus is achieved by the curious, indefinite pitch of the timpani against the voices. Effective use is made of timpani glissandi underneath a single melodic line. It is, with Anthony O'Daly unique in its cumulative and elegiac desperation." See: W22

B22i. Horowitz, Linda. "Literature Forum." Choral Journal 21:26-29 (December 1980)
"The text of this work...is pictorially set by Barber as a martial C minor lament for one of the fallen...This piece is certainly one of Barber's most dramatic and carefully constructed choral works and there is no way to listen to it without reacting to the horror and tragedy of the war it describes." See: W22

B22j. Hughes, Allen. "Landmarks." New York Times, April 30, 1961, sect. 2, p. 21.
"...a small, but very real masterpiece based on Stephen Spender's poem and scored for male chorus, percussion and brass" [Vanguard VRS 1065, VSD 2083] See: D22b

B22k. "Reviews of New Music." Musical Opinion 78:285+ (February 1955)
Review of the G. Schirmer/Chappell study score. "Not perhaps one of Barber's finest works, but certainly one of his most moving...There are many changes of tempo, but basically the work is a solemn march, underlining the personal tragedy that often lies in war." See: W22

B22l. Straus, Noel. "'Magnificat' Sung at Carnegie Hall." New York Times, December 17, 1945, p. 19.
Review of the Collegiate Chorale New York premiere (a cappella version). "Music so sincerely and deeply felt is extremely uncommon today, and it possessed such appeal that its success was immediate and unequivocal. In the unusually expressive and convincing creation, Mr. Barber showed a fertile imagination in regard to vocal sonorities and in the treatment of the solo tympani accompaniment, which was so perfectly adjusted to the voice parts that it provided a completely satisfying support, adding greatly to the impressiveness of the work as a whole." See: W22b

B22m. Waters, Edward N. "Harvest of the Year: Selected Acquisitions of the Music Division." Quarterly Journal of the Library of Congress 24:54-55 (January 1967)
"There are also two versions of Mr. Barber's A Stopwatch and an Ordnance Map, Op. 15, composed to words by Stephen Spender. The holograph has four-part male chorus and three timpani (published in 1942 by Schirmer) has neither date nor title. It also shows a sketch for a four-part musical chorus a cappella. The second version--and Mr. Barber's gift is surely entitled to be called a holograph--resulted from adroit manipulation. He cut up the 1942 publication, mounted it line by line or larger score paper, and above each line wrote new music for four horns, three trombones, and tuba. Schirmer also published the brassier settings in 1954, which contained the following note: 'This work was performed for the first time on December 16, 1945, by the Collegiate Chorale under the direction of Robert Shaw in New York City.'" See: W22

B23. TO BE SUNG ON THE WATER, OP. 42, NO. 2.

B23a. Horowitz, Linda. "Literature Forum." Choral Journal 21:26-29 (December 1980)
"This is a truly gentle and loving piece that requires great restraint and control from its performers." See: W23

B24. TWELFTH NIGHT, OP. 42, NO. 1.

B24a. Horowitz, Linda. "Literature Forum." _Choral Journal_ 21:26-29 (December 1980)
"Dissonant chords used frequently in this work help to create a feeling of harmonic bleakness which reflects the mood of the text." _See_: W24

B25. THE VIRGIN MARTYRS, OP. 8, NO. 1.

B25a. Horowitz, Linda. "Literature Forum." _Choral Journal_ 21:26-29 (December 1980)
"Barber chose Helen Waddell's English version of an old text after the Latin of Sigebert of Gemblous...The rhythmic intricacies characterizing this work make it a difficult though effective composition, an excellent choice for an advanced women's ensemble." _See_: W25

VOCAL MUSIC

B26. ANDROMACHE'S FAREWELL, OP. 39.

B26a. Chapin, Louis. "Debuts and Reappearances." _Hi Fi/Musical America_ 18:MA8 (February 1968)
"Martina Arroyo was soprano soloist...for the Barber, [Carnegie Hall, November 12-13, 1967] in which she spun out a mother's grief quite splendidly over the sonorous ample orchestration. The composer not only built into the music a kind of _Leitmotif_ on the rhythm and melody suggested to him by the Englishing of Euripides' first line, 'So you must die, my son,' but paid close, generous attention to the rise and fall of feeling through the forty-six lines that follow." _See_: W26b

B26b. Davis, Peter. "New Works." _Music Journal_ 21:68 (May 1963)
"It is perhaps ungracious to comment on Barber's extreme eclecticism at this stage of his career, yet in the orchestral introduction the ghosts of half a dozen early 20th-century composers marched past, finding themselves rather ill at ease in each other's company. When the voice enters, however, Barber finds his own with a Grand Tune that dominates the material in the opening and closing section of the work. The composer's skill and technique coupled with pleasing melodic lines, extremely grateful for the voice, carry through to the end of the work. As in all of Barber's pieces the construction is immaculate and the scoring imaginative. Although it is refreshing to find a contemporary composer unashamed of the large romantic gesture, it is unfortunate that one is left with the fixed

impression of a pleasant musical experience rather than the revelation of a great tragic character in true dramatic depth. Schippers conducted the work with proper bravura and sweep, while Arroyo sang the solo part with impeccable musicianship and style." See: W26a

B26c. Dickinson, Peter. "Songs." Musical Times 105:371-372 (May 1964)
Brief review of the Schirmer/Chappell score. "Compared with Stravinsky's attitude toward classical subjects, the self-pity and emotional indulgence of Barber's score, seem almost revolting. Parallels can be sought in Samson et Delila, and the persistent reliance upon one triadic phrase and one chord progression smells of the Leitmotiv. It is unworthy of Euripides." See: W26

B26d. Ericson, Raymond. "Recordings: A Batch of Moderns. New York Times, November 10, 1963, sect. 2, p. 14.
"For Andromache's Farewell, Mr. Barber has set for soprano solo a climactic speech from Euripides' The Trojan Women, in a translation by John Patrick Creagh. This, too, is a characteristic work, melancholy and harmonically on the lush side without falling into sentimentality. It is vocally grateful and effective, poignant rather than tragic, and a fine addition to the limited works for solo voice and orchestra. Martina Arroyo is the lovely voiced soprano in the Barber, managing some attractive high pianissimos, with Thomas Schippers conducting smoothly." [Columbia ML 5912, MS 6512] See: D26a

B26e. Flanagan, William. "Classical." HiFi Stereo Review 12:86 (February 1964)
"A setting of an excerpt from Euripides' The Trojan Women, the work is all about Samuel Barber's feelings on the matter of the late Richard Strauss. Andromache's Farewell, either in spite of, or because of Richard Strauss (I'm not quite sure which), is a thoroughly effective concert piece. If we've all suspected that Barber's gift for vocal writing has by now passed into the stage of mastery, this new piece tells us that we'd better believe it. The new work, furthermore, handsomely tailored, in a loose, motivic nineteenth-century fashion, and the orchestration is brilliantly eclectic. But the whole piece, when all's said and done, is a startlingly predictable, skillful, sonorous bore." [Columbia ML 5912, MS 6512] See: D26a

B26f. Kolodin, Irving. "Music to My Ears." Saturday Review 46:28 (April 20, 1963)
"Much of it was beautifully written and all of it was honestly felt, but the stalking specter of Strauss cast a long shadow...Martina Arroyo sang the demanding soprano part with strong sound and the needed thrust of volume. Better enunciation of the text would have emphasized her affinity with the sense of the subject." See: W26a

B26g. Levinger, Henry W. "Orchestras: Philharmonic Firsts." Musical America 83:22 (June 1963)

"...Samuel Barber's Andromache's Farewell, an example of American music at its best, with soprano Martina Arroyo the superb soloist...It is a deeply moving and highly dramatic score, a logical addition to Barbers oeuvre as we know and cherish it. Composer, conductor [Thomas Schippers] and soloist received an ovation." See: W26a

B26h. Sargeant, Winthrop. "Musical Events." New Yorker 39:153+ (April 13, 1963)

"Mr. Barber has created an intense and stirring study of feminine anguish, and the result had a powerful effect the other night." See: W26a

B26i. Schonberg, Harold C. "Music: Schippers Guest Conductor of Philharmonic." New York Times, April 5, 1963, p. 30.

"...Martina Arroyo was the opulent-sounding soprano soloist, it is an 11-minute scene using a long passage from Euripides's The Trojan Women. The words deal with Andromache's anguish on learning that her son is to be killed by the Greeks. Stylistically the music is remarkably Straussian. The Strauss of Electra is recalled. Perhaps, since both of the composers used a setting from Greek tragedy, the temptation is to read Strauss into Barber. But there is no getting away from the fact that Barber's use of the orchestra has a Straussian texture, and the opening flourish is intensely Straussian. So are many other later harmonics. On the whole the Barber is, on first hearing anyway, an exercise in rhetoric. It is skillful, of course, as befits so experienced a composer. Yet it lacks personality, profile and inner power. Indeed, the score is basically very conventional- conventional even in its dissonances. But the audience liked it very much, and recalled the composer several times with genuine enthusiasm." See: W26a

B26j. Shupp, Enos E., Jr. "Orchestra." New Records 31:3 (January 1964)

"Barber's commissioned work for the Lincoln Center, was a dramatic scene from a Greek tragedy. For all of its tragic drama it sounds like a tinkling cymbal to these ears after the Schuman symphony." [Columbia ML 5912, MS 6512] See: D26a

B26k. Sigmon, Carl "New Music: Pulling Out the Stops." Musical America 84:70 (January 1964)

"A carefully constructed motivic development enhances the continuity, which is all the more convincing for a slow middle section that dramatically employs a harmonic sequence, plain as an unwinding thread, and just as inevitable. One becomes so gripped and involved that the music comes to an end all to soon. The vocal writing is direct though felicitous, calling for a soprano of stamina and stature, and capable of encompassing the gamut of human emotion. The composer's own piano reduction is quite logical and playable, though difficult." See: W26

B261. Strongin, Theodore. "Joseph Eger Leads American Symphony." New York Times, November 13, 1967, p. 64.
"Mr. Eger did not tamper with the composer's intentions in each case, but he didn't add much, either. The music just rolled on and on, moderately lively but not gripping...Miss Arroyo was in radiant voice and sang with sympathetic musicianship." See: W26b

B31. DESPITE AND STILL, OP. 41.

B31a. Henahan, Donal. "Leontyne Price Excels in Recital Sans Opera." New York Times, April 28, 1969, p. 36.
Review of the April 27, 1969 Philharmonic Hall performance. "...the five songs are in Mr. Barber's utterly singable, rather impressionistic manner...One would guess that another singer could find more overtly dramatic ways to interpret this cycle, which Miss Price delivered effectively but with, again, that odd distancing that she falls into much too easily." See: W31a

B31b. Moushon, George. "Debuts and Reappearances." High Fidelity/Musical America 19:MA22 (July 1969)
Review of the premiere performance given by Leontyne Price April 27, 1969. "The new Barber cycle was of uncommon interest, for Leontyne Price has proclaimed her affinity with this composer on many occasions and recorded the Hermit Songs and Knoxville. On this occasion she responded well to the frankly melodic and eminently singable line--there was a wealth of rich tone in the first song and a miracle of agile coordination in the second. But I shall need to hear the work again before grasping its real character. So far the five poems upon which it is composed seem to have no linking logic or thematic connection: there are three by Robert Graves, one by Theodor Roethke, and one by James Joyce--this last is a bit of narration from Ulysses done in telegraphic style which tells of a young man and woman both guests at a Solitary Hotel and unable to communicate. The Roethke poem is My Lizard, the Graves trio A Last Song, In the Wilderness, and the poem which gives the new work its title, Despite and Still. The music is frank, forward, melodically bold if harmonically conservative; the thoughts remain disparate, compartmented and unrelated to each other. An enigma." See: W31a

B31c. Oberlin, Russell. "Solo Songs." Notes 26:849-50 (June 1970)
"...these songs are lyrical, vocal, and articulate and though in a somewhat lighter vein than usual, sumptuous. With his deft romantic brush, Barber draws some beautiful

atmospheric vocal lines against playable and effective
piano accompaniments. Although placed in a cycle in an
order making them model program fare as a group, any one of
the songs could stand alone on its own merits." See: W31

B33. HERMIT SONGS, OP. 29.

B33a. Albertson, John Emery. A Study of the Stylistic
Elements of Samuel Barber's "Hermit Songs" and Franz Schubert's "Die Winterreise". Thesis (D.M.A.)--University of
Missouri, Kansas City, 1969. 101 p.
"Barber's final output [to 1969] is a result of his
attempt to transform an essentially romantic idiom into a
modern one. The fusion of his lyricism with twentieth
century compositional techniques has created a musical
style which is reflective of our time and age. For his
ability to communicate emotion with eloquence and charm,
Samuel Barber stands out among composers of his generation.
Barber discovered some collections of medieval Irish poems
and stories and was impressed with the fresh charm and
innocence of what he had found. He read them all, and
selected from various collections ten poems, the shortest
consisting of two lines and the longest of twenty-two.
These were set to music as Hermit Songs, opus 29...Some
translations are literal, and others were especially made
for Barber by W. H. Auden and Chester Kallman. They very
greatly in subject and mood and the music varies accordingly, but all of it is in Barber's best style." See: W33

B33b. B., J. "Phyllis Antognini Sings American Songs."
New York Times, May 13, 1958, p. 25.
"Of special interest was Miss Antognini's singing of
Samuel Barber's Hermit Songs. This cycle of ten songs is
the work of a mature craftsman who from the outset of his
career demonstrated special aptitude for vocal writing.
Musically, the Hermit Songs are inordinately difficult, but
with such an interpreter as Miss Antognini they came off in
performance. They are difficult, not because the composer
lacks understanding of the voice, but because he understands it very well and accordingly taxes it almost to
capacity." See: W33d

B33c. Barnes, Clive. "Dance: Ailey Revives 'Suspensions.'" New York Times, December 15, 1971, p. 65.
"There was also a revival of 'Hermit Songs'...Set to
atmospheric music by Samuel Barber...Hermit Songs is a
complex solo of changing passions and deeply felt moods."
See: W33j

B33d. Berger, Arthur. "Americana Without Tears." Saturday Review 37:39 (August 27, 1955)
"Barber's Hermit Songs performed...by Leontyne Price
with the composer at the piano, are pleasant and highly
musical but they are coy at times, and outside of the

accompaniment figure for _Praise of God_ there are few surprises" [Columbia ML 4988] _See_: D33b

B33e. Broder, Nathan. "Review of Records: Columbia's
Modern American Music Series." _Musical Quarterly_ 41:551-
555 (October 1955)
    "Written in that composer's mature style, with its
well integrated mixture of traditional and contemporary
elements, it is, I think, one of the most distinguished
song-cycles in our century." [Columbia ML 4988] _See_: D33b

B33f. Davis, Peter G. "Repeat Performance." _High
Fidelity_ 18:122 (November 1968)
    "_The Hermit Songs_...are written in a leaner style--
agreeable miniatures of no great musical character...A very
young Leontyne Price sings the _Hermit Songs_ with a delightfully fresh musical innocence--a far lighter voice
than we are accustomed to hearing nowadays--and Barber's
accompaniments are immaculate." [Odyssey 32 16 0230, from
Columbia ML 4988] _See_: D33b

B33g. Ellsworth, Ray. "Americans on Microgroove. Part
II." _High Fidelity_ 6:61-62 (August 1956)
    "...sung by Leontyne Price with Barber at the piano.
These are texts written by thirteenth-century scholar-monks
on the margins of manuscripts, some of the mystical, most
of them ribald." [Columbia ML 4988] _See_: D33b

B33h. Flanagan, William. "Recording of Special Merit."
HiFi Stereo Review 21:105 (September 1968)
    "If the singer misses by a hair the slight jazziness
of the syncopations in Barber's delicious _The Monk and His
Cat_, she [singer Nancy Tatum] does full justice to _The
Crucifixion_. [London OS 26053] _See_: D33e

B33i. Frankenstein, Alfred. "Columbia and the Contem-
poraries--1955." _High Fidelity_ 5:57 (September 1955)
    "Barber's songs involve glorious texts-meditations of
medieval monks on life, religion, sex, and other things--
all very gracefully set." [Columbia ML 4988] _See_: D33b

B33j. Friedewald, Russell Edward. _A Formal and Stylistic Analysis of the Published Music of Samuel Barber._
Thesis (Ph.D.)--Iowa State University, 1957. 357 p.
    "A notational peculiarity of this set is the absence
of time signatures. In view, however, of the many changes
that would be required by conventional notation, this omis-
sion tends to make the metrical reading less confusing for
the singer. The composer is fastidious in his observation
of the pronunciation and duration of each syllable or word,
and there is never any question of the proper rhythms."
[p. 83] _See_: W33

B33k. Haggin, B. H. "Records." _Nation_ 181:122 (August
8, 1955)

"Samuel Barber's Hermit Songs...are, to my ears, only additional evidence of his ability to make endless numbers of black marks on paper." [Columbia ML 4988] See: D33b

B33l. Hill, Richard S. "Music." Quarterly Journal of Current Acquisitions [of the Library of Congress] 12:46 (November 1954)
    Item noting that the Library of Congress has received, "the autograph score of Samuel Barber's set of 10 Hermit Songs, opus 29, commissioned by the Founders Day Concert on October 30, 1953, and sung then by Leontyne Price, with the composer accompanying, has been received and added to the list of the works commissioned by the Coolidge Foundation during the founder's life." See: W33

B33m. Kisselgoff, Anna. "Dance: Ailey Versatility." New York Times, April 24, 1969, p. 42.
    Review of the April 20, 1969 Alvin Ailey American Dance Theater performance. "As the monastically garbed figure in Mr. Ailey's 'Hermit Songs,' Kelvin Rotardier conveys both devotion and passion in a performance that seemed to leave him at the same time spent and triumphant." See: W33l

B33n. Kohs, Ellis B. "Songs." Notes 12:333-334 (March 1955)
    "Vocally gratifying, these songs are straight-forward-ly lyrical and reveal a rare gift for characterization. Elegance of form is combined with an appropriate use of ecclesiastical modes." See: W33

B33o. Mann, William. "Choral and Song." Gramophone 46:1186 (February 1969)
    "...then Barber's The Monk and His Cat, cool and humorous but gentle in mood..." [Decca SXL 6336] See: D33e

B33p. March, Ivan. "Choral Music." Gramophone 55:1779 (April 1978)
    "To have a coupling of virtually unknown songs by Samuel Barber with a slightly more familiar Copland work in the tape catalog is welcome..." [Enigma Classics TC-VAR 1029] See: D33b

B33q. Miller, Philip L. "Other Reviews." American Record Guide 35:282 (December 1968)
    Barber used literal translation where this was feasi-ble; some of the poems, however, were given new versions by W. H. Auden and Chester Kallman...A technical peculiarity of this set is the absence of time-signatures. Strangely enough, this is less confusing to the singer than would be the many changes of time-signatures that would be required here by conventional notation. For the music is molded so closely to the natural pronunciation of the words that there is never any question of the proper rhythm." [Odyssey 32 16 0230] See: D33c

B33r. Parmenter, Ross. "Song Recital Given by Leontyne Price." New York Times, November 14, 1954, p. 30.
"Her voice is fresh, clear and agile, and she sings lighter music charmingly. But her range of expression is not yet wide enough, nor does it embrace a sufficient variety of styles for her work to make a deep impression. But she has sympathy, poise, good looks, accurate musicianship and a beautiful voice. Gluck, Rossini, Mahler, Manuel Rosenthal and Samuel Barber were her chief composers. The last named was in the house and he took over from David Stimer, the regular accompanist, to play the piano for his own cycle of Hermit Songs. These are ten moderately imaginative settings of anonymous Irish texts of the eighth to twelfth centuries." See: W33b

B33s. Redlich, H. F. "Music from the American Continent." Music Review 19:246-253 (August 1958)
A discussion of the music of Copland, Chavez, Diamond, and Barber. Concerning Hermit Songs he remarks, "The Hermit Songs reflect various rarified moods of religious introspection; they are self-torturing and serene in turn, expressing their emotional light and shade through a beautifully disciplined-though admittedly romantic-idiom." See: W33

B33t. Rickert, Lawrence Gould. "Selected American Song Cycles for Baritone Composed Since 1945-Part 2." NATS (National Association of Teachers of Singing) Bulletin 23:8 (December 1966)
Brief discussion of Hermit Songs, which "...represents a competent continuation in our generation of the great tradition of song cycle composition of the past. The Stravinsky influence has helped to give Barber's cycle a greater sensitivity to the stylistic pulse of the twentieth century. Barber sometimes, however, sacrifices his inherent lyrical beauty of expression for stylistic excesses." See: W33

B33u. Sabin, Robert. "Samuel Barber's Hermit Songs Issued." Musical America 74:30 (December 15, 1954)
"A work of marked beauty and unusual character is the cycle of Hermit Songs by Samuel Barber...[he] is always at his best in his vocal music. One has to study these Hermit Songs carefully to realize what a wealth of fine workmanship there is in them. The harmonic details have all of the richness and subtlety one would expect from this composer...American singers should welcome this work from one of our leading composers and see to it that it is widely heard." See: W33b

B33v. Schonberg, Harold C. "Records: Contemporary Americans." New York Times, July 10, 1955, sect. 2, p. 12.
"Samuel Barber's Hermit Songs...are sung by Leontyne Price with the composer at the piano. They are, for the

most part, simple and lyrical and perhaps try too hard to be simple and lyrical." [Columbia ML 4988] See: D33b

B33w. Steane, John. "Choral and Song." Gramophone 55:677 (October 1977)
"The piano writing is slightly richer [than Copland], more romantic, and Michael Isador plays with a sensitive touch. Sandra Browne sings well, but I would like to hear her in a different kind of programme--classical Italian songs for instance." [Enigma Classics VAR 1039] See: D33a

B33x. Tircuit, Heuwell. "Cries of 'We Love Leontyne.'" San Francisco Chronicle, March 6, 1975, p. 45.
"...the Barber songs, which she recorded shortly after premiering them in 1954 were (for me) the outstanding items of the evening. Her elocution was a marvel, and her ability to help the meaning of little phrases with quick subtle shifts of vocal color only go to support the sense of depth in her artistry." See: W33k

B33y. Waters, Edward N. "Harvest of the Year: Selected Acquisitions of the Music Division." Quarterly Journal of the Library of Congress 24:54-55 (January 1967)
"Here, too, is a reproduction of a copyists manuscript of Hermit Songs, opus 29, which Mr. Barber composed in 1953 on commission from the Library's Elizabeth Sprague Coolidge Foundation. It is extremely important document, for the composer inserted many holograph corrections and indications for performance." See: W33

B34. HERMIT SONGS, OP. 29. CHORAL TRANSCRIPTIONS. THE MONK AND THE CAT.

B34a. Horowitz, Linda. "Literature Forum." Choral Journal 21:26-29 (December 1980)
"The piece abounds with extremely complicated rhythms, particularly for the soprano...There are displaced accents, syncopations, meter changes and rhythmic subtleties that Barber has very carefully notated in order to create the carefree effect." See: W34

B34b. Ottaway, Hugh. "Modern Choral." Musical Times 109:63 (January 1968)
"The choral writing seems surprisingly laboured for this composer, whose feeling for voice is usually persuasive." See: W34

B36. KNOXVILLE: SUMMER OF 1915, OP. 24.

B36a. Belt, Byron. "Four Voices of America." Music Journal 25:89-90 (December 1967)
"Knoxville evokes a special aura of nostalgia and the questioning spirit of youth in Barber's superbly lyrical

and meaningful setting of Agee's great prose poem of an era rapidly disappearing even as the words were being written." See: W36

B36b. Daniel, Oliver. "Knoxville Revisited." Saturday Review 45:47 (September 29, 1962)
"It revealed all of Barber's familiar qualities: the long-lined melodic contours, the tasteful sense of orchestration, the absence of any striving toward artificial 'modernity.' Steber's performance was memorable. But with the deletion of all 10 inch discs from the catalogue, Knoxville: Summer of 1915 became a collector's item." [Columbia ML 2174] See: D36d

B36c. Davis, Peter G. "Repeat Performance." High Fidelity 18:122 (November 1968)
"It may be that in Knoxville Barber has stretched the text a bit beyond its emotional limits in one or two spots, but the treatment is so adroit and the nostalgic flavor of Agee's lines so well translated that the whole, immediate effect is pretty nigh irresistible." [Odyssey 32 16 0230, from Columbia ML5843] See: D36c

B36d. Diamond, David. "Samuel Barber." Notes 7:309-310 (March 1950)
"It is an extended work, beautifully made as only very few composers know how, of the most refreshing simplicity and intellectual honesty all too rare in American music of the past three decades...Barber's feeling for words to be sung is splendid. But finer still is the emotional release he has found in setting Agee's most delicate and haunting reflective sentiments. It is, of its kind, a small masterpiece of musical Americana...It is a joy to simply play through this work, to make it one's very own outside the concert hall. Perhaps that is the way of all great music." See: W36

B36e. Downes, Edward. "Eleanor Steber Offers Recital." New York Times, October 11, 1958, p. 18.
"Samuel Barber's song cycle Knoxville: Summer of 1915, which was commissioned by Miss Steber, was one of the most interesting parts of the program and showed how far the soprano's style ventures outside the conventional opera and recital program." See: W36c

B36f. Durgin, Cyrus. "Boston Pops Open as Symphony Season Closes Under Koussevitzky." Musical America 68:11 (June 1948)
Brief review of the April 9-10, 1948 performance with Steber/Koussevitzky. "Mr. Barber's music is melodic, metrically and structurally free, with close and very effective writing. Having heard it only in rehearsal and without recourse to a score, I would describe the effect of the music as simple, relaxed and expressive, although I

suspect that the technique has its complexities." See:
W36a

B36g. Ellsworth, Ray, "Americans on Microgroove. Part
II." High Fidelity 6:62 (August 1956)
"...a setting for soprano voice and chamber orchestra
of a prose poem by James Agee, is as tasteful a bit of
Americana as you are likely to find any where." [Columbia
ML 2174] See: D36d

B36h. Ericson, Raymond. "Old Fashioned But Not Saccha-
rine." New York Times, March 30, 1969, sect. 2, p. 30.
"This piece may end up the composer's finest, for it
is such a sensitive and successful exercise in nostalgia
for remembered innocence. It was written for Eleanor Steber...This was considered a definitive performance, but
Miss Price's singing is no less perceptive and is slightly
richer vocally. It contributes to a disc of unusual beauty." [RCA LSC 3062] See: D36b

B36i. Flanagan, William. "Classics." HIFI/Stereo Review
9:59 (August 1962)
"Were I asked about the desert island and the phonograph, as the question might pertain to American music,
Samuel Barber's Knoxville: Summer of 1915 would surely
qualify for my luggage. I've always found this to be the
single work that cuts beneath the veneer of coolness and
occasional superciliousness that characterizes Barber's
neo-Romanticism. The piece is beautifully made, meltingly
lyrical and has remained poignant over the fifteen years
since its composition." [St/and SLP 420] See: D36f

B36j. -----. "Classical: Samuel Barber's Best--Knox-
ville: Summer of 1915" Stereo Review 22:76-77 (June
1969)
"...Knoxville was composed during a period in which
Barber was very obviously trying on new styles and techniques. Knoxville--there is no mistaking it--is trying on
'Americana,' and specifically Americana a la Copland: if
the arpeggiated figuration closing the piece doesn't remind
you of the closing (and opening) of Appalachian Spring,
then you cant have heard the Copland work. But there is
virtually no composer's style that is hard to try on without getting egg on your face, and it is to Barber's credit
that Knoxville is not really Coplandesque at all, but
perhaps more 'Barber' than any other work of his I
know...[it] is a technical tour de force in that it has
mastered the prosodic eccentricities and complexities of
its text and, further, has done so within an immaculately
clear formal structure." [RCA LSC 3062] See: D36b

B36k. -----. "Classics." HIFI/Stereo Review 11:56 (July
1963)
"This setting of James Agee's prose poem, an excerpt
from the celebrated novel, A Death in the Family, is quite

likely Samuel Barber's masterpiece. No other work of his so glows with sensitivity and feeling, and no subsequent performance has topped this 1950 recording of the work." [ColumbiaML5843] See: D36d

   B36l. Friedewald, Russell Edward. A Formal and Stylis-tic Analysis of the Published Music of Samuel Barber. Thesis (Ph.D.)--Iowa State University, 1957. 357 p.
   "In addition to the cohesive nature of the form, the melodic material throughout is closely related by virtue of its chordal construction (Barber's predilection for chordal melodies has been pointed out earlier in this study.) The oscillation between F sharp minor and its related major tonic A gives additional evidence that the composer con-siders either chord as a substitute for the other." [p. 69] See: W36

   B36m. Galt, Martha. "New Music--With Emphasis on Eas-ter." Music Clubs Magazine 29:20 (February 1950)
   Brief review of the Schirmer piano-reduction score. "Like the composer's Dover Beach...he has achieved a per-fect relation between words and music...this is very keenly expressed through the medium of an original mind, which welded it into unity and beauty." See: W36

   B36n. Glanville-Hicks, Peggy. "New Music: Piano Score Edition Issued of Barber Vocal Work." Musical America 70:89 (January 15, 1950)
   Brief review of the piano reduction score by G. Schir-mer. "A wistful, nostalgic, vivid piece of prose by James Agee is the text; and Barber's music, without resort to tricks of atmospheric depiction, relates well to the ideas, underlining the mood of melancholy in the recollection of the familiar things of childhood...an effective piece for singers, in a genre and of a length not too often found." See: W36

   B36o. Goldberg, Albert. "'Three for July' by Camerata of L. A." Los Angeles Times, July 3, 1973, pt. 4, p. 8.
   "The choicest panel of this mismatched triptych pre-dictably proved to be Barber's nostalgic evocation of a small town family scene on a summer night, as described in James Agee's poetic prose. Delcina Stevenson's pure lyric soprano floated the vocal line with attractive sensibility and perceptiveness though with less than complete intel-ligibility, and Barber's delicate instrumentation received appreciative treatment by the good Camerata Orchestra, conducted by H. Vincent Mitzelfelt." See: W36f

   B36p. Griffiths, Paul. "Record Reviews." Musical Times 119:864 (October 1968)
   "...its nostalgic text justifies the luxuriant conserva-tism of the music. Molly McGurk floats a voluptuous line against the backdrop so richly painted by David Measham and his players." [Unicorn UNS 256] See: D36a

B36q. Haggin, B. H. "From Byrd to the Moderns." New Republic 148:26 (June 29, 1963)
"...the music, though irrelevant or contradictory to the text, could be impressive in itself; but Barber's music here, as elsewhere, is that of a man who can fit sounds into progressions which go from a beginning to an end, and which from beginning to end present nothing that is fresh or individual and as such worth attention." [Columbia ML 5843] See: D36d

B36r. "In Praise of Leontyne." Opera News 46:8-11 (January 23, 1982)
Pianist Van Cliburn and record producer Richard Mohr discuss Leontyne Price as she celebrates her 21st year at the Met. Mohr recalls: "I remember when she recorded one of my favorite records of all times, Samuel Barber's Knoxville: Summer of 1915...Leontyne just prior to that had lost her father. There is this marvelous line in the James Agee text, 'God bless my father, God bless my mother.' I said to here before we started the recording, 'I hope this text isn't going to upset you.' And she said, 'No, I'm going to sing it for my father.' You listen to that record today, and there are sounds that are beyond any human capability. It is spiritual, it is radiant."

B36s. Kammerer, Rafael. "Leontyne Price Soloist in Barber Work." Musical America 79:37-38 (December 1, 1959)
Review of the November 13, 1959 performance with Leontyne Price and Thomas Schippers. "Barber's score points up wondrously the magic of vanished summer eves, and Leontyne Price, beautifully seconded by Mr. Schippers and the orchestra, sang the vocal line evocatively, with a moving intensity and an inner ecstasy that tugged at the heart-strings...needless to say the eminent soprano and the young conductor were recalled again and again." See: W36d

B36t. Kolodin, Irving. "Recordings in Review: Steber's Berlioz and Barber." Saturday Review 46:50 (May 25, 1963)
"The Barber makes a fine sequential experience after the two concluding songs of Les Nuits on Side 2; the sound hangs in the air like a living thing, sure, full-bodied, and absolutely suited to the material (it was written on a commission by her)." [Columbia ML 5843] See: D36d

B36u. Kupferberg, Herbert. "Record Reviews." Atlantic 212:121 (July 1962)
"Samuel Barber's Knoxville: Summer of 1915, with a text by the late James Agee, has taken on the stature of an American musical classic, as has Eleanor Steber's singing of it...Columbia might have indicated clearly on the jacket that these are, in fact, reissues and not new recordings." [Columbia ML 5843] See: D36d

B36v. Leigh, E. S. V. "Concerts." New Records 47:5 (April 1979)

"Molly McGurk has an engaging, artless voice that is well suited..." [Unicorn UN1 72016] See: D36a

B36w. McDonagh, Don. "Alvin Ailey Ballet on Love and Death Danced in Brooklyn." New York Times, April 23, 1969, p. 41.
"Transience--in life, love, friendship and simple social justice--has been the source of many of Alvin Ailey's finest dances. Last night...the Alvin Ailey Dance Theater performed a beautiful revival of one such ballet: Mr. Ailey's 'Knoxville: Summer of 1915'...The ballet was first performe in 1959 for an absurdely short run of one evening. In 1968 it was revised for performance at the Edinburgh Festival, and it is this version which we now see." See: W36e

B36x. Miller, Philip L. "Other Reviews." American Record Guide 35:282 (December 1968)
"Knoxville was composed in 1947; in 1950 Miss Steber recorded it for Columbia. Her performance has been much admired, and this is its second reissue. During a period when it was temporarily not available she recorded the piece again with the Greater Trenton Symphony under Harsanyi, issuing it on her own St/And label. Since her company is no longer functioning, that second try may be itself a collector's item; but her first--i.e., this one--remains the classic." [Odyssey 32 16 0230] See: D36c

B36y. "New Publications in Review." Musical Courier 141:54 (February 15, 1950)
"His harmonies are on the conservative side, with a really lovely section in A major opening and closing the work, and a sympathetic lyricism pervading the whole. In the present edition the piano reduction is Barber's own, with instrumental indications cued in." See: W36

B36z. Osborne, Conrad L. "Classical." High Fidelity 12:76 (August 1962)
"It is a highly poetic piece of writing [the text], but it is not poetic in the way Barber seems to want it to be. The final lovely lines...are climactic, but climactic, I should think in a muted, fading way. Barber's sweaty, vocally ungrateful little outburst here strikes one as a slightly adolescent interpretation of the lines. All this adds up to a cycle that is overblown, that tried to make points that aren't there--this despite Barber's frequently deft touch and the pleasant nostalgic air with which he invests the piece." [St/and SLP 420] See: D36f

B36aa. -----. "Classical." High Fidelity 13:82 (November 1963)
"Both vocally and orchestrally, this version of the Barber piece is far more appealing than the later performance...Miss Steber's soprano here sounds fresh, sweet, and full with some floated high tones reminiscent of her

Sophie days--and it is well balanced against the orchestra by the 1950 Columbia engineering (still excellent today, by the way). Actually, I would prefer a less cultured, more 'American'-sounding approach to the Agee text--I don't think rolled r's really have any place here--but Steber was, after all, the creator of the solo part." [Columbia ML 5843] See: D36d

B36bb. Osborne, Conrad L. "Classical." High Fidelity 19:82 (June 1969)
"My own problem with Knoxville is that I am always more moved by the Agee prose than I am by the Barber set-ting; yet in fairness it must be said that the writing is honestly felt, nicely scored, and possessed of a mild but genuine fragrance of its own. I always wonder why it was set for soprano." [RCA Red Seal LSC 3062] See: D36b

B36cc. Porter, Andrew. "Opera." Gramophone 47:302 (August 1969)
"...Knoxville, whose lazy rocking ritornello tune goes on running through the mind for days, is a hunting, en-dearing composition...The text...is the close of an auto-biographical essay by James Agee: 'It has become that time of evening when people sit on their porches, rocking gently and talking gently and watching the street...' Lovable words. Lovable music. And a generous warm-spirited compo-ser who has matched them perfectly." [RCA Red Seal SB 67989] See: D36b

B36dd. Quillan, James W. "The Songs of Samuel Barber." Repertoire 1:17-22 (October 1951)
"A quotation at the top of the first page of music gives an indication of the nostalgic quality of the text to follow...Barber has captured this nostalgia to a degree that is uncanny." See: W36

B36ee. "Reviews of New American Music." Music Clubs Magazine 29:16 (December 1949)
Very brief review of the Schirmer piano-reduction score. "This is a thoroughly charming and desirable work in modern conservative vein for high voice, rather long, substantial, melodious." See: W36

B36ff. "Reviews of New Music." Musical Opinion 78:225 (January 1955)
Review of the G. Schirmer/Chappell score. "Occasional-ly, in the use of a 'motto' figure, harmonic or rhythmic, one is reminded of Britten, but for the most part Barber's style is emphatically his own, and a rich, rewarding style it is." See: W36

B36gg. S., R. "Strickland Leads Contemporary Works." Musical America 76:18 (March 1956)
"It is a vision of an America that is fast disap-

pearing and a marvelous glimpse into a child's heart. Miss
Stahlman sang the solo part movingly..." See: W36b

B36hh. Sagmaster, Joseph. Cincinnati Symphony Orchestra Program Notes, March 15-16, 1974 [unpaged]
    "Agee's free style poem is treated as a recitative,
with a varied metrical beat. At the close, as the child is
taken to bed, the music becomes quiet and closes in phrases
for woodwinds, horns, harp and strings." [Evelyn Lear/Tho-
mas Schippers performance] See: W36g

B36ii. Saxby, Richard. "Samuel Barber" [album notes
for Unicorn UNS 256 disc]
    "Barber creates the atmosphere he wants at once and
sustains it without effort for almost twenty minutes,
showing how far he has developed, even since the Violin
Concerto. The episode of the streetcar, with its almost
Stravinskian glitter, is especially noteworthy for the
excitement of the harmonics and the vividness of the
rhythms but what remains in the memory is the way one is
immediately captured and held by that opening motif whose
repetitions are so effective and moving. A hint of folk-
song evokes the childlike innocence of the narrator and
establishes that this is an American town. The words may
be prose but the music indeed is poetry. It should provide
a temptation for more exploring in what is for most British
people virtually uncharted territory." See: D36a

B36jj. Schillaci, Daniel. "For the Record." New West
6:118 (April 1981)
    "The music is in the prose, there is nothing to 'com-
plete.' Yet Barber, drawing on his melodic gift at its
freshest, evokes the right sense of innocence and earthly
effulgence." [RCA Red Seal LSC 3062] See: D36b

B36kk. Simmons, Walter. "Classical Recordings." Fanfare 2:22+ (March/April 1979)
    Knoxville: Summer of 1915 is a quite uncharacteristic
excursion (for Barber) into the realm of American-flavored
nostalgia (at its most sensitive and poignant, to be sure),
and ironically its great popularity has led many into the
erroneous impression that the work represents Barber at his
most quintessential. Moreover, this single piece has become an exceedingly influential work as well, a veritable
prototype for an entire school of progeny (Corigliano,
LaMontaine, and Floyd, among other) drawn to this slightly
reserved, self-effacing, yet exquisitely lyrical approach
to poetic settings, and to instrumental music too. What
makes this ironic is that the Knoxville style is not really
pure Barber, as many elements were distilled from Copland
and Stravinsky for this particular work." [Unicorn UN 1-
72016] See: D36a

B36ll. "Summer, 1915." Newsweek 31:84-85 (April 19,
1948)

"Koussevitzky had urged Sam Barber, easily one of our finest young composers, to write a work for voice and orchestra. And Miss Steber, for whom Barber had wanted to compose something, commissioned it. So Koussevitzky, Miss Steber and the Boston Symphony (who had taken to it from the first rehearsal) gave Knoxville: Summer of 1915 a beautiful, compelling performance...The music Barber wrote is modern, but ridden with melody and perceptive of the mood Agee created. The part for soprano is perfectly suited to Miss Steber's extraordinary legato and impeccable musicianship. Although the critics were divided on the work itself, Miss Steber's performance drew the highest marks." See: W36a

B36mm. Taubman, Howard. "Music: American Gain." New York Times, November 14, 1959, p. 13.
"Knoxville: Summer of 1915 is a profoundly American work, not simply because it deals with an American subject, but because it brings to life a time and mood. James Agee's prose poem recalling a child's intimations of sorry in the sweet security of his family's nearness is as moving as was his extended development of the subject in his posthumous novel, A Death in the Family. And Samuel Barber's music, in its refinement and perception, fills out and enriches the emotion...Under Thomas Shippers direction, the piece had an affecting performance. The soloist was Leontyne Price, who sang with such a grasp of the work's spirit that one was hardly aware of vocalism. When one thought about it, one realized that the control and shading of the voice were delicate and the phrasing admirable. But one's interest was drawn to the heart of the work's emotion; that is an interpreters proudest achievement. Mr. Schippers led the orchestra in a fine-fibered reading. The balance with the soloist was first rate; one reacted to an artistic totality. Mr. Barber's music is not idiosyncratic; it pursues no theories. In its simplicity, tenderness and honesty it goes to the essence of the subject. In externals one could find derivations from other sources; in its penetration it is thoroughly and touchingly American." See: W36d

B36nn. "Two by Americans." Time 74:72 (November 23, 1959)
Barber's Knoxville was at its best when it was least pretentious, matching with quiet lyricism Agee's poetic vision of a remote summer evening in the South..." See: W36d

B36oo. "Vocal." New Records 19:13 (May 1951)
"There is a general mood about the work that most certainly evokes the time, the place, and the season. Nostalgic, misty, and dreamlike..To some listeners it will bring back days they have experienced...to others it will be a meaningless meandering composition of small import." [Columbia ML 2174] See: D36d

B36pp.   Waters, Edward N.   "Music." Quarterly Journal of Current Acquisitions 15:15 (November 1957)

"The manuscript pages show three different versions of this important and popular work. One is a penciled score for voice and orchestra, dated April 4, 1947; a second version, also penciled, is for voice and piano and bears the same date; the third version, again in pencil, is for voice and smaller orchestra. The last-mentioned manuscript is incomplete, lacking approximately the first half, but this makes it no less welcome. The three versions together form a highly significant unit in the output of one of America's major composers." See: W36

B36qq.   Whittall, Arnold.   "Orchestral."   Gramophone 56:182 (July 1978)

"The text of Knoxville, by James Agee, presents a child's view of family life in a small Tennessee town. It has some tiresome quasi-poetic flights, but Barber's setting is touchingly unaffected; if over-provided with cadence points." [Unicorn UNS 256] See: D36a

B41. MELODIES PASSAGERES, OP. 27.

B41a.   Friedewald, Russell Edward.   A Formal and Stylistic Analysis of the Published Music of Samuel Barber. Thesis (Ph.D.)--Iowa State University, 1957.   357 p.

"These five songs are comparatively short, and with the exception of the fourth, no obvious tone painting is employed. The distinguishing feature of each song lies above all in its consistent delicacy and lack of pretentious mannerisms." [p. 76] See: W41

B41b.   George, Earl. "Solo Songs." Notes 10:497 (June 1953)

"In setting some of Rilke's French poems Samuel Barber has...so immersed himself in what he has apparently felt to be the appropriate Gallic idiom that little of his own identity remains perceptible. But the results are, as usual, masterful and convincing, often more so than his French models." See: W41

B41c.   Goldman, Richard F. "Current Chronicle: New York." Musical Quarterly 38:435-437 (July 1952)

"The distinction of Barber's songs lies above all in a consistent delicacy and lack of pretentious mannerism. The music seems natural and simple, though it is neither. It is the work of an experienced, assured, and subtle craftsman whose taste is equal to his technique, and whose sensibilities are in balance with his ingenuity. There is nothing new in the elements with which Barber works, either for Barber or for other composers; there is a fine quality of live, intelligent prosody, a harmonic consistency that preserves freshness within the limits of conventional tonality. But it is rare to find these elements in so fine a balance that one is not tempted to hear them or think of them as elements at all. Each song is that kind of whole which is more than the sum of its parts; each 'frames itself.' and achieves a musical communication that requires no translation or analysis, but merely attention...Barber's music remains, in these songs, neither startling nor novel. But its qualities remain far beyond competence, or what is now praised as 'craftsmanship.' Barber's music has always had a feeling of rightness about it, of achieving an intention completely, of curiously combining directness and sophistication. It is perhaps possible to sense, especially in the last of these songs, still further refinements to come." See: W41

B41d. H., C. "Bernac and Poulenc in Town Hall Recital." New York Times, February 11, 1952, p. 21.
Brief review of a recital by Pierre Bernac and Francis Poulenc at which Barber's Mélodies Passagères was presented for the first time. "The American Mr. Barber's music was written to French lyrics by the German poet, Rilke. The style was well suited to the text, being close to the romantic tradition of French composers." See: W41b

B41e. "New Publications in Review." Musical Courier 146:29 (November 1, 1952)
"The style is influenced by modern French idioms, the vocal line of semi-parlando sort...the piano accompaniment is fairly simple, including ostinato effects in The Bell Tower section, with sustained chords in the bass. Well worth the effort of a sensitive interpreter." See: W41

B41f. Ramey, Phillip. "Songs of Samuel Barber and Ned Rorem" [album notes for New World Records NW 229 disc]
The extensive notes in this album contain an interview with Samuel Barber. In part: Phillip Ramey: "You used a French text for your Mélodies Passagères. American composers have generally avoided setting foreign languages." Samuel Barber: "Americans generally avoid speaking foreign languages, so it's not surprising. Almost everything I've done has been in English, but I happen to speak fluent French, so there seemed no reason not to set those Rilke poems. I was living in France at the time [1950-51] and was, I suppose, in a French mood. Those particular poems were written while Rilke was living in Paris (he was secretary to Rodin), and he actually wrote them in French." See: D41a

B41g. "Reviews of New Music." Musical Opinion 76:33 (October 1952)
Brief review of the G. Schirmer/Chappell score. "Intricate weaving of parts, so beloved of Barber, is in evidence in all but 'Tombeau dans un parc,' where the voice has a serene recitative against a simple chordal accompaniment from the piano." See: W41

B41h. Sabin, Robert. "New Songs and Cycles by American Composers." Musical America 72:26 (December 15, 1952)
Brief review of the G. Schirmer/Chappell score. "Barber has always been at his best in his songs, and if these settings are not as melodically inspired or as emotionally evocative as some of his others, they are nonetheless sensitive in coloring and felicitous in verbal and musical accent." See: W41

B46. NUVOLETTA, OP. 25.

B46a. Carson, Leslie. "Secular Music." Musical Courier 147:39 (February 15, 1953)
"Nuvoletta, a setting by Samuel Barber of an excerpt from James Joyce's Finnegan's Wake, is an amusing, if highly individual song depicting in unconventional words (as is this author's later trait) the whimsical departure from this world of the bewitching heroine. It is surprisingly poetic, with a disillusioned, tender undertone. A work for sophisticates only, it has a tessitura ranging from B sharp below the staff to A sharp above it, and at one place there is an elaborate cadenza." See: W46

B46b. Daniel, Oliver. "Take Me to Your Lieder." Saturday Review 48:84 (October 30, 1965)
"...it is a pretentious and rather fussy display piece that, for all its care, is too low in musical content to sustain interest." [Desto DST 6411/2] See: D46b

B46c. Flanagan, William. "Samuel Barber Song Draws Text from Joyce." Musical America 74:224 (February 15, 1954)
"A wonderfully ingratiating long song with a text taken from Joyce's Finnegan's Wake has come from Samuel Barber...Although this new song, called Nuovoletta[sic] is by no means as long or as impressive as Knoxville, it is still a triumph of a similar musico-poetic enterprise; it is also smoothly lyrical, splendidly workmanlike, and often quite funny. If I were a singer, I shouldn't be able to wait to perform it." See: W46

B46d. Quillan, James W. "The Songs of Samuel Barber." Repertoire 1:17-22 (October 1951)
"A sort of rondo for voice and piano, with a vocal cadenza wholly original, it speeds along in a rapid three-eight rhythm. No matter that the words are sometimes strange, the music is positively captivating and a joy to perform. Barber must have had a rare good time composing this song; it is full of unexpected details." See: W46

B46e. Ramey, Phillip. "Songs of Samuel Barber and Ned Rorem" [album notes for New World Records NW 229 disc]
Phillip Ramey: "Have you ever set a poem that you didn't entirely understand?" Samuel Barber: "Yes. The

song <u>Nuvoletta</u> is a case in point. The text is from James
Joyce's <u>Finnegan's</u> <u>Wake</u>. I'm not unlearned in Joyce. I've
read quite a few books on him. But what can you do when
you get lines like 'Nuvoletta reflected for the last
time on her little long life, and she made up all her
myriads of drifting minds in one; she cancelled all her
engagements, she climbed over the banisters, she gave a
chilly, childly, cloudy cry' except to set them instinctively, as abstract music, about like a vocalise?" [New
World Records NW 229; incidentally, even though discussed
in the album notes, <u>Nuvoletta</u> is not contained on the disc]
<u>See</u>: W46

     B46f. Rich, Alan. "Songs of American Composers." <u>High</u>
<u>Fidelity</u> 15:103 (April 1965)
     "Much of the music is treasurable. Samuel Barber's
setting of a passage from <u>Finnegan's</u> <u>Wake</u> is justly famous
for its wit and high art." [Desto SLP 7411/2, SLS 7411/2]
<u>See</u>: D46b

     B46g. Starkie, Walter. "James Joyce and Music." <u>Satur-</u>
<u>day</u> <u>Review</u> 43:47 (March 26, 1960)
     "<u>Finnegan's</u> <u>Wake</u> is an easier medium for composers and
the most successful wedding of words and music of the whole
record is <u>Nuvoletta</u> set by Samuel Barber, who gives us
radiant and ethereal music as 'Nuvoletta climbs over the
banister and gives her childe cloudy cry.' Patricia
Neway's singing of this and <u>Anna</u> <u>Livia</u> <u>Plurabelle</u> is a
splendid tour de force of diction, drama , and lyricism."
[Lyrichord LL83] <u>See</u>: D46a

B51. SONGS (3), OP. 2.

     B51a. Flanagan, William. "Collections." <u>HiFi/Stereo</u>
<u>Review</u> 18:99 (January 1967)
     "Needless to say, we hear nothing of Samuel Barber's
more sophisticated later products (like the delicious
<u>Hermit</u> <u>Songs</u>, but get instead the early familiar pot-
boilers..." [Duke University Press DWR 6417B, <u>Bessie</u> <u>Bob-</u>
<u>tail</u> only] <u>See</u>: D51c

     B51b. Friedewald, Russell Edward. <u>A</u> <u>Formal</u> <u>and</u> <u>Stylis-</u>
<u>tic</u> <u>Analysis</u> <u>of</u> <u>the</u> <u>Published</u> <u>Music</u> <u>of</u> <u>Samuel</u> <u>Barber</u>.
Thesis (Ph.D.)--Iowa State University, 1957. 357 p.
     "The three songs that are included in Opus 2 show the
lyrical qualities of Barber's early musical thought. The
emphasis is on clear tonality, on a simple, flowing vocal
line, and although not derived from folk songs,they nevertheless show the spontaneity that is often associated with
them." [p. 3] <u>See</u>: W51

     B51c. Miller, Philip L. "An Anthology of American Art
Song." <u>American</u> <u>Record</u> <u>Guide</u> 32:784 (May 1966)
     "Samuel Barber early made a lasting name with a number

of successful songs. Four good examples given here range from 1934 to 1941." [Bessie Bobtail only] [Duke University Press DWR 6417B] See: D51c

B51d. Moore, Dale. "Favorite American Concert Songs by Samuel Barber and others" [album notes for Cambridge CRS 2715 disc]
"Whether sung by a young student in the studio or by an established singer in formal concert this song cannot help but please. It is really as unbelievable a 'first song' as Brahms' Liebestreu." [The Daisies only] See: D51e

B51e. Quillan, James W. "The Songs of Samuel Barber." Repertoire 1:17-22 (October 1951)
"These pose no technical problems for the pianist; however for the singer, Bessie Bobtail requires more breath control and more dramatic sense than most amateurs possess. The Daisies and With Rue My Heart Is Laden are graciously lyrical..." See: W51

B52. SONGS (3), OP. 10.

B52a. Ditsky, John. "Classical Recordings." Fanfare 6:93 (May/June 1983)
This is "...a rich sampling of Samuel Barber's songs, including pieces from both early and late in the late composer's career." [Sleep Now and I Hear an Army only] [Etcetera ETC 1002] See: D52f

B52b. Friedewald, Russell Edward. A Formal and Stylistic Analysis of the Published Music of Samuel Barber. Thesis (Ph.D.)--Iowa State University, 1957. 357 p.
"The text of Rain Has Fallen conveys a nostalgic mood, and the musical setting explicitly reflects this quality...In the vocal part of Rain Has Fallen the composer captures the melancholy, lyrical quality of the poem with the short haunting motive that is stated twice (the motive is varied in the second phrase) in each section...It is a powerful setting of a poem [I Hear an Army] which is in essence a 'dream-vision.' A vigorous, strident figure for the piano, starting forte, most vividly brings to life the opening lines of the poem." [pp. 20, 25, 30] See: W52

B52c. H., A. "New Music: Songs: Schirmer (Chappell)." Musical Times 81:66 (February 1940)
"Three remarkable compositions by Samuel Barber are commended to the serious student of modern songs. They are settings of poems from James Joyce's Chamber Music. Their difficulties, often the initial ones of sight-reading, are entirely those of interpretation and do not include extremes of pace, vocal range or pianism...By the way, Barber's accompaniments, though as modern as you will care for, are not of what has been called the 'errant weevils in cheese' type." See: W52

B52d. Quillan, James W. "The Songs of Samuel Barber."
Repertoire 1:17-22 (October 1951)
     "Here the composer has completely succeeded with a
powerful setting of the 'dream-vision.'" See: W52

B52e. Waters, Edward N. "Music." Quarterly Journal
of Current Acquisitions [of the Library of Congress] 18:15
(November 1960)
     Among the current acquisitions by the Library of Con-
gress Mr Waters reports, "That distinguished American composer, Samuel Barber (b. 1910), continued to add to the
manuscripts he has placed here by presenting two short
works.   The first is the song, I Hear an Army [op. 10, no.
3] (piano accompaniment), which comes in both pencil and
ink versions. It was composed in 1936 and is the third and
last of Three Songs to Poems from 'Chamber Music' by James
Joyce. (Mr. Barber had previously presented the manuscripts
of the first two songs)." See: W52

B53. SONGS (4), OP. 13.

B53a. Blyth, Alan.   "Choral and Song." Gramophone
60:946 (February 1983)
     "However apt they may be to the texts in hand, Bar-
ber's songs seem somewhat tame and uninspired in the company of Britten." [Conifer ETC 1002] See: D53f

B53b. Downes, Olin.   "Recital is Given by Povla
Frijsh." New York Times, April 8, 1941, p. 33.
     Review of the April 7, 1941 Town Hall performance. "A
song in English, which just missed being important, by
Samuel Barber, 'A Nun Takes the Veil'...much liked by the
audience." See: W53b

B53c. Eaton, Frances Q.   "Povla Frijsh, Soprano."
Musical America 63:14 (November 10, 1943)
     "Review of the October 24, 1943 New York City perfor-
mance, but with no direct reference to Barber or the
individual song [A Nun Takes a Veil]. "She has a knack for
evoking the whimsy and the subtle aura of such material,
and her admirers reward her with hearty affectionate applause." See: W53c

B53d. Frankenstein, Alfred. "Recitals and Miscellany."
High Fidelity 16:91 (June 1966)
     "Samuel Barber's lyricism is occasionally plausible.
Hanks is a very acceptable if not tremendously exciting
singer. He has a nice tone, projects a lyric line well,
has a fair command of nuance, gets in trouble with his
intervals now and then. Ruth Friedberg is a superlative
pianist, and one would like to hear her in an album of her
own. The sound throughout is excellent." [Duke University
Press, DWR 6417B] [Sure on This Shining Night only] See:
See: D53d

B53e. Friedewald, Russell Edward. A Formal and Stylistic Analysis of the Published Music of Samuel Barber.
Thesis (Ph.D.)--Iowa State University, 1957. 357 p.
"The vocal line is a long, flowing melody from the
beginning to the end, and the piano writing is an important
aspect of the over-all design rather than a mere accompanying part [Sure on This Shining Night]...The feeling of
this darkly passionate poem has been fully captured by
Barber's somewhat turgid setting. [Nocturne] [p. 42, 45]
See: W53

B53f. H., A . "New Music: Songs: Schirmer (Chappell)."
Musical Times 82:336 (September 1941)
"The nearest approach to such a personal forging of
style among the song writers is that of Samuel Barber, who
has a sensitive and economical command of pictorial background...Both the words and their settings are for those
who know them, but one is rewarded by the attempt to learn
them...Of his Four Songs only one is poor, viz., Sure on
This Shining Night, in which amateurish attempts at canon
between voice and R. H. piano impoverish both melody and
forward thrust of harmony...In Yeat's Secret of the Old,
the spirit of whimsy is delicately realized by simple
means, such as the punch of first and fourth quaver in a
prevailing 5-8 scheme: dignity and resignation are portrayed with masterly economy in the shortest and finest of
the four, a setting of G. M. Hopkins' A Nun Takes the Veil.
A lyric from Prokosch's Carnival set under the title of
Nocturne shows the composer at grips with more sententious
modern poetry than in the other songs." See: W53

B53g. Harrison, Lou. "Recitals in the Fall." Modern
Music 21:36 (November-December 1943)
In his review of a recital by Povla Frijsh Mr. Harrison remarks, "Samuel Barber contrived the dullest song in a
long time in his setting of [Gerald Manly] Hopkins' A Nun
Takes the Veil. The vocal line is an aimless rise and fall
without a moment of melodic distinction, and it is furthermore, accompanied by piano material of an exactly similar
degree of banality." See: W53c

B53h. Orr, C. W. "Reviews of Music." Music Review
2:335-336 (November 1941)
"His melodic line is awkward and unvocal, and the
writing for the piano without much distinction. Indeed,
the accompaniment of the Yeats song recalls the old
'vamping' style that was such a present help in trouble to
the man at the piano who was doing his best in old-
fashioned concert parties. At the same time one feels that
Mr. Barber is gifted and sincere enough to do better than
anything shown here. He should try again." See: W53

B53i. Osborne, Conrad L. "Recitals and Miscellany."
High Fidelity 12:93 (May 1962)
"Though there is some sensitive musicianly singing

here, there is little imagination or coloring of the
voice's attractive tone." [Da Vinci D-203] See: D53l

B53j. Quillan, James W. "The Songs of Samuel Barber."
Repertoire 1:17-22 (October 1951)
"...with the simplest of means, Barber has evoked the
mood of the Hopkins poem [A Nun Takes the Veil]. With only
a few rolled chords in the accompaniment he has suggested
music in a convent chapel...In The Secrets of the Old we
find much in evidence Barber's happy faculty of fitting the
music to the rhythm of the works...[Sure on This Shining
Night "...one of the loveliest of all the composer's songs.
It is one long, beautiful melody from beginning to end.
The piano answers the phrases in the voice part until the
last page, when the voice answers the piano...This darkly
passionate poem [Nocturne has been fully captured by Barber's somewhat turgid setting. It is the most ambitious
song in this opus and is the most effective in performance." See: W53

B53k. Rorem, Ned. "A Selected Gallery of the Composers" [album notes for New World Records NW 243 disc]
"Consider this setting, from 1939, of the rather non-
descript verses of James Agee...It is neither the simple
tune nor the primary harmonics of Sure on This Shining
Night that render it bland...but the ear searches in vain
for a personal signature. The piano may echo snatches of
Canteloube's Auvergne orchestrations, much admired in those
days, but the music could have been written by anyone. I
would not presume such harshness were not Barber an American glory. His instrumental music dating from this
period, his operas, ballets, concertos and above all his
song cycles during the following three decades are from the
pen of a musician who, so far as elegance is concerned,
stands alone." See: D53b

B53l. Schulman, Michael. "On the Record." Performing
Arts in Canada 15:52 (Winter 1978)
"Her [soloist Joan Patenaude] Canadian roots find much
more congenial stylistic soil closer to home in nine songs
by Samuel Barber (who is, arguably, somewhat less than a
'great opera composer'). She is especially effective in
three fine songs that let her 'act' vocally, Sure on This
Shining Night, The Secrets of the Old, and Solitary Hotel
[the last named is op. 41, no. 4], respectively set to
words by Agee, Yeats, and Joyce." [Musical Heritage Society MHS 3770] See: D53h

B53m. Weinraub, Bernard. "Marian Anderson Sings Finale,
But Cry is Bravo, Not Farewell." New York Times, April 19,
1965, p. 1.
"She stepped across the stage yesterday afternoon and
the applause rose from the audience in a sweeping and
throbbing wave. Her eyes glistening, her lips in a sight
smile, she whispered, 'Thank you, thank you, thank you,' as

two elderly women stood up in the paraquet. Suddenly and
dramatically the entire audience--2,900 persons--stood,
clapping, cheering and acclaiming the woman on stage--
Marian Anderson." Miss Anderson included <u>Nocturne</u> on her
program. <u>See</u>: W53k

**B54.   SONGS (4), OP. 13.   CHORAL TRANSCRIPTIONS.   A NUN
TAKES THE VEIL (HEAVEN-HAVEN).**

   B54a.   Horowitz, Linda.   "Literature Forum."   <u>Choral
Journal</u> 21:26-29 (December 1980)
      "The mood of this piece is personal and introspective
and Barber uses shifting meters to aid his sensitive setting of an essentially strophic text." <u>See</u>: W54

**B55.   SONGS (4), OP. 13.   CHORAL TRANSCRIPTIONS.   SURE ON
THIS SHINING NIGHT.**

   B55a.   Horowitz, Linda.   "Literature Forum."   <u>Choral
Journal</u> 21:26-29 (December 1980)
      "A 1961 choral transcription of his lovely vocal com-
position, originally composed in 1941." <u>See</u>: W55

B56.   SONGS (2), OP. 18.

   B56a.   Friedewald, Russell Edward. "A Formal and Stylistic Analysis of the Published Music of Samuel Barber."
Thesis (Ph.D.)--Iowa State University, 1957.   357 p.
      "The text of the poem [by Robert Horan] is somewhat
bizarre almost surrealistic, the musical setting being
conceived in such a manner as to reflect this quality very
effectively.   There are many false relations, and there is
virtually no feeling of harmonic progression in the traditional sense...The second song in Opus 18, entitled <u>Monks
and Raisins</u>, was written in 1943...The composer sets the
poem in a rapid seven-eight meter.   The form of the song is
ternary with a short rhythmic introduction and coda..These
two songs in Opus 18...represent a landmark in the career
of Barber as a song writer.   He seems to cast off the
chains of extreme conservatism by the extraordinary complexity of interplay between the voice and piano.   He
handles the unusual rhythmic patterns with complete confidence..." [pp. 55, 59, 61] <u>See</u>: W56

   B56b. Horan, Robert.   "American Composers, XIX: Samuel
Barber."   <u>Modern Music</u> 20:167 (March-April 1943)
      "In a most recent song, set to a text by José Garcia
Villa [<u>Monks and Raisins</u>], an unusual metre is employed
with a naturalness and wit.   The entire song, with the
exception of one measure, is in 7/8.   The pulse of the song
is almost reminiscent of Calypso rhythms..." <u>See</u>: W56

B56c. Quillan, James W. "The Songs of Samuel Barber."
Repertoire 1:17-22 (October 1951)
"For some strange reason these utterly delightful
songs have been overlooked and neglected by artists when
planning their programs for New York City as well as across
the country." See: W56

B57. SONGS (3), OP. 45.

B57a. Brewer, Robert. "Neue Kammermusik in New York."
Melos 41:238 (July-August 1974)
"Dietrich Fischer-Dieskaus vergeistigte Vortragskunst
und Charles Wadsworths pianistische Finesse sicherten der
Neuheit einhelligen Erfolg." ["Dietrich Fischer-Dieskau's
refined art and Charles Wadsworth's pianistic skill assured
this new work unmixed approval."--R.F.] See: W57

B57b. Ditsky, John. "Classical Recordings." Fanfare
6:93 (May/June 1983)
In reviewing this recording, Ditsky notes: "These are
lush settings of poets such as Joyce, Yeats, Agee, and
Milosz, and are consistent in approach with the smattering
of Barber's vocal writing already available on discs. Maurice has a rich and full-dimensioned voice, and Garvey is
an adept accompanist." [Etcetera ETC 1002] See: D57b

B57c. Schonberg, Harold C. "Music: Season's Finale."
New York Times May 2, 1974, p. 64.
"Mr. Barber's settings reflect his conservatism, his
lyricism and his practical hand as a composer. It was
interesting to hear them as sung by Mr. Fischer-Dieskau,
who seldom sings songs in English. His diction was fine
(though the words were not shaped as precisely as they
emerge in his lieder), his artistry impeccable." See: W57a

B59. THE WATCHERS.

B59a. "Homer and Daughter in Pleasing Recital." New
York Times, January 30, 1927, sect. 2, p. 6.
"In the English group, Mme. Homer proved how vocal and
musical the language really is, how expressive it is and
what a fund of pathos and humor it possesses. Samuel
Barber's The Watchers (in manuscript) had to be repeated."
See: W59b

ORCHESTRAL MUSIC

B61. ADAGIO FOR STRINGS, OP. 11.

B61a. "Barber." Music Survey 4:377 (October 1951)
"An interesting study in the crescendo and sustained climax and a very lovely piece of music, worth many of its composer's later and more pretentious efforts. Its beginning and ending on the dominant is a stroke of genius in the handling of this simple framework." [Decca X 305] See: D61g

B61b. Barnes, Clive. "Dance: 2 Old, 2 New by National Ballet." New York Times, March 30, 1967, p. 53.
Review of the National Ballet of Washington performance. "The main new work was 'Through the Edge'...[which] is set to Samuel Barber's 'Adagio for Strings,' very possibly the most sadly flatulent piece of popularly acclaimed music written this century." See: W61i

B61c. Berger, Arthur. "Spotlight on the Moderns." Saturday Review 34:61 (February 24, 1951)
"...Barber's well-made Adagio for Strings is so much like the Prelude to Faure's Pelleas and Melisande and the home-spun English style that it is sad to contemplate how widely it represents American music abroad." [London LPS 298] See: D61g

B61d. Bernheimer, Martin. "Chamber Symphony Closes Its Season." Los Angeles Times, April 21, 1970, pt. 4, p. 10.
"Barber's Adagio for Strings has become so familiar as an all-purpose cultural theme song that it is a bit difficult for this listener to take seriously in the concert hall. Temianka seemed to take it very seriously, however, with heavy accents, thick textures and a slow-slow tempo. The orchestra responded with its best effort of the evening." See: W61n

B61e. Bronston, Levering. "Orchestra." New Records 44:5-6 (June 1976)
"Marriner gives the Barber a measured, almost funeral pace, the music sounding as fresh and inspired to me as it did when I first heard the Toscanini recording almost thirty years ago." [Argo ZRG 845] See: D61a

B61f. Brown, Royal S. "Recitals and Miscellany." High Fidelity 26:132 (October 1976)
"Marriner and his forces concentrate strongly on unified sound, a tendency that perks in the most excessively vibrant shimmer imparted to the climax of the deeply elegiac Barber Adagio. And although this approach makes for rewarding listening, especially combined with the excellent Argo engineering, it strikes me that Marriner makes everything just a bit too smooth, both in the vertical textures, whose component parts are not delineated enough, and in the transitions." [Argo ZRG 845] See: D61a

B61g. Chislett, William A. "Nights at the Round Table." Gramophone 58:1002 (January 1981)

"There may be more inspiring tributes to Barber on his eightieth [sic, seventieth] birthday than this version of his Adagio for Strings, but there will be no more agreeable one." [Philips Festivo 6570 181] See: D61w

B61h. "Collections." Gramophone Shop. Record Supplement 14:7 (April 1951)
"Stunning recordings of some contemporary music..The familiar Adagio is brilliantly set forth by Mr. Neel and his string orchestra." [London LPS 298] See: D61g

B61i. Darrell, R. D. "Recitals and Miscellany." High Fidelity 27:128 (October 1977)
"Each of the six pieces represents a different national provence--The U.S., England, France, Spain, Russia, Austria--and each has distinctive appeals...mellifluous Barber Adagio." [Angel S 37409] See: D61r

B61j. Davis, Peter G. "Concert: Brooklyn Philharmonia in Ives, Sessions and Beethoven." New York Times, January 16, 1981, sect. 3, p. 19.
"Mr. Foss also added an extra, unscheduled American piece to the program, Samuel Barber's Adagio for Strings, as a tribute to the composer, who is gravely ill with cancer." See: W61q

B61k. Douglas, Basil. "Gramophone Notes." Musical Times 91:273 (July 1950)
"It was written for Toscanini, who also recorded it; his performance was so intense that he drove most of the poetry away. Boyd Neel's performance is not quite intense or poetic enough, and yet I prefer it to Toscanini's, for the playing is first rate and at least something of the spirit of the work is recaptured." [Decca X 305] See: D61g

B61l. Downes, Olin. "Barbirolli Offers American's Music." New York Times, January 26, 1940, p. 12.
"It has not only genuine and noble feeling but the sustained line which is unfortunately rare today. How many composers dare to stand or fall by the merits of a slow movement which must rely for its effect upon sheer invention and the ability to develop a thought? Here is high purpose and a quality of taste gratifying today and promising well for the future. We hold no particular brief for Mr. Barber, but in certain respects other native sons could afford to emulate him." See: W61c

B61m. -----. "Toscanini Plays Two New Works." New York Times, November 6, 1938, p. 48.
"Mr. Barber had reason for thankfulness for a premiere under such leadership. And the music proved eminently worth playing...There is an arch of melody and form. The composition is most simple at the climaxes, when it develops that the simplest chord, or figure, is the one most significant...This is the product of a musically creative

245

nature, and an earnest student who leaves nothing undone to achieve something as perfect in mass and detail as his craftsmanship permits." See: W61a

B61n. Ericson, Raymond. "Concert: Ilana Vered." New York Times, March 10, 1980, sect. 3, p. 12.
   The New York Philharmonic, conducted by Morton Gould played the Adagio for Strings, and the Waltz and Galop from Souvenirs in commemoration of Mr. Barber's 70th birthday. Mr. Barber was still recovering from a recent illness and could not attend. See: W61p

B61o. Frankenstein, Alfred. "Collections and Miscellany." High Fidelity 4:57 (May 1954)
   "Barber's Adagio is a bit of solemn romanticism richly exploiting the full sonorities of the strings." [Capitol P-8245] See: D61j

B61p. -----. "Recitals and Miscellany." High Fidelity 12:72 (July 1962)
   "They are all too familiar to demand discussion; suffice it to say that they are beautifully played here and well recorded." [Philips 900 001] See: D61w

B61q. Gilbert, J.-M. "Divers." Disques ser. 2, no. 39 1951:351.
   "Œuvre de jeunesse de Barber l'Adagio pour cordes est d'un intense romantisme, généraux, habilement transcrit du Quatuor à cordes, op. 11 pour un ensemble d'archets. Boyd Neel imprime à sa phalange une intense dignité lyrique et une puissante organisation des plans sonores." ["A work from Barber's youth, the Adagio for Strings is of an intense romanticism, noble, adroitly transcribed from the String Quartet, op. 11, for an ensemble of bows. Boyd Neel imparts to his phalanx an intense lyrical dignity and a powerful organization of sonorous designs."--L.M.] [London LPS 298, Decca LX 3042 (French)] See: D61g

B61r. Greenfield, Edward. "Orchestral." Gramophone 42:135 (September 1964)
   "The Barber Adagio is also rather heavily done (no one else's performance had yet approached Toscanini's) but it is the only available version in stereo." [HMV Concert Classics SXLP 20058] See: D61jj

B61s. -----. "Orchestral." Gramophone 61:155 (July 1983)
   "This is a beautiful collection of American music, lovingly and brilliantly performed. With Barber's lovely Adagio I was afraid that Bernstein would 'do a Nimrod' and present it with exaggerated expressiveness. Although the tempo is very slow indeed the extra hesitations are not excessive and the Los Angeles Strings play with angelic refinement and sweetness..." [DG 2532 085 (digital)] See: D61t

B61t. Grunfeld, Fred. "Barber's Adagio for Strings,
Op. 11" [album notes for Victor LM 2105 disc]
    "Samuel Barber's Adagio is all of a piece, though it
progresses through a tricky succession of rhythms...pro-
vides the occasion for a brilliant display of the virtuosity for which the Boston Symphony's string players have
been justly renowned ever since the days of Muck and
Nikisch." See: D61f

B61u. Hall, David. "Classical Discs and Tapes."
Stereo Review 37:123 (October 1976)
    "Barber's Adagio for Strings gets its best recorded
performance ever, excluding not even the celebrated reading
by Toscanini who premiered the music in its string-orches-
tra version. Here is not only the Toscaninian flawless
intonation, but also superb modern recording and rock-
steady unhurried pacing, a combination that makes for a
realization of hair-curling intensity." [Argo ZRG 845]
See: D61a

B61v. -----. The Record Book. New York: Citadel
Press, 1946. 1063 p.
    "Originally the slow movement of a String Quartet in B
Minor, this Adagio by the gifted young American composer,
Samuel Barber, has achieved great popularity in concert
performance. The reasons are obvious on first hearing, for
it is music of great lyric intensity and sincere feeling.
As might be expected Toscanini gives it everything he's got
(which is plenty) and is backed up by superb playing and
fine recording. Put this down as a 'must.'" [Victor 11
8287 (78 rpm)] See: D61y

B61w. Harrison, Max. "Concert." Times (London) March
25, 1982, p. 11.
    "Although Samuel Barber's Adagio for Strings has been
a popular classic since the days of Toscanini's advocacy,
and must have been performed all over the place, it was
quite salutary to hear it from the Leipzig Gewandhaus
Orchestra under Kurt Masur last night. This German orchestra lent a different emphasis from the usual one to the
nostalgic pathos of the long finely spun lines. A carefully balanced tension between widely arching melodies and
rich harmony yielded a frail, elegiac quality so that
American innocence was touched with an almost Mahlerian
world-weariness." See: W61r

B61x. Harvey, Trevor. "Orchestral." Gramophone 54:1704
(May 1977)
    "The Barber Adagio has a very long build-up to the big
moment of tension and climax beautifully calculated--I
wondered for a time if any build-up at all was coming, but
when it did its effect was the more tense." [Angel S 37409]
See: D61r

B61y. Horan, Robert. "American Composers, XIX: Samuel

Barber." <u>Modern</u> <u>Music</u> 24:164 (March/April 1943)
"The <u>Adagio</u> <u>for</u> <u>Strings</u> ...with its disarming simplicity, its sonority and its climax on a constant chord, is
the sort of music one might associate with the early
paintings of Chirico [Giorgio de, 1888-   ]. It has an
equal isolation; one imagines this music at home in Chirico's deserted courtyards and pink buildings, among those
shadowy children that disappear suddenly under archways
and around corners like startled animals." <u>See</u>: W61

B61z. Johnson, David. "Classical." <u>High</u> <u>Fidelity</u> 7:78
(September 1957)
"Barber's evocation of the sarabands of Johann Sebas-
tian Bach is performed with moving intensity." [Victor LM
2105] <u>See</u>: D61f

B61aa. Jones, Isabel Morse. "Korjus Wins Throng at
Auditorium." <u>Los</u> <u>Angeles</u> <u>Times</u>, March 4, 1939, pt. 2, p.
7.
"The <u>Adagio</u> <u>for</u> <u>Strings</u> is as fine a piece of atmospheric writing as America has produced since Charles Martin
Loeffler's death." [Otto Klemperer conducting the Los Angeles Philharmonic Orchestra] <u>See</u>: W61b

B61bb. Kolodin, Irving. <u>New</u> <u>Guide</u> <u>to</u> <u>Recorded</u> <u>Music</u>.
Garden City, N.Y.: Doubleday, 1950. 524 p.
"There is sound reason why this was the first work by
an American that Toscanini chose to record; its predominately conservative patterns are warmly reflected in the
eloquence of his playing." [p. 35] [Victor V 11 8287
(78rpm)] <u>See</u>: D61y

B61cc. Layton, Robert. "Records Reissued." <u>Gramophone</u>
51:997 (November 1973)
"Admittedly there are more eloquent accounts of the
Grieg, Hindemith and Barber works available, but these
accounts are well shaped and conscientious." [Decca
Eclipse ECS 688 (from mono BR 3039 and mono LXT 5153)]
<u>See</u>: D61nn

B61dd. Lester, William. "New Music for Organ." <u>Diapa-</u>
<u>son</u> 40:28 (November 1, 1949)
"One of the most inspired products of this prominent
composer, well reset for the organ by an expert in that
line [William Strickland]. The result is a meditative
lyrical movement of real beauty well worthy of attention
and hearing." <u>See</u>: W61

B61ee. McDonagh, Don. "Premiere of 'Youth,' Ballet of
Lost Love Given by Harkness." <u>New</u> <u>York</u> <u>Times</u>, November 8,
1967, p. 57.
"Boy meets girl and boy loses girl is the framework of
this haunting mood piece set to Samuel Barber's 'Adagio for
Strings.'" <u>See</u>: W61k

B61ff.   Macdonald, Malcolm. "Chamber Music." Gramophone 44:431 (February 1967)
    "String quartet single-movement length fill-ups lie very
thinly on the ground; a good one has been found in the
Barber Adagio, originally from a complete quartet of 1936,
but probably more familiar to audiences in general in its
later version for string orchestra. Here it is given
splendidly, with an intensity of tone at the climax which
will allow the piece its full effect even to ears accustomed at this point to the obviously greater power and
strength of a string orchestra." [HMV HQS 1061] See: D61q

B61gg. -----. "Orchestral." Gramophone 54:182 (July
1976)
    "There is also playing of the very fist order in
Samuel Barber's Adagio, with an intensity of string tone at
the climax hardly to be believed possible with the number
of players likely involved." [Argo ZRG 845] See: D61a

B61hh. -----. "Records Reissued." Gramophone 51:102
(June 1973)
    "It is unlikely that substantially better versions,
even considered individually, are going to be found than on
this very well recorded disc." [Philips Universo 6580 045
(from SABL 216)] See: D61w

B61ii.   McNaught, W. "Gramophone Notes." Musical Times
86:149 (May 1945)
    "This work has come to the front for good reason.
Though it shows no eagerness to gain the ear by fluent or
striking melodies or by colourful progressions, yet it
makes a direct appeal by a quality best described by calling it deeply musical. Moreover, it holds the attention
by steady growth and plan: not many composers put such
faith in sustained equable strength and responseful movement. At a first hearing you may not think it an eventful
piece, except near the climax at the end of side 1; but on
better acquaintance it takes shape as a long drawn single
event, with an unhurried rise and fall and growing in
cogency by its patient unfolding...The Adagio is played by
the N.B.C. Symphony Orchestra under Toscanini. [HMV DB
6180] See: D61y

B61jj. Majeski, John F., Jr. "Samuel Barber's Adagio
Led by Cantelli." Musical America 75:22 (April 1955)
    "Sonorous string sound characterized the Barber, but
Mr. Cantelli delivered the work as if he were directing the
Pathetique. Every last inch of emotion was wrung out of
this music where more simplicity was needed." See: W61f

B61kk. March, Ivan. "RCA Victrola." Gramophone 59:1292
(March 1982)
    "There is less electricity in the Barber Adagio but
Münch creates a convincing, spacious nobility at the cli-
max. [RCA Victrola VCS 2001] See: D61f

B61ll. Müllman, Bernd. "Schallplatten." Melos NZ 3:64 (January-February 1977)

"Das Adagio für Streicher, eine Bearbeitung das langsamen Satzes aus dem zweiten Streichquartett (op. 11) Machte ihn erstmals bekannt, weltwert, als dieser Satz als Trauermusik nach dem Tode Roosevelts erklangs." ["The Adagio for Strings, a revision of the slow movement from the second string quartet (op. 11), made him known for the first time, worldwide, when this movement was played as funeral music after the death of Roosevelt."--H.B.] [CBS 73 434] See: D61dd

B61mm. "I Musici" [album notes for Philips PHS 900 001 disc]

"Barber's Adagio has an obsessive tune and almost doleful harmonics, but the slow sustained movement of the piece is perfectly managed and disciplined, and the slow-motion rise and fall of single instrumental parts out of and back into the general texture of sound is exceedingly impressive." See: D61w

B61nn. Noble, Jeremy. "Orchestral." Gramophone 40:10 (June 1962)

"Barber's Adagio for Strings demands an intensity and flexibility that are quite impossible without a conductor and not always possible with one...anyone who first made the works acquaintance through the old 78 recording by Toscanini is bound to find this performance pretty unsatisfying." [Philips SABL 216] See: D61w

B61oo. "Orchestra." New Records 25:5 (August 1957)

"Think of all the nice words you can--they all apply to this disc: charming, ingratiating, rewarding, melodious, and so on." [Victor LM 2105] See: D61f

B61pp. Rawlinson, Harold. "Famous Works for String Orchestra, no. 20: Adagio for Strings." Strad 60:372+ (April 1950)

Brief remarks on performing the work and possible explanations for the composition's wide popularity. See: W61

B61qq. Reed, Peter Hugh. "Fascinating Novelties in New Records." Etude 61:31 (January 1943)

"The thoughtful restraint in this music is rare among modern composers; for Barber's music does not seem to be affected by the restlessness of our times." The article contains an excellent early photograph of Samuel Barber. See: W61

B61rr. Robertson, Alec. Analytical Notes and First Reviews." Gramophone 31:232 (December 1953)

"The music is eloquently played and will exercise its spell on those who surrender to its sad contemplative mood." [Columbia LX 1595 (78 rpm)] See: D61kk

B61ss.   Sabin, Robert. "Berlin Philharmonic Completes
Tour."   Musical America 75:23-24 (April 1955)
    "One of the best performances of the evening was that
of Samuel Barber's Adagio for Strings...Mr. Karajan shaped
its long, sinuous phrases firmly, while being careful not
to inhibit the singing freedom of his strings. The composer came to the stage to acknowledge the applause and thank
the orchestra." See: D61g

B61tt.   Salzman, Eric.   "Samuel Barber." HIFI/Stereo
Review 17:77-89 (October 1966)
    His [Arturo Toscanini] championing of this music
promptly put Barber--at the age of twenty-eight--in the
front rank of American composers. The Adagio immediately
became a repertoire work. It has the curious distinction
of becoming not merely a 'classic' but entering into general musical awareness in an almost subliminal way: it is
one of those universally accepted and recognized sound
images that are identifiable by people who have no concept
of what it actually is. It has been used for background
music innumerable times--Barber once discovered it being
used for a French television commercial. It was played in
American and England a few minutes after the announcement
of President Roosevelt's death; in South Africa it was
played to commemorate the passing of Jan Christian Smuts.
It has, in fact, gone around the world, and it must easily
rank as one of the half-dozen or so most performed American
compositions." See: W61, W61a

B61uu.   Schonberg, Harold C.   "Music: Berlin Encore."
New York Times, March 31, 1955, p. 24.
    "Mr. Barber's adagio was sweetly sung by the Berlin
strings, as rich-sounding a collection as has been heard in
this country." See: W61g

B61vv.   Sharp, Geoffrey N.   "Gramophone Records." Music
Review 6:123 (1945)
    "It is warm, lyrical music with a strong sense of
direction which leads us to expect great things of Mr.
Barber in the future." [HMV DB 6180, 78 rpm] See: D61y

B61ww.   Slonimsky, Nicolas.   "Four Melodic Masterpieces
of Samuel Barber" [album notes for CBS 32 11 0005, 32 11
0006 disc]
    "The music has a fairly archaic air: it is an essay in
austere polyphony, slowly rising in dynamic intensity
through a series of lingering chordal suspensions leading
to languorous cadences...The dirge-like serenity of the
Adagio suggests tranquility in grief. Unexpectedly, this
unpretentious movement from a string quartet became a
threnody...it was selected again and again to be performed
on occasions of public mourning." See: D61ee

B61xx.   The Stereo Record Guide, vol. 3. Ivan March,
editor. London: Long Playing Record Library, 1963 [pp.

661-1102]
    "...the climax of Barber's Adagio must be one of the
most intense moments of string playing ever captured on a
disc." [p. 977] [Capitol SP 8542] See: D61h

    B61yy. Turner, Charles. "The Music of Samuel Barber."
Opera News 22:7+ (January 27, 1958)
    "It has none of the characteristics usually associated
with American music--no hard-driven rhythms, jazz or otherwise, no explosive energy, no dissonances or harmony that
Bach might not have used. Its rhythm is freely flowing,
seemingly conceived in an age centuries before metronomes
were invented and the melodic lines are made of the simplest bits of diatonic scales, spiraling gradually upward.
Technically its only very contemporary feature is its form,
which seems just right for the piece. It might be pre-
Bach, classic, romantic or modern; but its highly personal
quality stamps it entirely Barber. There it nothing else
quite like it in American music." See: W61

    B61zz. "U. S. Composer Gets Toscanini's Approval." New
York Times, October 27, 1938, p. 26.
    News story and photograph of Barber. "For the first
time since he assumed directorship of the National Broadcasting Company's Symphony Orchestra, Arturo Toscanini will
perform the music of an American composer at one of the
weekly broadcasts. On Saturday evening, November 5, [1938]
he will conduct the world premiere performance of the
Adagio for Strings and Essay for Orchestra. See: W61a

    B61aaa. Waters, Edward N. "Music." Quarterly Journal
of Current Acquisitions 13:26 (November 1955)
    "Samuel Barber...gave the autograph score of two of
his best works--the Adagio for string quartet and the
Violoncello Concerto, op. 22. The former is the slow movement of his Quartet, op. 11, and provides the music of his
famous Adagio for Strings, so well known in orchestral
literature." See: W61

    B61bbb. Youngren, William "Ensemble." Fanfare 4:223-
24 (November/December 1980)
    "...the powerful and moving Barber Adagio, which I had
not heard since Toscanini performed it in the 1940's, is
really worth the candle. But the playing! Throughout this
very uneven batch of music I Musici exhibits a flawless
elegance, an aerated buoyancy, a sustained eloquence, and a
sheer tonal beauty that brings tears to one's eyes."
[Philips Festivo 6570 181] See: D61w

B62. ADVENTURE.

    B62a. "Composers Corner." Musical America 74:31 (De-

252

cember 1954)
"Samuel Barber received a challenging assignment from the producers of the CBS television program Adventure, who wanted music to demonstrate a number of aboriginal instruments from the American Museum of Natural History collection on November 28. Given a two-week deadline, the composer delivered a score calling for such artifacts as a nose flute, a water gong, and Burmese cymbals." See: W62

B62b. Waters, Edward N. "Harvest of the Year: Selected Acquisitions of the Music Division." Quarterly Journal of the Library of Congress 24:54-55 (January 1967)
"The score...was completed on November 25, 1954. Aptly titled Adventure it calls for an extraordinary orchestra of flute, clarinet, horn, harp, and a number of exotic 'instruments from the Museum of Natural History.' These include African sansas, a Balinese water drum, African xylophones, gourds filled with peas, hollow tree trunks, pressure drums, and still others for special effects." See: W62

B63. A BLUE ROSE.

B63a. Rutland, Harold. "A Blue Rose and The Angels." Musical Times 99:92 (February 1958)
The Junior Company of the Royal Ballet used Souvenirs as the music for its ballet A Blue Rose presented on Boxing Day (December 26, 1957) at Covent Garden, London. "Samuel Barber's Souvenirs, the suite used for the music...is so attractive and deftly written that it is difficult to understand why it was not drawn upon before for such a purpose." See: W63a

B64. CANZONETTA, OP. 48.

B64a. "New Wave Music Joins Jazz to Spice Festival Programs." (Charleston, S.C.) News and Courier, May 29, 1983 (located in NewsBank, Review of the Arts [microform], Performing Arts, 1983, 99:B6-7, fiche).
Review of the May 28, 1983 Piccolo Spoleto performance. "...a lovely and elegiac work that needed a richer and smoother string sound that [sic, than] the orchestra could supply, also a more liquid oboe technique than Eric Ohlsson provided." See: W64b

B64b. Porter, Andrew. "Musical Events." New Yorker 57:112 (January 18, 1982)
"Samuel Barber's last composition, completed in short score in 1978, soon after the Third Essay for Orchestra, was an eight-minute piece for oboe and string orchestra, intended to be the middle movement of an oboe concerto--one of the Philharmonic's series of concerto commissions for its own members to play. But the outer movements were

253

not written. The piece, put into full score after Barber's death last year by his pupil and friend, Charles Turner, now stands on its own with the title <u>Canzonetta</u>. The Philharmonic, under Zubin Mehta, gave the first performance last month, with Harold Gomberg, the orchestra's first oboe from 1943 to 1977, as the soloist. It is a graceful and endearing work, based on a charming and shapely lyrical melody, deftly treated...Barber was a fastidious and sure artist. <u>Canzonetta</u> is slight but elegantly written." <u>See</u>: W64a

B64c. Rockwell, John. "Philharmonic: 4 Pieces by Modern Composers." <u>New York Times</u>, December 20, 1981, p. 74.
"There was a world premiere on the program, in the form of Samuel Barber's posthumous <u>Canzonetta</u> for oboe and string orchestra [op. 48]...The brief movement was sweet and modestly luxurious in its lyricism, and Mr. Gomberg played it truly. Curiously though, for so seemingly uncontroversial a work, the performance was preceded by controversy, when Mr. [Charles] Turner called the <u>New York Times</u> to complain that the performance, by altering some passages and introducing a cadenza, had falsified Barber's intentions. But by Friday, some corrections had been made, and Mr. Mehta asserted that Mr. Turner had been mollified." <u>See</u>: W64a

B65. CONCERTO FOR PIANO AND ORCHESTRA, OP. 38.

B65a. Barker, Frank Granville. "Virtuoso Night Out." <u>Music and Musicians</u> 13:41 (August 1965)
Review of the June 21, 1965 London performance, Royal Festival Hall; John Browning, piano; Cleveland Orchestra, George Szell, conductor. "This is not a work of any real depth or enduring qualities, but as America's answer to Khachaturian it was immediately likeable as a romantic virtuoso piece." <u>See</u>: W65h

B65b. Barnes, Clive. "Dance: Two Premieres by Alvin Ailey." <u>New York Times</u>, November 24, 1969, p. 62.
"I found something even more in Pauline Koner's duet, 'Poeme,' set to the second movement of Samuel Barber's Piano Concerto--the movement, if you recall it, with the Galli-Curci-aspirant flute--and yet charming, moving, and as perfectly formed as an Oriental miniature created by skills and then lovingly eroded by time. Ideally danced by George Faison and Linda Kent...it had a succinct beauty and a suggestion, with all its fears and veil-removal of the ecstacy of love." <u>See</u>: W65k

B65c. "Britten Honored by Music Critics." <u>New York Times</u>, May 20, 1964, p. 37.
News article announcing that Samuel Barber's Piano Concerto No. 1 had been awarded the New York Music Critics Circle award for an orchestral composition for the musical

season of 1962-63 and 1963-64. See: W65

B65d. Broder, Nathan. "Current Chronicle: New York."
Musical Quarterly 49:94-97 (January 1963)
"This was one of Barber's major works. Its idiom is
the smooth blending of tradition with contemporary procedures that he employed in Medea, the Second Symphony,
and the Piano Sonata. The writing for piano is brilliant
and idiomatic, that for orchestra colorful, trenchant, and
full of telling touches..." See: W65

B65e. -----. "Piano Concerto." Boston Symphony Orchestra Program Notes, September 28, 1962, p. 78+
"A piano concerto is about the only music form Samuel
Barber has not undertaken until now. He is known to
audiences in Boston for a number of works which like this
one have had their first performances by this Orchestra.
In this way Serge Koussevitzky...was one of the first
conductors to recognize his qualities..." See: W65b

B65f. Carter, Susan Blindermann. The Piano Music of
Samuel Barber. Thesis (Ph.D.)--Texas Tech University,
Lubbock, Texas, 1980. 188 p.
"The entire Concerto remains traditional in the sense
of formal design and tonal centers. In addition Barber's
classical economy provides a cohesive unity within each
movement. The effective use of contrapuntal writing and
motivic transformations also contribute to the greatness of
this work." [p. 135] See: W65

B65g. Cohn, Arthur. "Recorded Classical Music." New
York: Schirmer Books, 1981. 2164 p.
"Pianistic to the hilt, it contains no-nonsense tonal
romanticism, dramatic tossing between the solo voice and
the piano in the first movement, natural melody in the
Cadenza, and a Finale of touch-and-go character, with its
meter excited by quintuple arrangement." [p. 98-99] See:
W65

B65h. Dickinson, Peter. "Record Reviews." Musical
Times 117:913 (November 1976)
"There is a musical satisfaction to be had from both
these works and they are capably played, especially the
Piano Concerto, which was written for John Browning." [CBS
61621] See: D65b

B65i. Downes, Edward. "The New York Philharmonic Guide
to the Symphony." New York: Walker, 1976. 1058 p.
"Almost immediately it became one of Barber's most
highly regarded and widely performed works. In less than a
year it had been heard in Boston, London, Brussels, the
festivals of Spoleto and Tanglewood, and was scheduled for
forty further performances in the British Isles, on the
European continent and in North and South America." [p.
28] See: W65

B65j. Flanagan, William. "Classical." HIFI/Stereo Review 14:78 (January 1965)

"The work itself, taken as much as possible out of the context of its spectacular public success, is a puzzling one to evaluate. It is perhaps superfluous to say that the piece is made with the most robust, sure-footed sort of craftsmanship--we would expect nothing less from Barber...The work's pianistic brilliance is built into it with the same inevitability that one finds counterpoint built into a Bach fugue. And while the piano writing is perhaps, in a certain inescapable sense, lacking in any intrinsic originality, it is still full of invention, rich in detail, and even at its showiest quite gravely considered...But once one has put Barber's concerto aside, it is somehow difficult to recall its sound, its texture, even its ambience." [Columbia MS 6638, ML 6038] See: D65a

B65k. Frank, Peter. "Classical Recordings." Fanfare 1:7 (January 1978)

"The Barber Concerto...is full-blown romanticism trimmed entirely of schmalz. The graceful line of the melodic writing carries a yearning passion in the first movement, an introspective quietude in the second, and a furious driving motoric drive in the third, all of which add up to an emotional experience as dramatically, vicerally fulfilling as a really good movie and/or seduction." [Turnabout QTV 34683] See: D65b

B65l. Frankenstein, Alfred. "Symphony Soloist's Daring Maneuver." San Francisco Chronicle, March 20, 1964, p. 45.

"Write it in the book ---
Proclaim it from the housetops ---
Publish it in the streets ---
An instrumental soloist with the San Francisco Symphony played something new!

The person who achieved this prodigy was a tall handsome young pianist named John Browning, who possesses a fine technique, a beautiful tone, and the performance rights to Samuel Barber's recently composed concerto...I found the work rather more impressive than previous symphonic efforts from the same hand. As usual, the slow movement--nostalgic, lightly lyrical, restrained by superlative taste--was the best; but the last whipped up a temperamental storm which is most unusual for Barber and the whole had a pepper and power one has not come to expect from this source. The texture of this piece is very heavily elaborated throughout the orchestral part as well as for the pianist but equally a test for the entire orchestra and for collaboration between soloist and conductor. On each of these counts--solo performance, and the meshing of the two--Browning, Joseph Krips and the ensemble hit one of the very high points of the current season." See: W65g

B65m. Goldberg, Albert. "Schenck, Joselson at Pasadena

Symphony." <u>Los</u> <u>Angeles</u> <u>Times</u>, February 11, 1984, pt. 6, p. 1, 6.

"The Barber Concerto put the conductor to as severe a test as it did the pianist, and that is important, for accompanying is an important part of a conductors function...Joselson at the Steinway was the right man in the right place. He played with an obsessive conviction that made it all sound more important than it really is...he can tear off octaves and interlocking passages with diabolic disdain of difficulties. He can also turn a melody melting and embroider it with limpid arabesques. He was a hugh success with the audience." <u>See</u>: W65q

B65n. Greenleaf, Christopher. "Guide to Records." <u>American</u> <u>Record</u> <u>Guide</u> 41:10 (February 1978)

"Samuel Barber's <u>Piano</u> <u>Concerto</u> is a horrifically difficult work for both the pianist and the conductor. It is also a very important composition and vital proof that the concerto as a form is far from exhausted. It may well be the most significant concerto for any instrument to come into existence since the war and is a deeply impassioned plea for <u>musicality</u> in contemporary composition." [Turnabout QTV 34683] <u>See</u>: D65d

B65o. Guglielmi, Edoardo. "Il VI Festival del Duo Mondi di Spoleto." <u>Musica</u> <u>d'Oggi</u>, nuova serie, 6:171 (July-August 1963)

Brief review of a performance given by John Browning, with Dietfried Bennet conducting. "In questo <u>Concerto</u>, dal linguaggio sempre limpido ed immediato pur nella solenne grandiosità d'impianto, segnaleremo l'estrema delicatezza e l'espressione raccolta del secondo tempo, di un fine disegno quasi pittorico, alla Ravel, e l'estrosa brillante costruzione degli altri due tempi." ["This <u>Concerto</u> is notable for clarity and accessibility, notwithstanding the solemn grandeur of its form. We are especially impressed by the extreme delicacy and expressiveness in the second part, marked as it is by a fine design which is almost picture-like in the style of Ravel, as well as by the original and brilliant constructions of the other two parts."--R.F.] <u>See</u>: W65d

B65p. Haggin, B. H. "Choreographic Evocations." <u>New</u> <u>Republic</u> 152:31 (January 30, 1965)

"The Piano Concerto of Samuel Barber, which has had an enormous publicity-press build-up since its first performance during the inaugural week of Lincoln Center, turns out to be another characteristic product of this composer who is no creator--one in which he uses a lot of notes in the gestures of saying the impressive thing he really doesn't have to say." [Columbia MS 6638] <u>See</u>: D65a

B65q. Hall, David. "Classical Discs and Tapes." <u>Stereo</u> <u>Review</u> 40:92 (May 1978)

"Samuel Barber's 1962 piano concerto, for all the

brilliance of its solo writing and the craftsmanship lavished on its musical architecture, does not, for me, jell
as a totality. I hear echoes in it of the First Symphony's
dramatic rhetoric, the Violin Concerto's lyricism, and the
Dance of Vengeance from Medea, but no genuine synthesis,
either in this well-played new version or the very formidable decade-old one with John Browning..." [Turnabout QTV
34683, S 34683] See: D65d

B65r. Hanson, John Robert. Macroform In Selected Twentieth-Century Piano Concertos. Thesis (Ph.D.)--Eastman
School of Music, The University of Rochester [New York],
1969. 404 p.
"Barber's style remains quite faithful to sense of key
center and use of tertian harmonic material. There is
considerable contrapuntal interest in this concerto. Mode-
rating harmonic elements are the avoidance of common root
movement patterns, some use of polychordal and non-tertian
combinations, and occasional brief but effective employment
of synthetic scalar material...While motivic technique of
the concerto is based on classical principles, the range of
intensity, the melodic and harmonic flavor, and the bravura
piano part all contribute to the 'neo romantic' quality."
[p. 20-21] See: W65

B65s. Harrison, Jay S. "The New York Music Scene."
Musical America 83:178+ (December 1963)
"Judged by the number of performances it has received
it is one of the most successful works written in the last
25 years. But it is also more. In my view it is the best
piano concerto ever written by an American...That it is
murderously difficult is not the point--any composer worthy
of the name can write a fiendishly hard number: there is
no trick in it. But Barber has begun by turning his difficulties to a musical advantage, to make them serve the
context of the work, not merely appear as so many ex-
crescenes stuck upon it. Every dazzling phrase, every
wild-eyed scale, every contortionist figuration comes alive
as part of the whole and is not an isolated show of pianistic fancy. Thus, not a measure of the number detracts from
the concerto as an entity...As for Mr. Browning's performance, it was, to put it bluntly, sensational. He is a
virtuoso to the keyboard born and dismissed the concerto's
treacheries of finger as though they scarcely existed. It
was art concealing art." See: W65f

B65t. Heller, Richard R. "Neues aus Wiener Konzert-
salen." Osterreichische Musikzeitschrift 33:46 (January
1978)
"Samuel Barbers vom ORF-Symphonieorchester und dem
Solisten James Tocco unter der Leitung von Leif Segerstam
erstaufgeführtes Klavierkonzert op. 38...steht in der sym-
phonischen Orchestertradition und bedient sich einer
durchaus publikumswirksamen Tonsprache, in der 'Amerikanis-
men' unüberhorbar vorhanden." ["The premiere of Samuel

Barber's piano concerto opus 38...with the ORF Symphony Orchestra and soloist James Tocco under the direction of Leif Segerstam stands in the symphony orchestra tradition and uses a language of tone which is very effective and in which one cannot fail to note certain 'Americanisms.'"--R.F.]

B65u. Helm, Everett. "Lincoln Center." Musical America 82:18-19 (November 1962)
"This is a virtuosic piece, highly effective for the piano and expertly written. Its basically traditional style contains something for everyone--except the most radically oriented. Browning played the grateful piece with bravura and a fine feeling for its effect of contrast and color." See: W65a

B65v. Hughes, Allen. "Music." New York Times, November 8, 1975, p. 22.
"A little more than 13 years ago Mr. Leinsdorf and John Browning gave the premiere of the Barber Concerto with the Boston Symphony at Philharmonic (now Fisher) Hall. With Mr. Browning as soloist this weekend, the work is obviously getting authentic performance. Those who have never heard it before will not find it difficult to take from a modern-music standpoint. Though a product of the mid-20th century, it is a Romantic work at heart and in its musical language. Mr. Browning played the concerto triumphantly, the composer was on hand to hear it, and the audience seemed to like it very much." See: W65m

B65w. Hume, Paul. "Dorati and the NSO." Washington Post, March 12, 1980, sect. D, p. 8.
"The Piano Concerto, which won Barber his second Pulitzer prize--the first was for his great opera, Vanessa --followed, with James Tocco as soloist. First heard in 1962, the concerto has seemed steadily to increase in stature since that time. Its exquisite textures, as impressive in the massing of the strings as in the woodwind choir of the finale, are balanced by a keen sense of structure, a factor that is never forced on the listener but that contributes substantially to the feeling of unity that fills the whole. Tocco, an artistic powerhouse in the work, not more for the dramatic thrust he provided easily in its largest pages than for the finesse in his gradations of sound and of the fleet beauty of the filigree writing that lifts so many pages to special heights." See: W65n

B65x. Kafka, Barbara S. "Samuel Barber: Piano Concerto, Opus 38" [album notes for Turnabout QTV 34683 disc]
"This Concerto is a technical tour de force for both the composer and the performer [Abbott Ruskin] and richly deserves the Pulitzer Prize for Music that it won in 1963." See: D65d

B65y. Kammerer, Rafael. "Americans All (North and

Bibliography

South)." <u>American Record Guide</u> 31:392 (January 1965)
    "Aside from being a brilliant virtuoso vehicle for the
soloist, Samuel Barber's Concerto is probably the finest
work of its kind to have been written by an American composer since MacDowell.   It has enough popular appeal,
too, to rival the Tchaikowsky and Rachmaninoff Concerti."
[Columbia ML 6038, MS 6638] <u>See</u>: D65a

    B65z. Kolodin, Irving. "Music to My Ears: Barber
Concerto--Campora, di Stefano." <u>Saturday Review</u> 46:33
(November 23, 1963)
    "Thanks to his particular kind of fortitude in fol-
lowing the bend of his own talent and allowing others to
bend under the burden of aping fashion, Barber has evolved
a tonal language that has artistic individuality as well as
meaningful vocabulary. This would not necessarily work for
anyone else, but it works for him, because it is a natural
growth from the music he was writing twenty-five years ago
and more...Clearly Browning had added to his knowledge of
the work in the year he has been playing it, especially in
some details of the first and third movement. He plays it
with confidence and affection..." <u>See</u>: W65f

    B65aa. -----. "Recordings in Review." <u>Saturday Review</u>
47:70 (October 31, 1964)
    "Contrary to one of the most formidable platitudes,
familiarity with Samuel Barber's <u>Piano Concerto</u> breeds
esteem. Indeed, in this performance, the work has more
profile, a larger variety of expressive resources than had
been recalled from its much-acclaimed introductory performance...What emerges most clearly from the additional
hearings are the compactness and discipline of the writing.
Indeed, it has a refinement and elegance of cut that recalls, more than anything else, the workmanship of Ravel.
This is most meaningfully apparent in the Canzona (slow
movement), in which a bud of a melodic idea is cultivated
not merely into a blossom, but into something of a full
bloom. It is by far the most distinguished movement of the
concerto, and a fitting older, graver partner for the fine
<u>Adagio</u> of Barber's 1934 String Quartet. There will, sooner
or later, come a performance by a pianist other than
Browning, but his will remain the model for some time to
come." [Columbia MD 6638] <u>See</u>: D65a

    B65bb. Kriegsman, Alan M.   "The Washington Ballet's
Starry Night." <u>Washington Post</u>, October 10, 1981, sect. 1,
p. 1, 9.
    World premiere of a new ballet set to the music of
Barber's <u>Concerto</u>. Mr. Kriegsman comments, "It is a strong
handsome, riveting ballet in a mold not unlike many of
Goh's finest previous works...<u>Configurations</u>, which has
Samuel Barber's 'modernistic' but decidedly romantically
Piano Concerto as its score, is abstract, to be sure...But
it also defines tensions, attractions and currents between

260

Its dancers that evoke specific transactions of feeling."
See: W65o

B65cc. Kupferberg, Herbert. "Record Reviews." _Atlan-_
tic 215:134 (February 1965)
"These two contemporary works and make admirable companion pieces. In fact, the coincidences are almost startling. Both composers are fifty-three years old; both write
in an idiom which is a nice blend of the modern and the
traditional; both concertos begin with a statement by the
solo instrument while the orchestra waits silently. But
there are differences. The Barber piece has greater scope
and proportions. It is a major composition, with a confident start, a triumphant and somewhat jazzy finale, and a
richly textured slow movement in which the piano spins a
lovely strand of sound through the orchestral fabric."
[Columbia ML 6038, MS 6638] See: D65a

B65dd. Layton, Robert. "Orchestral." _Gramophone_
52:1639 (March 1975)
"The piano concerto, dazzlingly played by John
Browning, does not possess the astonishing freshness of
inspiration that distinguishes the Cello Concerto...and it
does stray into a kind of general-purpose post-romantic
virtuosity that does not make the heart beat faster. The
slow movement is the finest." [Columbia SAX 2575, reissued
as CBS Classics 61621] See: D65b

B65ee. Macdonald, Malcolm. "Orchestral." _Gramophone_
43:55 (July 1965)
"Barber's is a large-scale concerto...written in the
first place with John Browning in mind as soloist, it
exploits to great effect the extremely well-controlled
finger facility on offer. Not that in effect it is a
showpiece for the piano, tho it is no _sinfonia_ _concertante_
either; but it is the strength and agility of instrument
and player alike which are on trial rather than their
poetry. Some relaxation is found in the middle movement;
but a fresh access of energy drives the finale to its end
through an unfaltering and electrifying quick 5/8."
[Columbia SAX 2575] See: D65a

B65ff. "Music." _New York Times_, May 7, 1963, p. 35.
An announcement that Samuel Barber has won his second
Pulitzer Prize, this time for the _Piano Concerto_, Op. 38
which had its world premiere September 24, 1962 at Philharmonic Hall, Lincoln Center. John Browning was soloist and
the Boston Symphony Orchestra was conducted by Eric Leinsdorf. See: W65a

B65gg. "New Piano Concerto." _Times_ (London) January 9,
1963, p. 11.
"The concerto is amply designed, professionally laid
out: it holds variety, strong climaxes, powerful interesting sounds. The piano-orchestra relationship is roughly

the same as Rachmaninov's, ranging from defiant duel to expressive dialogue; the piano writing is wickedly brilliant using much variation technique. The sense of the music is perfectly clear but, oddly, is clearer to the eye than to the ear--and this is most certainly no cerebral writing. There is no moment where sound and sense act instantaneously on each other and press out some new, vital, complex idea, such as happens, say in the cadenza of Shostakovich's cello concerto." [review of a radio broadcast with John Browning as soloist] See: W65a

B65hh. Rayment, Malcolm. "Orchestral." Records and Recordings 18:21 (April 1975)
    "The Piano Concerto, one of several works commissioned to celebrate the centenary of the publishing firm of G. Schirmer, was completed in 1962. Although it is far more mature [than the violin concerto], it also is something of a mixture of styles. The central slow movement, which might almost have been written almost 100 years earlier, is followed by a Finale in quintuple time that seems to have been much influenced by Bartok. Within the first movement itself there are almost equally strong contrasts. John Browning gave the first performance and has been closely associated with the work ever since; the extremely demanding solo part needs a pianist of his calibre." [CBS Classics 61621] See: D65b

B65ii. Rich, Alan. "Classical." High Fidelity 14:80 (December 1964)
    "As organization music goes, these pieces are both superior examples. There is nothing inherently wrong with professionalism when meaningfully applied, and it is in both the present works. Samuel Barber has written a big, splashy, old-fashioned concerto that must have tremendous appeal to a young-hearted old-fashioned virtuoso (which Browning is rapidly becoming). There are many reminders, all pleasant, of its musical ancestors. All the work really lacks, and the lack is only relative to some of Barber's other scores, is distinctive melodic substance. It settles too often for the gesture rather than the deed. The slow-movement does develop an attractive lyric line, but the outer movements are built for the most part out of small, scrappy fragments that do not ignite one another." [ColumbiaML 6038, MS6638] See: D65a

B65jj. Richards, Denby. "Radio." Music and Musicians 11:45 (February 1963)
    "One of Barber's greatest gifts is his melodic inventiveness...In the second movement of the Piano Concerto we are given the full Barber treatment. Woodwind interchange phrases of the theme, which is then taken up by the strings until the piano's sentimental return...John Browning played with assurance and understanding. He is, undoubtedly one of the most interesting young musicians in America. Berthold Goldschmidt and the Philharmonia Or-

chestra gave first-class support to what may be considered
a musical 'scoop' for the Third Programme." See: W65c

B65kk. Sargeant, Winthrop. "Musical Events." New
Yorker 39:127-128 (November 16, 1963)
"I have heard the work a number of times, and have
found it one that improves with repeated hearings. Its
first movement contains some of the most original and
fascinating symphonic development produced during the past
half century; the second shows Barber to be the master of a
type of sophisticated melody that, for all its modernisms,
can evoke a poetic response from the audience; and its
finale is a stirring, demoniac movement, full of fire that
one knows was felt rather than contrived. Mr. Browning
performed prodigies of virtuosity with the piano part, and
Mr. Krips kept everything beautifully balanced and clean in
the orchestra." See: W65f

B65ll. Schonberg, Harold C. "Music: Barber Concerto."
New York Times, September 25, 1962, sect. 2, p. 32.
"The concerto is based, roughly, on such contemporary
works as Prokofiev's Third; and indeed, much of the piano
writing is strongly Prokofieffian. No standard key relationships are present, the writing for solo piano is a
mixture of romanticism and everything but tone clusters,
and the five-four finale is a first cousin to the toccata-
like conclusion of the Prokofieff Seventh Sonata. This is
a real virtuoso concerto, with some staggeringly difficult
writing. It also has a strong melodic profile, a lyric
slow movement and a sense of confidence in the entire
conception--the confidence that comes only from an experienced composer engaged in a work that interests
him...Mr. Browning stormed the work, surmounted the peaks
and proved himself to be a virtuoso with a fine sense of
line. In music like this he is an eminently satisfactory
pianist." See: W65a

B65mm. Shupp, Enos E., Jr. "Concerto." New Records
45:6 (January 1978)
Barber's Piano Concerto has had a hard time achieving
popularity, although it is a bristling work of skilled
craftsmanship. Its difficulties include an exceptionally
prominent orchestral part which should have a more polished
and professional orchestra than the M.I.T., however good it
is in its class. Ruskin, of course, is equal to any task,
and has the music very well in hand, however this edition
is no match for the Browning/Szell recording." [Turnabout
QTV 34683] See: D65d

B65nn. -----. "Orchestra." New Records 32:5 (December 1964)
"Samuel Barber's Piano Concerto is the most likely
contender that we have heard to pull today's top artists
out of the pot-boilers rut. If every pianist who overworks
Tchaikovsky and Rachmaninoff with all the orchestras from

Seattle to Miami does not latch onto the Barber, he is missing a sure-fire bet. This concerto has everything a concerto should have and has it with _quality_. John Browning premiered the work and this fine young artist gives the selection a reading of vigor and assurance." [Columbia ML 6038, MS 6638] _See_: D65a

B65oo. Steinbrink, Mark. "Footnotes." _Ballet News_ 3:8 (October 1981)
Brief article which indicates that "Rehearsals began last month for a new ballet by the ubiquitous Choo San Goh. Set to Samuel Barber's _Piano Concerto_, the work is being created for Mikhail Baryshnikov and Marianna Tcherkassky. Audiences will get a chance to see the piece on October 9 [1981] at a benefit for Washington Ballet where Goh is assistant artistic director. The work will receive its official premiere with American Ballet Theatre in Minneapolis on October 15 and theoretically will then pass into the ABT repertory." _See_: W65o

B65pp. Thompson, Kenneth. "Radio in Retrospect." _Musical Opinion_ 86:285 (February 1963)
Review of the January 8, 1963 London broadcast. "Here is a piano concerto almost in the grand manner, unabashedly and persuasively romantic--the spearhead of a new movement to the return of general, not specialised, intelligibility?" _See_: W65c

B65qq. Tracey, Edmund. "London Music." _Musical Times_ 104:192-193 (March 1963)
"The concerto is a conventionally florid affair...The solo part, with its massive chords and scalic cascades, was clearly both difficult and enjoyable to play, and John Browning played it with stunning virtuosity. Berthold Goldschmidt conducted the Philharmonia." _See_: W65c

B65rr. Willis, Thomas. "A Major Talent Comes of Age as Browning Repeats Barber." _Chicago Tribune_, October 8, 1965, sect. 2A, p. 1.
"This neo-romantic concerto...takes a retrospective look at Rachmaninoff and Ravel, balancing the strong melodic line of the one on the shimmering orchestration of the other...Mr. Browning took command at the outset, with a dignity and affirmation of authority which signals a major talent reaching its majority." _See_: W65l

B66. CONCERTO FOR VIOLIN AND ORCHESTRA, OP. 14.

B66a. Ardoin, John. "Two Moderns by Gerle." _Musical America_ 83:277-278 (December 1963)
"Only Gerle presents the work in the direct communicative manner the score calls for. Other recorded versions bog the first movement down in syrupy drawn-out phrases, making effete and sugary what is direct and economical.

Gerle handles this movement as it is marked--Allegro moderato--not as it is too often played--Andante romantico. He knows well the line between expounding and sentimentalizing. The succeeding two movements show two aspects of Gerle's art: the rich, warm sound he lavishes on the andante second movement, and the breath taking whirlwind he makes the perpetual-motion finale. It is enough to make one stand and cheer the phonograph speakers." [Westminster WST 17045] See: D66b

B66b. B., F. "The Promenades." Musical Times 85:221 (July 1944)

"Samuel Barber's Violin Concerto introduced by Eda Kersey on June 23 proved by far the most satisfactory piece of American music we have had since the war. It is original without eccentricity, the composer appearing to be quite happy in evolving melodies and harmonies that without being in the least conventional retain the traditional character of these elements, melody being lyrical and harmony, however cunning and distinguished, yet subservient to the melodic design. If the Concerto has a fault it is that the last movement, a sort of perpetuum mobile, stands outside the rest. In listening to a great concerto or symphony we have the impression that the composer when writing the first note had already in mind all the rest, consciously or unconsciously. The Barber Concerto would seem to have been composed in two parts, the first embracing the lively first movement and the delicate romance which forms the second, and then tacking about to sail on a different course to find the right breeze for the finale." See: W66d

B66c. "Barber Concerto." New York Times, June 29, 1980, sect. 2, p. 22.

"It seems that the concerto [according to Herbert Baumel] had been commissioned by Samuel Feis, an industrialist, for Iso Briselli. On seeing the score, Briselli said that the final movement, a moto perpetuo, was 'unplayable,' and Feis refused to pay Barber the $500.00 still outstanding on the commission. A pianist at Curtis, Ralph Berkowitz, asked Baumel one day if he could play the last movement for a few people. 'I looked it over,' Mr. Baumel writes, 'practiced it for an hour or so, and returned to school in the afternoon to play it for Sam Barber, Gian Carlo Menotti, Mary Louise Curtis Bok (not yet Mrs. Zimbalist) and her friend Mrs. Braun in Josef Hoffmann's studio. I proved to their delight that I could play it at any tempo they wanted me to...Now Barber would be able to collect the full sum.'" See: W66

B66d. Barstow, Cris. "Concert Notes." Strad 93:619 (January 1983)

"It would be rewarding to hear Jaime Laredo in a better concerto than the Barber, a work which could not reveal depth of musicality, but nonetheless displayed his

stylish sense of phrase and some attractive tonal qualities, particularly in the low register and in spite of the
relatively unfavorable acoustic." See: W66j

B66e. Bernheimer, Martin. "Two Twentieth-Century Masterpieces" [album notes for Columbia MS 6713 disc]
    "Two thirds of the Barber Violin Concerto reflect the
composer's 'youthful' style. Graceful cantabile melodies,
easy-to-take harmonic procedures, relatively simple rhythmic formulas and Mendelssohnian lyricism dominate the first
two movements. In the finale, however, a 'new' Barber
makes his unexpected appearance. Dissonances crop up where
they are least expected, the rhythmic patterns suddenly
become irregular and unpredictable, and the mood of classic
serenity gives way to the agitation of perpetual motion."
[Columbia MS 6713] See: D661

B66f. "Composers Honored." New York Times, May 18,
1958, p. 23.
    "Two awards for original works by contemporary com-
posers played by the Philadelphia Orchestra during the
1957-58 season have been made to Samuel Barber of Mount
Kisco, N. Y., and Mme Arthur Honegger, widow of the Swiss
composer, now living in Paris. Mr. Barber received
$3,000.00 for his violin concerto...The compositions were
selected by the first chair men of the orchestra. The
awards are the gift of an anonymous donor to encourage the
creation and appreciation of contemporary music." See: W66

B66g. "Concert and Opera: Violin Concerto by Samuel
Barber to Have Premiere in February." New York Times,
December 29, 1940, sect. 9, p. 7.
    News article announcing the premiere of Barber's vio-
lin concerto. See: W66a

B66h. Cooke, Deryck "Orchestral." Gramophone 43:145
(September 1965)
    "Even on its own level of amiable neo-romanticism in a
near nineteenth-century idiom, this is an uninspired and
poorly constructed piece; Barber an unequal composer, has
written much better music than this, and one can only
wonder why he has not withdrawn the work since it can
hardly enhance his reputation." [CBS SBRG 72345] See:
D661

B66i. Dickinson, Peter. "Record Reviews." Musical
Times 117:913 (November 1976)
    "There is musical satisfaction to be had from both
these works, and they are capably played..." [CBS 61621]
See: D66j

B66j. Downes, Edward. The New York Philharmonic Guide
to the Symphony. New York: Walker, 1976. 1058 p.
    "Looking nostalgically to the past and impatiently to
the future, this Concerto is a pivotal work. Its two

contrasting musical styles reflect a crisis in Samuel Barber's development which coincided with a crisis in world
history: the outbreak of World War II. It would be hard to
show a direct, one-to-one relationship between the German-
Soviet invasion of Poland in September, 1939 and the change
in Barber's musical style; but one does not have to be a
mystic to feel that a connection does exist, no matter how
ripe Barber may have been for a change." [p. 30-31] See:
W66

    B66k. Downes, Olin. "Ormandy Directs at Carnegie
Hall." New York Times, February 12, 1941, p. 25.
    "The violin concerto of Samuel Barber, a work am-
bitiously conceived, and written with honesty and talent,
impresses at a first hearing as a form too big for the
composer successfully to fill. The concerto is long for
its contents, despite many a good moment, as for instance
in the second part, where a melodic sequence rises with
constantly more stress and dramatic impulse to an intense
climax. The finale, which is dark and sardonic, asks much
of the violinist, which is true of other pages, including
those of overweighty orchestration." See: W66a

    B66l. Epstein, Benjamin. "Pacific's Opener Fulfills
Promise." Los Angeles Times, October 8, 1983, sect. 6, p.
2.
    "In the violin concertos of Samuel Barber and Gian-
Carlo Menotti--a pairing which, given the intense lifelong
friendship between the two composers, represents a stroke
of programming ingenuity--he [Keith Clark, conductor] captured the youthful innocence and rapture as well as the
power--albeit to a greater degree in the Barber piece...An
artist of Ruggiero Ricci's stature, of course, is not going
to be far off the interpretive mark." See: W66k

    B66m. Ericson, Raymond. "Discs: Congolese Mass vs. a
Local Stunt." New York Times, October 27, 1963, sect. 2, p.
17.
    "The Barber concerto projects much the same atmosphere
[slow, sustained, rhapsodic] for two movements and in a
third falls back on a conventional fast bit of perpetual
motion. The works are sensitively scored to collaborate
with the singing violin tone in producing aural fleshpots."
[Westminster XWN 19045, WST 17045] See: D66b

    B66n. Flanagan, William. "Classical." HiFi/Stereo
Review 15:65 (July 1965)
    "It is easy enough to dismiss the Barber Violin Con-
certo, which was first heard as recently as 1941, as an
academic post-Romantic throwback. But hearing the work,
listening to it on its own terms, confronted by its fresh,
honest, youthful romanticism, it requires a man of more
certainty than I about what we have achieved or not a-
chieved musically in this century to put it irrevocably
down as a work of small matter. Furthermore, it sings its

sweet song with a lovely innocence that some of us find lacking in the rather cool, defiant post-Romanticism of the more recent Barber."[Columbia ML 6113, MS 6713] See: D66j

B66o. Flanagan, William. "Classical." Stereo Review 22:87 (April 1969)
"A lyrical eclectic by nature, Barber laid his influence on the line in the Concerto--a bit of Sibelius, a moment surprisingly like Shostakovich--but there is also a good deal of Barber's elusively personal youthful lyricism." [Philips PHC 9105] See: D66a

B66p. Frankenstein, Alfred. "Classical." High Fidelity 6:53 (June 1956)
"Barber's Violin Concerto consists of a wonderful lyric slow movement surrounded by a salonlike first movement and a fairly trivial finale. Kaufman's superb playing is well recorded, but the orchestra is pushed uncomfortably far into the background." [Musical Masterpiece Society 105] See: D66g

B66q. -----. "Classical." High Fidelity 6:85 (October 1956)
"Nothing makes a better case for Samuel Barber than his elegant, intensely lyrical, subtly colorful violin concerto, and no one makes a better case for this work than Louis Kaufman." [Concert Hall CHS 1253] See: D66f

B66r. -----. "Classical." High Fidelity 15:70 (June 1965)
"The tuneful, easy going, sentimental concerto of Samuel Barber, on the other side, affords an amusing contrast to Hindemith's great work..." [Columbia MS 6713] See: D66i

B66s. -----. "Classical." High Fidelity 19:67 (April 1969)
"Although I have never previously thought of Barber's widely played Violin Concerto as a major work, Mlle. Bernard and her associates are obviously of that opinion--and they are very convincing about it. The rich melodious lyricism of the piece--or at least of the first two movements--is marvelously wrought here. These performances make it sound like a cross between Copland and Puccini if that can be imagined; if you can't imagine it, listen to this record. But the perpetuum mobile finale is, regrettably, not up to the heights of what goes before." [Philips World Series PHC 9105] See: D66a

B66t. Fuller, Donald. "Forecast and Review." Modern Music 18:168 (March-April 1941)
"Samuel Barber's Violin Concerto is a sad story for our times. There is certainly feeling for the long line but what goes into it is not very choice. The first two movements have genuine, unaffected simplicity, yet the

intimate quality is kept at such a low pitch that the fire almost goes out. The finale however throws all restraints to the winds. It is harmonically and rhythmically con-fused, stylistically out of keeping with the preceding material. Even the virtue of a rather pale unity is thus lost." See: W66a

B66u. Gorer, R. "Review of Music." Music Review 11:327 (November 1950)
"The total effect of Mr. Barber's Concerto would be greater if the middle movement were less good. As it is it makes the first and last movements rather unsatisfactory. This judgement is not really fair. Though neither movement is of the type to set the Delaware on fire, they are per-fectly competent and the soloist can display his bravura in the last movement, though the material is not, perhaps, the most interesting imaginable. The first movement has some rather curious bits of scoring, as when the soloist and the clarinet play arpeggii at each other and occasionally the violin has to attempt to make itself heard over a fortis-simo tutti, but by and large the movement seems satisfacto-ry. the andante is a powerful and moving movement, inspired to a certain extent by the Largo from the Symphonie Es-pagnole, but what better model could one take? In any case the movement is in no derogatory sense derivative. A detail of scoring, associating the piano with the brass, seems to me unfortunate." See: W66

B66v. Griffiths, Paul. "Record Reviews." Musical Times 119:864 (October 1978)
"...This is still heady Romantic stuff, securely tonal and everything a violin concerto should be. Ronald Thomas plays it with love, and the excellent recording makes the West Australian SO sound almost a world-class orchestra." [Unicorn UNS 256] See: D66k

B66w. Hall, David. "Classical." HIFI/Stereo Review 12:71 (February 1964)
"As for the Barber concerto, the work was written so as to put the soloist in high relief. Again, Gerle and Zeller serve the music well, reaching a brilliant peak in the finale." [Westminster WST 17045, XWN 19045] See: D66b

B66x. Horan, Robert. "American Composers, XIX: Samuel Barber." Modern Music 20:166 (March-April 1943)
"The theme of the first movement is open and expansive and very tender. In the more brilliant perpetuo mobile of the final movement, where tension and increased excitement are desired, the rhythmic scheme becomes much more compli-cated and the harmonic one correspondingly stringent. Critics in general have naively labelled the last movement as 'more modern,' dissociating it in design from the rest of the work and failing to apprehend the fact that the dissonance involved is merely more necessary." See: W66

B66y. Jones, Ralph E. "Orchestra." New Records 28:7
(December 1960)
"Dating from 1939, this work has a more lyrical
character than the ponderously dramatic First Symphony; yet
it, too, has its moments of tension and dissonance...the
disc will be of interest chiefly to Barber devotees and
students of the violin." [CRI 137] See: D66h

B66z. Kammerer, Rafael. "Gerle: Barber and non-
Beechamized Delius." American Record Guide 30:516 (February 1964)
"What gives special significance to the coupling is
the fact that while these concertos must be numbered among
the greatest works in the repertoire, they are very seldom
heard. Westminster in this disc is due much credit for
this far from 'sure-fire' release. Its choice of performers was a happy one too, and the sound could not be
bettered. A brilliant technician, Gerle, is also a
musician of fine sensibilities. The beauty and warmth of
his tone and his evident sympathy for the respective idioms
is everywhere in evidence. He is particularly successful
in communicating the haunting loveliness and nostalgic
overtones of the slow movements." [Westminster XWN 19045,
WST 17045] See: D66b

B66aa. Keener, Andrew. "Orchestral." Strad 93:159-160
(May 1982)
"What we are left with is a work which, neo-romantic
yet individual, combines the lyrical freshness and intensity of its first two movements with the bravura of its
finale, a challenge alike to the virtuoso and the poet;
those unequipped for both aspects will have little overall
success with Barber's Violin Concerto." See: W66

B66bb. Kendall, Raymond. "Philharmonic Honors Schuman
and Barber." Musical Courier 162:16 (December 1960)
"Barber was represented by his Violin Concerto, a
highly appealing work and often movingly melodious score,
in which Aaron Rosand, the gifted American violinist,
making his debut with the Philharmonic, presented a lyrical
and expressive reading. This work, which reveals the composer's melodic powers quite strongly, antedates some of
his more recent writing for stage and concert." See: W66e

B66cc. Klein, Howard. "Recordings: The Shower of Isaac
Stern." New York Times, April 18, 1965, sect. 2, p. 15.
"Pairing the Barber and the Hindemith together was a
good idea, for the works complement each other. The gentle
songfulness of the American composer has a tender poignancy
not found in the German academician's stirring concerto.
Stern brings to each what seems necessary for thorough
performances. Since emotional eloquence is the violinist's
trump, the Barber has more immediate appeal, but the Hindemith, with its acerbic, thin-lipped sobriety wears
better." [Columbia ML 6113, MS 6713] See: D66i

B66dd. Kolodin, Irving. "Thanks to Kaufman." <u>Saturday Review</u> 39:39 (September 29, 1956)
"It is in every way a work of substantial crafts-manship and thoughtful content which, with the 'cello con-certo, gives Barber's instrumental literature a decidedly playable pair of works. In some of its broader melodic aspects it has a kinship with the Elgar concerto, but the vocabulary is Barber's own, also the sense of structure makes the totality as satisfying as it is." [Concert Hall CHS 1253] <u>See</u>: D66d

B66ee. Layton, Robert. "Orchestral." <u>Gramophone</u> 52:1639 (March 1975)
"...It has such natural lyrical feeling and generosity of spirit that its scant representation on record is puz-zling...The score has the warmth and freshness that characterise the best of Barber's early music; it has a rich fund of invention and the slow movement has a youthful innocence that is touching. Isaac Stern plays it with passionate commitment and Bernstein and the New York Phil-harmonic are at their most responsive." [CBS SBRG 72345, reissued as CBS Classic 61621] <u>See</u>: D66j

B66ff. -----. "Orchestral." <u>Gramophone</u> 53:1331 (Feb-ruary 1976)
"...his music has a greater freshness than has much other music of its period with a higher norm of dissonance and wider repertory of expressive devices...The slow move-ment of the concerto is an inspired piece, full of warmth and innocence, and whatever his achievement may be, Barber strikes me as being the most naturally musical composer America has produced..." [Rediffusion Composer's Recordings SD 137] <u>See</u>: D66h

B66gg. Leigh, E. S. V. "Concerto." <u>New Records</u> 47:5 (April 1979)
"The sound in the Barber <u>Violin Concerto</u> is spacious; the performance, dream-like. I miss the fervor of the Stern performance (Columbia MS 6713), but Ronald Thomas does a good job, forgiving occasional intonation slips." [Unicorn UN1 72016] <u>See</u>: D66k

B66hh. Mellers, Wilfrid. "Gramophone Records" <u>Musical Times</u> 106:867 (November 1965)
"Barber's Concerto...is a dreadful piece, sloppy in its lyricism, self-indulgent in harmony and texture. Pret-ty pentatonic doodlings of the type associated with the lesser 'western' movie are inflated to symphonic propor-tions; far from being a masterpiece, the Concerto seems to me to do scant justice even to Barber's modest talent. Presumably, however, Stern and Bernstein believe in it, for the performance seems better than could be expected." [CBS SBRG, BRG 72345] <u>See</u>: D66i

B66ii. Mills, Charles. "Over the Air." <u>Modern Music</u>

22:139 (January-February 1945)
"Stokowski and his New York City Symphony Orchestra gave a performance over WNYC of Samuel Barber's Concerto for Violin and Orchestra. The slight, innocuous materials of this piece and their subsequent treatment, naive and politely cute at best, hardly make up a concerto in any normal sense of the word. The work seems more like a three part bagatelle, neatly scored throughout with intelligent musicianship in a conventional sort of way, and especially well managed in the slow movement which has a fine cadence, suave in sonority and comparatively fresh in quality."

B66jj. Moore, David W. "Guide to Records." American Record Guide 43:16 (May 1980)
"This work is a lovely poetic one, with the exception of its disturbing perpetual-motion finale in which Samuel Barber suddenly thrusts us into the disorienting atmosphere of the Second World War, it is Barber at his most touching and heart-warming, characteristics his later works from the 50's on seem to have in increasingly small measure" [Orion ORS 79355, originally Concert Hall 1253] See: D66e

B66kk. Moore, J. S. "Concerts." New Records 47:4-5 (February 1980)
"Unfortunately Orion saw fit to 'enhance' the...recording (with Louis Kaufman) for stereo, giving it the usual 'inside a tuna can' sound, far less preferable than the superb mono from which this recording comes. The playing on the disc, however, makes one forget the bad technical judgement of the record company. Louis Kaufman, not a name on the tip of every violin lovers' tongue, produces all the romance one has ever desired to hear. The Barber is a master-work of interpretation and fine tonal development. Kaufman carries each phrase, each explosive climax--in fact the entire work--to the heights one rarely hears in this quintessential 20th-century romantic concerto." [Orion ORS 79355, originally Concert Hall 1253] See: D66e

B66ll. "Music Reviews." Strad 60:186 (October 1949)
Brief review of the revised edition of the concerto in a reduction for violin and piano published by Schirmer. "His music is diatonic and melodious and his fiddle writing is much more grateful to the player than most new work. Judged from the piano reduction, the ideas seem a little trite, but no doubt the orchestral score would reveal more points of interest." See: W66

B66mm. "Music Reviews." Strad 61:338 (January 1951)
Review of the revised version published by Chappell. "The idiom is diatonic and the writing for the solo instrument is grateful--as far as can be judged from a piano reduction, the orchestra is well provided for, but the ensemble will not be easy." See: W66

B66nn. "Notes on the News!" _International Musician_ 57:18 (July 1958)
Note that Barber was granted $3,00.00 for his _Violin Concerto_, played by the Philadelphia Orchestra during its 1957-58 season. _See_: W66

B66oo. Pleasants, Henry. "Opera and Orchestra in Phila-delphia." _Modern Music_ 18:181 (March-April 1941)
"Barber's _Violin Concerto_, which is slightly better than the Schmidt symphony [Franz Schmidt's Symphony in E flat], and a man of livelier imagination than his teacher, Scalero, but both his imagination and his craftsmanship are of a conventional order, without significant distinction. It is music of talent, but hardly of fibre, and will proba-bly continue to win prizes and general approbation." _See_: W66a

B66pp. "Promenade Concert: A Violin Concerto From America." _Times_ (London) June 26, 1944, p. 8.
"The concerto is not given to any form of outward display. It is scored for small orchestra, its three movements are comparatively short, and both the orchestral coloring and actual harmonic language avoid harshness. But beneath the external reticence of expression, it is imme-diately apparent that the music was born of deep feeling. The first two movements are wistfully introspective in character, and provide admirable opportunities for the violin to brood in terms of characteristic cantilena. The contrasting agitation of the finale is achieved by sheer bustle from the soloist, with irregular rhythmic ejacula-tions from supporting orchestra. The weakness of the work is that this last movement achieves only the status of a scherzo. At this point the concerto seems to need a real finale, in which all the preceding restraint and modesty could be thrown aside, and the music brought to an emo-tional climax such as the composer is obviously capable of producing and the listener instinctively seeks." _See_: W66d

B66qq. Rayment, Malcolm. "Orchestral." _Records and Recordings_ 18:21 (April 1975)
"The first two movements are lyrical and little con-cerned with virtuosity. This is left to the Finale, a fairly short and hectic movement in which the solo part is a perpetuum mobile. This rather brittle music, a little suggestive of Prokofiev, may seem out of place after the preceding movements." [CBS Classics 6162] _See_: D66j

B66rr. Reed, Peter Hugh. "Orchestra." _American Record Guide_ 23:6 (September 1956)
"This is a re-issue from a Concert Hall Limited re-lease of about five years ago...The feature attraction here is Barber's _Violin Concerto_, a neo-romantic work despite some technical devices reminiscent of Stravinsky." [Concert Hall CHS 1253] _See_: D66d

B66ss. Schonberg, Harold C. "Music: A Birthday Party."
New York Times, October 15, 1960, p. 27.
"Mr. Barber is quite a different species of composer
[as compared with William Schuman, also programmed]--an
out-and-out romantic. This is true of even some of the
more dissonant scores he has written. The Violin Concerto,
though has no dissonance. Its harmonics are of the nineteenth century and its treatment of the solo violin is
along the lines of orthodox concertos. It is a sweet and
lyrical work. What saves it from being merely a romantic
derivation is the strong, quite personal melodic gift of
the composer...Mr. Rosand used a modest approach to the
Barber concerto. His playing was rather small scaled but
within its framework, altogether agreeable." See: W66e

B66tt. Shupp, Enos E., Jr. "Concerto." New Records
31:6 (December 1963)
"A beautifully lyric work, characteristic of Barber's
songful writing, the concerto was written in 1939, when the
composer was twenty-nine. It abounds in ingratiating
phrases and is an immediately appealing work." [West-
minster XWN 19045, WST 17045] See: D66b

B66uu. -----. "Concerto." New Records 33:7 (July
1965)
"Isaac Stern and Leonard Bernstein offer a performance
of even greater opulence [than that of Robert Gerle and the
Vienna State Opera Orchestra, Robert Zeller, conductor] and
of course the music remains a delight, even growing with
repeated hearings." [Columbia ML 6113, MS 6713] See: D66i

B66vv. Wilkinson, Nigel. "Prom String Concertos."
Music and Musicians 25:58-59 (November 1976)
"For the modern virtuoso the work may create only
minimal problems, but this did not detract from the superb
advocacy of Ralph Holmes, the evening's soloist...It was a
thoroughly satisfying rendition in a memorable Prom." See:
W66g

B67. CONCERTO FOR VIOLONCELLO AND ORCHESTRA, OP. 22.

B67a. "Barber Concerto Gets Critics' Prize." New York
Times, June 28, 1946, p. 16.
News article reporting the awarding of the fifth an-
nual award by the Music Critics Circle of New York to
Samuel Barber for his concerto for violoncello and orches-
tra. See: W67

B67b. Berger, Arthur. "Spotlight on the Moderns."
Saturday Review 34:62 (May 26, 1951)
"The concerto stands high among the available works
for cello, and in the hands of so excellent a soloist as
Zara Nelsova the idiomatic writing for the instrument spins

itself out like silk thread..." [London LPS 332 (10")]
See: D67a

B67c. Brozen, Michael. "Classical." High Fidelity
16:85 (December 1966)
"The Cello Concerto is Barber of 1945, in his neoclas-
sical-cum-Americana phase. By now the materials sound a
little naive--contemporary American music has gone in other
directions in the last two decades--but the treatment is
always sophisticated and well thought out. The polish of
the music contrasts interestingly with the ruggedness of
the performance by Raya Garbousova. This and the self-
effacement of Frederic Waldman's Musica Aeterna Orchestra
make the solo a sometimes overly strong protagonist..."
[Decca DL 10 132, DL 710 132] See: D67a

B67d. "Concerto." New Records 19:5 (November 1951)
"It is, for once, contemporary music that sets out to
be beautiful and not ugly, and it succeeds admirably. One
would be willing to credit it to some well known composer
of a century ago, except that the modern technique is in
evidence too often..." [London LPS 332 (10")] See: D67a

B67e. Dale, S. S. "Contemporary Cello Concerti. XV:
Samuel Barber." Strad 84:529-535 (January 1974)
"Like Toscanini, Barber has always held that the true
function of music is melos, melody, and he has never for an
instant been swayed by any fashionable trends to make non-
music...The concerto for cello represents Barber at his
finest...the work is unusually dissonant for Barber, but
still written within the conventions of diatonicism and
chromaticism. The work calls for perfect technique: it
abounds in double stops, harmonics interspersed with
singing passages for which Barber is justly renowned."
See: W67

B67f. Diether, Jack. "Other Reviews." American Record
Guide 33:320 (December 1966)
"Besides its very felicitous and idiomatic solo writing, its chief appeal lies in the catchy syncopated main
theme, which does duty in both the first and second movements. In fact the finale, the only movement on which this
theme does not bestow its folksy presence, is by far the
least compelling. The Concerto is one of Barber's most
conservatively lyrical works withal..." [Decca DL 10 132,
DL710 132] See: D67a

B67g. Downes, Olin. "Bostonians Play 2 American
Works." New York Times, April 14, 1946, sect. 1, p. 46.
"...one was aware of a composer finding himself and
speaking with an unprecedented directness and confidence of
manner...The gay and piquant character of the opening and
its spicy rhythm is presently given competition and melodic
intensity by the solo instrument...But this movement [the
slow movement], grows in melodic interest and in intensity

275

of mood, and for its coda--a young modern American absolutely dares to express himself poetically. The last movement is remarkable for its structure and also for its sudden emergence of measures more serious, even tragical, than the prevailing tenor of the composition." See: W67c

B67h. Downes, Olin. "Raya Garbousova Concert Soloist." New York Times, December 5, 1947, p. 31.
"And Mr. Barber's Concerto, heard for the second time, let us down, or better said, perhaps, confused us. Was it a different treatment of the score or a different degree of perceptivity in ourselves from the time when the concerto was first presented here in 1946?...Mr. Mitropoulous, who conducted with the greatest care and his customary authority, gave Miss Garbousova every possible cooperation. She played with the warmth and distinction, the technical intelligence which have given her her present high position among her colleagues of the concert platform. Nevertheless, with all these favorable circumstances the concerto at the second hearing felt overlong for its contents, with many good melodic ideas, but not enough physiognomy. Because of this conflict of impressions between a first and second hearing of a modern work, let us say that estimates of it from this quarter shall be adjourned until a third hearing." See: W67d

B67i. F., H. "Analytical Notes and First Reviews." Gramophone 29:4-5 (June 1951)
Review of a recording featuring violoncellist Zara Nelsova. "The first movement is long, but inventive, powerful but nostalgic; it is never clumsy in operation as 'cello concertos tend to be. The working out maybe is over elaborate, but the movement is carried by Barber's rare power to imagine a melody that contains in itself a moving musical beauty...The second movement is extremely touching, with its haunting swing of thirds and its nostalgic hovering between major and minor; there are melting moments here. The third movement is harmonically less usual and much more spikey in melodic outlines; it seems to me to be thoughtful, but also melancholy and nagging by turns." [Decca LX 3048 (10")] See: D67c

B67j. Fine, Irving. "English in Boston; Stravinsky's Symphony." Modern Music 23:210 (Summer 1946)
Review of the premiere performance, April 5, 1946. "This was an effective and attractive piece, the difficult medium handled with skill. I liked best of all the siciliano-like second movement. Tonally it was clear; arrivals at new keys were treated as events, and while it was closer to Barber's more conservative earlier music, it seemed purer in style than the first and last movements. Here Barber is still in the process of evolving a more contemporary style and the stylistic inconsistencies are marked by a certain formal diffuseness, especially in the last movement." See: W67a

B67k. Finney, Ross Lee. "Orchestral Music." Notes 11:146-147 (December 1953)

Review of the Schirmer miniature score. "Samuel Barber's Concerto for Violoncello and Orchestra is one of the most convincing works that this talented American composer has written and one of the finest concertos for the instrument composed during this century." See: W67

B67l. Flanagan, William. "Recordings of Special Merit." HiFi/Stereo Review 18:75 (April 1967)

"The Barber Concerto (1945) is, to be sure, one of the earlier manifestations of his stylistic burgeoning out from the lyrical conservatism of his earlier music--it is, in its way, even a little thorny and convoluted as musical structure--but it is still rooted in the post-Romantic tradition." [Decca DL 710 132, DL 10 132] See: D67a

B67m. Freed, Richard. "A Little Barber Festival." Stereo Review 42:115 (May 1979)

"Cellists who lament the scarcity of concertos for their instrument somehow seem to overlook the fine one Barber composed in 1945, in which his expressive lyricism and his sense of color are both at their most directly appealing." [Varese Saraband VC 81057] See: D67a

B67n. Friedewald, Russell Edward. A Formal and Stylistic Analysis of the Published Music of Samuel Barber. Thesis (Ph.D.)--Iowa State University, 1957. 357 p.

"While there are many passages in this work that owe a great deal to the Capricorn Concerto (1944), it is apparent that the composer is extending rather than merely repeating the compositional techniques that he used in his earlier work. The solo writing in this composition, when compared with that of the Violin Concerto, which was written six years earlier, consistently calls for greater virtuosity on the part of the performer. In addition to the many cantilena passages, it bristles with multiple stops, harmonics, and difficult patterns requiring rapid shifts in position." [p. 218-219] See: W67

B67o. Goldberg, Albert. "Debut Orchestra Performs." Los Angeles Times, April 20, 1970, pt. 4, p. 19.

"If cellists thus far have fairly unanimously avoided the work it is not because of any lack of gratefulness for the solo instrument. The cello was one of the versatile Barber's early preoccupations and he concocted a formidable array of difficulties for the hapless performer. The trouble is that the musical substance hardly supports the technical hazards; only the last movement flowers on a well developed scale, after a weak and rambling first movement and a moderately pleasant slow section. [Paul] Tobias, however, seemed to harbor no doubts of the importance of his task. He played with contagious urgency, brilliant tone and dauntless technical command and the orchestra gave him excellent support." See: W67g

B67p. Greenfield, Edward. "Classical Reissues." Gramophone 43:455 (March 1966)
     "...the snapping Hungarian rhythm of the main theme
suggests a tribute (whether unconscious or not) to Bartok.
The slow movement too is passionately lyrical and though
the finale sounds a degree more contrived--almost as though
Barber was daunted at the thought of finding an adequate
completion--the whole concerto should certainly be in the
regular repertory everywhere." [Decca Ace of Clubs ACL 264,
from Decca LX 3048] See: D67c

B67q. Klenz, William. "Samuel Barber." Notes 8:392
(March 1951)
     Review of the Schirmer piano score and part. "...It
is, of course, too soon to predict the enduring success of
this particular concerto with either the public or performers, although it is surely an important contribution in
which the highest level of modern instrumental technique is
exploited in a distinguished work. The three movements...are organic forms embracing classic elements of
exposition, development, and recapitulation, but without
reference to any fixed formula. The texture is by turns
astringent and rich as suits the needs of the moment.
Always, there emerges the craftsman counselled and en-
lightened by intention and conviction." See: W67

B67r. L., K. "Orchestral." Records and Recordings 9:44
(April 1966)
     "Though at times it smacks strongly of Bartok the
whole work seems more closely integrated and the slow
movement is intensely lyrical. With so little available
for the solo cello, this work deserves to be far better
known....the 'Cello Concerto is likely to become a family
favorite." [Ace of Clubs ACL 264, reissue of Decca Eclipse
ECS 7071] See: D67d

B67s. Layton, Robert. "Orchestral." Gramophone 51:488
(September 1974)
     "The work possesses an astonishing freshness, lyricism
and a natural charm which grows stronger over the years.
There are few modern concertos that have such a marvelous
main tune as does the opening of the Concerto, and Barber's
scoring is beautifully transparent and full of colour. The
performance has the stamp of the composer's own authority
to commend it..." [Ace of Clubs ACL 264, reissue of Decca
Eclipse ECS 707] See: D67c

B67t. -----. "Samuel Barber" [album notes for Chandos
ABRD 1085 disc]
     "...if I were pressed to name the most lyrical of
modern concertos, it would have to be that of Samuel Barber...It radiates the freshness and innocence of Barber's
finest music and were it not for the rhetorical vehemence
of some of the solo writing, it would, I'm sure, enjoy
classic status." See: D67f

B67u. Locklair, Wriston. "Leonard Rose Plays Barber
Concerto." Musical America 79:22 (March 1959)
     "The concerto has several things to recommend it: the
development in the first movement, with numerous double
stops, rapid bowings and pizzicato phrases, is a challenge
to the soloist, and the melodic content of the closing
movement reveals Barber's special leaning toward good
strong writing. Mr. Rose gave a fine performance of the
concerto." See: W67e

B67v. Moore, David W. "Guide to Records" American
Records Guide 42:16 (June 1979)
     "...Garbousova finds the going difficult; therefore so
does the listener. I recall going to a lesson with Leonard
Rose while he was preparing this work for his New York
Philharmonic performance; he sweat bullets over it. In
his opinion at the time, this was the most difficult concerto he had ever played. Indeed, it is extremely challenging, with tremendous leaps from register to register
and all to be played with Barber's typical Sibelian passion. This piece, particularly the Finale, always did
remind me of Sibelius' most wintery early style...It is a
fine piece of Barber, one of the last fine pieces he wrote
with the passion and dark fervor that made him the most
moving American composer of his generation." [Varese Saraband VC 81057, reissue of Decca DL 10 132, DL 710 132]
See: D67a

B67w. Roddy, Joseph. "A Presence of Cellos." High
Fidelity/Musical America 15:86J-K (March 1965)
     "It is a work Barber put together twenty years ago,
and it still lacks airs and graces. Although it is her
piece, Garbousova could draw little pleasure from it, and
gave none." See: W67f

B67x. Sabin, Robert. "New Music Reviews." Musical
America 71:30 (August 1951)
     "This concerto puts the soloist through strenuous
paces, and goes through the traditional developments with
professional skill. Yet it remains one of Barber's most
labored, thematically dry and academically stilted scores.
One searches almost fruitlessly for the color, the imaginative power and the eloquence he has achieved in his scores
for the theatre and in other compositions." See: W67

B67y. Simmons, Walter. "Classical Records." Fanfare
3:43-44 (May/June 1980)
     "Barber composed his Cello Concerto...during a transi-
tional period when he attempted to infuse his hitherto
unbridled romanticism with a bit of the bracing acerbity of
his neo-classical colleagues...the portions of the work
that spring from the composer's melodic predisposition, the
second movement especially, are quite lovely, and the work
as a whole is a fair enough concerto. But it clearly lacks
the intense conviction of the earlier Violin Concerto or

279

the formal strength and stylistic balance of the later
Piano Concerto...Raya Garbousova's performance is adequate
and shows a great deal of sincere effort, but her pitch
goes awry at times, and her tone is not always evenly
controlled." [Varese Saraband VC 81057] See: D67a

B67z. Taubman, Howard.   "Music: Cello Concerto." New
York Times, January 31, 1959, p. 12.
    "This work...discloses some of the strongest facets of
the composer's art as well as some of the weak ones. Mr.
Barber writes with deep sympathy for strings, and the
rhapsodic affinities of the 'cello are made to order for
his most felicitious vein. Particularly in the slow movement he sings with romantic ardor, undisturbed by the
pressures of fashions. One feels that Mr. Barber is
expressing his true identity as a composer." See: W67e

B67aa. Waters, Edward N. "Music." Quarterly Journal
of Current Acquisitions [of the Library of Congress] 13:26
(November 1955)
    "Samuel Barber...gave the autograph scores of two of
his best works--the Adagio for string quartet and the
violoncello concerto, Op. 22...The latter is well on its
way to becoming a standard work in the limited repertoire
available to cellists. Both scores are representative of
the art of one of America's foremost composers, a creator
whose lyrical gifts are surpassed by no one of the present
day." See: W67

B68. ESSAY FOR ORCHESTRA, OP. 12.

B68a. B., F. "Orchestra: Schirmer." Musical Times
82:430 (December 1941)
    "[It] deserves to be better known on this side of the
Atlantic. It is too short to create a sensation, but not
too short to show the skill of the composer in mixing
orchestral colours, or to be thoroughly enjoyed. It should
prove extremely effective with its piano part dexterously
woven into the texture, and its brilliant writing for
strings and wood-wind." See: W68

B68b. Downes, Olin. "Schuman Song Led by Koussevitzky." New York Times, April 4, 1943, p. 43.
    "Mr. Barber's [work] is excellent writing, not earth-
shaking, or in anyway prophetic of revolution, but in its
form and logic of treatment, and refreshing sense of direction, of the composer knowing exactly what he wants to
do, and skilfully doing it..." See: W68e

B68c. -----. "Szell on Podium for Philharmonic." New
York Times, December 8, 1950, p. 40.
    "[It] is more than a testimony to his qualities as a
composer. The introduction has a romantic beauty, line and
color all of its own. But its pendant is the charming and

fanciful scherzo which follows. The design is clear; the final reminiscence of the introduction completes it. If it is a 'first essay' of a modest composer it is also a triumph of inventiveness and refined workmanship." See: W68f

B68d. Downes, Olin. "Toscanini plays Two New Works." New York Times, November 6, 1938, p. 48.
    "The Essay for Orchestra modestly named is well integrated, with clear instrumentation, and with development of the ideas that unifies the music in spite of changes of tempo and marked contrasts of orchestration." See: W68a

B68e. Griffiths, Paul. "Chorus of Virtuosity." Times (London) September 7, 1981, p. 11.
    "It was a magnificent musical spread that Sir George Solti and the Chicago Symphony Orchestra spread before us on Friday...Then came a regional speciality, Samuel Barber's first Essay, which was odd in its mix of typical twilight melancholy with vitality, but which hardly represented the American compositional cuisine at its strongest." See: W68k

B68f. Hall, David. The Record Book. New York: Citadel Press, 1946. 1063 p.
    "The Essay for Orchestra is a more mature work [than Dover Beach] and a stunning piece of orchestral music. One is impressed by the composer's sincerity, directness, strength of utterance, and above all imagination." [p. 764] [Victor 18 062, 78 rpm] See: D68c

B68g. Horan, Robert. "American Composers, XIX: Samuel Barber." Modern Music 20:164 (March-April 1943)
    "The Scherzo of the First Essay, although self-consistent, would appear to be misplaced in this form. It is the weaker and less virile side of Barber's romanticism and seems to lack the conviction that the form implies. Or perhaps it is that he is less able to manipulate his intention in the orchestra in passages of Scherzo quality. The lightness comes out a bit thin, although the scoring is clean and energetic." See: W68

B68h. Jones, Isabel Morse. "Korjus Wins Throng at Auditorium." Los Angeles Times, March 4, 1939, pt. 2, p. 7.
    "The Essay for Orchestra" is subjective, mystic, and strangely stirring to the emotions." [Otto Klemperer conducting the Los Angeles Philharmonic Orchestra] See: W68b

B68i. Lieberson, Goddard. "Over the Air." Modern Music 16:65-66 (November-December 1938)
    "It is gratifying to have American music in the expert hands of Maestro Toscanini, but unfortunately, this great conductor has a faculty for singling out that music which represents the concessionary style of our native

art...These pieces of Samuel Barber fall neatly into line
with the other American music which Toscanini has chosen in
the past. It is contemporary only in the sense that the
composer is still alive. There is but a fraction of the
whole which even suggests an individual technic; and instead of melodic creativeness and harmonic invention, Mr.
Barber has substituted his wealth of listening to the works
of other composers...And so Maestro Toscanini, in whose
hands lies the opportunity to vindicate our native music by
his good taste and musicianship, has again shown American
music to be what it is most often not--uncreative, colorless, and sub-European." See: W68

B68j. Reed, Peter Hugh. "Record Notes and Reviews."
American Record Guide 7:435 (August 1941)
     Commenting on Toscanini's choice of two Barber works,
played in November, 1938, Mr. Reed writes, "This choice
caused considerable resentment among left-wing musicians,
for they felt that Barber was too conservative for such a
distinction, but on the general public the works made a
favorable and musicianly impression. The left-wings' resentment was hardly justified, for it would seem to us that
Samuel Barber's music is as substantially American, as
anything they may advance. Barber's material is conservative in the sense that he is apparently not interested in
extreme dissonance or radical rhythmic devices, but it does
not necessarily follow that he has not something new to
say." [Victor 18 062] See: D68c

B68k. Taubman, Howard. "Records: Modern Scores." New
York Times, August 19, 1941, sect. 9, p. 6.
     "Mr. Barber does not hesitate to write in what some of
the advance guard would call a conservative idiom, but if
that is how he happens to feel, why not? The form of the
Essay is compact, and its content is rhapsodic, impassioned
and boldly dramatic." [Victor 18 062] See: D68c

B68l. Thomson, Virgil. "Superficially Warlike." In
his Music Reviewed. New York: Vintage Books, 1967. 422 p.
[originally appeared in the New York Herald Tribune, April
4, 1943]
     "Private Samuel Barber's Essay for Orchestra, No. 1,
is a pretty piece but not a very strong one. It resembles
more a meditation than it does the kind of reasoned exposition one usually associates with the prose form of that
name. Perhaps Mr. Barber thinks of the word in its contemporary sense of a reflective composition on some relatively
trivial subject. Certainly his musical material here is
not striking. Neither, unfortunately, is his development
of it, though there is always in this composer's music,
grace." [p. 94-95] See: W68

B68m. "Toscanini Gets Around to Tchaikowsky After 45
Years; Starts on Barber Early." Newsweek 12:30 (November
14, 1938)

"Whereas Toscanini saw fit to delay his American reading of the Russian work until it was nearly a half a
century old, he put two of the American's compositions on
the air before the ink was dry. One of them--_Essay for
Orchestra_--was composed only last spring. The 28-year-old
musician who captured this big sprig of laurel is a tall
black-haired young man with vague brown eyes that have
grown used to looking at honors handed him...He is a baritone and once sang on the radio, but composition is his
real passion. An enthusiastic pedestrian, he works out
most of his creations while walking." _See_: W68a

B69. FADOGRAPH OF A YESTERN SCENE, OP. 44.

B69a.   Apone, Carl.   "Pittsburgh: A 'New' Old Hall is
Born." _High Fidelity/Musical America_ 22:MA25-26 (January
1972)

"His _Fadograph of a Yestern Scene_ is a brief piece of
one movement...The title comes from a line in James Joyce's
Finnegan's Wake. Joyce's prose makes frequent journies
into the subconscious and Barber seems to follow similar
paths in the impressionistic exercise.   To be sure, as in
his other writings, there is compactness and discipline
here.   But while the score has dignity, shuns large
volumes, and is sometimes softly affectionate, it hardly
casts the intended spell.   There is little that is viable,
little that holds the attention. This is more like a man
doodling than digging.   The language is hardly in the
twentieth-century vocabulary, and future historians will
puzzle at its place on the opening of a new hall in America
in 1971." _See_: W69a

B69b.   Ericson, Raymond.   "Pittsburghers Led by Steinberg Play New Barber Work." _New York Times_, November 7,
1971, sect. 1, p. 83.
"The evening's novelty, Samuel Barber's _Fadograph of a
Yestern Scene_, in its New York premiere could be described,
without deprecation, as short and sweet...Whether by design
or not, it seems like a reflection, both like and unlike,
of earlier Barber works, notably parts of _Vanessa_." _See_:
W69b

B69c.   Niemann, Suzanne.   "The Journal Reviews: Carnegie
Hall." _Music Journal_ 30:74 (January 1972)
"[It] opened Pittsburgh's Heinz Hall for the Performing Arts in a reflective mood rather than with a
flourish, provoking thought in a time when there is too
much fanfare. However, unlike James Joyce's _Finnegan's
Wake_ from which the title is taken, the short work does not
bar the uninitiated from understanding and enjoyment."
See: W69a

B71. MEDEA, OP. 23.

B71a. Barnes, Clive. "Dance: Miss Graham's Choreography." New York Times, November 5, 1965, p. 30.
"Samuel Barber's somber music, which sends even its allegro melodies scurrying across the stage like bewildered mice, provides a darkly conventional backdrop upon which Miss Graham splashes the color of her dance. Here in these dances, is this dramaturgy, is the full flavor of Miss Graham's tragic muse." See: W71d

B71b. Cohn, Arthur. Recorded Classical Music. New York: Schirmer Books, 1981. 2164 p.
"Music of archaic and contemporary contrasts, displaying Barber in his most dynamic stance. More than once in this seven-movement piece...the harmonics take on a polytonal tang." [p. 96-97] See: W71

B71c. DeMotte, Warren. "Classic." HiFi Stereo Review 4:54 (April 1960)
"It has the Barber melodiousness, and it also has power and tension." [Mercury SR 90224, MG 50224] See: D71a

B71d. Donovan, Richard. "Samuel Barber." Notes 7:431 (June 1950)
"Here and there the harmony seems to lack flexibility, but the composer undoubtedly had good reasons for his choice of key plan. As a concert piece the work may not be quite as appealing to a general audience as some of Barber's other orchestral works. Sweeping, impassioned melodies, so beloved by the mass of listeners, would be quite inappropriate here, and are fortunately absent. This music, nevertheless, is eloquent and interesting enough to stand by itself, apart from the action of the ballet. It is effectively scored, and the idiom is one that will communicate in language intelligible to reasonably experienced concert-goers, the dramatic qualities of the subject." See: W71

B71e. F., H. "Analytical Notes and First Reviews." Gramophone 29:4-5 (June 1951)
"Medea as a suite does not, it seems to me, quite come off, though the patterns of the music are quite intelligible without the dancers' motions. The opening is impressive and the third section has a fine heroic quality; at times one cannot avoid noticing a French influence; the ending is powerful." [Decca LX 3049 (Great Britain), 10 inch] See: D71d

B71f. Frankenstein, Alfred. "Classical." High Fidelity 10:58 (June 1960)
"Barber is essentially a charm-composer and power is not one of his virtues, but the Medea theme and the demands of Martha Graham's choreography, for which it was written,

conspired to bring forth a most exceptional degree of power in this score. It is probably Barber's finest dramatic work, or at least it seems so as Hanson plays it." [Mercury MG 50224, SR 90224] See: D71a

B71g. Friedewald, Russell Edward. A Formal and Stylistic Analysis of the Published Music of Samuel Barber. Thesis (Ph.D.)--Iowa State University, 1957. 357 p.
"The avoidance of a literal interpretation of the Medea-Jason legend is reflected in the treatment of the musical material." [p. 312] See: W71

B71h. Fuller, Donald. "Columbia's Festival: Hindemith's Lilacs. Modern Music 23:200 (Summer 1946)
"Barber's usual craftsmanship is limited here to aptly supplying a demand, the counterpoint to Miss Graham's frenzy.   Thus we are treated to an interminable series of nervous, gasping phrases, which strive for no real goal and seem to insinuate but unconstructively. Barber has certainly thrown back the point with devastating realization of the emotional climate, but one misses his sense of the long line and the broad period, his lyrical gift." See: W71a

B71i. Krokover, Rosalyn. "New Publications in Review." Musical Courier 141:28 (May 1, 1950)
"Barber has divided his score into seven sections that suggest the action of the Greek tragedy from the time the characters appear until Medea commits mass murder. A knowledge of the Graham balletics is not necessary to appreciate the atmosphere and brooding quality that Barber conveys. His scoring is wonderfully precise, the workmanship secure and mature." See: W71

B71j. Martin, John. "Cave of the Heart Danced by Graham." New York Times, February 28, 1947, p. 26.
"It is a more full-bodied score than is customary in the Graham repertoire, and both in this respect and in its fine feeling for the theatre it provides a real support for the action." [Decca LX 3050 (Great Britain), 10 inch] See: D71d

B71k. "Record Supplement for May, 1951." Gramophone Shop. Record Supplement 14:1-2 (May 1951)
"It is a rather stark work, brilliantly scored and stunningly performed in this recording with the composer directing." [London LPS 333 (Great Britain), 10 inch, Decca LX 3049 (Great Britain), 10 inch] See: D71d

B71l. S. "Orchestra." New Records 19:3 (July 1951)
"The score of Medea was commissioned for Martha Graham and was first danced by her and her company in 1946. Miss Graham uses the title Cave of the Heart for her ballet...Barber seems to have accomplished with notable success what he set out to do...we found it more interesting

and palatable than most late Stravinsky." [London LPS 333 (Great Britain), 10 inch] See: D71d

B71m. Schab, Gunter. "Europaische Erstauffuhrung: Medea von Samuel Barber." Das Musikleben 6:173 (May 1953)
     Review of the 1953 Cologne performance.

B71n. Shupp, Enos E., Jr. "Orchestra." New Records 28:5 (March 1960)
     "The Medea Suite loses little, if anything, in its concert dress (though balletophiles will recall the tremendous impact of the ballet itself); the now-famous Dance of Vengeance is the focal point of a very thrilling score." [Mercury MG 50224, SR 90224] See: D71a

B71o. The Stereo Record Guide, vol. 3. Edited by Ivan March. London: The Long Playing Record Library, 1963. 1102 p.
     "Medea, which was in the mono catalogue before in a recording under the composer's direction, was a ballet written for Martha Graham. As Barber himself has said, 'the suite follows roughly the form of a Greek tragedy,' and it contains some of his most intensely serious music as well as some of the most expressive. But as with all good ballets the rhythmic element is vital...An invaluable record when American music is still inadequately represented in the British catalogue." [p. 682] [Mercury AMS 16096, SR 90224] See: D71a

B72. MEDEA'S MEDITATION AND DANCE OF VENGEANCE, OP. 23A.

B72a. D., E. "Boston Symphony Heard in Concert." New York Times, December 16, 1956, p. 85.
     "The work reinforced the strong impression it made at its first performance here by the Philharmonic-Symphony under Dimitri Mitropoulos last February. Mr. Munch led it yesterday with explosive intensity." See: W72b

B72b. Davis, Peter G. "Repeat Performances." High Fidelity 19:107 (June 1969)
     "After the Debussy, unsatisfactorily performed though it may be, Barber's Medea music sounds tawdry and obvious and the excellent, letter-perfect performance only points up the fact." [RCA Victrola VIC 1391, from RCA Victor LM 2197] See: D72a

B72c. "Festival Hall: Celebrity Concert." Times (London) February 1, 1957, p. 3.
     "Samuel Barber's Medea was last night's novelty, or at least a symphonic poem, Medea's Meditation and Dance of Vengeance, derived from a ballet composed for Martha Graham. One could see that it would suit her type of dance-drama...It is skilful and colourful music starting with suggestions of the primitive on percussion and passing

through Strauss's to Stravinsky's kind of reflection on Mediterranean antiquity. It just, but just, passes the test of independent viability on the concert platform and does not tell us much about Barber." See: W72c

B72d. Frankenstein, Alfred. "Guest Conductor Here: Schippers in Fine Debussy." San Francisco Chronicle, March 2, 1962, p. 36.
"At the end Schippers presented Medea's Meditation and Dance of Vengeance by Samuel Barber, which impressed me as unmitigated trash and left a bad taste, although many present obviously liked it. They gave Schippers one of the season's warmest ovations when it was over." See: D72h

B72e. G.-F., C. "In My Opinion: The London Concert World." Musical Opinion 80:393 (April 1957)
Review of the January 31, 1957 London performance. "...this is fluent music of high professional competence and shows an abundance of colouristic resource but no stylistic distinction..." See: W72c

B72f. Goldberg, Albert. "American Music Heard at Bowl." Los Angeles Times, August 17, 1961, pt. 4, p. 8.
The work comes "...off better with the visual realization for which...[it was] designed than...in concert performance. But there still remains a sultry theatricalism to Barber's music that makes an effect..." [Howard Mitchell conducting the Los Angeles Philharmonic Orchestra at the Hollywood Bowl] See: W72f

B72g. Hume, Paul. "Dorati and the NSO." Washington Post, March 12, 1980, sect. D, p. 8.
"The evening...opened with a celebration of the 70th birthday of Samuel Barber, an event that occurred last Sunday. For his notable contributions to every area of music, orchestral, song, opera, ballet, chamber music, choral and solo instrumental literature, Barber should indeed be honored by this country. It is reassuring that American orchestras everywhere are marking the signal anniversary. Dorati began the evening with Medea's Meditation and Dance of Vengeance from the ballet score that Barber wrote for Martha Graham in 1946. Those fortunate enough to have seen Graham dance this work under its final balletic title Cave of the Heart, will never forget the overpowering effect of Barber's music and the great dancer at her peak. The two famous excerpts from the score with their emotional balance and gorgeous coloring, have rightly held a high place on American orchestral programs ever since the composer arranged them." See: W72r

B72h. Kolodin, Irving. "Beecham's Mozart, Barber's Medea, Peters's Lucia." Saturday Review 39:27 (February 18, 1956)
"As synthesized and completely rewritten [from the earlier ballet], the new work has a certain kinship with

the famous Strauss _Dance of the Seven Veils_ from _Salome_, in
the sense that it begins quietly and attains a bruising
conclusion. However, the artifices here are Barber's own,
and remarkably well manipulated to achieve his purpose.
Mitropoulos had, in it, just the kind of score to absorb
all his faculties." _See_: W72a

   B72i. Levinger, Henry W. "New York Concert and Opera
Beat." _Musical Courier_ 153:14 (March 1, 1956)
   "It is a work of great consequence...this symphonic
work is a completely fresh creation...Barber has written an
important and exciting new orchestral piece which was
played brilliantly by the orchestra and brought to the
composer an enthusiastic ovation by the audience." _See_:
W72a

   B72j. "_Medea_ by Barber." _Time_ 67:42 (February 13,
1956)
   "It turned out to be a meatier work for full symphony
than as a dance accompaniment, with the same virtues--and
the same faults--that have made Barber, 45, one of the most
performed of contemporary American composers. Among the
virtues: a firm command of the orchestra, which produced a
vividly mysterious opening figure on the xylophone and two
flutes that appear to bump and separate like a pair of
slow-motion dancers. Chief fault: thematic aimlessness.
After the promise of the opening bars, the next part of the
brief score is limp and weary--a routine expression of
Media's mother love. Only when the heroine goes into her
'dance of vengeance' do things liven up again...The music
got more conventional in texture as it got noisier, but
ultimately, sheer noise was sufficient: as the last club-
bing chord thundered out the Philharmonic's subscribers
gasped and then burst into applause." _See_: W72a

   B72k. Müllmann, Bernd. "Schallplatten." _Melos NZ_ 3:64
(January-February 1977)
   "Die Medea-Studie, nach mehreren Bearbeitungen gereift
und gehärtet, zeigt den amerikanischen Komponisten auf der
Hohe seiner zweiten Schaffensperiode, die mit den vierziger
Jahren begann." ["The study of Medea, matured and established after several revisions, displays the American composer at the height of his second creative period which
started with the forties."--H.B.] [CBS 73 434] _See_: D72c

   B72l. "Reviews of New Music." _Musical Opinion_ 80:221
(January 1957)
   Brief review of the G. Schirmer/Chappell study score.
"The work is one long crescendo of emotion, superbly and
excitingly scored." _See_: W72

   B72m. Rutland, Harold. "Thomas Schippers." _Musical
Times_ 98:157 (March 1957)
   Barber's work, which he recorded for large orchestra
two years ago (nine years after the first production of the

ballet), holds more interest for the listener; it has power
and find craftsmanship." See: W72c

B72n. Sabin, Robert. "New Barber Work Has World Premiere." Musical America 76:223 (February 15, 1956)
    "The score...is one of his best works. The impact of
the great dancer stirred the composer to a stinging directness of emotion and sense of tragic grandeur that brought
something new into his music. In this new rescoring for
large orchestra he feels that he has created a 'completely
new work.' It is written in one continuous movement,
drawing material from the original score that is directly
related to Medea. While the original score is both structurally and dramatically a more satisfying work, this new
tone poem is magnificently scored and has tremendous intensity. Mr. Mitropoulous' tempos were sometimes too fast,
but he conducted it in inspired fashion." See: W72a

B72o. Weinstock, Herbert. "Boston Symphony Orchestra"
[album notes for RCA Victor LM 2197 disc]
    "It is dedicated 'To Martha Graham,' and carries, in
addition to the indications in Italian, these English instructions: 'Broadly, from the distance,' 'moving moderately,' 'slower,' 'mysterious, moving ahead,' 'anguish-
ed,' 'sombre with dignity,' 'with gradually increasing
intensity,' 'moving ahead slightly,' and 'with mounting
frenzy.' These markings indicate the musical means by
which the piece traces Medea's emotions: tenderness, toward
her children, suspicions of--and then anguish at--her husband's betrayal, her consequent decision to take vengeance,
and finally, frenzy..." See: D72b

B73. MUSIC FOR A SCENE FROM SHELLEY, OP. 7.

B73a. Barry, Edward. "Ravinia's 1936 Festival Ends;
Praise Janssen." Chicago Tribune, August 3, 1936, p. 17.
    "The Barber music offered conductor and orchestra both
a chance to demonstrate their virtuosity. It ranges
through the entire dynamic scale, and is built from material so tenuous as to require the greatest care in handling." See: W73b

B73b. "Concert and Opera Asides." New York Times, April
16, 1939, sect. 10, p. 7.
        News item in which it is noted that Samuel
Barber's Music For a Scene From Shelley, recently performed
by the Helsinki Municipal Symphony Orchestra, is the first
American work to be played in a regular symphony concert in
Finland. The "...work aroused much favorable comment in
Finnish music circles, and probably significantly weakened
in Finland the prejudice against American musical talent
common throughout Europe. Mr. Barber's music was conducted
by Martti Simila, a young Finnish artist." See: W73e

B73c. Copland, Aaron. "Scores and Records." Modern Music 14:100 (January-February 1937)
"The Scene From Shelley...which is the best of the three [Dover Beach, Sonata for cello and piano], in its nicety of taste, balance and finish, recalls the early work of Randall Thompson. One cannot help wishing that something or someone would inveigle Mr. Barber out of the safe and sane channels he seems to be content to tread." See: W73

B73d. Downes, Olin. "Janssen Presents New Native Music." New York Times, March 25, 1935, p. 13.
"The qualities of Mr. Barber's music which do him much credit are those of poetical feeling, an instinct for form and--a theme. The style is experimental, and so is the development. Polytonal effects thrown about the principal theme do not appear to be the most natural to it. But what young composer would not wish, in the modern manner, to try his wings? The composer seeks the special color and the evocation of mood that he wants in a genuinely musical way. Furthermore, there is logic of statement and a main melody of considerable length and arch and feeling." See: W73a

B73e. E. "Janssen Gives Barber Novelty." Musical America 55:14 (April 10, 1935)
"The young man has written an appealing work on certain lines from Prometheus Unbound, investing a broad melody with shimmering color and tender mood. Great originality is not apparent, but great promise is." See: W73a

B73f. Eyer, Ronald. "Music by Americans." Musical America 73:17 (April 15, 1953)
"...among that composer's best-known works and...[has] received wide acceptance both in the concert hall and in previous recordings." [American Recording Society ARS 26] See: D73a

B73g. Frankenstein, Alfred. "Classical." High Fidelity 11:49 (July 1961)
"By far the best thing here is Music for a Scene from Shelley, a short orchestral piece of great intensity and finesse, beautifully played and nicely recorded." [Vanguard VRS 1065, VSD 2083] See: D73b

B73h. Harvey, Trevor. "Opera." Gramophone 46:272 (August 1968)
The work "...isn't so strong--a much earlier work--but it is passionate and it works to a fine climax." [Philips Vanguard VSL 11019] See: D73b

B73i. Leigh, E. S. V. "Concerto." New Records 47:5 (April 1979)
"This is the only stereo recording of Music for a Scene from Shelley listed in Schwann. The spacious sound

gives the piece an other-worldly aspect, which is partly appropriate." [Unicorn UN 1 72016] See: D73d

B73J. "New Works High Lights Concert." Los Angeles Times, July 24, 1937, pt. 2, p. 7.
    "His music...is filled with poetic mystery. It is strangely northern in instrumentation and marked by inspiration. It is intimate music and yet peculiarly suited to playing out of doors." See: W73c

B73k. Stinson, Eugene. "Janssen Ends Ravinia Series with Sibelius' Second Symphony." Chicago Daily News, August 3, 1936, p. 17.
    "...it was effective and suitable music of fascinating workmanship. Mr. Barber has not used methods that are particularly new, but he certainly speaks with his own voice and has, it seems, most likely, something quite his own to say." See: W73b

B73l. Tetreault, Ronald. "Shelley at the Opera." ELH 48:158 (Spring 1981)
    "Although Prometheus Unbound has never received full-scale operatic treatment, parts of it have been set to music, most notably by Samuel Barber and Sir Hubert Parry." See: W73

B73m. Whittall, Arnold. "Orchestral." Gramophone 56:182 (July 1978)
    "...it moves confidently from an already expansive opening to an almost extravagantly rhetorical climax. Touches of Sibelian grandeur can be heard on the way, and the piece is probably over scored, but Measham controls Barber's steady crescendo with skill and draws full bloodied playing from the West Australian Symphony Orchestra." [Unicorn UN 1 72016, previously UNS 256] See: D73d

B74. DIE NATALI: CHORAL PRELUDES FOR CHRISTMAS, OP. 37.

B74a. Ardoin, John. "Munch Premieres Barber Work." Musical America 81:43-44 (February 1941)
    "Two of Barbers most distinct characteristics, his superb rhythmic sense and his feeling for orchestral color, work wonders in the recasting of the familiar carols he uses in this work...The spirit of the chorale prelude is one of homogeneity of material and/or mood within a contrapuntal framework. A series of preludes would have to follow this premise in order to work well together and convince the listener. When foreign textures are suddenly introduced, as in Die Natali, the basic spirit of the choral prelude is nullified...Barber has often designed engaging and admirable settings, but the linking together of the carols, a formidable task, does not form a congenial whole." See: W74a

B74b. "Barber's Die Natali. Times (London) December 19, 1961, p. 5
Short notice that Die Natali would be broadcast on December 30, 1961 on the Network Three by the BBC Northern Orchestra, conducted by Stanford Robinson, making its English and European premiere. See: W74c

B74c. Brown, Royal S. "Classical." High Fidelity 25:85 (December 1975)
"Samuel Barber's warm and charming Die Natali (Christmas Day), subtitled Choral Preludes for Christmas and premiered in 1960, represents another extremely welcome recording first. A musical montage employing a number of well-known Christmas carols presented in kaleidoscopically shifting contrapuntal and instrumental textures. Die Natali causes the colors of Christmas to swirl within the mind of any listener who has been brought up on these hauntingly evocative tunes. Needless to say, the Barber work makes this disc all the more attractive for this particular season." [Louisville LS 745] See: D74a

B74d. Cohn, Arthur. Recorded Classical Music. New York: Schirmer Books, 1981. 2164 p.
"This work is far afield (in technique, meaning, creative objective and stylistic stability) from the many Christmas-carol settings that have appeared--simple and straight, rhapsodic mix, collective suite. Barber's choice of eight carols forms a large fantasy tapestry utilizing canon, theme-and-variations, and cyclic techniques. The orchestration and metrical interplay are further assets in this, one of the composer's best pieces." [p. 96] See: W74

B74e. Durgin, Cyrus W. "National Report: Boston." Musical America 81:16 (February 1961)
"The idea for such a piece must have occurred to dozens of composers, but Mr. Barber seems to be the only one to have dome something about it. His method was scholarly: presenting of the times according to the manifold devices of counterpoint. The result is a biggish work for big orchestra which, however, never really rolls out the tunes with Christmas joy or jubilation. Mr. Barber did work up a certain degree of Orientalism in rhythms and color, and those episodes are the ones which have more motion. Too much of the work seems aimless; though it may look wonderful on paper, the sound is often amorphous, and the rhythm, too. The piece also is very sour, harmonically." See: W74a

B74f. Lewando, Ralph. "Boston Symphony Premieres New Work by Samuel Barber." Musical Courier 163:13 (February 1961)
"Barber has lavished his genius upon a setting of favorite carols...Strange is the union of themes of extreme simplicity with a complex harmonic and countermelodic pro-

cedure. The amazing variety of their treatment in modern
idiom often is confusing. Although the listener is sometimes overwhelmed by the volume and richness of orchestral
tone, one or another of the solo instruments...carries
along the thematic thread cleverly. The work seems likely
to be around a long time, especially during coming Christmas observances." See: W74a

B74g. "Music." Time 77:42 (January 13, 1961)
"The remarkably successful piece is essentially a
patchwork of familiar Christmas carols artfully embedded in
unfamiliar harmonics...The mood for the most part is reflective, the tone intensely lyrical, as most of Barber's
best work is. The only truly shocking section of the piece
is also one of the most effective: the brasses suddenly
explode into a jazzy freewheeling that hardened Yuletiders
will eventually recognize as Good King Wenceslas." See:
W74a

B74h. Parsons, Arrand. Chicago Symphony Orchestra
Program Notes, December 19, 1968, p. 13-15.
"The Latin title of the work, suggesting an anniversary, indicates 'Christmastide,' as a note in the score
reports. The work itself consists of a succession of
chorale preludes, or instrumental treatments of some of the
familiar Christmas carols. The various sections are joined
and are played without pause." See: W74e

B74i. Reynolds, Gordon. "Last Look at Christmas."
Music 102:725 (November 1961)
"Samuel Barber's prelude on Silent Night (Novello),
arranged by the composer from the score of his Die Natali
(Chappell), is a most effective composition which makes
even this threadbare tune work for its living." See: W74

B74j. Sagmaster, Joseph. Cincinnati Symphony Orchestra
Program Notes, December 17-18, 1971, p. 299-300.
"In this work Barber develops a continuing series of
chorale preludes from Christmas carols, using such contrapuntal devices as the canon and double canon." [Eric Kunzel, conductor] See: W74g

B74k. Sargeant, Winthrop. "Musical Events." New
Yorker 36:106 (January 14, 1961)
"It may not be one of his most ambitious works, but it
is an altogether engaging one. It puts several Christmas
tunes, including the entirely familiar Silent Night through
a course of symphonic treatment that is technically very
sophisticated and intellectually interesting without being
in the slightest degree satirical. The result is a delightful piece d'occasion, full of poetic feeling as well
as technical virtuosity, and I am sure it will become a
popular item on symphonic programs." See: W74a

B74l. Schonberg, Harold C. "Music: New Yule Work."

New York Times, January 5, 1961, p. 28.
    "Sensitively harmonized and orchestrated Die Natali is
the kind of piece than any competent craftsman can turn out
rapidly on order. Mr. Barber, being the professional he
is, has avoided a stock arrangement of a television-commer-
cial nature. There is nothing vulgar in this piece save
for one spot--a rather glaring jazz like treatment of Good
King Wenscelas. It is otherwise, tidy, pleasant and atmospheric; and it probably will be turning up in symphony
concerts all over the country come next Christmastide."
See: W74a

B75. NIGHT FLIGHT, OP. 19A.

    B75a. Angles, Robert. "Samuel Barber" [album notes for
Unicorn RHS 342 disc]
    "During the Second World War, Barber served in the
U.S.A.A.F. and wrote his Second Symphony on specific com-
mission from them. The slow movement has become Night
Flight, a remote, ethereal nocturne." See: D75a

    B75b. Brown, Royal S. "Classical." High Fidelity
27:95 (March 1977)
    "...but Night Flight, the reworked slow movement of
the composer's repudiated (but not unrecorded) Second Symphony (1944) all but falls apart at the seams..." [Unicorn
RHS 342] See: D75a

    B75c. Layton, Robert. "Orchestral." Gramophone 54:409
(September 1976)
    "Night Flight is the slow movement of the Second
Symphony, which Barber himself recorded in the early days
of LP...If you possess this disc, hang on to it since the
composer has withdrawn the Symphony, save for its middle
movement, recorded here. I might say this seems to me a
dreadful thing to do, a kind of artistic infanticide."
[Unicorn RHS 342] See: D75a

B76. OVERTURE TO "THE SCHOOL FOR SCANDAL," OP. 5.

    B76a. Arlen, Walter. "Boston Orchestra's Flawlessness
Thrills Distinguished Audience." Los Angeles Times, May 5,
1953, Women [section], p. 1.
    "Samuel Barber was chosen to represent American music
with his overture, The School for Scandal. This ingratiating and mellifluous work sounded as if it were coming from
a well-oiled machine, so carefully tailored and effortless-
ly enjoined was its format. Mr. Munch conducts with characteristic wide gestures, anticipating every nuance in the
music and receives minute responses from every section,
every member of the orchestra." See: W76l

    B76b. B., F. "New Music." Musical Times 82:406
(November 1941)

"The composer knows both the orchestra and his own mind. Nothing appears to be taken for granted, and there are combinations of instruments that should mightily please the connoisseur...Only the best orchestras could hope to do justice to Mr. Barber's exceptionally well-balanced scoring." See: W76

B76c. Bernheimer, Martin "Music Review: Pop John Williams on Philharmonic Podium." Los Angeles Times, pt. 5, "Calendar," November 12, 1983, p. 1.
In his usual sarcastic style Mr. Bernheimer questions, "Why would our cultured guardians want to devote an entire evening's diet to such junk food as Samuel Barber's crunchy School for Scandal overture (a replacement for the originally scheduled Divertimento of Leonard Bernstein), the aforementioned Williams Concerto [for violin] and--horror of horrors--Gustav Holst's Planets, a banal thumpety-thump 1916 ooze orgy now prized by some observers as a preview of spacy Star Wars attractions?" See: W76o

B76d. "Composer Wins Again." New York Times, April 12, 1933, p. 24.
News article announcing that Samuel Barber has won the Joseph H. Bearns Music Prize for the second time in five years; this time for the Overture to "The School for Scandal." See: W76

B76e. Downes, Edward. The New York Philharmonic Guide to the Symphony. New York: Walker, 1976. 1058 p.
"How fresh and spontaneous this Overture sounds. Despite its exuberant virtuosity it is in a sense a student work, for it was written when Barber was twenty-one...Its music does not follow any story line. Nor was it composed for any specific production of Sheridan's comedy. It was simply suggested by the wit and laughter of that nimble masterpiece. The music is Classical in spirit, in its transparent clarity of form, and the luminous texture of its orchestral sounds." [p. 34] See: W76

B76f. Downes, Olin. "Barbirolli Leads Music by Barber." New York Times, March 31, 1938, p. 14.
"The overture, well and gracefully written, is highly creditable for a first orchestral work by a young American. But here is the curious thing: it is no more American in flavor than Wolf-Ferrari. It is in essence an Italian comedy overture, slight in material, clearly composed, transparently orchestrated, conceived in the humorous vein...This overture is evidently a formative work by a young artist of talent who has yet to discover his metier." See: W76b

B76g. -----. "Boston Symphony at Carnegie Hall." New York Times, February 16, 1941, p. 39.
"It is Italianate somewhat in its approach to the comedy mood, and this is probably due to certain musical

influence which Mr. Barber experienced in his student period. His model is close to the _Falstaff_ of Verdi and the scores of Italian opera buffa composers of the later period. This influence lends a passing flavor to the motives themselves and to the method of attack. We do not mean that M. Barber is imitative or directly influenced by other men. He has his own things to say. He says them here with contagious spirit." _See_: W76e

B76h. Downes, Olin. "Munch Conducts Barber Overture." _New York Times_, February 19, 1950, p. 65.
"Charles Munch opened the concert of the Boston Symphony Orchestra yesterday afternoon with Samuel Barber's brilliant and genial overture...[It] was not intended by the composer as a curtain-raiser in the theatre. It is conceived rather as an evocation of the spirit of Sheridan's play. This spirited overture never made a stronger impression than it did yesterday, not only because of its inherent worth, but because of Mr. Munch's exhilarated performance." _See_: W76f

B76i. Eyer, Ronald. "Music by Americans." _Musical America_ 73:17 (April 15, 1953)
"...among that composer's best-known works and...[has] received wide acceptance both in the concert hall and in previous recordings." [American Recording Society ARS 26] _See_: D76a

B76j. Friedewald, Russell Edward. _A Formal and Stylistic Analysis of the Published Music of Samuel Barber_. Thesis (Ph.D.)--Iowa State University, 1957. 357 p.
"According to a 'program note' in the orchestral score the _Overture to 'The School for Scandal'_, was suggested by Richard Brinsley Sheridan's drama of the same title. While the work reflects the rather comical, sardonic atmosphere of the drama, no attempt seems to have been made to portray any of Sheridan's characters." [p. 273] _See_: W76

B76k. Fuller, Donald. "Forecast and Review: Season's Height, New York 1941." _Modern Music_ 18:168-169 (March-April 1941)
"With its nice first theme for the violins, it should make a good curtain-raiser for almost anything light and gay." _See_: W76d

B76l. Hughes, Allen. "Youth Symphony Fetes Herbert, Cellist." _New York Times_, February 12, 1973, p. 24.
"Although the playing of the violins was untidy in the Barber work, the general performance level of this remarkable training orchestra was high." _See_: W76j

B76m. Kolodin, Irving. _New Guide to Recorded Music_. Garden City, N. Y.: Doubleday, 1947. 524 p.
"This work could be as properly named for any other

Restoration comedy, but Janssen makes much of its bright patterns." [p. 26] [Victor 11 8591, (78 rpm)] See: D76e

B76n. M., M. "Analytical Notes and First Reviews." Gramophone 32:9 (June 1954)
"The gaiety of the School for Scandal overture throws for us a new light on him [Samuel Barber]. The quick-witted vein is an attractive one, and the piece is well presented by the orchestra." [Mercury MG 40002] See: D76b

B76o. McPhee, Colin. "Scores and Records." Modern Music 19:47 (November-December 1941)
"...vivacious and brilliant to a degree where thoughts of Sheridan pale and run to cover." See: W76

B76p. -----. "Scores and Records." Modern Music 22:59 (November-December 1944)
"Victor releases Samuel Barber's Overture to 'The School for Scandal', an over-elaborate piece of orchestration that has all the blaze and brilliance of a final set-piece in a display of fireworks and little else to remember." [Victor 11-8591, 78 rpm] See: D76e

B76q. Sagmaster, Joseph. Cincinnati Symphony Orchestra Program Notes, December 7-8, 1973 [unpaged]
"This work is not an introduction to a performance...but rather a concert overture reflecting the spirit of the play." [Carmon De Leone, conductor] See: W76k

B76r. Slonimsky, Nicolas. "Four Melodic Masterpieces of Samuel Barber" [album notes for CDS 32 11 0005, 32 11 0006 disc]
"From the outset the music reflects the theme of sly merriment, the shining metallic sonorities of trumpets, triangle and cymbals accentuating the brightness of the scene. As the festive metallic sound subsides, a pastoral theme is sounded by the oboe. But a school for scandal must have its wily elements as its farce. The tonality is dislocated and twisted, suggesting intrigue; the gaiety is resumed with an invigorating rhythmic bounce." See: D76f

B76s. Stevens, Halsey. "Program Notes." [Los Angeles Philharmonic] Symphony Magazine March 30-31, 1950, p. 657.
"But the School for Scandal overture reveals Barber's lyric gift without the encumbrance of a conscious effort in the direction of modernity; his melodies are straight forward and flowing, his scoring colorful, and his harmonic and formal structures traditional." See: W76g

B77. SECOND ESSAY FOR ORCHESTRA, OP. 17.

B77a. Canby, Edward Tatnall. "Classical reviews." Audio 59:97 (November 1975)
"All this is just what you are looking for if you are

"All this is just what you are looking for if you are the swooning type, or if you enjoy Romantic music for big orchestra written the day before yesterday. This is a reissue of an LP that was originally on the CBS label, not Columbia. Don't ask me." [Columbia Odyssey Y 33230] See: D77b

B77b. Carner, Mosco. "Reviews of Music." Music Review 7:52 (February 1946)
"Barber is no pioneer and no experimentalist nor does he seem concerned with any topical 'social realism' and Zeitgeist as some of his American fellow composers are. His Second Essay confirms this impression, showing a mind that is interested in giving a rounded and well-balanced form to ideas which, while perhaps not very significant in the strictest sense of the term, are most attractive and flow with natural spontaneous ease. Call them romantic if you like, with a modicum of astringency in them due to a few modern discords and an interesting polyrhythmic counterpoint." See: W77

B77c. Cohn, Arthur. Recorded Classical Music. New York: Schirmer Books, 1981. 2164 p.
"In his Opus 17 Barber's lyricism is darker and more impetuous than in most of his other works." [p. 96] See: W77

B77d. Downes, Edward. The New York Philharmonic Guide to the Symphony. New York: Walker, 1976. 1058 p.
"Completed during World War II, Barber's Second Essay came at a turning point in the evolution of his style toward works of no less spontaneity than his First Essay for Orchestra or his earlier Overture to 'The School for Scandal' but of greater harmonic tension and more probing spirit." [p. 33] See: W77

B77e. Finkelstein, Sidney. "Samuel Barber" [album notes for Vanguard VSD 2083 disc]
"The Second Essay for Orchestra, Op. 17, is one of those works as deep as they are long, with a concentrated musical drama, richness of texture and tightness of struc- ture that merits for it the title of 'symphony.'...Notable is the unity within variety that Barber achieves through the transformation of one motif into another, and the subtle linking of all the motifs together." See: D77d

B77f. Frankenstein, Alfred. "Classical." High Fideli- ty 11:49 (July 1961)
"The famous Second Essay is also a first class work and its performance is not bad, but the recording is poor." [Vanguard VRS 1065, VSD 2083] See: D77d

B77g. Friedewald, Russell Edward. A Formal and Stylis- tic Analysis of the Published Music of Samuel Barber. Thesis (Ph. D.)--Iowa State University, 1957. 357 p.

"The Essay, opus 17, though longer and more complex than the first, retains the qualities of succinctness and unity of mood. The principal thematic material consists of a main theme revolving about the tonic of F minor, a second subordinate theme, and a cadential motive." [p. 297] See: W77

B77h. Fuller, Donald. "Forecast and Review." Modern Music 19:254 (May-June 1942)
"[It] is the best of this composer's work to date. I think Barber has been reading his Copland and Harris scores and it has been good for him. The horizon has also broadened, and he now appears capable of real thematic invention, manifest mostly in melodic variety. In this finished piece with its quiet persuasive personality, there is integrity in feeling, form, and style." See: W77

B77i. Harvey, Trevor. "Opera." Gramophone 46:272 (August 1968)
"At something less than ten minutes, it is the equivalent of a powerful first movement of a symphony...The whole movement is worked out with the greatest coherence of thought and range of mood." [Philips Vanguard VSL 11019] See: D77d

B77j. Jones, Isabel Morse. "Menuhin, Philharmonic Orchestra." Los Angeles Times, January 7, 1944, pt. 2, p. 8.
"It is proud music written by a man who knows how he wants his music to sound, unusual as it is. There is none of the arrogance of the ultra-modernist who scoffs at poetry because he knows little of it. This is music from a contemporary and very musical American Shelley. The listeners liked it upon first hearing [performed by Alfred Wallenstein conducting the Los Angeles Philharmonic Orchestra] and gave it remarkably warm approval." See: W77c

B77k. Menen, Aubrey. "Opinion: Am American Renaissance: the Impossible Dream?" Vogue 171:315-316+ (November 1981)
"Yet listen to the Second Essay. It has boldness checked by anxiety, it has glimpses of vast horizons brought back suddenly to the personal here and now. It sings, yet it complains. It has sadness, but no real unhappiness. It is all of a piece but comes to no pat conclusion. It is--what? Adolescent." See: W77

B77l. Müllmann, Bernd. "Schallplatten." Melos NZ 3:64 (January-February 1977)
"Der II Essay schliesslieh gerät...wieder zur stimmungsbeschreibenden Musik, die hier von Schippers besonders 'eingehend' z.T. auch amerikanisch-optimistisch angelegt ist. Ferne Erinnerung an die 'Lästerschule' taucht auf--ein Werk, fesselnd durch seine Viel-seitigkeit, das zu Assoziationen aussermusikalischer 'Bilder' verleitet."

which is here presented by Schippers in an especially intense reading, at times with an American-optimistic touch. There are also reminders of the Lästerschule music--A work, in short, which attracts by its many-sidedness, and leads to associations with images outside the music."--R.F.] See: D77b

B77m. Parmenter, Ross. "Music: Orchestra of America Opens 2d Season." New York Times, November 17, 1960, p. 45.
    Program honoring the 75th birthday of Wallingford Riegger, the 60th of Aaron Copland, and the 50th of Samuel Barber. "Mr. Barber's piece was a work that has entered the standard repertory, his Second Essay for Orchestra [conducted by Richard Korn]" See: W77j

B77n. Rutland, Harold. "New York Philharmonic." Musical Times 100:671 (December 1959)
    "In Samuel Barber's Second Essay for Orchestra one remarked at once the fine, clean sound of the strings, and indeed the impressive tone of the whole orchestra, though the woodwind players seemed to be less outstanding than those of certain of our orchestras..The Essay, a neo-romantic piece with arabesque-like-themes, made a more pleasing impression than did the other American work...Charles Ives's The Unanswered Question." See: W77h

B77o. Sagmaster, Joseph. Cincinnati Symphony Orchestra Program Notes, March 20-21, 1970, p. 576.
    "The work marked a turning point in his [Barber's] career. It is more dramatic, with deeper musical thinking, and greater harmonic tension than his earlier composi-tions." [Izler Solomon, conductor] See: W77k

B77p. ------. Cincinnati Symphony Orchestra Program Notes, March 15-16, 1974 [unpaged]
    "...Barber modelled his 'Second Essay' on a literary form, beginning with a central thought, developing that thought and then bringing it to a logical conclusion." [Thomas Schippers, conductor] See: W77l

B77q. Schonberg, Harold C. "Music: Philadelphians." New York Times, April 29, 1975, p. 40.
    "In the Barber and the Brahms, he [Eugene Ormandy] shaped everything with care and love. The Barber...has a touch of Debussy, a touch of Copland, and some tuneful and conservative fantasy-like sequences." See: W77n

B77r. Taubman, Howard. "Walter Conducts Trio of Seconds." New York Times, April 17, 1942, p. 20.
    "His work, in a short space, creates and sustains a mood. Its thematic material is unashamedly lyrical, but also dignified. It is worked out for the orchestra with the economy of knowledge and assurance. Perhaps the compo-

sition is a shade too solemn, but a composer is entitled to his own thesis. Mr. Walter and the orchestra gave the essay a spacious, sonorous performance. Whether it was just what the composer wanted it is impossible to say. But Mr. Barber was there to take a bow and to thank Mr. Walter and the men." See: W77a

B77s. Tucker, Marilyn. "Buckley's Oakland Opener--A Confident Start." San Francisco Chronicle, October 13, 1983, p. 62.
"In the Barber Essay, Buckley elicited a big, generous sound from the orchestra, with cleanly articulated solo passages from oboe, clarinet, horn and flute. His conducting style is direct and on the mark, with no choreographic nonsense to clutter up the picture. There is an obvious lyric vitality that gives positive direction and lift to the music." See: W77q

B78. SOUVENIRS, OP. 28.

B78a. Barnes, Clive. "Dance: Harkness Ballet Season Opens." New York Times, November 7, 1969, p. 43.
"The company confirmed the mettle of its performing standards with a cheerfully rumbustious account of Todd Bolender's lightly amusing 'Souvenirs,' a Feydeau-like farce with innumerable characters and almost as many bedrooms." See: W78j

B78b. Berger, Arthur. "Spotlight on the Moderns: Berg, Schoenberg and Krasner." Saturday Review 37:57 (April 24, 1954)
"Barber's Souvenirs, an innocuous assortment of deliberately old-fashioned salon music. The playing throughout is of the highest order." [Columbia SL 198] See: D78a

B78c. Dawes, Frank. "For Two Pianos." Musical Times. 106:128 (February 1965)
"Barber's Souvenirs were first composed in 1952 as piano duets and subsequently scored for orchestra, so this new arrangement bring them back to somewhere near their original form. There are six pieces, all ballroom dances of pre-first war vintage...Their amusing touches of parody are nothing like the barbed satire of Walton's Facade, for instance. They would make a nice change from Arensky." See: W78

B78d. Ericson, Ray. "Collections and Miscellany." High Fidelity 4:54 (July 1954)
"Six dances make up Samuel Barber's Souvenirs, an exceedingly lightweight score designed to charm with nostalgia. The composer has written in terms of 'a setting reminiscent of the Palm Court of the Hotel Plaza in New York, the year about 1914, epoch of the first tangoes;

Souvenirs--remembered with affection, not in irony or with the tongue in cheek, but in amused tenderness.' The music uses some mild harmonic and rhythmic distortions, but it never resorts to the cute: it is almost a pure re-creation of the past with the crudities and vulgarities lost in a happily sentimental haze." [Columbia ML 4855] See: D78a

B78e. Frankenstein, Alfred. "Classical." High Fidelity 9:49 (May 1959)
"_Souvenirs_ is the score to a light satirical ballet about goings-on of a scandalous and semiscandalous kind in a grand metropolitan hotel, circa 1914. The music has that tasteful, beautifully wrought, bitter-sweet quality so characteristic of Barber, and he handles its dance rhythms with admirable variety and point." [EMI Capitol G 7146] See: D78e

B78f. -----. "In Brief." High Fidelity 20:118 (April 1970)
"The scores of these two ballets might well have been shelved along with their choreography--both have long since been dropped from the repertory...It is inconceivable, however, that _Souvenirs_ is the work of a composer as skilled and tasteful as Samuel Barber. It sounds like the work of some Russian hack." [Desto DC 6433] See: D78d

B78g. "Gold, Fizdale Offer Music for 2 Pianos." New York Times, March 12, 1953, p. 23.
"The newest was Samuel Barber's ballet suite _Souvenirs_ written in 1952, and heard for the first time here at this performance. The six sections of the new Barber work are marked 'Waltz,' 'Schottisch,' 'Adagio,' 'One-step,' 'Hesi-tation-Tango,' and 'Galop.' They are expertly wrought and show no lack of inventiveness. At the same time one is uncomfortably reminded of Shostakovitch's _Polka_ from _The Golden Age_. It is true that Mr. Barber's piece has not the blatant vulgarity of Shostakovitch's unnecessarily boorish creation. But no one, not even a Pulitzer Price composer, can write a successful waltz with tongue in cheek. One must be thoroughly in earnest about it, and it is not clear that Mr. Barber is." See: W78e

B78h. Harrison, Max. "Instrumental." Gramophone 60:597 (November 1982)
"Less familiar are the _Souvenirs_, composed for piano duet in 1952. These exist in other forms--for two pianos, arranged by Arthur Gold and Robert Fizdale, for example-- and Barber himself orchestrated them and made this solo piano version...Barber's _Waltz_ and _Tango_, say, are no better in quality or intentions than the sort of light music which they take as models...It is hard not to feel that there is a considerable element of unconscious pat-ronization involved. However, plenty of listeners will be happy with the simple tunefulness of _Souvenirs_. [Nonesuch Digital D 79032] See: D78c

B78i. Kozinn, Allan. "Samuel Barber" [album notes for Nonesuch Digital D 79032 disc]
"Easy going and nostalgic, it examines some familiar dance forms in six short sections. The present version, for solo piano, is Barber's own, and also dates from 1952. It is something of a rarity, however, and although it retains all the charm and wit of the orchestral and two-piano version, it remains both the least frequently heard version of Souvenirs, and the lest frequently played of Barber's piano works. In fact, this is the premiere recording of the solo version." See: D78c

B78j. Luten, C. J. "Wonderful Teamwork." American Record Guide 20:284 (May 1954)
"...Barber's Souvenirs, a work which recalls many of the social dances of 1914 and which will probably wind up supporting choreography. This piece--so airy, gracious, inventive, and lighthearted--is certain to please even those who generally only admire Barber's lyric gifts." [Columbia ML 4855] See: D78a

B78k. Lyons, James. "Souvenirs" [album notes for Desto DC 6433 disc]
"Barber composed exquisitely subtle music. Bolender's choreography is skillful period camp. The effectiveness of the ballet lies in the compatibility of these contrasts." See: D78d

B78l. Morton, Lawrence. "Samuel Barber." Notes 12: 483-484 (June 1955)
"Six dances make up Barber's suite...These are no longer stylish dances, but the music is stylish in the manner of the year of its composition, 1952. That is, there are melodic intervals and bass-based harmonies that are, let us say, post-Stravinskian even while the dance rhythms (not excluding the delightful 5/4 section of the Waltz) are those of an earlier century." See: W78

B78m. "Recitals of the Week: Piano Duets." Times (London) December 15, 1952, p. 9.
"They had two novelties to offer, suites expressly written for them by Rieti and Barber; but these were facile trifles, vehicles only of the players' extraordinary accomplishment." See: W78d

B78n. "Reviews of New Music." Musical Opinion 77:651 (August 1954)
Review of the G. Schirmer/Chappell study score. "This is likely to rival the Adagio for Strings in popularity, even though it is not one of the composer's finest works, nor truly representative of his style." See: W78

B78o. Sabin, Robert. "New York City Ballet." Musical America 75:5 (December 1, 1955)
"Barber's music is tepid, but it serves excellently as

background for Mr. Bolender's madcap work." <u>See</u>: W78c

B78p. Schonberg, Harold C. <u>Chamber and Solo Instrument Music</u>. New York: Knopf, 1955. (The Guide to Long-Playing Records, vol. 3) 280 p.
"Barber's work consists of six fairly short pieces, all in dance form...I find them tiresome. After several playings, the slick, superficial elegance wears off and the poverty of invention is laid bare." [p. 22] [Columbia SL 198] <u>See</u>: D78a

B78q. -----. "Records: Two Piano." <u>New York Times</u>, May 2, 1954, sect. 2, p. 9.
"The Barber <u>Souvenirs</u> which may be seen as a ballet one of these days, takes some American dance forms and prettifies them. Some listeners hearing the Barber work will gurgle, coo, and say: 'How cute and adorable!' Others will call the music trite, sterile and lacking in any real ideas." [Columbia SL 198 (ML 4853, ML 4855)] <u>See</u>: D78a

B78r. Shupp, Enos E., Jr. "Orchestra." <u>New Records</u> 27:3 (June 1959)
"Barber's <u>Souvenirs</u> is the orchestration of a set of piano duets that carry a story of goings-on in a fashionable resort hotel." [Columbia G 7146] <u>See</u>: D78e

B79. SYMPHONY NO. 1, OP. 9.

B79a. "Barber Symphony Approved in Rome." <u>New York Times</u>, December 14, 1936, p. 28.
"The symphony is endowed with subtle melodic phrases which, in the second movement, are rich in pathos and modulation...Mr. Barber's harmonic and orchestral resources were such that they atoned for a not too happy contrast of brass and strings." <u>See</u>: W79a

B79b. Berger, Arthur. "Scores and Records." <u>Modern Music</u> 23:66 (Winter 1946)
"...Barber complacently accepts what may be called the conservatory style--the big noise, the fragmentary motive blown up and over-worked, the uninstigated climax--all of these to be found in the <u>First Symphony</u> (Columbia), which opens like the score of a Class B thriller. Bruno Walter, in preparing the recording with the New York Philharmonic could, I imagine, have applied much the same methods that he would to a work of the repertory from Schumann to Strauss, his specialty." [Columbia X 252] <u>See</u>: D79i

B79c. Brown, Royal S. "Classical." <u>High Fidelity</u> 27:95 (March 1977)
"Schermerhorn and the Milwaukee Symphony are much more successful in maintaining the symphony's tensions, but the playing, particularly in the strings, is considerably duller than Unicorn's clean but rather depthless reproduc-

tion." [Turnabout TV S 34564] <u>See</u>: D79h

B79d. Brown, Royal S. "Classical." <u>High Fidelity</u> 27:95 (March 1977)
"Barber's First Symphony...is a beautifully unified, four movement-in-one work with an almost Shakespearean dramatic pacing...The Measham/London Symphony performance is slack, eliciting little feeling of continuity or dramatic coherency." [Unicorn RHS 342] <u>See</u>: D79g

B79e. Cohn, Arthur. <u>Recorded Classical Music.</u> New York: Schirmer Books, 1981. 2164 p.
"Though Barber's Symphony combines classical ideology with a romantic enlargement of harmony it also has some latter-day touches--the orchestration contains Sibelian colors and the lusty drive of many a passage is kin to the music of Shostakovich." [p. 97] <u>See</u>: W79a

B79f. Crimp, Bryan. <u>The Record Year 1</u>. London: Duckworth, 1979. 541 p.
"Barber's over-riding vein of lyricism is evident throughout, a lyricism which is never derivative and always unmistakably his own." [p. 327] [Unicorn RHS 342] <u>See</u>: D79g

B79g. Downes, Olin. "Bloch Work Given by Philharmonic." <u>New York Times</u>, April 5, 1937, p. 17.
"Sam Barber's 'Symphony', successful at its recent first performance in New York, was repeated. The composer bowed from the platform. The symphony improves with acquaintance, and confirms the impression of a composer of talent." <u>See</u>: W79c

B79h. Epstein, Benjamin. "Audience Eats Up Music, Apple Pie." <u>Los Angeles Times</u>, February 21, 1984, pt. 6, p. 4.
Review of the February 18, 1984 Pacific Symphony Orchestra performance. "Conviction and poignancy marked Barber's Symphony No. 1." <u>See</u>: W79r

B79i. Frankenstein, Alfred. "An American Symphony." <u>San Francisco Chronicle</u>, January 11, 1963, p. 37.
"Mitchell plays much American music, if my observation is correct, of the more conservative and easily accepted kind. Barber's first symphony certainly falls into that category, but it also has considerable virtues." <u>See</u>: W79i

B79j. -----. "Classical." <u>High Fidelity</u> 6:61-62 (May 1956)
"Whatever reservations one may have about Howard Hanson as a composer, one must go all out in admiration of his conductorial gifts. His performance of the Barber symphony forces a complete revision of one's attitude toward that far from obscure work. Previous recordings and performances have made it seem pale and well-mannered and guaranteed

to do nothing much to anybody. Hanson, however, makes it
sing, gives it body and strength and a genuinely impressive
symphonic thrust. Needless to say, this result could scarcely have been achieved without superb co-operation from
Mercury's recording staff." [Mercury MC 400014] See: D79a

     B79k. Frankenstein, Alfred. "Classical Music on Long
Playing." High Fidelity 2:50 (January-February 1953)
     "Barber's first symphony is a vigorous, beautifully
constructed and beautifully scored piece of work. It is
one of his earliest compositions, dating from 1935, and
remains one of his most distinguished. It is in one movement, subdivided into four sections, lasts 18 minutes, and
makes a powerful, splendidly articulated statement."
[Classical Editions CE 1011] See: D79j

     B79l. Freed, Richard. "A Little Barber Festival."
Stereo Review 42:115 (May 1979)
     "Barber's powerful one-movement First Symphony has
never received a more compelling performance on records,
and even more surely it has never received so lifelike a
recording. Measham's brilliant version with the London
Symphony must make us wonder anew why the work is so little
heard in our concert halls." [Unicorn UN1 72010] See:
D79g

     B79m. Friedewald, Russell Edward. A Formal and Stylis-
tic Analysis of the Published Music of Samuel Barber.
Thesis (Ph.D.)--Iowa State University, 1957. 357 p.
     "Although termed a symphony in one movement, it is
actually divided into four clear-cut parts corresponding to
the movements of the classical pattern. The entire work is
constructed from three subjects that are introduced in the
exposition. The second part of the symphony (Scherzo) is
based upon the principal subject; the third part (Andante
tranquillo) is derived from an augmentation of the second
subject and fragments of the first; the fourth part (Finale) is a passacaglia, whose theme is based upon the
principal subject. The chief unifying feature is, obviously, this close thematic correlation between all parts; no
melodic or thematic material can be found that does not
bear a discernible relationship of the three subjects al-
luded to above." [p. 243] See: W79

     B79n. Goldberg, Albert. "Apathy Marks Concert at
Bowl." Los Angeles Times, August 29, 1964, pt. 2, p. 8.
     "It is an eclectic piece, with constant reminders of
other composers, yet it has elements of originality in form
and construction, and while the expressive content is never
profound it is sometimes agreeable enough in idea and
orchestration to hold the listener's attention." See: W79n

     B79o. Horan, Robert. "American Composers, XIX: Samuel
Barber." Modern Music 20:162 (March-April 1943)
     "It is with the Symphony in One Movement, written in

1935-36, that Barber's handling of form becomes personal. There is a kind of impeccable logic which unifies this work in design. The units are compressed and astringent from the formal standpoint. The general structure may be analyzed as follows: three themes are announced, as in a classical exposition, but after a brief development, instead of a recapitulation, the first theme in diminution, becomes the basis of a Scherzo section; the second, in augmentation, becomes the basis for the Andante section; and the third appears over the Passacaglia which is constructed of the first theme. In this fashion, a logical synthesis of the four-movement symphonic form is achieved." See: W79

B79p. Kolodin, Irving. New Guide to Recorded Music. Garden City, New York: Doubleday, 1947. 382 p.
"Barber's good fortune with conductors continues in this work, one of the few recent works which Walter has liked sufficiently to record." [p. 27] [Columbia X 252] See: D79j

B79q. Layton, Robert. "Orchestral." Gramophone 53:1331 (February 1976)
"The Symphony for all its frank lyricism and bold rhetoric is conceived sectionally rather than organically and some of its gestures ring hollow..." [Rediffusion Composers' Recordings SD 137] See: D79f

B79r. -----. "Orchestral." Gramophone 54:409 (September 1976)
"The work may not be wholly successful structurally (each of its individual sections is too vividly characterized) but it has an imaginative vitality that is unfailingly compelling." [Unicorn RHS 342] See: D79g

B79s. Mann, William S. "Reviews of Music." Music Review 13:246 (August 1952)
Review of the G. Schirmer/Chappell score. "It is a moving, closely woven yet emotionally expansive work built on two themes. That, and any further comment, ought to be stale news by now, when we have had some years to become acquainted with it." See: W79

B79t. "Music: Rodzinski's Audience Acclaims Barber's Latest Work." Newsweek 9:28 (April 3, 1937)
"His latest symphony shows a deft knowledge of instrumentation and a sound originality. Introducing three themes of interesting variety, he expounds them with many different colors...In addition to its technical virtues, the symphony possesses strong feelings not generally found in contemporary music." See: W79

B79u. Parsons, Arrand. Chicago Symphony Orchestra Program Notes, February 6-7, 1981, p. 7.
"If there is one style that might emerge as an in-

fluence on this Symphony, it is perhaps that of Sibelius;
not only are there structural similarities but there is a
musical coloring, sometimes an orchestral sound, reminiscent of the Finnish symphonist." See: W79p

B79v. Persichetti, Vincent. "Revueltas Reaches Philadelphia." Modern Music 21:177 (March-April 1944)
"The revised Symphony In One Movement of Samuel Barber
still has the kind of doubling in its scoring that deadens
the bolder passages when they should have been projected.
The opening is restless rather than forceful and calms down
to a slow oboe stretch that lacks the lyric qualities
promised. Two faults that Barber has since fought off are
in full evidence throughout the scherzo section. He chances upon an attractive passage and presumes that his listening guests would like copies in their favorite colors;
thus abruptly he spans the gap between sections and discon-
nects his critical followers. Behind these weaknesses is a
wealth of creative talent, recently freed in the Second
Essay." See: W79

B79w. Pleasants, Henry. "First-Time Fever." Modern
Music 16:84-85 (January-February 1939)
"I am not one of Barber's more ardent admirers, but it
is hard to believe that a composition so much discussed as
his Symphony In One Movement has not been played at least
once by every orchestra in the land. At the most it has
had a half a dozen performances, chiefly under the direction of Mr. Rodzinski who introduced it first with the
Cleveland Symphony and later with the New York Philharmonic-Symphony and the NBC Orchestra. Barber was born
within thirty miles of Philadelphia...and yet this work
finally got around to Philadelphia only in December 1938,
nearly two years after its first American performance."
See: W79e

B79x. "Promenade Concert." Times (London) August 7,
1941, p. 6.
"Here the form imposes the virtue of conciseness, the
themes are cyclically treated in the four sections, and if
the final drawing of conclusions involves some pretty dras-
tic counterpoint, there is no doubt about its intelligibility, cohesion and cogency." See: W79g

B79y. "Reviews of New Music." Musical Opinion 74:533
(July 1951)
Review of the Chappell study score. "This, to my
mind, is one of the most important of modern symphonic
works, ranking very close to Walton's Symphony. In spite
of the Neo-Romantic idiom and the refreshing vitality and
buoyancy of the ideas, the work is closely-knit..." See:
W79

B79z. S. "Orchestra." New Records 24:5 (May 1956)
"Hanson digs into the No. 1 as one dedicated to dis-

playing how great a piece of American music can be, and
makes a mighty good case for it." [Mercury MG 40014] <u>See</u>:
D79a

B79aa. S., N. "Barber Symphony Heard in Revision."
<u>New York Times</u>, March 9, 1944, p. 15.
    "That Mr. Barber's revised symphony [conducted by
Bruno Walter] was able to hold its ground and not appear
anticlimatic after the Schumann masterpiece spoke worlds in
its favor. If it lacked the melodic invention, simplicity
and freshness of that opus, it nevertheless was so skilled
in its craftsmanship, so knowingly orchestrated and filled
with character that it scored heavily with its hearers,
even if it was forced to bear comparison with the Schumann
creation." <u>See</u>: W79h

B79bb. "Salzburg Will Hear American Symphony." <u>New
York Times</u>, May 2, 1937, sect. 2, p. 10.
    "For the first time in the history of the Salzburg
Festival a symphonic work by an American composer will be
performed, it was disclosed...by Dr. Artur Rodzinski, director of the Cleveland Orchestra." <u>See</u>: W79d

B79cc. Shupp, Enos E., Jr. "Concerto." <u>New Records</u>
42:5 (January 1975)
    "Samuel Barber's <u>Symphony No. 1</u> could well stand a
modern recording, which it gets here in quad. The Milwaukee Symphony Orchestra has risen fast in its 18 years, and
particularly in the past six years under Kenneth Schermerhorn. They sound like a first-rate ensemble in the Barber
symphony, given an eloquent reading by their conductor who
has the knack of this work quite thoroughly in his bones--
it is convincing." [Turnabout QTV 34564] <u>See</u>: D79h

B79dd. -----. "Orchestra." <u>New Records</u> 47:4 (April
1976)
    "A grand modern recording of Barber's one movement
<u>Symphony No. 1</u> is past due and is to be welcomed. This one
fills the bill with distinction. It is a performance born
of understanding, and it communicates persuasively to the
listener. Although in his mid-twenties when he wrote this
work (1936) in Rome, the symphony is a sure-footed, perfectly crafted piece which has a universality about it that
defies being tagged with a national origin. It is richly
melodic, however, concise, and is somewhat in the Romantic
vein. Measham has exactly the right feel for it, and the
performance is a beauty." [Unicorn UN 1 72010] <u>See</u>: D79g

B79ee. Simmons, Walter. "Classical Recordings." <u>Fan-
fare</u> 2:22, 24 (March/April 1979)
    "The Symphony No. 1, <u>Essays</u> 1 and 2 and <u>Music for a
Scene from Shelley</u> are among Barber's most perfect works,
totally sincere in their rich, Gothic melodrama, and fully
consummated in their formal design. In addition, they are
integrated dramatic entities, rather than melodies strung

309

together. Measham's ability to bring these pieces to life, and to project their great intensity, is feeble beyond belief. The orchestra sloshes around aimlessly, groping blindly among murky textures. Tempos are ponderous, melodies are completely undifferentiated, and climaxes come and go unnoticed." [Unicorn UN 1 72010] See: D79g

B80.   SYMPHONY NO. 2, OP. 19.

B80a. Burk, John N. "Concert Bulletin" for Boston Symphony Orchestra, March 3, 1944, p. 1061-1066.
Program notes for the March 3, 1944 performance under Serge Koussevitzky. "The composer...has made no attempt to describe a scene or tell a story, since the emphasis in this work is on the emotional rather than the narrative factor. It is in no sense program music." See: W80a

B80b. "The Case of Sam Barber." Newsweek 23:94+ (March 13, 1944)
"Though Barber flew often during the symphony's writing, he made no attempt to tell a narrative or descriptive story through his music--although a screaming trumpet and crashing percussion in the third and final movement suggest the blockbusters of an air raid. In the second movement, an electric 'tone generator' simulates the radio beam, but Barber insists that it has a purely musical meaning. The difference between the rather old-fashioned romanticism of Barber's first symphony and the harsh and rugged lines of the new second is undoubtedly what being in the Army would do to an extraordinarily sensitive 33-year-old artist." See: W80, W80a

B80c. Davis, Peter G. "Repeat Performances." High Fidelity 21:106 (February 1971)
"The Second Symphony deserves more frequent exposure: for a composer who has often disappointed when called upon for a Major Statement, its taut structure and expressive maturity are most imposing." [Everest 3282] See: D80b

B80d. Downes, Olin. "New Barber Work Honors Air Force." New York Times, March 10, 1944, p. 21.
Review of the March 9, 1944 Boston Symphony Orchestra performance under Serge Koussevitzky. "It is a 'modern' score, if modernity is assumed to be absent unless typified by dissonance. In structure this is the most close-knit and concise of his works we have heard. The first movement is clear and strong in outline and the last sounds brilliantly. Whether the slow movement is longer than its ideas justify, and whether this tonal speech is as native to Corporal Barber as earlier idioms which he has successfully treated, is to be better decided after more than one hearing." See: W80a

B80e. "Events in the World of Music." New York Times, March 5, 1944, sect. 2, p. 5.
News item noting that Barber's Second Symphony will be performed in Carnegie Hall on March 9, 1944 with Serge Koussevitzky conducting the Boston Symphony Orchestra. "Royalties for all performances will be turned over to the Army Air Forces Aid Society." See: W80b

B80f. F., H. "Analytical Notes and First Reviews." Gramophone 29:4-5 (June 1951)
"First impressions of the Symphony (which I feel sure I have hear somewhere somehow before) are of strength without any noisy assertiveness, of an exteriorised and philosophical dignity supported by introspective argument, of a real beauty too, especially in the richly peaceful slow movement. I felt that finales are not really Barber's strong point, and that while this is of a piece with the rest of the work, it is not a satisfactory ending." [Decca LX 3050] See: D80a

B80g. Friedewald, Russell Edward. A Formal and Stylistic Analysis of the Published Music of Samuel Barber. Thesis (Ph.D.)--Iowa State University, 1957. 357 p.
"The angular melodies of this symphony, its pulsating ostinati and the spiraling figure of its Finale, give it a decided mechanistic power. In addition to being far larger in scope than the First Symphony, it is consistently more dissonant and the tonal centers are less clearly defined. and the general atmosphere of Air Force camps and airplanes, it is not denied by the composer himself. He does, however, frown upon the 'aeronautical' interpretations that commentators sometimes dwell upon, and 'wishes it to be listened to as a purely abstract work.'" See: W80

B80h. Greenfield, Edward. "Classical Reissues." Gramophone 43:455 (March 1966)
"The themes are splendidly clear-cut and at this new hearing I was struck for the first time by the similarity of the first theme here to Puccini's 'hello' theme as the curtain rises on Fanciulla del West." [Decca Ace of Clubs ACL 264] See: D80a

B80i. Harrison, Lou. "Season's End, May 1944." Modern Music 21:233-234 (May-June 1944)
"This piece has moments of great interest and several of convincing beauty. Barber has a healthy disregard for good taste and sometimes the inevitable jolts are disturbing; at others, they result in a surprising life and beauty. I liked the opening measures, the development and the coda of the first movement. The coda is especially striking with its high pedal point and the strange tense resolution. The use of major seconds skipped about in the woodwinds, mixed with piano, was quite interesting also. The second movement culminates in a strongly lyrical section of massed polyphony, which though sincere and moving,

311

is suddenly interrupted by a mysterious radio signal that merely makes one wish he knew the Morse code. The finale was a more conventional but still vigorous section, opening with several striking bravura runs for the violins." See: W80

B80j. Heinsheimer, Hans W. "The Composing Composer: Samuel Barber." ASCAP Today 2:4-7 (Autumn 1968)
      "'Why is it that all your concert works are success-ful, that they all seem to stay alive, no matter how old you are--all with the exception of your Second Symphony. This one we just can't get off the ground.' There was, again, no hesitation. 'The reason is very simple,' Barber said. 'It is not a good work.'...While such an admission was unusual enough, what followed was even more startling. 'Let's go back to the office and destroy it,' he said. And that is what we did. We went back, got all the music from the library...and Samuel Barber, with a gusto that in-creased our admiration for him from one torn page to the next, tore up all these beautifully and expensively copied materials with his own hands." See: W80

B80k. Henehan, Donal. "Samuel Barber, Composer, Dead; Twice Winner of Pulitzer Prize." New York Times, January 24, 1981, p. 1, 16.
      "The composer's other major disappointment [another was Antony and Cleopatra] was his Second Symphony, which the Air Force commissioned while he was in the service in 1944. Hans Heinsheimer, his onetime editor at the publish-ing house of G. Schirmer, tells how Mr. Barber was flown from airfield to airfield so he would soak up the proper atmosphere for such a work. The composer evidently did not find the Air Force's method conducive to inspiration, and the results, in his own estimation, was an inferior work. Some years later, he insisted on going to the Schirmer warehouse and personally tearing up all available scores of the symphony." See: W80

B80l. Jacobs, Arthur. "A British Music Critic in New York--II." Musical America 71:6 (April 15, 1951)
      "As revised, the symphony no longer carries its former programmatic connotation, and the use of a specially-made 'tone-generator' instrument is no longer required in the score. The only unusual feature of the present instrumen-tation is a piano, and the reason for its presence is not always clear...The music has solidity, variety, and oc-casional eloquence; but however skillful Barber illuminates the traditional symphonic terrain the hearer is left won-dering whether this terrain has not already had enough, or more than its share of exploitation." See: W80e

B80m. Keys, Ivor. "Reviews of Music." Music and Let-ters 33:89 (January 1952)
      "One can see in this Second Symphony the qualities that have helped him to establish himself thus far. They

include a straightforward attitude to form, a picturesque
and masterly handling of the orchestra (the piano appearing
as an instrument) and in general an unfettered vivacity of
expression and an infectious enjoyment of the process of
composition. In a word, the music is happily extrovert."
See: W80

B80n. Kozinn, Allan. "Samuel Barber: The Last Interview and the Legacy. Part I." High Fidelity 31:44-46+
(June 1981)
   "With greater reliance on dissonance and modernistic
rhythmic irregularity than any previous Barber score, the
work seemed to signal a new direction. In the early
1960's, though, Barber withdrew the symphony, saying only
that 'it wasn't very good'...Although it has its thrilling
moments and is for Barber, adventurous, it's too densely
packed and lacks cohesiveness." See: W80

B80o. L., K. "Orchestral." Records and Recordings
9:44 (April 1966)
   "The Symphony is a brittle work beginning with a
Copland-like fanfare and going on to a Vaughan Williams-
like second subject. The slow movement is said to have
been suggested to the composer by his war-time experience
of night-flying...The finale, a theme and variations, is
almost pure Walton in its spiky rhythms and relentless
climaxes. The slow movement, with its intricate subdivi-
sions of an 8/8 bar, is by far the most interesting and
rewarding." [Decca Ace of Clubs ACL 264] See: D80a

B80p. Luten, C. J. "A Barber Carnival." American
Record Guide 17:297-298 (May 1951)
   "Throughout the Symphony No. 2 there is an absence of
memorable melody and of sufficient contrapuntal vigor. Its
orchestration is often unpleasantly thick in texture because of the excessive use of instrumental doublings. Its
angular harmony, the only modern reference present, is
uninterestingly conventional." [London LPS 334 (10 inch)]
See: D80a

B80q. "New Publications in Review." Musical Courier
142:42 (December 1, 1950)
   "Despite some sharp harmonic clashes, this is essentially a big post-romantic symphony with its philosophy
rooted in conservatism; and is one of the best works of its
kind that the present generation has produced." See: W80

B80r. Persichetti, Vincent. "Philadelphia." Musical
Quarterly 35:296 (April 1949)
   "Alexander Hilsberg presented Samuel Barber's Second
Symphony, a work that marks Barber's first venture into
truly creative composition. The symphony has the vitality
and ingenuity of his Capricorn Concerto and Medea. The
dissonant harmonies sound forced at times but warm-blooded
melodic and rhythmic lines are bold and free." See: W80c

B80s. Redlich, Hans F. "New Music: A Critical Interim Report." Music Review 16:160-168 (May 1955)
Discussion of new works by ten contemporary composers. Of Barber's Second Symphony, Redlich notes: "It is written in a severe near-academic style (not so far removed from the scholarly, but anaemic detachment of Walter Piston), with jazz influence and 'folkiness' all but excluded...But the academic rigor of his style does not prevent Mr. Barber from occasional impressive flights into greater conceptual freedom...However, as in so many works of younger American composers, thematic matter as well as the planning of the general harmonic angle frequently lack evidence of a truly creative personality." See: W80

B80t. "Reviews of New Music." Musical Opinion 73:583 (July 1950)
Review of the G. Schirmer/Chappell full score. "I shall certainly look forward to hearing many performances of this fine work, which is decidedly an event for American music, and more." See: W80

B80u. "Reviews of New Music." Musical Opinion 74:589+ (August 1951)
Review of the G. Schirmer/Chappell study score. "Barber has always had a complete command of technical resource and while this work has not the direct appeal of the First Symphony, its brilliance and audacity will ensure it many performances." See: W80

B80v. S. "Orchestra." New Records 19:3 (July 1951)
The work is "...a good example of modern music in that it is built on rather traditional lines using a sonata-form first movement, and variations and fugato in the third movement...It is not easy to grasp on first hearing, but its message is worth repetition, and the chances are better than fair that this work will someday be a part of the standard orchestral repertoire." [London LPS 334 (10 inch)] See: D80a

B80w. Simmons, Walter. "Classical Recordings." Fanfare 7:134-135 (September-October 1983)
The 1940s were "...the time of the ill-fated Symphony No. 2, which marked something of a new course. Though a crisis of self-confidence impelled Barber to withdraw the symphony (not a bad piece, by any means), subsequent works continued the new sound." See: W80

B80x. Singer, Samuel L. "Philadelphia: Orchestral Premiere Marks Fete on 25th Anniversary of Curtis." Musical Courier 139:24 (February 15, 1949)
"In three movements Barber's Symphony has something to say, and it is not derivative. Throughout it bears the mark of 'modernism'--in fact, it opens on dissonant chords--but there are many passages of melodic, singing beauty, with puckish touches in the first movement. The

last two movements have greater structural clarity than the opening, where in an effort to speak boldly the composer sometimes mistakes mere noise for power. There is excellent writing for strings and woodwinds in the slow movement, while the finale builds to climaxes with canny effect." <u>See</u>: W80c

B80y. Smith, Moses. "Americans and Shostakovitch in Boston." <u>Modern Music</u> 21:252 (May-June 1944)
"I have been prejudiced against Barber ever since the time years ago when I heard a gooey indiscretion for quartet. In subsequent works, more expertly and slickly written, I have observed what seemed to me the same continued concern for surface effect. Not so in the <u>Second Symphony</u>. In this work, dedicated to the Army Air Forces, Barber strikes out boldly and admirably on a new path. The music is often harsh and astringent. It is of our time, and that means time of war. I refer to over-all impression, not to its specifically programmatic character, about which there is much talk, naturally. No music of the concert-hall--or the opera-house, for that matter--was ever saved or ruined by its program. Specifically, in the slow movement...he employs an electric instrument to imitate the sound of a radio-beam. It was a device, and remained only a device. It makes one think of blind flying, as the composer probably wanted it to do, but it added nothing to the emotional intensity of the music. At the beginning of the third movement, on the other hand, Barber has a remarkable introduction, consisting of a spiral figure for strings, played in fantasy-style. This is supposed to represent a plane spiraling earthward, but here the device, <u>qua</u> music, is engrossing and exciting." <u>See</u>: W80

B81. THIRD ESSAY FOR ORCHESTRA, OP. 47.

B81a. Alps, Tim. "Concerto: Modern." <u>Music and Musicians</u> 28:66 (January 1980)
"Barber uses the term 'Essay' in the literary sense of the word of 'pithy brevity' with a 'tendency to explore a single aspect of a subject'...The Third Essay is longer than either of its predecessors but the unity of thought is the same. The soft opening timpani motif provides the basic rhythmic and melodic material for the whole work which is in one movement. The ideas are built up by playing with different orderings of small groups of notes and these gradually extend and grow to form long lyrical chains before closing up again to end as they began. The harmonic language never really extends beyond Scriabin, but the broad, sumptuous tunes are undeniably compelling and of course any work must ultimately stand or fall by the terms it sets itself and this work is strongly constructed and richly imagined." <u>See</u>: W81

315

B81b. Freed, Richard. "New Creations by Corigliano and Barber Magnificently Celebrate the New York Philharmonic." Stereo Review 46:56-57 (May 1981)
"The Third Essay...was Barber's last work for orchestra and, I believe, his last completed composition in any form. It displays obvious connections with the two earlier Essays of 1937 and 1942, and at the same time is just as conspicuously different from them. It is at once more urgent and more expansive, and it has a greater emphasis on (one might even say it is a wilder celebration of) orchestral virtuosity. While lyricism is less to the fore than in the earlier Essays, Barber's distinctive vein of romanticism is clearly identifiable, together with some coloring that suggests so unexpected an influence as Scriabin. It is, in any event, a stunning valediction, and it is carried off with irresistible conviction and brilliance to burn." [New World Records NW 309] See: D81a

B81c. Lange, Albert. "Guide to Records." American Record Guide 45:21 (October 1981)
The work is "...a single, self-contained movement of symphonic proportions, which touches variously upon dramatic, tender, and impassioned episodes characteristic of Barber's Symphony No. 1, among other works. Lushly orchestrated (at times, though, a bit too creamy) and crisply conceived, the music unfortunately lacks a unifying thread, and the themes are not top-drawer Barber (who was certainly one of the most lyrical melodists of our time)." [New World Records NW 309] See: D81a

B81d. Smith, Patrick J. "Debuts & Reappearances." High Fidelity/Musical America 29:MA32-33 (January 1979)
"This polished and accomplished work is not really unfamiliar, as it is fully in the style of the composer, which has shown a remarkable homogeneity from his earliest success, the overture to The School for Scandal. If anything, a nostalgic lyricism pervades this work to an even greater extent, so that the piece sounds like something unfrozen from a time warp...The work is aloof and unconcerned with today's music-making as is its composer and it is this sunset nostalgia rather than the specifics of its makeup that give the Third Essay an oddly touching remembrance of things past." See: W81a

B82. TOCCATA FESTIVA, OP. 36.

B82a. Aprahamian, Felix. "Orchestral." Gramophone 43:552 (May 1966)
"Not without a few dull, meandering and unfestive patches for the solo instrument, the Toccata provides, nevertheless, a useful addition to the slender list of concerted works for organ." [CBS SBRG 72364] See: D82a

B82b. Bronkhorst, Charles Vary. "New Records." American Organist. 46:22 (February, 1963)

"About 14 minutes long, this one-movement is well conceived to exhibit the organ's many possibilities in contrast and combination with orchestra. [Columbia MS 6398, ML 5798] See: D82a

B82c. Day, Wesley A. "New Organ Dedicated at Philadelphia Academy of Music." Diapason 51:3 (November 1, 1960)

"...Toccata Festiva...carefully proportioned and so constructed that all of the characteristics of the organ are used, with and without the orchestra. A stunning pedal cadenza precedes the final section which in turn effectively utilizes all resources of organ and orchestra, of soloist, conductor and instrumentalists! The Toccata Festiva is a major contribution to the literature for organ and orchestra." See: W82a

B82d. Hughes, Allen. "Music: Soloists Highlight Tully Organ Dedication." New York Times, April 15, 1975, p. 29.

"Miss Crozier, another symbol of uncompromising quality among organ virtuosos for more than three decades, was soloist in Barber's Toccata Festiva, an extended, one movement work composed for the Philadelphia Orchestra in 1960. She performed it handsomely and was especially impressive in the pedal cadenza, which she played with as much attention to its expressive import as to its display aspects." See: W82d

B82e. Jones, Ralph E. "Organ." New Records 31:12 (March 1963)

"Aside from some interesting orchestral sonorities, there is a fascinating pedal cadenza, which remains impressive despite the absence of the visual image." [Columbia ML 5798, MS 6398] See: D82a

B82f. L., K. "Orchestral." Records and Recordings 9:55 (April 1966)

"...though only a piece d'occasion, is well constructed and offers some interesting ideas. After the surging introduction and organ fanfares, a long striking cantilena emerges. A turbulent middle section based on ideas in the introduction culminates in an extended pedal cadenza of prodigious difficulty. Later the cantilena melody returns in the form of a pseudo-chorale. In this work the organ writing is far more idiomatic than in either of the others [Poulenc and R. Strauss] and it calls for considerable virtuosity...Power Biggs plays superbly and with the utmost control; he brings off the most frightening passages with tremendous panache but in quieter sections he reveals true musicianship and artistry." [CBS BRG 72364, SBRG 72364] See: D82a

B82g. Maw, Nicholas. "20th Century." Musical Times 103:181 (March 1962)

"Samuel Barber's _Toccata Festiva_ is a big, occasional piece full of flourishes and fanfares. The orchestra is large, with a percussion section of four players. The organ part will sound brilliant but it is not unduly diffi-cult, except for a pedal cadenza where the player needs fleetness of foot to get over all the notes in time." _See_: W82

B82h. Peterson, Melody. "UCLA Symphony in Royce Hall Program." _Los Angeles Times_, November 23, 1973, sect. 4, p. 22.
"...[It] strikes one as a substandard work from this composer of generally distinctive romantic-modern music. No amount of musical consideration by organist Thomas Har-mon could conceal its paucity of thematic invention. Nor could virtuosity, even in the lengthy, demanding registra-tively varied pedal cadenza, make a dramatic entity of a basically ponderously rambling one." _See_: W82c

B82i. Salzman, Eric. "Classical." _High Fidelity_ 13:88 (April 1963)
"The contrast between the graceful, light touch of Poulenc and the heavy-handed Barber _Toccata_ is striking. This latter composition was written for the occasion of the inauguration of the new Philadelphia organ and, in fact, it turns out to be just a little too occasional. This is not an impressive or an engaging work either in its ideas or in the way they are delivered. The performance is, however, noteworthy." [Columbia ML 5798, MS 6398] _See_: D82a

B82j. Schauensee, Max de. "National Report: Philadel-phia Barber Premiere." _Musical America_ 80:23 (November 1960)
"The composition, expertly written, proved sonorous and majestic in scope, giving the organist, Paul Callaway of Washington Cathedral, plenty of opportunity to exploit the instrument and to display his considerable technique, which was particularly impressive in a long pedal cadenza." _See_: W82a

B82k. Singer, Samuel L. "Philadelphia Dedicates New $150,000 organ." _Musical Courier_ 162:20 (November 1960)
"The organ is a brilliant concert vehicle, with empha-sis on the reeds...It was first heard at the opening con-certs with Paul Callaway, organist of the Washington Cathe-dral, as soloist in Samuel Barber's _Toccata Festiva_, com-missioned for the occasion. Barber's work effectively displayed the resources of both the organ and the organist, although its purely musical value is questionable." _See_: W82a

B82l. Smith, Rollin. "American Organ Composers." _Music_ [American Guild of Organists] 10:18 (August 1976)
"[It] is in one movement and centers upon a simple

theme which undergoes a number of ingenious transformations." See: W82

B82m. "Stoplists." American Organist 43:19 (December
1960)
"Samuel Barber's toccata is, as it should be, a virtuoso piece; but it is far more than merely this. Here is
an important addition to the organ-orchestra literature.
It is the work of a craftsman, who knows what he is about.
The carefully designed inter-play between organ and orchestra, between voices in each 'instrument' are exceptionally
and imaginatively well conceived. There is drama, pulse,
driving rhythm, singing line, beauty, shape and purpose
here. It goes without saying that this work deserves many
hearings." See: W82, W82a

BAND MUSIC

B83. COMMANDO MARCH.

B83a. Bauman, John. "Ensemble." Fanfare 2:129
(July/August 1979)
"The Commando March..., which he wrote in 1943 while
assigned to the Air Corps Band...is aggressively brash and
a good march to open the disc." [Telarc 10043 (digital)]
See: D83a

B83b. Cohn, Arthur. Recorded Classical Music. New
York: Schirmer Books, 1981. 2164 p.
"A band march written by a leading contemporary composer is an extraordinary incident in any case, but unless
one has the particular talents of a Sousa, the incident is
a waste of musical powder and shot." [p. 98] See: W83

B83c. Fennell, Frederick. "Macho Marches" [album
notes for Telarc DG 10043 (digital) disc]
"The commando was a new kind of soldier, one who did
not march in straight lines, across parade ground; he
struck in stealth with speed, disappearing as quickly as he
came. He inspired a different kind of music and
Barber...provided that in this wide departure from tradition." See: D83a

B83d. Grunfeld, Frederic V. "It Ain't Necessarily
Oompah: The Concert Band." High Fidelity 4:82 (October
1954)
"The Commando March by ex-airman Samuel Barber is an
old-fashioned quickstep sporting a crew cut." [Mercury
MG 40006] See: D83c

B83e. Lyons, James. "Instrumental." American Record

Guide 20:200   (February 1954)
    "I must say I never expected to hear Barber's Commando
March again; we were importuned with it too many times
during the late war and I, for one, would as leave file it
away until the next one." [Mercury MG 50079] See: D83c

    B83f. Payne, Ifan. "Direct or Digital." American Re-
cord Guide 42:53-54 (September 1979)
    "Fennell's conducting is unsophisticated but lively
enough." [Telarc DG 10043 (digital)] See: D83a

    B83g. Smith, Moses. "Boston Goes All Out for Pre-
mieres." Modern Music 21:103-104 (January-February 1944)
    "Originally written for band, [this work] was prepared
for orchestra by the composer at the suggestion of Serge
Koussevitzky.   The orchestration was lavish but quite appropriate. And the piece was good and fast and spirited, as
a march ought to be." See: W83b

CHAMBER MUSIC

B85. CAPRICORN CONCERTO, OP. 21.

    B85a. Anderson, W. R. "Round About Radio." Musical
Times 87:339 (November 1946)
    "Samuel Barber's Capricorn concerto lasts under a
quarter-hour. It is for flute, oboe, trumpet and strings
in concerto grosso style. The spirit is less immediately
enjoyable than the Adagio we have heard several times.   I
thought the music rather desiccated and squeaky." See: W85

    B85b. -----. "Round About Radio." Musical Times
88:323 (September 1947)
    "Another American work, Barber's Capricorn concerto
(about a quarter-hour) is a mixture of what occurred to me
as little pictures somewhat after the Moussorgsky Exhibition order, with religioso insertions. Like so much American music, it doesn't seem to jell, for us; that emphasizes
the great foreignness of each nation, as seen by the
other." See: W85

    B85c. Berger, Arthur. "Scores and Records." Modern
Music 23:66 (Winter 1946)
    The Concerto's idiom is more valid and malleable [than
the Second Symphony]. Its Brandenburgian last movement
gets away from slavery to a nuclear motive and spins more
exciting lines, with an asymmetry and attention to rhythmic
interest that recalls the later Stravinsky. The score does
not, by nature, aim for absorbing developments, but it
makes us look forward to what Barber will do next." See:
W85

B85d. Ericson, Raymond. "Music: Festival's 11th." New York Times, November 12, 1964, p. 40.
Review of the Festival Orchestra of New York perform-ance, Carnegie Hall. "Mr. Barber's perky 'Capricorn Concer-to,' which dates from 1944, is both lively and lyrical in its neoclassic style." See: W85d

B85e. Eyer, Ronald. "New York Philharmonic Launches Season." Musical America 76:23+ (November 1, 1956)
"Samuel Barber's off-beat concerto for flute, oboe and trumpet was executed with immense virtuosity by...first-chair men of the orchestra. This is a busy, airy, fast-moving piece...displaying the modern possibilities of the three instruments in solo and in ensemble, which it does exhaustively if not particularly movingly. It probably will never get a better performance." See: W85c

B85f. Frankenstein, Alfred. "Classical." High Fidel-ity 10:58 (June 1960)
"[It] is a vivacious, peppery piece for flute, oboe, trumpet, and strings. The Eastman-Rochester virtuosos, and the recording virtuosos in the Mercury studio do very well by it." [Mercury MG 50224, SR 90224] See: D85a

B85g. Friedewald, Russell Edward. A Formal and Stylis-tic Analysis of the Published Music of Samuel Barber.
Thesis (Ph.D.)--Iowa State University, 1957. 357 p.
"This work is characterized by a rather dry, brittle quality, which is in sharp contrast to those works be-longing to Barber's first (so-called neo-romantic) period.
[p. 207] See: W85

B85h. Harrison, Lou. "Forecast and Review." Modern Music 22:31 (November 1944)
"Samuel Barber's new Capricorn Concerto is a brilliant work, and takes the cake for orchestration this month. The charming combinations he achieves with the wind concertino are very telling indeed and produce a bubbling opalescence.
The music is well worked, although very Stravinskian, and makes intentional and persistent use of that old academic bugaboo, the general pause. Actually, Barber has done an obvious but seldom thought of thing. When he comes to the end of a section of material, instead of making the fluid and highly professional transition into the next idea, he simply stops. Dead silence for a fraction of a second and then everything begins at once with the new material already in full action. The device is effective and frank.
It is used over and over and becomes an integral stylistic feature. Except for this, though, the piece might have been signed by Stravinsky of a few years back. Barber has tremendous technical grasp and an essential urge to expression, but seems fascinated in turn by each of the famous masks and mantles. If he ever catches up with himself he certainly will be a composer of power and in-terest." See: W85, W85a

B85i.   Henken, John. "Schwarz Conducts L. A. Chamber."
Los Angeles Times, January 30, 1984, pt. 6, p. 2.
    "Samuel Barber's Capricorn Concerto is as derivative
as Gounod's Symphony, relying on Copland and Stravinsky in
large measure. But it put the L. A. Chamber Orchestra
strings in a better light and gave genial work to three
accomplished orchestral soloists: David Shostac, flute;
Allan Vogel, oboe; and Mario Guaneri, trumpet." See: W85e

B85j.   Mills, Charles. "Over the Air." Modern Music
23:74 (Winter 1946)
    "Samuel Barber's Capricorn Concerto [broadcast over
C.B.S.] uses a little concertante ensemble of trumpet,
oboe, violin and flute. It exemplifies strikingly what a
productive study of Copland will do for a young musician
who has been brought up in the tradition of big, fat sounds
and pompous effects. The title of the piece refers not to
the zodiac sign but to Barber's summer home, called Capricorn, where the work was written. This delightfully clear
and brilliant score is most adaptable to radio use." See:
W85

B85k.   P. "Saidenberg Little Symphony." Musical America
64:24 (October 1944)
    "...it is little more than a flip exercise of humorous
rhythmic and instrumental formulas (with special attention
to a trumpet) which have been done far better at one time
or another by Stravinsky, Shostakovich and their fellows."
See: W85a

B85l.   "Record Supplement for April, 1949." Gramophone
Shop. Record Supplement 12:2 (April 1949)
    "[It]...is a terse but brilliantly colored work which
follows the general pattern of the concerto grosso. Flute,
trumpet and oboe form the small group of instruments which
oppose the larger group of the orchestra. There is an
obvious influence of Stravinsky and Aaron Copland in this
music, but the work is no mere duplication of other composers' ideas. The rhythmic freedom and the treatment of
the woodwinds are particular examples of this outward influence; but beyond these surface influences, the treatment
of the musical ideas and the ideas themselves are Barber's
own...This is an excellent performance by the Saidenberg
Little Symphony." [Concert Hall CH A4] See: D85b

B85m.   S. "Orchestra." New Records 19:3 (May 1951)
    The work "...is scored in concerto grosso form for
flute, oboe, trumpet and strings and was written especially
for the Saidenberg Little Symphony. It is written in the
form of Bach's famous Brandenburg Concertos." [Concert Hall
Society 1078] See: D85b

B85n.   Shupp, Enos E., Jr. "Orchestra." New Records 28:5
(March 1960)
    Capricorn Concerto offers the soloists a chance to

play games against the background of strings; it must be demonically difficult to perform and is as exciting to see as it is to hear." [Mercury MG 50224, SR 90224] See: D85a

B85o. Smith, Cecil Michener. "Big Names in Chicago." Modern Music 22:121 (January-February 1945)
"While there can be no doubt that Barber observed closely much that Stravinsky has to show younger composers, he nevertheless invents his own themes, maintains them by his own special kind of rhythmic urgency, and orchestrates them with his own pointed economy. More than most of his contemporaries Mr. Barber understands the difference between beginning, middle and end. He evolves movements out of his material which are reasonable, consecutive, and cumulative, and he does not disdain to be friendly and communicative along the way." See: W85

B85p. The Stereo Record Guide. Volume 3. Ed. by Ivan March. London: Long Playing Record Library, 1963. 1099 p.
"[It] is a concerto grosso on the lines of Stravinsky's Dumbarton Oaks, not so openly attractive as that but concentrating great power in the slow fugal passage at the beginning." [Mercury AMS 16096, SR 90224] See: D85a

B85q. Straus, Noel. "Saidenberg Leads Little Symphony." New York Times, October 9, 1944, p. 17.
"[It] was conceived in a lighter vein [than Henry Cowell's Hymn and Fuguing Tune] and modernistic in its method of treatment. Though it had nothing particularly original to import and was largely episodic and fragmentary in its three divisions, it served its purpose well enough in rather inconsequential but clever fashion." See: W85a

B86. DOVER BEACH, OP. 3.

B86a. Clark, Robert. "First Recording of a Masterpiece: Schoeck's Notturno." HiFi/Stereo Review 21:109 (October 1968)
"Next to Notturno, Barber's Dover Beach (1931) is, for this listener, something of a wallflower. I have thought the poem a schoolmasterish bore ever since it was first thrust upon me by a college literature syllabus; the genteel effusions of Barber's music are, I'm afraid, a perfect match for it. Still, the work has a surface attractiveness, and shows that skill with English prosody that was to become one of Barber's chief assets." [Columbia KS 7131] See: D86c

B86b. Ellsworth, Ray. "Americans on Microgroove--Part II." High Fidelity 6:62 (August 1956)
"Dover Beach, once a collector's item on 78 rpm (because Barber himself sang it with the Curtis String Quartet), now [1956] available on LP as part of Paul Hume's Critic's Choice collection. [RCA LCT 1158] See: D86b

B86c. Frankenstein, Alfred. "Classical Music on Long Playing." High Fidelity 2:50 (January-February 1953)
"Dover Beach, for baritone and string quartet, is a remarkable achievement, translating the thoughtful atmosphere of Matthew Arnold's pessimistic poem into musical nostalgia that bears repeating. [Classic Editions CE 1011] See: D86e

B86d. Friedewald, Russell Edward A Formal and Stylistic Analysis of the Published Music of Samuel Barber. Thesis (Ph.D.)--Iowa State University, 1957. 357 p.
"It is evident that the composer was very meticulous in following the rhythm of the poem, and it appears, too, that he has captured its mood and expressiveness. Repeated notes are frequently used in the vocal line, which is predominately conjunct in nature." [p. 18] See: W86

B86e. Goodwin, Noël. "Samuel Barber." Times (London), July 7, 1980, p. 13.
"...the setting of Matthew Arnold's Dover Beach, the cry of a young heart in a hostile world, itself so characteristic of Barber, lacked its due poignancy and shades of feeling in the singing of Vivien Townley. Her tone sounded curiously bleached, and her words were seldom intelligible even from a seat in the fourth row." See: W86i

B86f. Hall, David. The Record Book. New York: Citadel Press, 1946. 1063 p.
"A very sensitive setting of Arnold's poem by one of the younger American composers. These records also show him to be a very fine baritone." [p. 621] [Victor 8898, 78 rpm] See: D86b

B86g. Harrison, Max. "Chamber Music." Gramophone 61:54 (June 1983)
"Dover Beach was...the piece with which Samuel Barber first gained attention. It is nostalgic, adolescent music, yet the composer can scarcely be blamed for that, as he was only 21 when he wrote; he sang it most touchingly...on a recording (Victor 8898, 78 rpm) that was never issued here [Great Britain]" See: D86b

B86h. Hinton, James, Jr. "Recitals and Miscellany." High Fidelity 6:128 (January 1956)
"...however much one may admire Samuel Barber's Dover Beach as a song, his singing as singing may not be an experience that everyone will want to repeat over and over --but, again, nobody said it was." [Victor LCT 1156] See: D86b

B86i. Hume, Paul. "Samuel Barber" [album notes for Classics Edition CE 1011 disc]
"Dover Beach...was written while the composer was studying at Curtis Institute. More than that it was recorded, with the baritone-composer as soloist by the Curtis

String Quartet. That recording has been unobtainable for many years. Those fortunate enough to have heard the record treasure it for its evidence of Barber, the singer, as well as its historic value." See: D86e

B86j. Jones, Robert. "Give Me Those Oldtime Singers." New York Times, August 18, 1968, sect. 2, p. 24.
"It does no disservice to Dietrich Fischer-Dieskau to point out that interest in his latest...recording centers on repertory more than it does on the singer. Samuel Barber's Dover Beach has long been due an up-to-date recording. It is a beautiful work and certainly more than a warm-up Knoxville: Summer of 1915 whose reputation tends to overshadow this earlier (1931) piece." [Columbia KS 7131] See: D86c

B86k. Kirkpatrick, John. "Bennington's Festival of the Arts." Modern Music 18:53 (November-December 1940)
"[It] has real character. It didn't quite succeed in sustaining an unvarying interest throughout its length, but it did achieve something positive and beautiful." See: W86

B86l. Kolodin, Irving. The New Guide to Recorded Music. International Edition. Garden City, New York: Doubleday, 1950. 524 p.
"A notation for the oddment hunter; a work recorded by Barber in the early period, when he had not decided to devote himself wholly to composition." [p. 36] [Victor 8898, 78 rpm] See: D86a

B86m. -----. "Recordings in Review: Juilliard Plus Fischer-Dieskau." Saturday Review 51:48 (July 27, 1968)
"Those who esteem Fischer-Dieskau as essentially, a lyric rather than a dramatic artist are also likely to put this disc among the most satisfactory of the many to his credit. It is absorbing to compare his version of Dover Beach with the one made by Barber (in the Thirties) before he retired from public performance as a singer to devote himself wholly to composition." [Columbia KS 7131] See: D86c

B86n. Osborne, Conrad L. "Classical." High Fidelity 18:108 (November 1968)
"Dover Beach is the very best side of Barber--nothing pretentious or posy, but an emotionally direct, brilliantly crafted setting of Matthew Arnold's great poetry. Because it settles for being what it is--stays within its own frame, you might say--it acquires a degree of force and truthfulness that many of Barber's more recent compositions (however well written, and he does write well) do not attain. One would not mistake Fischer-Dieskau for either an American or an Englishman, and without the text I find some of the phrases incomprehensible. But then, the text is provided..." [Columbia KS 7131] See: D86c

B86o.   Ramey,   Philip.   "Dover Beach" [album notes for
Columbia AKS 7131 disc]
   "In his setting for voice and string quartet of Matthew Arnold's poem Dover Beach, Barber demonstrates   pre-
cocious sensitivity to the text.   The work is true chamber
music, in which the string ensembles share equal rights
with the voice; at times, in fact, each of the strings has
an almost independent role, creating the impression of five
individual voices."   See: D86c

   B86p.   Robertson,   Alec.   "Choral and Song."   Gramophone
46:695 (November 1968)
   "Samuel Barber composed his setting of Matthew Arnold's wonderful poem, Dover Beach in his twenty-first
year...There are many fine descriptive touches in the
string quartet accompaniment, picturing, for example, the
grating roar of the pebbles on the shore and there is a
superb outburst of emotions from singers and strings in the
final stanza 'Ah, love, let us be true to one another.'"
[CBS 72687] See: D86c

   B86q.   Simmons,   Walter.   "Classical Recordings."   Fanfare 6:92 (May/June 1983)
   "The music reflects eloquently the high-minded pessi-
mism of Matthew Arnold's   poem, conveying a gloomy Victorian atmosphere quite congenial to the young composer's
aristocratic but highly sensitive temperament...Guinn's
expression seems somewhat constricted...offering little in
the way of interpretive nuance."   [Nonesuch 78017]   See:
D86d

B87.   MUTATIONS FROM BACH.

   B87a.   Bryan,   Paul R.   "Band Music."   Notes 26:365 (December 1969)
   "To those who labor in less exalted fields of musical
endeavor, the appearance of a new work for winds by a major
composer is an exciting event.   Samuel Barber has rarely
heeded the plea of those who would have him write for
winds, so his Mutations from Bach comes as a pleasant
surprise.   Unfortunately the work is somewhat disappointing
because it contains very little Barber...[His] contribution
is more subtle and can be seen in the masterful welding
together of the material and in the extremely effective use
of the instruments."   See: W87

   B87b.   Frost,   Ana.   "As Others See Us; A Rumanian in New
York." [Translated by Paul Shapiro from Musica (Rumania)
No. 6, June 1969] American Musical Digest 1:45   (December
1969)
   "Barber neither changes nor adds anything, but combines the few thematic lines of the Bach Chorale into a
unitary work in which there are several solos, the most
ingenious of which is the trumpet solo in its highest

register." See: W87

B87c. Macdonald, Malcolm. "Orchestral." Gramophone 54:58 (June 1976)
"...an arrangement, rather than a composition, of Bach movements based on the chorale Christe, du Lamm Gottes which does not seem to lie quite naturally for brass. For all that it completes the programme effectively, bridging the two extremes of the period covered." [Unicorn RHS 339] See: D87a

B87d. O'Loughlin, Niall. "Modern Brass." Musical Times 109:1050 (November 1968)
"Mutations from Bach is a blend of a chorale set by Bach with short meditative interludes by Barber. The instrumentation (4 horns, 3 trumpets, 3 trombones, tuba, timpani) is of course, Barber's and well laid out." See: W87

B88. SERENADE FOR STRINGS, OP. 1.

B88a. Bookspan, Martin. "Record Reviews: Classical" Consumer Reports 46:339 (June 1981)
"The Samuel Barber score is the composer's Opus No. 1...its three movements have the lyrical ease that characterizes all of his work. [Nonesuch Digital D 79002] See: D88a

B88b. Cohn, Arthur. Recorded Classical Music. New York: Schirmer Books, 1981. 2164 p.
"An Opus 1 is sometimes a spilling of unnecessary creative blood believed in by the creator but fraught with mishaps and miscalculations. Barber's Opus I is well ordered and is in no way pedantic." [p. 98] See: W88

B88c. Dettmer, Roger. "Orchestral." Fanfare 4:232 (March/April 1981)
"The Barber Serenade, created for string quartet, dates from his teen years at the Curtis Institute. Either in 1928 or 1929 he 'adapted' it for string orchestra as Op. 1 in his canon. For a student piece it is assuredly proficient, but otherwise without personality or even precocity." [Nonesuch Digital D 79002] See: D88a

B88d. Friedewald, Russell Edward. A Formal and Stylistic Analysis of the Published Music of Samuel Barber. Thesis (Ph.D.)--Iowa State University, 1957. 357 p.
"This work, as well as several other compositions of the early period, looks back to the late romantic era for its inspiration. The melodic writing is interesting, the texture is varied, and the piece achieves its modest aims." [p. 156] See: W88

B88e. Hall, David. "Classical Discs and Tapes." *Stereo Review* 46:111 (February 1981)

"This is an admirable collection of attractive music, and it's digitally mastered too. Pensively lyrical and elegantly dance like elements are contrasted in the *Serenade for Strings*, which Samuel Barber composed in 1929 while still in his teens." [Nonesuch Digital D 79002] *See*: D88a

B88f. Harrison, Max. "Orchestral." *Gramophone* 59:1257 (March 1982)

"It is very assured, but although quite likeable--more so for the present writer, than much of his later work--it holds less interest than the other music here." [Nonesuch Digital D 79002] *See*: D88a

B88g. Harvey, Trevor. "Opera."" *Gramophone* 46:272 (August 1968)

"...it owes a debt to Tchaikovsky...pleasant listening." [Vanguard VSL 11019] *See*: D88c

B88h. Mills, Charles. "Over the Air." *Modern Music* 20:213 (March-April 1943)

"Another Symphonic Strings [Alfred Wallenstein, conducted over the Mutual Network] broadcast offered Samuel Barber's *Serenade for Strings*, Opus 1. This obviously early work, originally scored for quartet, was probably better in that version. It is essentially lyric in character and not unattractive, but still sounds woefully conventional and romantic in a lukewarm way." *See*: W88

B90. SONATA FOR VIOLONCELLO AND PIANO IN C MINOR, OPUS 6.

B90a. Anderson, W. R. "Round About Radio." *Musical Times* 85:46-48 (February 1944)

"This (1938) work is in three movements, of a darkish colour in general: some eloquence, plenty of feeling; rather disjunct, at first hearing. It is not 'extreme,' but acid or angular, in places." *See*: W90

B90b. Broder, Nathan. "Gregor Piatigorsky, 'Cellist." [album notes for RCA Victor LM 2013 disc]

"If there is one quality that truly marks Barber's musical style, it is lyricism...In the later ones [compositions] it is more subtle, more profound, and sometimes touched with tragedy." *See*: D90h

B90c. Brown, Royal S. "Classical." *High Fidelity* 27:95 (March 1977)

"The early (1932) cello sonata shows Barber's more mellowly lyrical side, with a remarkable theme in rising minor sixths opening the work and a number of haunting melodies and intriguing figures as it progresses...Both works are technically well-played by the Clark-Schuldmann duo, although I am not partial to Harry Clark's reedy cello tone." [Musical Heritage Society MHS 3378] See: D90a

B90d. Budden, Julian. "Chamber Music." Gramophone 44:320 (December 1966)
"Barber's sonata of 1932, for all its cavalier treatment of traditional harmony and key relationships, shows a heart no less fundamentally romantic. The ghost of the Londonderry Air haunts the Adagio and the second subject of the first movement is an unashamed 'Hommage a Sibelius.' It is an early work...but it can boast of a wealth of attractive ideas." [Saga STXID 5272] See: D90b

B90e. "Chamber Music." New Records 19:6 (August 1951)
"Raya Garbousova handles the darkly emotional part assigned her...with just the right amount of control. Erich Kahn's piano work, while not meant to be an accompaniment, skillfully abets the 'cello's deep tones, reminding one of a dark, rich fabric shot through with bits of gold thread." [Concert Hall Society 1062] See: D90d

B90f. Cohn, Arthur. Recorded Classical Music. New York: Schirmer Books, 1981. 2164 p.
"An important part of this Sonata's design is the telescoping of the inner slow and Scherzo movements into one. The two outer movements are in set forms; the first is in sonata arrangement, with lines that sing in a traditional manner and neat romantic harmonies, the last consists of a series of connected variations on a theme, though it is not so titled. But this movement's construction is exceedingly tight-knit. Its sections unfold with no recapitulated material." See: W90

B90g. Cowling, Elizabeth. The Cello. 2nd ed. London: B.T. Batsford, 1983. 240 p.
"The Barber sonata is an early work in a lyrical romantic vein and very appealing to an audience. Its three movements offer considerable contrast, and the writing throughout has solved the balance between the cello and piano by careful handling of the accompaniment when the cello has the important material. The sonata is affirmative, strong, and passionate; in other words, it is eloquent." [p. 161] See: W90

B90h. Edel, Oliver. "Sonatas for Cello and Piano." Repertoire 1:50-51 (October 1951)
"Samuel Barber [here] writes with strength and passion for both piano and cello. He does so without sacrificing either sonority of piano or softness of cello; and he succeeds in maintaining a striking balance between the two instruments...Of distinct importance, too, is its suitability to the task of creating in audiences a confidence in, and sympathy for contemporary composition." See: W90

B90i. Frankenstein, Alfred. "Classical." High Fidel-

ity 6:88 (October 1956)
    "The romantic, melodious, and felicitous sonata by
Barber stands up to it [the Hindemith work] quite well,
however, and affords it excellent contrast. The performances are superb and the recording is flawless. [RCA Victor
LM 2013] See: D90h

    B90j. Frankenstein, Alfred. "Records in Review." High
Fidelity 1:55-56 (Spring 1952)
    "One expects this kind of dramatic, percussive and
exquisitely calculated composition from Randall Thompson,
but the vitality, not to say monumentality, of the Barber
sonata is rather surprising. It is an early piece and a
rather Brahmsian one, but a work of decided strength despite its obvious derivativeness." [Concert Hall Society
CHS 1092] See: D90d

    B90k. Freed, Richard. "Classical Discs and Tapes."
Stereo Review 45:77 (September 1980)
    "Of the four current versions, this newest one is by
all odds the smoothest and most persuasive--surely the most
fetching account of the work on record since the old Concert Hall recording by Raya Garbousova and Erich Itor
Kahn...Solow and Dominguez are fine players, and they seem
both serious and delighted about the give-and-take required
to bring these pieces off. The sound is good, too."
[Pelican LP 2010] See: D90j

    B90l. Friedewald, Russell Edward. A Formal and Stylis-
tic Analysis of the Published Music of Samuel Barber.
Thesis (Ph.D.)--Iowa State University, 1957. 357 p.
    "This three movement work is expressive in the late
Nineteenth Century, romantic style. The piano part, almost
equal in importance to that of the cello, requires a large
expansive technique." [p. 166] See: W90

    B90m. H., M. "American Duo." Times (London) September
30, 1968, p. 7.
    Review of the September 28, 1968 Brys/Sack per-
formance. "The middle brow romanticism of Samuel Barber's
op. 6 Sonata fared somewhat better, the innocence, nostalgia, and rather facile expressiveness so typical of his
earlier music coming over quite well, though the cello's
tone was inclined to deteriorate at faster tempos, especially in the final Allegro Appassionata." See: W90m

    B90n. Hays, Doris. "Cello Sonatas" [album notes for
Finnadar Records 90076-1 disc]
    This work "...offers a Pandora's box of harmonic and
structured means. Barber chose some Beethoven, some
Brahms, some Debussy to make his sound...The combination of
Barber's eminently singing cello lines with his sometimes
quixotic harmonic texture in the piano part gives the
Sonata a memorable quality." See: D90f

B90o. Hoover, Joanne Sheehy. "Performing Arts: Wolf Trap Concert Soloists." Washington Post, August 9, 1979, sect. B, p. 10.

"Some of the evening's most passionate playing came from 19-year old Charles Curtis, a past winner of the International Bach Competition in Washington. A performer who puts his total being into every note, Curtis turns each line into a charged statement. With pianist Earl Wild, he plunged into a melodic Samuel Barber Sonata, producing gorgeous, flowing lines as well as some delightfully pointed moments in the second movement toccata passages." See: W90o

B90p. Jones, Isabel Morse. "Enjoyable Chamber Music Concert Given." Los Angeles Times, December 10, 1943, pt. 1, p 11.

"It shows the influence of the song world he lived in then [Italy] and was accustomed to from the first time he heard his greatly gifted aunt, Louise Homer. It moves steadily along to a climax in the first movement, enters into a meditative mood in the Adagio of the second, is very smart and clever in the Presto and romantically inclined in the second short Adagio. The finale is a summation of all that goes before." [Performance with Stephen De'ak, violonello, and John Crown, piano] See: W90h

B90q. Lyons, James. "Chamber Music." American Record Guide 23:10 (September 1956)

"It is a surfeit of lyricism, full of song and sun-light (both Italianate) and more poetry than one expects from the unwieldy cello." [RCA Victor LM 2013] See: D90h

B90r. Parmenter, Ross. "Husband-Wife Duo Plays Cello, Piano." New York Times, October 29, 1963, p. 32.

"They are both serious musicians who place music before personal display. Miss Nilya is a clear, accurate and fluent pianist, and Mr. Bemko is a fair cellist who is at his best when the music is slow, songful and expres-sive...Because they presented worthy music that is not heard very often and because of their fundamental dedica-tion, they produced a certain amount of musical pleasure." See: W90l

B90s. Persichetti, Vincent. "Philadelphia Takes a Flier." Modern Music 21:106 (January-February 1944)

"The first of two concerts of the Philadelphia Chapter of the National Association of American Composers and Con-ductors gave us the Samuel Barber Sonata for Cello and Piano, a work that held promise of really important things to come. Even though the sure-footed rhythmic personality of the first movement towers over the loosely constructed second and third, a certain romantic flow holds the sonata together." See: W90

B90t. "Recitals of the Week." Times (London), June 25,
1937, p. 14.
   "A new sonata by the American composer, Samuel Barber,
was played for the first time here, with the composer at
the piano. Although late romantic in temper...the music
did not sound derivative...It did not strike one as a great
or specially remarkable work, but it was attractive as an
introduction to a thoughtful and gracious musical
personality." See: W90g

B90u. Reed, Peter Hugh. "Chamber Music." American
Record Guide 14:154 (January 1948)
   "While no great emotional depth is revealed, the capability of the composer's workmanship and his strict adherence to a stylistic formula is to be admired. Garbousova and Kahn perform with fervor and conviction. Excellent
recording." [Concert Hall Limited Set No. 1, Series B]
See: D90d

B90v. S., E. "Jules Eskin Offers 'Cello Recital Here."
New York Times, December 10, 1959, p. 30.
   "The three sonatas on the program were performed with
the excellent assistance of John Thomas Covelli at the
piano and they were projected with fine musicianship. But
the Barber 'Cello Sonata, op. 6, is a weak rewrite of
Brahms." See: W90j

B90w. S., M. M. "London Concerts." Musical Times
78:645 (July 1937)
   "What rare playing it was!--rich in tone, ripe in
musicianship, masterful without self-assertion...Yet,
though the Sonata may not grip, it attracts and deserved
the warm applause bestowed on it." See: W90g

B90x. Shupp, Enos E., Jr. "Chamber Music." New
Records 41:7 (March 1973)
   "Barber's very youthful work, the 'Cello Sonata, was
written while he was still a student, but it is a fine,
romantic work which is idiomatic for the instrument and
smartly crafted. It is given a performance of exceptional
tonal beauty and penetration by Mrs. Greco." [Orion ORS
7297] See: D90e

B90y. Simmons, Walter. "Classical Recordings." Fanfare 2:22, 24 (March/April 1979)
   "It is a lovely piece, alternatively gentle and passionate, and quite extended in scope, wearing its tender
romanticism proudly. But cellist Clark is as in the dark
interpretively as Measham...His tempos are so slow that the
work's fragile beauty becomes sluggish and simplistic. The
opening Allegro is played as a slow Andante, so that the
following Adagio is ridiculous." [Musical Heritage Society
MHS 3378] See: D90a

B90z. Simmons, Walter. "Classical Recordings." Fanfare 3:43-44 (May/June 1980)
    "The essential features of his style--the long, mem-
orable, highly affecting melodic lines that become the
primary compositional focus: never coarse--appeared early
and are found in their pure form in this lovely sonata.
Like most of Barber's early works, it makes no concession
at all to "modernism"; its formal progression is quite
episodic; and technical matters, such as the balance between the two instruments, are sometimes handled awkwardly.
But the Cello Sonata is a spontaneous and genuinely motivated piece of music, and has rightfully become one of the
most widely performed 20th-century works for cello."
[Pelican LP 2010] See: D90j

B90aa. -----. "Classical Recordings." Fanfare 7:134-
135 (September/October 1983)
    "In recent years, Samuel Barber's Sonata for Cello and
Piano has become increasingly established as a repertoire
staple--no surprise for a work that offers an unimpeded
flow of warm, expressive melody as its chief musical cur-
rency. The sonata was composed in 1932 at the Menotti
family home in Italy, and exhibits the almost exclusive
reliance on lyrical beauty and emotional expression characteristic of the works of Barber's 20s." [Finnadar 90076-1]
See: D90f

B90bb. "Some Chamber Works." American Record Guide
18:107 (December 1951)
    "The cello sonata, an earlier work owing much to
Brahms, is gratifyingly written for the cellist...Ricci and
Mittman do justice to the sonata. The recording is tonally
faithful." [Stradivari STR 602] See: D90i

B90cc. Stevens, Denis. "Duet Sonatas Without Wind Instruments (From 1700)." In Chamber Music. Ed. Alec
Robertson. Baltimore, Md.: Penguin Books, 1957. 427 p.
    The sonata "...has become an established work in the
cellists' repertory since 1932 when it was first published. Its freshness and lyricism, allied to traditional
forms and design, place it firmly among the finest cello
sonatas of the century." [p. 286] See: W90

B91. STRING QUARTET IN B MINOR, OP. 11.

B91a. Brown, Royal S. "Classical." High Fidelity
26:110 (October 1976)
    "It would be nice to be able to report that the outer
sections of Samuel Barber's 1936 String Quartet are worthy
of the famous Adagio second movement. Unfortunately, this
is not the case. In spite of some rather Beethovenish
energy and an attractive snippet here and there, the first
movement comes on basically as a choppy mishmash of pedestrian rhythmic figures and surprisingly ordinary (for Bar-

ber) themes, while the final movement, which follows the Adagio without pause, does little but restate the material in an even more perfunctory manner. In this setting, the gloriously flowing, long-phrased, and decidedly melancholic Adagio stands out even more strongly for the masterpiece it is. It is certainly worth hearing in its original version, particularly as performed by the Cleveland Quartet whose members have sensitively fathomed the expressivity of the twentieth-century Romanticism, adding to their interpretive finesse a well-nigh perfect blending of string sonority." [RCA Red Seal ARL 1 1599, quadraphonic ARDI 1599] See: D91d

B91b. Cohn, Arthur. "David Diamond--Magnificent Creativity." American Record Guide 32:507 (February 1966)
"Barber's Opus 11 (written 30 years ago) is of large shape, organic, deriving its flow and continuity from the interlocutions that stem from the opening unison theme. The famous Adagio for Strings is heard here in its original state. It stands up as a small gem, no matter that popularity cannot be depended on to define the greatest music. The Beaux-Arts performances are subtle, strongly colored, and positively identified with the styles of the composers. In total, Epic can be proud of this release." [Epic LC 3907, BC 1307] See: D91a

B91c. -----. "How News Comes to Philadelphia." Modern Music 15:237 (May-June 1938)
"No one can deny the technical equipment of this young man, but one may inquire whether he realizes that the year is 1938 and things are not so placid as his carefully tailored quartet would make us believe." See: W91d

B91d. Flanagan, William. "Classical." HIFI/Stereo Review 7:65 (December 1961)
"It's rather interesting to hear what a group of Russians musicians do with the neo-Brahmsian conservatism of the early Samuel Barber--especially since this is the quartet from which derives the independently famous Adagio for Strings. The results, taken altogether, are good, though the music emerges somehow more Russian in sound than one is accustomed to hear." [Artia MK 1563] See: D91b

B91e. -----. "Samuel Barber String Quartet, Op. 11." [album notes for Epic LC 3907 disc]
"It is a work evincing a solid grasp of fundamentals, a quality that Barber's teacher Rosario Scalero, was celebrated for demanding from his students. Nonetheless the Quartet provides unmistakable evidence that the young composer had a voice of his own and the capacity to use it. Furthermore, in spite of the fact that it is meticulously-- even cautiously--well made, it sings with ardor, brio and freshness." See: D91a

B91f. Frankenstein, Alfred. "Classical." High Fidelity 11:74 (December 1961)
    "If I am not mistaken this disc has the distinction of
containing the first piece of American music to be recorded
in Russia, by a Russian ensemble, for Russian
consumption...The Barber quartet is an early work, but it
is interesting as the source of the famous Adagio for
Strings of which Schwann lists ten recordings in the
orchestral version." [Artia MK 1563] See: D91b

B91g. -----. "Classical." High Fidelity 16:84 (January 1966)
    "Samuel Barber's op. 11--apparently the only string
quartet he has ever written--is a very early work, composed
in 1936. It is in that fluent, reserved, cleancut, warmly
academic style with which Barber established his reputation...As is invariably the case when a quartet movement is
made familiar in a string orchestra version, the original
sounds infinitely finer, more subtle and meaningful, when
it is finally unveiled. At least it does when it is played
by the Beaux-Arts String Quartet and recorded as well as it
is here." [Epic LC 3907, BC 1307] See: D91a

B91h. Freed, Richard D. "Diamond Comes Home." New
York Times, December 26, 1965, sect. 2, p. 21.
    "Like the Tchaikowsky and Borodin quartets in D, the
Barber is a work whose slow movement has long enjoyed an
independent life in a transcription for string orchestra.
In this case, the famous Adagio for Strings was arranged by
the composer himself. It is certainly welcome here in its
original context, but tends to overshadow the substantial
allegro that precedes it and the tiny one that follows
it...A significant release." [Columbia LC 3907, BC 1307]
See: D91a

B91i. Goodwin, Noël. "Samuel Barber." Times (London)
July 7, 1980, p. 13.
    "...in the String Quartet...where among other felici-
ties the playing of the Sinfonietta members even over-
weighted the controlled balance of the music's character
and gave listeners a rare chance to enjoy the celebrated
Adagio movement in its original scale and context."
See: W91h

B91j. Hall, David. "Classical." HIFI/Stereo Review
16:88+ (February 1966)
    "To those readers who have admired Barber's Adagio for
Strings it will be interesting to know that its original
version is included in the Quartet between the dramatic
first and last movements." [Epic BC 1307, LC 3907]
See: D91a

B91k. Harrison, Max. "Chamber Music." Gramophone
61:54 (June 1983)
    "Barber's only Quartet came...in 1936, and it is of

some interest to hear the famous Adagio in its original place (not that this is the first recording of the complete work). Small, conservatively romantic pieces that appeal strongly to those many who do not like what has happened to music during the present century, they will continue to attract listeners--who will find these new performances entirely sympathetic..." [Nonesuch/Conifer N 78017] See: D91e

B91l. Kolodin, Irving. "Recordings Reports II: Miscellaneous LPs." Saturday Review 44:48 (October 28, 1961)
"Whether or not Barber is the first American to have a work of this scope recorded in the Soviet Union, it is not easy to recall a predecessor. The Borodin ensemble performs the work with thorough comprehension as well as abundant technical resource, especially the slow movement." [Artia MK 1563] See: D91b

B91m. -----. "Recordings Reports II: Miscellaneous LPs." Saturday Review 48:92 (October 30, 1965)
"Barber's brief quartet (fifteen minutes) is known to some for its slow movement, which has become independently celebrated as the Adagio for Strings...In both the Diamond and Barber work, the group...displays a unanimity of sound and a disciplined intensity that puts them among the world's foremost interpreters of such music." [Epic 3907] See: D91a

B91n. Salzman, Eric. "Classical Discs and Tapes." Stereo Review 37:136 (November 1976)
"The Barber String Quartet is just the sort of Nice Nelly chamber music that Ives hated and, in fact, wrote his Second Quartet to satirize! Nevertheless, in some odd way, the two works harmonize in these excellent back to back Cleveland Quartet performances...In spite of the new-Romantic and quasi-baroque character of much of this music, there is a kind of modal hymn background that gives the quartet an underlying solidity Barber's work sometimes lacks." [RCA ARL 1 1599] See: D91d

B91o. Schonberg, Harold C. Chamber and Solo Instrument Music. New York: Knopf, 1955. (The Guide to Long-Playing Records, vol. 3) 280 p.
"The quartet is a conservative work in two movements, full of promise, and is well played by the Stradivari group." [p. 21] [Stradivari 602] See: D91g

B91p. Shupp, Enos E., Jr. "Chamber Music." New Records 33:8 (December 1965)
"The Barber work is a youthful and slender effort...although it is not second-rate music by any standards. The famous Adagio for Strings, familiar in string orchestra arrangement, first saw the light of day as the second movement of this quartet." [Epic LP 3907, BC 1307] See: D91a

B91q. Shupp, Enos E., Jr. "Chamber Music." New Records 44:6-7 (September 1976)

"The Barber Quartet, Op. 11, is not having its first recording, but is the sole entry in the current Schwann, so it will be a first chance for many persons to hear the original version and the entire work from which the famous Adagio for Strings is transcribed. The two-movement quartet is an enjoyable work, conventional and always melodious. It is in two movements, although the Adagio (second) closes with a return to the first movement subject to give it a strong conclusion." [Victor ARL 1 1599] See: D91d

B91r. Simmons, Walter. "Classical Recordings." Fanfare 6:92 (May/June 1983)

"In both form and substance, the work is one of the most essentially romantic string quartets ever written, relying almost exclusively on the intrinsic beauty of its musical material and on the effectiveness of its discursive impulses...This Concord performance is superior to any I have ever heard..." [Nonesuch 78017] See: D91e

B91s. Smith, Moses. "Bowdoin College Series." Modern Music 16:262 (May-June 1939)

"...played by the Curtis String Quartet, which also did duty by Samuel Barber's suave sonorities and platitudes in his B-minor Quartet..."

B91t. "Some Chamber Works." American Record Guide 18:107 (December 1951)

"Barber's early quartet does not have as strong a profile as some of his later music, but there is a seriousness of purpose in its lyrical romantic writing which commands respect." [Stradivari STR 602] See: D91g

B91u. Taubman, Howard. "Samuel Barber Work Heard." New York Times, March 16, 1938, p. 20.

"Although Mr. Barber's composition has been played in this country and abroad, this was the first time that it came within the local reviewer's orbit. It should not be the last. For here is a score that deserves to be heard again, whatever its shortcomings. In the main, it combines sincerity of purpose, freshness of feeling and a capacity to realize new ideas. There is no need to expect a masterpiece to issue full-fledged from the brain of a young composer. It does not even matter if the composer never writes a masterpiece at all. It should be enough if his talents are well above the average, if he has something to say and if he is trying to say it in his own way. Mr. Barber's quartet indicated that he meets these requirements. Every element of this quartet is not of equal merit, but that is only natural. The Curtis ensemble..gave Mr. Barber's score an integrated, carefully wrought performance." See: W91d

B92. SUMMER MUSIC, OP. 31.

B92a. Bassett, Leslie. "Samuel Barber." <u>Notes</u> 15:148-
149 (December 1957)
    "<u>Summer Music</u> will find a secure place in the reper-
toires of woodwind quintets possessing mature technical and
interpretive ability. It is a sonorous and attractive work
in one movement containing a variety of sections of dif-
fering tempo and mood. Although the form is balanced by
the return of earlier passages, the work has a rhapsodic
quality and admirable freedom. The style is fresh, though
far from radical, similar to several of Barber's better-
known works in nostalgic vein." <u>See</u>: W92

    B92b. Bookspan, Martin. "Collections." <u>HIFI/Stereo
Review</u> 4:99 (March 1960)
    "Barber's work is a pleasant diversion, easy to take
and lastingly effective." [ConcertDisc CS 216] <u>See</u>: D92b

    B92c. Cohn, Arthur. "Four Works For Wind Instruments."
<u>American Record Guide</u> 26:714-715 (May 1960)
    "Barber's work is music of craftsmanship, but it is
less than acutely creative. The substratum of composers,
good ones at that, is the coterie of the eclectic. Barber
illustrates the codification of this opus. Diplomatically
composed music is a desirable commodity. Here it is. I
damn myself willingly, by asserting that the symphonies of
Joachim Raff also obtained (once upon a time) wide hearing.
'Better to be now than never' is an argument I cannot
discount, however. Nor can I the brilliant rendition heard
on this recording." [Columbia MS 6114] <u>See</u>: D92f

    B92d. Daniel, Oliver. "Bloch, Ben-Haim, Barber and
Dahl." <u>Saturday Review</u> 42:44 (December 12, 1959)
    "Barber's diatonic lyricism is a soothing contrast to
the more naughty world of many of his dodecaphonic con-
freres." [ConcertDisc CS 216] <u>See</u>: D92d

    B92e. Frankenstein, Alfred. "Classical." <u>High Fideli-
ty</u> 10:68 (January 1960)
    "The <u>Summer Music</u> of Samuel Barber is a pleasantly
impressionistic piece that provides an excellent foil to
the other...works." [ConcertDisc CS 216] <u>See</u>: D92d

    B92f. Goodwin, Noël. "Samuel Barber." <u>Times</u> (London)
July 7, 1980, p. 13.
    "The wind instruments began it with a refreshingly
cool account of the <u>Summer Music</u> of 1956, in which the span
of a single movement encompasses an intricately-worked
texture expressive of actual or remembered feelings that
are no less valid because the emotion is easily shared."
<u>See</u>: W92k

    B92g. Hall, David. "Classical." <u>HIFI/Stereo Review</u>
4:65 (May 1960)

"Samuel Barber's _Summer Music_ (1956) sounds curiously bitter-sweet after the idyllic sounds and open texture of Carl Nielsen; but it is a no less masterly piece of writing for all that, albeit a minor addition to the Barber catalog." [Columbia MS 6114] _See_: D92f

B92h. Kolodin, Irving. "Recordings Report II: Miscellaneous LPs." _Saturday Review_ 43:52 (March 26, 1960)
"Here is the rare and most rewarding of recorded experiences--two unfamiliar works of almost equal quality, performed in flawless manner by men who are as good artists as they are technicians. As their names (Robert Cole, flute; Anthony Gigliotti, clarinet; Mason Jones, horn; Sol Schoenbach, bassoon; and John de Lancie, oboe) will suggest, they are all members of the Philadelphia Orchestra. Barber's fanciful beautifully written work (a Detroit commission in 1956) fuses his best qualities--melodic invention and contrapuntal dexterity--with binding instrumental texture." [Columbia MS 6114] _See_: D92f

B92i. M., R. "Notable Pleasures." _Times_ (London) October 16, 1968, p. 16.
"It was the Samuel Barber which gave the most substantial pleasure. Its lyrical abundance sensitively adapted to the expressive potential of each instrument." _See_: W92h

B92j. McV., D. "Music for June Evening." _Times_ (London) June 10, 1967, p. 9.
"The concert had begun with a wind quintet formed from the orchestra in Barber's _Summer Music_, garrulous but agreeable..." _See_: W92h

B92k. Morgan, Robert P. "Recitals and Miscellany." _High Fidelity_ 27:110 (December 1977)
"It seems characteristic of the 1950's that of the two works included from that decade, one points forward while the other looks backward. The latter is Barber's beautiful _Summer Music_ (1957), a highly virtuosic vehicle that is even more traditional in tonal orientation and more sectional in structure than the Fine and Berger...the Barber is bathed in a warm and intensely lyrical romanticism." [Vox SVBX 5307] _See_: D92b

B92l. Noble, Jeremy. "Orchestral." _Gramophone_ 41:420 (March 1964)
"His _Summer Music_ as one might expect is a charming, unashamedly reactionary piece, beautifully written; for my taste it goes on rather too long." [Saga XIP 7009] _See_: D92e

B92m. O., W. A. "Chamber Music." _New Records_ 28:7 (April 1960)
"It is quite relaxing music, well performed by the stellar musicians of the Philadelphia Woodwind Quintet." [Columbia ML 5441, MS 6114] _See_: D92f

B92n. "Reviews of New Music." Musical Opinion 80:599 (July 1957)
"This is undoubtedly one of Barber's finest works. It is a pity that its difficulty will preclude frequent performance--but then, there are always gramophone records." See: W92

B92o. Salzman, Eric. "Records: Sessions' First at Last." New York Times, June 19, 1960, sect. 2, p. 16.
"Summer Music, op. 31, is one of his most charming works and the elegance of this pleasant idiomatic music is captured by the performers, who are all members of the Philadelphia Orchestra." [Columbia ML 5441, MS 6114] See: D92f

B92p. -----. "Three Works of Ben Weber on LP." New York Times, December 13, 1959, sect. 2, p. 18.
"The Barber is a conservative, pleasant piece, the length of which and changes of character seem capricious." [Concert-Disc CM 1216, CS 216] See: D92d

B92q. Schonberg, Harold C. "2 Premieres Mark Woodwind Concert." New York Times, November 17, 1956, p. 17.
"Mr. Barber's new work was attractive, quite romantic in conception and tuneful throughout. Much of it sounded like a nocturne for wind quintet, and in some spots there even were suggestions of Grieg. But a few clever rhythmic shifts and sharp-sounding harmonics reminded the listener that the music was very much of our day...They [New York Woodwind Quintet] are a dependable group of musicians, seriously engaged in exploring a rather neglected segment of the repertory." See: W92b

B92r. "20th Century American Music for Woodwind quintet" [album notes for Vox SVBX 5307 disc]
"Though Barber is most often identified with string music, in his Summer Music for Woodwind Quintet (1957) he reveals a unique insight into the special qualities of winds, and he writes intricate and elegant music of careful design. The Summer Music suggests an outdoor atmosphere, but it is highly sophisticated entertainment music, full of rhythmical complexity, and demands alternating shifts of mood and tempo." See: D92b

SOLO INSTRUMENTAL MUSIC

B93. BALLADE, OP. 46.

B93a. Carter, Susan Bindermann. The Piano Music of Samuel Barber. Thesis (Ph.D.)--Texas Tech University, Lubbock, Texas, 1980. 188 p.

"...the _Ballade_ is a ternary structure with the outer homophonic sections framing a more contrapuntal and dramatic middle section. This piece reveals a return to Barber's more conservative approach, similar to his earlier compositions." [p. 164] _See_: W93

B93b. Chissell, Joan. "Steve Mayer." _Times_ (London), November 2, 1977, p. 12.
"From America he brought a _Ballade_, op. 46, by Samuel Barber, hitherto unperformed in England...[It] sounded more neo-Romantic then[sic] new. But it was true piano music and immediately communicative." _See_: W93b

B93c. Dommett, Kenneth. "The Piano Music of Samuel Barber" [album notes for Hyperion A 66016 disc]
"Thematic evolution rather than classical development is a feature of Barber's handling of small forms and is the structural 'cement' of the..._Ballade_." _See_: D93b

B93d. Harrison, Max. "Instrumental." _Gramophone_ 58:1212 (March 1981)
"The _Ballade_ is a piece about which I have never been able to make up my mind. It is the most recent item here, dating from 1977, and composed for the Fifth Van Cliburn International Quadrennial Piano Competition. Miss Brownridge plays the quiet opening passage, which recurs, with delicacy and perception, and can well contain the problems of the _Allegro con fuoco_." [Hyperion A66016] _See_: D93b

B93e. Poole, Geoffrey. "Music Review." _Musical Times_ 121:713 (November 1980)
"When piano music is not written for children the stimulus is often a piano competition, as was the case with the _Ballade_ by Samuel Barber, in his most approachable vein (American Delius)." _See_: W93

B93f. Sifferman, James Philip. "Samuel Barber's Works for Solo Piano." Thesis (D.M.A.)--University of Texas at Austin, 1982. 129 p.
"The title _Ballade_ harks back to the 19th century like Barber's _Nocturne_, but its musical characteristics display stylistic features more in common with the so-called impressionistic music of Debussy and Ravel than with the earlier tradition of Chopin or Brahms." [p. 95] _See_: W93

B94. EXCURSIONS, OP. 20.

B94a. A., R. "Piano." _Musical Times_ 91:357-358 (September 1950)
"Consisting of involved rhythms characterized by regional American idioms and suggesting 'local' instruments, they are certainly fascinating. Only a fine pianist could tackle these with any success." _See_: W94

B94b. "André Previn" [album notes for Columbia ML 5639 disc]
"Unlike the majority of twentieth century American composers, Barber owes little or nothing to American folk idiom for the development of his style. It is all the more surprising to find him using this idiom with such adeptness in Excursions." See: D94g

B94c. B., J. "Darson Presents Recital for Piano." New York Times, November 18, 1956, p. 86.
"Mr. [Thomas] Darson displayed his dexterity...in Samuel Barber's Excursions, op. 20." See: W94g

B94d. Berger, Arthur. "Scores and Records." Modern Music 22:267 (May-June 1945)
"Samuel Barber's Excursions (G. Schirmer) also deals with the colloquial, but North American brand. Barber has set down separately in his four pieces a few familiar banjo or guitar devices, the blues, something resembling anti-macasar pianism with a theme that might also be Calypso, and finally, some very slick harmonica playing...Though Barber has integrated the elements of each style, they have undergone too little transformation. There is no dissection; the primitive, static harmony is uncritically preserved." See: W94

B94e. Carter, Susan Blindermann. The Piano Music of Samuel Barber. Thesis (Ph.D.)--Texas Tech University, Lubbock, Texas, 1980. 188 p.
"Each piece is a stylized setting of a popular American folk idiom. The opening piece is a boogie-woogie; the second, a blues piece; the third, a set of variations on a cowboy song; the last a barn dance [p. 32]...As Barber's sole example of stylized folk idioms, Excursions occupies a unique position among his piano works." [p.49] See: W94

B94f. Cohn, Arthur. Recorded Classical Music. New York: Schirmer Books, 1981. 2164 p.
"Barber's set of investigations are American in spirit, with a desire to express dance color, dance design, dance freedom. And they do this well." [p. 99] See: W94

B94g. Downes, Olin. "Horowitz Offers Czerny Variations." New York Times, March 29, 1945, p. 18.
"A contemporary quality was furnished by the modernity and humor of the three felicitous pieces, Excursions, by Samuel Barber." See: W94c

B94h. Frankenstein, Alfred. "Classical." High Fidelity 11:57 (August 1961)
"Barber's Excursions are extremely clever studies in American folklore--boogie-woogie, blues, ballad and barn dance...The recording throughout is superb. All in all, one of the most distinguished piano records of the year." [Columbia ML 5639, MS 6239] See: D94g

342

B94i. Harrison, Max. "Instrumental." Gramophone 58:1212 (March 1981)

"Most attractive are the Excursions, and I suspect that these short pieces may prove more durable than some of Barber's other works. They evoke idioms of popular deriva-tion...Miss Brownridge plays excellently, but she does not, I think, have enough contact with the original styles to do an entirely convincing job." [Hyperion A 66016] See: D94c

B94j. Henahan, Donal. "Pleasant Pianism From Zola Shaulis." New York Times, January 19, 1974, p. 21.

"...admirable in many ways, though also somewhat colorless, was the pianist's performance of Barber's Excur-sions. This is Barber in a witty, semi-popular mood, and Miss [Zola] Shaulis took a terribly somber view of the matter." See: W94o

B94k. Kisselgoff, Anna. "Dance: Premiere of Feld Ex-cursions." New York Times, October 20, 1975, p. 45.

"The Eliot Feld Ballet has a hit on its hands. 'Ex-cursions,' a whiz of a ballet that will take your breath away, is presumably Mr. Feld's contribution to the Bicen-tennial season, and at its premiere Saturday night, Mr. Feld fired the shot that will be heard 'round the dance world. 'Excursions,' set to Samuel Barber's piano music of the same title, is an outstanding and sparkling work. There was something properly exuberant about the way Mr. Feld coaxed Mr. Barber onstage at the premiere to share the bows at the Newman Theater...Mr. Barber's 1944 cycle of four piano pieces...and its vibrant mood of open frontier optimism has been captured most cogently by the choreo-grapher." See: W94p

B94l. Lowens, Irving. "Recitals and Miscellany." High Fidelity 27:115 (March 1977)

"...Neatly shaped performance." [Orion ORS 76237] See: D94b

B94m. "Record Supplement for May, 1951." Gramophone Shop. Record Supplement 14:1-2 (May 1951)

"...Rudolf Firkusny gives a tonally splendid perform-ance of Four EXcursions, a group of short piano pieces based on regional American folk material." [Columbia ML 2174] See: D94d

B94n. Richie, Donald. "Voice." American Record Guide 17:280 (April 1951)

"The composer has called his four piano pieces 'excur-sions in small classical forms into regional American idioms.' The fourth has been recorded before (in Vox Album 174, withdrawn) but together, they seem to have more meaning. This may, however, be due to the extremely polished performance by Firkusny, whom Columbia has favored

with a very life-like recording." [Columbia ML 2174] <u>See</u>:
D94

B94o. Schonberg, Harold C. <u>Chamber</u> <u>and</u> <u>Solo</u> <u>Instrument</u>
<u>Music</u>. New York: Knopf, 1955. (The Guide to Long-Playing
Records, vol. 3) 280 p.
   "Pleasant, idiomatic piano pieces that achieved a
short vogue several years ago." [p. 21] [Columbia ML 2174
(10 inch)] <u>See</u>: D94d

B94p. Sifferman, James Philip. <u>Samuel</u> <u>Barber's</u> <u>Works</u>
<u>for</u> <u>Solo</u> <u>Piano</u>. Thesis (D.M.A.)--University of Texas at
Austin, 1982. 129 p.
   "While Barber refers to the four pieces as being in
'classical forms,' they are freely so. Not one of them can
be 'pigeon-holed' as being strictly a rondo, variation,
sonata, or some other traditional form. It is the use of
American folk and popular idioms which form the point of
interest in each piece." [p. 5] <u>See</u>: W94

B94q. Straus, Noel. "Firkusny Scores in Piano Pro-
gram." <u>New</u> <u>York</u> <u>Times</u>, January 19, 1946, p. 19.
   "Of the three [<u>sic</u>, four] numbers making up Mr. Barber's <u>Excursions</u>, the 'Honkey-tonk,' 'Blues,' and 'Calypso'
were played. The 'Calypso' is the most praiseworthy of
these exacting experiments with folk material, and the most
difficult. Mr. Firkusny made light of its formidable combination of rhythms in a performance as expert as those
meted out to Debussy's atmospherically treated <u>Terrance des</u>
<u>Audiences</u>." <u>See</u>: W94d

B94r. "Vocal." <u>New</u> <u>Records</u> 19:13 (May 1951)
   "<u>Four</u> <u>Excursions</u>, which bears no further title by way
of explanation, are evidently Mr. Barber's impressions of
journeys into the folkways of America. Regional characteristics are skillfully employed in these novel piano
pieces." [Columbia ML 2174] <u>See</u>: D94d

B97. NOCTURNE: HOMAGE TO JOHN FIELD, OP. 33.

B97a. C., O. J. "Penelope Spurrel." <u>Times</u> (London),
September 30, 1968, p. 7.
   "She was sensitive in phrasing and tone in a Nocturne
by Barber." <u>See</u>: W97b

B97b. Carter, Susan Blindermann. <u>The</u> <u>Piano</u> <u>Music</u> <u>of</u>
<u>Samuel</u> <u>Barber</u>. Thesis (Ph.D.)--Texas Tech University, Lub-
bock, Texas, 1980. 188p.
   "While Barber's <u>Nocturne</u> is an homage to Field, the
dedication appears to pay tribute to Fields as the origi-
nator of the form, but is actually more influenced by
Chopin...Barber preserves the form and character of the
nineteenth-century nocturne, but employs contemporary harmonies and procedures. [p. 102] In the <u>Nocturne</u> Barber

achieves a synthesis of tonality and serialism. In addition, he has successfully combined his characteristic lyrical style with twelve-tone writing. The very title and
its dedication to John Field, reflects Barber's romantic
approach to composition." [p. 106-107] See: W97

B97c. Dommett, Kenneth. "The Piano Music of Samuel
Barber" [album notes for Hyperion A 66016 disc]
     "Barber's ability to compress much into a small com-
pass is most evident in the Nocturne, which John Browning
introduced in 1959. In strict ABA form and about forty
bars long with a cadenza linking the middle section to the
reprise of the first, the piece pays tribute to the Irish
inventor of the Nocturne in virtuoso writing which explores
the entire range of the instrument." See: D97b

B97d. Garvelmann, Donald. "A Good Survey--But Flawed."
American Record Guide 40:9 (May 1977)
     "It is good to hear Barber's homage to John Field, his
Nocturne, so nicely spun-out." [Vox Box SVBX 5303] See:
D97f

B97e. Harrison, Max. "Instrumental." Gramophone
58:1212 (March 1981)
     "Barber's Nocturne is a...stylistic exercise, though
in a manner of early Chopin, rather than John Field to
whom, it ostensibly renders homage." [Hyperion A 66016]
See: D97b

B97f. -----. "Instrumental." Grampohone 60:597 (November 1982)
     "The Nocturne receives sensitive handling also,
though, as I have said before in these pages, it is little
more than a stylistic exercise, and in the manner of early
Chopin, rather than Field." [Nonesuch Digital D 79032]
See: D97e

B97g. Kozinn, Allan. "Samuel Barber" [album notes for
Nonesuch Digital D 79032 disc]
     "Like a Field nocturne, Barber's boasts a freely
rhapsodic melody in the right hand, while the left hand
provides a simple, steady accompaniment. Here again, Barber plays at 12-tone writing in the melody departing from
his tone rows where he sees fit. The bass line outlines a
chordal progression that becomes increasingly chromatic in
the middle section, and then after a short cadenza, returns
to its more subdued and diatonic form for the reprise of
the opening section." See: D97e

B97h. Sifferman, James Philip. Samuel Barber's Works
for Solo Piano. Thesis (D.M.A.)--University of Texas at
Austin, 1982. 129 p.
     "...certain features of Barber's Nocturne bear greater
resemblance to Chopin's nocturnes than to those of Field.
Perhaps Barber's dedication was simply meant to acknowledge

John Field as the 'father' of the genre." [p. 89] See: W97

B98. PIANO SONATA, OP. 26.

B98a. A., R. "Piano." Musical Times 91:357-358 (September 1950)
"...a sonata which displays the influence of Hindemith. Apart from this there are many passages of scintillating beauty, notably in the second movement, which bear the stamp of a real personality. Three staves are frequently used, indeed one feels that in places four hands would be more effective than two. A fine Fugue (the inevitable Hindemith touch) concludes a work of distinction that only the rare pianist of intellect, and complete technical efficiency, could essay." See: W98

B98b. Aikin, Jim. "Records." Keyboard Magazine 7:64 (August 1981)
"Barber was not a prolific piano composer—this record contains all four of his solo piano pieces...In the Ballade and the Sonata in particular, his ability to weave extraordinary bitonal and dissonant chords into straight forward romantic texture creates music of wonderful color and depth...Brownridge's playing is expressive and perfectly balanced, and the result is a memorable recording." [Hyperion A 66016] See: D98b

B98c. Ardoin, John. "Recitals in New York." Musical America 80:20 (January 1, 1960)
"While her playing was always in good taste, Miss [Zita] Carno reflected little of the Sonata's bigness or moody character. Still, there was no doubt that an important talent had come to public attention at this recital." See: W98bb

B98d. -----. "Van Cliburn." Musical America 83:38 (November 1963)
"The outer movements of the Barber though pressed, worked well, but the rubatos in the scherzo were downright willful." See: W98jj

B98e. Arlen, Walter. "Young Pianist Plays With Taste, Authority." Los Angeles Times, January 20, 1958, pt. 4, p. 11.
"...everyone was much taken with it, and rightly so, for it is not only a formidable pianistic vehicle...but also a composition of great musical merit. Barber here is at his most dissonant and always logical...The music...communicates readily, in spite of its unfamiliar idiom." [Performance by John Browning] See: W98v

B98f. B., J. "Doppmann Heard in Piano Program." New York Times, October 6, 1954, p. 36.

"William Doppmann...distinguished himself by winning both the Walter W. Naumburg Musical Foundation Award and the Michaels Memorial Award. Since both these awards are sought by the very finest of the nation's young musicians, Mr. Doppmann's first appearance promised to be something out of the ordinary. It was...Even in an age that takes technical fluency almost for granted at a recital debut, the young pianist has unusual speed and accuracy." See: W98n

B98g. B., J. "Magaloff, Pianist Presents Recital." New York Times November 24, 1953, p. 35.
    "Mr. Magaloff performed the work with a dexterity that easily surmounted its bristling technical difficulties, and with a fine sympathetic understanding of its poetical essence." See: W98l

B98h. ------. "Music: Double Opera Bill in Village." New York Times, December 5, 1956, p. 50.
    "His powers as a technician were demonstrated from the beginning of the program, and established beyond question by his performance of the Samuel Barber Piano Sonata, Op. 26. This formidable work, written for and first performed by Vladimir Horowitz, calls for virtuosity of a transcendental sort. Last night Mr. Pollack performed it with seeming ease. The brilliance and lucidity of the young artist's playing, especially in the final movement, which bristles with technical and musical difficulties, was little short of astounding." See: W98p

B98i. Bloch, Joseph. "Some American Piano Sonatas." Juilliard Review 3:9-14 (Fall 1956)
    "The Barber surely belongs in the first rank of twentieth century sonatas; it is a superb piece from any point of view, the pianist's, the composer's, or the audience, with advanced, but not insurmountable problems for all three." See: W98

B98j. Briefer, Charles. "Marjorie Mitchell" [album notes for Decca 710 136 disc]
    "Barber is basically a romantic, but a high-strung one. No matter how broad a melody he spins, there is an underlying tension--a continuous ferment." See: D98q

B98k. Broder, Nathan. "Current Chronicle: New York." Musical Quarterly 36:276-279 (April 1950)
    "Samuel Barber's Piano Sonata...represents Barber's final emancipation from the neo-Romantic traits that dominated his early compositions and is thus the cumulation of a development that has taken a decade to reach its goal...the work is emotionally profounder than many of his earlier pieces and technically farther advanced than any of them. Its grand sweep, its largeness of utterance, reminds this listener of Beethoven, and its intensity made him think of Bartok. It is the first work of Barber's that

347

employs 12-tone writing, of which there is some in the
first movement and a good deal more in the third. While
the texture is almost entirely chromatic and dissonant, the
themes are sharply defined and stand out clearly." [drawn
from a Horowitz performance review] See: W98, W98c

B98l. Carlson, Tom. "Samuel Barber" [album notes for
Mace MXX 9085 disc]
"As a whole, the Sonata demonstrates an exultant mastery
of piano composition in the modern idiom, with its elements
of 12-tone harmonics and uses of chromaticism, and is
increasingly becoming a staple in the repertories of many
of today's pianists." See: D98f

B98m. Carter, Susan Blindermann. The Piano Music of
Samuel Barber. Thesis (Ph.D.)--Texas Tech University,
Lubbock, Texas, 1980. 188 p.
"The dramatic change in Barber's style is displayed in
this particular composition by a more complex texture,
dissonant harmony, rhythmic innovations and his first use
of twelve-tone serialism." See: W98

B98n. Chittum, Donald. "The Synthesis of Materials and
Devices in Non-serial Counterpoint." Music Review 31:123-
135 (May 1970)
A structural analysis and comparison of the fugue
section in Barber's Piano Sonata and Bartok's Music for
String, Percussion and Celesta. "To sum up, then, the
devices used throughout the fugue are suggested in the
exposition or earlier in the fugue. The subject suggests
certain structural ideas which influence melody and thematic treatment, contrapuntal intervals, chordal structure
and progression, the pitches of imitations and stretti, and
overall tonal relations. Thus the absence of harmonic
tonality is, to some extent, counterbalanced through a
greater synthesis of various dimensions of the development
and organization." See: W98

B98o. Cohn, Arthur. Recorded Classical Music. New
York: Schirmer Books, 1981. 2164 p.
"Traditional forms, but containing controlled twentieth-century temper. There is a key center (E flat
minor), but aesthetic freedom allows Barber to dip into
twelve-tone waters, a bit in the dramatic and energetic
opening movement and much more in the emotive and dark-
toned Adagio mesto. The Scherzo is snide and seems to be
program music without a program. A virtuosic Fugue completes the work, a polyphonic product that Poulenc indicated 'knocks you out [vous met knock-out] in some five
minutes." [p. 100] See: W98

B98p. Davis, Peter G. "John Browning on Piano is a
Model of Orderliness." New York Times, February 3, 1975,
p. 32.
"Mr. Browning's playing was a model of orderliness

too. Not a note seemed out of place, all the composers'
dynamic instructions were duly observed and tempo relationships made perfect sense. As an example of modest self-
effacingly objective music-making, this recital set some
rare standards." See: W98vv

B98q. Diether, Jack. "Howard Aibel." Musical America
79:31 (December 1, 1959)
"Mr. Aibel gave an impression of clarity and cohesiveness, stressing the sturdy structural elements and etching
the principal lines unforgettably." See: W98z

B98r. Dommett, Kenneth. "The Piano Music of Samuel
Barber" [album notes for Hyperion A 66016 disc]
"If evidence were needed that Barber could write contemporary virtuoso music of an essentially lyrical nature,
the Sonata provides it...The work has been described as a
'virtuoso paradise,' but it is more than that. In it
technique has been employed solely for musical ends, and
the result is a rare achievement, a modern American piano
sonata that has won a place in the international repertoire." See: D98b

B98s. Downes, Olin. "Goldsand Offers Program on
Piano." New York Times, November 26, 1952, p. 20.
"For Barber's Sonata, which is not only a contempora-
neous work of exceptional interest, but a tour de force for
the virtuoso, he had all necessary resources at his command. This sonata is no affectation of modernism, but the
natural language of modern music--or one of its phases--
and a language used readily and commandingly by a young
American of today. One has, however, a question in mind
about this very interesting work. Is its second movement,
the lightest of the four, really necessary? The same
sonata in three movements, with the present scherzo omitted, would be ideal in length and completely coherent and
consistent in its structure." See: W98j

B98t. -----. "Horowitz Offers Barber's Sonata." New
York Times, January 24, 1950, p. 27.
"This sonata, between the quality of the performance
and the quality of the music, had also a prodigious
success. It makes on initial acquaintance a very striking
impression...We consider it the first sonata really to come
of age by an American composer of this period. It has
intense feeling as well as constructive power and intellectual maturity. It is stated naturally and convincingly in
the language of modern music..." See: W98c

B98u. Epstein, Benjamin. "Laredo at Wadsworth Theatre." Los Angeles Times, October 11, 1983, pt. 6, p. 6.
"The Sonata has long been a staple of the Laredo
repertory; she played it for Barber himself in her graduation recital at the Curtis Institute on March 9, 1960, the
composer's 50th birthday. Her approach to the work almost

a quarter-century later is an eloquent one, emphasizing the lyric rather than the electric, a warm sensuality rather than no-holds barred virtuosity--which does not by any means imply that there were not many gripping moments on a merely digital level." See: W98bbb

B98v. Frankenstein, Alfred. "Classical." High Fidelity 11:72 (January 1961)
"When a Sviatoslav Richter comes to the United States you expect the American recording firms to record him the minute he lands, but you do not expect American pianists in Russia to be recorded in that country. That, however, is what happened here...His [Daniel Pollock] performances of all three sonatas are very brilliant, but the tinny recording makes them sound shallow. So interesting a departure deserves better luck, mechanically speaking." [MK-Artia 1513] See: D98t

B98w. Friedewald, Russell Edward. A Formal and Stylistic Analysis of the Published Music of Samuel Barber. Thesis (Ph.D.)--Iowa State University, 1957. 357 p.
"The work is emotionally more profound than many of Barber's early works and technically farther advanced. [p. 133] It is the first work of Barber's in which twelve-tone series are worked into the texture. [p. 134] Barber gives his sonata unity by the transfer of motives from the preceding movements and by returning in the finale to the tonality of the opening movement." [p. 155] See: W98

B98x. G., H. "Daniel Pollack." Musical Courier 155:15 (January 1, 1957)
"Mr. Pollack is emotionally too detached. In the mammoth Barber Sonata...where interpretive passion is necessary to keep the work from sounding like an endless succession of thundering tonal masses, this fault was most noticeable." See: W98p

B98y. Garvelmann, Donald. "A Good Survey--But Flawed." American Record Guide 40:9 (May 1977)
"And to give us only single movements from the Charles Ives and Samuel Barber Piano Sonatas is ill-advised, since this deprives us of hearing these movements in the intended context of their wholes. Besides, why whet the listener's appetite in this way, especially when there are already available several excellent complete recordings of these sonatas?" [Vox Box SVBX 5303] See: D98v

B98z. Gerber, Leslie. "Cliburn: Supple, Virile, Prokofievian Barber (and Prokofiev, Too)." American Record Guide 38:355 (April 1972)
"Much of the same success attaches to the Barber Sonata in which Cliburn tempers by his suppleness of tone an essentially outgoing, virile approach to this most Prokofievian music...As for Horowitz, I must admit that he clangs more clangorously than Cliburn...but not being sub-

ject to the Horowitz charisma I must commit the heresy of preferring Cliburn's playing for its wider dynamic and emotional range. Although alternate performances of either work offer other virtues, this recording is certainly a distinguished addition to the too-small discography of major contemporary piano works in successful performances by major pianists." [RCA LSC 3229] See: D98e

B98aa. Goldsmith, Harris. "Recitals and Miscellany." High Fidelity 13:145 (October 1963)
"Barber's Sonata was new in 1958 when Horowitz premiered it and made the present recording. Now, it turns up on just about every debut recital. In my opinion the piece is basically synthetic, but Horowitz's masterful account of it is fraught with true pianistic voltage." [RCA Victor LD 7021] See: D98i

B98bb. H., C. "Lympany, Pianist, Heard in Recital." New York Times, October 9, 1951, p. 32.
"And there were wonderful moments, too, in Samuel Barber's Sonata, Op. 26...particularly in the brief, feathery second movement. But this work was not for Miss Lympany, at least not on this occasion. Its first and last movements produced rather shapeless complexes of sound in the middle register, with sharp punctuations high and low and the pianist could not bring the slow section into focus. Without hearing this composition elsewhere, one hesitates to fix blame on the performance, but it might be a better piece than it sounded last night." See: W98h

B98cc. Haberkorn, Michael H. A Study and Performance of the Piano Sonatas of Samuel Barber, Elliott Carter and Aaron Copland. Thesis (Ed.D.)--Columbia University Teachers' College, New York, New York, 1979. 122 p.
"Examination of the Barber Sonata for Piano, Op. 26 discloses a design which is sympathetic to the Classical period's four movement organization...While the sonata employs meter signatures, they are altered with each movement in the context of heightened expressivity...The sonata is traditionally key oriented, but utilizing the chromatic idiom of the turn of the century along with dissonances of more recent development." [p. 114] See: W98

B98dd. Hall, David. "Classics." HIFI/Stereo Review 6:62 (February 1961)
"In terms of Barber's own development as a composer, his piano sonata combines the most significant aspects of his romantic, intellectual and the Americanist expressions, via a granite first movement, a feather-light Scherzo, an intense Adagio and a fantastically virtuosic fugue." [Artia MK 1513] See: D98t

B98ee. Hamburger, Paul. "Concerts." Music Survey 3:200 (March 1951)
A review of the first performance in Great Britain by

Robert Wallenborn. "I believe Barber's compositional con-
science--a strong conscience I should say--is satisfied the
moment he had found a workable plan for the distribution of
his material. But this is too soon: a sonata is not built
for efficiency, even if this be the efficiency of form at
its most abstract. The second step, namely the mutual
penetration of form and material, a process both unique and
defiant of established rules in every new movement every
written--this step is not taken by Barber. This becomes
specially clear at those places where Barber thinks he
knows where he is and what he is about, i.e. when his
formalistic conscience has been satisfied...Over his self-
righteousness he goes comfortably to sleep--although that
doesn't stop him writing brilliant piano passages." See:
W98f

   B98ff. Harrison, Max. "Instrumental." Gramophone
53:1221 (January 1976)
     "Despite the sub-Schoenbergian chromaticism (which
matches the sub-Stravinskian textures of the earlier Capricorn Concerto), it soon becomes apparent, if this work is
set besides the equivalent pieces of Ives, Griffes, Copland, Sessions and Carter, that all we have here is old
wine in an old bottle. In fact, Barber's usual middlebrow
romanticism prevails, and...it is discouraging that this
does not prevent Horowitz from playing the work for all it
is worth--indeed, for rather more than that." [RCA Victrola
VH 1014] See: D98l

   B98gg. -----. "Instrumental." Gramophone 58:859
(December 1980)
     "Terence Judd was obviously destined to be one of the
greatest pianists of his generation and his death at 22 was
a tragedy...It is a long way from Haydn to Balakirev and a
great deal further from Liszt or Ravel to Samuel Barber or
Ginastera, but the interpretative range demonstrated here
is remarkable for one so young, however great his purely
technical accomplishment." [Chandos DBR 3001] See: D98n

   B98hh. -----. "Instrumental." Gramophone 58:1212
(March 1981)
     "It has always seemed to me that this piece is pianis-
tically rather more trouble to play than it is worth musically, and can best be justified by a transcendental interpretation like that heard on RCA [Horowitz]." [Hyperion A
66016] See: D98b

   B98ii. Hebble, Robert. "Joseph Battista." Musical
Courier 157:18 (January 1, 1958)
     "By the time he came to the Samuel Barber Sonata...he
had really warmed up to the pitch of this giant of contemporary piano literature. Battista's powerful technique and
authority made this rendition of Barber's sinuous score a
great treat to hear. Only the delicate allegro vivace was

perhaps a bit over-played for its scherzo-like quality."
See: W98t

B98jj. Henahan, Donal. "Barber's Piano Sonata Revis-
ited--Cliburn and Browning vs. Horowitz." High Fidelity
22:83 (January 1972)
    "Cliburn's Barber, more nearly than Browning's, fits
the Horowitz mold. He solves the complications of the
fugue particularly well. RCA's piano sound (and Cliburn's,
of course) is rich at bottom and evenly distributed all the
way up, losing out only at the top octave where the best
piano recordings take on overtones of sheen and shimmer.
Cliburn, like Browning, takes off some of the aggressively
brittle edge that Horowitz gives the score, looking for
lyrical curves to balance the percussive dryness that per-
meates so much of the sonata... Browning takes an unusually gentle and expansive approach broadening phrases sensitively and lingering over favored details. He also whips
up an aptly Prokofievian excitement in the third movement, and takes a cue from a quotation in the finale to
turn Barber's Prokofiev mask around and show us the face of
Gershwin on the other side. There is a flash of recognition here that lets us hear how strikingly similar are
these two apparently different American composers, how
alike in their blending of tough and tender, their angular
line, their harmonic bite." [RCA LSC 3229, Desto 7120]
See: D98c, D98e

B98kk. -----. "The Keyboard Cult of Mother Piano."
New York Times, February 6, 1972, sect. 2, p. 32.
    "John Browning takes a somewhat relaxed, though still
properly high-tensioned approach, and his disc would be
completely recommendable except for tinny sound and an-
noying background noise...Van Cliburn gives the Barber
Piano Sonata a glittering, muscular performance, not quite
so probing as Browning's, but full of excitement. Cliburn's piano sound is much superior." [Desto 7120, RCA LSC
3229] See: D98c, D98e

B98ll. "The Horowitz Collection" [album notes for RCA
ARM 1 2952 disc]
    "Any fugue today may be looked upon with suspicion as
an outmoded form, quite inappropriate for the expression of
the modern scene. But the fugue in this sonata, though it
dazzles the listener as a brilliant and intricate tour de
force, is more than a sensational essay. It comes as a
logical climax to the emotions generated and exploited in
the preceding movements. And it is optimistic music,
brightly affirmative, a kind of healthy credo." See: D98h

B98mm. "House in Mt. Kisco." Time 55:34-35 (February
6, 1950)
    "Last week...Barber's Piano Sonata, Op. 26, got a
rousing reception at Manhattan's Carnegie Hall. Played by
Vladimir Horowitz, whose steely, piston-precise fingers can

make the most of whatever music they attack, the four
movement work gave concertgoers the clean-cut craftmanslike
profile they had learned to expect from Barber's music.
Only in the Bach-like final fugue--and then mostly because
of his choice of form--was Barber's conservative but original composition blurred by the wraith image of a dead
master." See: W98c

B98nn. Hughes, Allen. "De Gaetano Shines in Piano
Debut." New York Times, November 9, 1975, p. 69.
   "One way of summing up Robert de Gaetano's New York
debut at Tully Hall...is to say that he was ultrasuccessful
in ultrapianistic...Barber's Sonata, with a beautifully
played Adagio as a high point, ended the program." See:
W98ww

B98oo. -----. "Jane Carlson, Pianist, Excels in Ton-
alis." New York Times, March 25, 1976, p. 45.
   "The Barber Sonata came off well enough, although Miss
Carlson did not articulate it quite so cleanly as some
pianists do...but she won out and kept the music shapely in
the process." See: W98xx

B98pp. Jablonski, Edward. "Two 20th-Century Masterpieces" [album notes for RCA LSC 3229 disc]
   "The sonata has been called by one critic 'a virtuoso's paradise;'...at the same time it is recognized as a
composition of great musical substance. While Barber has
been saddled with the label 'Neo-Romantic,' his musical
speech in this four movement sonata is decidedly contemporary; it could only have been written today--and it could
only have been written by Samuel Barber. He even draws
ingeniously upon twelve-tone serial procedures. But never
is the clarity of his writing or his innate lyricism smoth-
ered by mere technique; the 'sound' is at once distinctive-
ly personal and American. The results is a masterpiece
that belongs in the company of other great American piano
sonatas--by Charles Ives, Charles Griffes, Aaron Copland
and other. But also it stands alone, like a solitary
beautiful mountain." See: D98e

B98qq. Jacobson, Bernard. "Classical." High Fidelity
17:82 (June 1967)
   "Not having heard it for a while, I have grown accustomed to thinking of Samuel Barber's Piano Sonata as one
of the best things he has done. On renewing acquaintance I
find it less individual and less arresting than I had
thought, and in any case Miss Mitchell's performance has to
cope with memories of one of Horowitz's most spectacular
interpretations." [Decca DL 10 136, DL 710 136] See: D98q

B98rr. Kagan, Susan. "Instrumental." Fanfare 1:126
(May/June 1979)
   "Horowitz is not known as a champion of contemporary
music, but his premiere performances of two major 20th-

century sonatas were extraordinary successes. The Barber
Sonata is a well-crafted four movement work in an
essentially conservative harmonic idiom, bristles with
thorny passages. The extremes of its technical demands on
the performer--steely fingers and precise rhythms in the
first and last movements, rippling roulades of passage-work
in the waltz-scherzo, melodic lyricism in the slow movement
--are perfectly met by Horowitz." [RCA Red Seal ARM1 2952]
See: D98h

B98ss. Kammerer, Rafael. "Joseph Battista...Pianist."
Musical America 78:38 (January 1, 1958)
"That Mr. Battista could purr and coax on the keyboard
as well as thunder was well demonstrated in his performance
of the Ravel [Valses Nobles et Sentimentales] and Barber
works...his Barber can be summed up in one word--'terrific'!" See: W98t

B98tt. -----. "Marjorie Mitchell." Musical America
81:53-54 (March 1961)
"Miss Mitchell not only had the Prokofieff [No. 3] and
Barber Sonata in her head and fingers, she made them a part
of her very being and her performances of these works were
the most exciting and revealing that I have heard." See:
W98gg

B98uu. -----. "Nikita Magaloff, Pianist." Musical
America 73:7 (December 15, 1953)
"His playing of [the]...Sonata...was utterly fantas-
tic. The burning intensity he brought to bear upon this
work, the spectrum of tonal colors he invested it with, and
the virtuosity displayed here ran the gamut of pianistic
art at it modern best." See: W98l

B98vv. Kendall, Raymond. "Howard Aibel." Musical
Courier 160:17 (December 1959)
"Samuel Barber's Sonata showed what the young pianist
could do in the modern field, and he surmounted the task
creditably." See: W98z

B98ww. Kerr, Russell M. "New Publications." Musical
Courier 141:29 (February 1, 1950)
This is "...one of Barber's most powerful works and
one of the most virtuosic piano sonatas of the
generation...some of the most brilliant and satisfactory
piano writing that any American composer has achieved."
See: W98

B98xx. Kirkpatrick, John. "Samuel Barber." Notes
(second series) 7:448 (June 1950)
"Barber's piano sonata...is a virtuoso piece for both
player and composer, showy, precisely focussed, and expertly turned. All four movements are fairly elaborate and
epitomize their expected role in the traditional
plan...Considered in line with the great tradition of sona-

ta writing, which still speaks from heart to heart, this seems dangerously close to being a magnificent scenery-sonata." See: W98

B98yy. Klein, Howard. "Nicolai Petrov, Russian Pianist, Makes Local Debut at Carnegie." New York Times, November 5, 1965, p. 32.
"The closing work was the Adagio and Fugue from the Barber Piano Sonata. Here again, Mr. Petrov showed a powerhouse of technique." See: W98oo

B98zz. Kozinn, Allan. "Samuel Barber" [album notes for Nonesuch Digital D 79032 disc]
"In this ambitious score, Barber uses a palette that allows him to mix an underlying tonality (the work revolves around an E-flat minor tonal center) with bold chromatic strokes and even dashes of 12 tone rows. The one element typical of Barber here is the work's pervasive lyricism, which shines through even the most stunningly virtuosic sections." See: D98p

B98aaa. Krebs, Albin. "Notes on People: A Sonata to Celebrate Samuel Barber's 70th." New York Times, March 1, 1980, p. 24.
News article announcing that Ruth Laredo will perform the Barber Sonata at a program celebrating his 70th birthday. Ruth Laredo performed the same work on Barber's 50th birthday, known then as Ruth Meckler. See: W98zz

B98bbb. Krokover, Rosalyn. "New Publication." Musical Courier 141:29 (February 1, 1950)
"Barber here has composed one of his most powerful works, and one of the most virtuosic piano sonatas of the generation. The writing is very difficult - in some cases frankly exhibitionistic--but is always kept in check by a stringent musicianship. Some hints of Prokofieff, perhaps, are present; but there is more Barber than anything else. In the second movement he breaks into impish suggestions of a waltz, though for the most part the writing is 'absolute.' Some interesting harmonic clashes touch up the almost improvisatory slow movement, which rises to an imposing climax and might be called the core of the work. The last movement has some of the most brilliant and satisfactory piano writing that any American composer has achieved." See: W98

B98ccc. Lancaster, J. B. "Other Reviews." American Record Guide 27:303 (December 1960)
"The nature of the work is one of imaginative counterpoint and angular formality, and therefore a product altogether admirable to Russian ears, accustomed as they are to composers who have undergone a normal university course in theory of twelve years, compared to our miserable four (if that)." [Artia MK 1513] See: D98t

B98ddd. Laredo, Ruth. "Samuel Barber" [album notes for Nonesuch Digital D 79032 disc]
"The sonata, op. 26 is one of the great works written in this century--truly a legacy for the piano. It is a tragic work, emotionally rich, with grandeur, wit and the special eloquence of Sam Barber's personal style." <u>See</u>: D98p

B98eee. Levinger, Henry W. "New York Concerts." <u>Musical Courier</u> 141:42 (February 15, 1950)
"Most important event of Horowitz's recital given before an audience filling hall and stage, was the premiere of Samuel Barber's <u>Sonata in E flat minor</u>, op. 20 [sic] (1949). The tremendous difficulties were victoriously conquered, and the musical content seemed to have become Horowitz's own language. The <u>Sonata</u> is an important contribution to contemporary piano music. Its idiom shows modernism with traditional ties. The basic feeling is romantic, with a slow movement of poignant lyricism and a scherzo of almost Chopinesque elegance. The first movement, based on a single powerfully rhythmed theme, which goes through various transformations, has dramatic drive. The finale, a gigantic Fugue, utilizes the old form with mastery. The audience gave an ovation to composer and pianist." <u>See</u>: W98c

B98fff. Levy, Marvin. "Miklos Schwalb." <u>Musical America</u> 77:34 (December 1, 1957)
"...in the striking Barber <u>Sonata</u>, Op. 26, which is almost standard repertory, one felt that the performance did not quite measure up to the possibilities of the piece." <u>See</u>: W98r

B98ggg. Milburn, Frank, Jr. "John Browning." <u>Musical America</u> 78:28-29 (December 1, 1958)
"As for the Barber sonata, its effect was brilliant. Massive in its climaxes, intense in its intellectual concentration, the interpretation again affirmed that Mr. Browning should have a bright future ahead of him." <u>See</u>: W98x

B98hhh. -----. "Seymour Bernstein." <u>Musical America</u> 77:33 (May 1957)
"The Barber <u>Sonata</u> was the high point of the program. Here the pianist grasped the dramatic impact of the work, and the first and second movements were particularly exciting as bravura display." <u>See</u>: W98q

B98iii. Olsen, William A. "Piano." <u>New Records</u> 40:13 (March 1972)
"Samuel Barber's <u>Sonata</u> (1950) is a 'masterpiece' and has been bracketed with the piano works of Ives, Griffes and Copland." [Victor LSC 3229] <u>See</u>: D98e

B98jjj. Parmenter, Ross. "The World of Music Commis-

sions." New York Times, December 11, 1949, sect. 2, p. 9.
     News article telling of upcoming performances of three
commissioned works. "The third work has a more complicated
background. It is Samuel Barber's E flat minor piano
sonata that requires almost half an hour to perform. Its
commission came from the League of Composers using money
donated by Richard Rodgers and Irving Berlin. The man who
will introduce it is Vladimir Horowitz, who is so interested in the sonata that he has agreed to the plans of its
publisher, G. Schirmer, Inc., to give it a hearing before
an invited audience three weeks before the New York premiere at Carnegie Hall on January 23." See: W98

     B98kkk. Plaistow, Stephen. "Instrumental." Gramophone
51:696 (October 1973)
     "It is one of those virtuoso pieces which are rather
to obviously a 'vehicle,' a catalogue of gestures...I think
Barber suffers badly here from his proximity to Prokofiev."
[RCA LBS 4095] See: D98e

     B98lll. "Pollack Plays in Beijing." Los Angeles Times,
January 28, 1980, pt. 5, p. 4.
     "...warm applause...[greeted] the lively sonata, opus
26..." See: W98yy

     B98mmm. Rabinowitz, Peter J. "Instrumental." Fanfare
5:238 (September/October 1981)
     "This recital disc was recorded and released as long
ago as 1975...The Barber Sonata is an old favorite of mine
and though I felt a certain lack of melodic definition at
first, this rendition proved effective in the end...The
disc has its noisy moments, to be sure, but for anyone
lacking the Barber and interested in lesser-known American
pianists, this item is worth picking up." [Transonic 3008]
See: D98o

     B98nnn. Redlich, H. F. "Reviews of Music." Music
Review 11:329 (November 1950)
     "...a serious attempt to revive the classical Sonata
scheme within the framework of a very progressive music
idiom. The composer deliberately eschews atonality, cling-
ing so persistently to the tonic of E flat minor, that--
especially in the first movement--the music itself seems to
be marking time...The two middle movements consist of a
graceful scherzo in 6/8 time with a trio section in Buso-
ni's ghostly Waltz rhythm (à la 'Nächtlichen,' from the
Elegies, 1910) and a melancholy adagio with polytonal en-
claves and imaginative coloratura in the right hand, skillfully interlacing the impressive monotony of sprawling
quaver intervals in the left. This certainly deserves the
attention of pianists still interested in the progress of
music." See: W98

     B98ooo. S., E. "Brockman Plays Here." New York Times,
January 19, 1959, p. 23.

"When he [Thomas Brockman] had firm control of the long lines, as in the Barber sonata, the result was more than poetic, it was also powerful." <u>See</u>: W98y

B98ppp. Sabin, Robert. "New Music Reviews: Samuel Barber Composes Effective Piano Sonata." <u>Musical America</u> 70:332 (February 1950)
Review of the G. Schirmer score. "Other American piano sonatas may be more profound, intellectually consistent, and durable than this one, but none is more appealing. Mr. Barber's music is an excellent challenge to the die-hards who are perpetually complaining that contemporary piano music is unidiomatic, emotionally dry, and inexpressive." <u>See</u>: W98

B98qqq. Salter, Lionel. "Instrumental." <u>Gramophone</u> 41:282 (December 1963)
"...perhaps the most outstanding of all is the Barber sonata (of which Horowitz was the original interpreter), despite some unpleasantly clangy tone in fortes; the feather-light Scherzo is a dream, and the sheer pianistic virtuosity of the finale leaves one gasping." [RCA Victor RB 6554-5] <u>See</u>: D98k

B98rrr. Schonberg, Harold C. "Battista Heard in Piano Recital." <u>New York Times</u>, December 8, 1957, sect. 1, p. 83.
"There was some powerful playing in the Barber sonata. Under Mr. [Joseph] Battista's skilled fingers the music had drive and excitement. Perhaps there is more romanticism to the writing than he suggested. The steely tonal approach made it sound like Prokofieff." <u>See</u>: W98t

B98sss. -----. <u>Chamber and Solo Instrument Music</u>. New York: Knopf, 1955. (The Guide to Long-Playing Records, vol. 3) 280 p.
"Barber, in this work, obviously set out to compose a big, splashy, neo-romantic display piece. What resulted, however, is a synthetic that goes through all the motions but has no inner life. In Horowitz the composer has an interpreter who can do as much as anybody alive for the music." [p. 22] [RCA Victor LM 1113] <u>See</u>: D98j

B98ttt. -----. "Firkusny Excels in Piano Program." <u>New York Times</u>, November 26, 1951, p. 21.
"He commands a lovely tone. His technique is admirable. His variety of touch is a perpetual pleasure. He's one of the few pianists who can really handle pianissimo passages and the accuracy of his ear in dynamics puts him in a special category. Mr. Firkusny is not a 'big' pianist, though sometimes he tries to be. This is a mistake on his part. In several places in the Schumann work and in the last movement of the Barber Sonata he let matters get a little out of hand in his attempt to achieve a grand and noble line." <u>See</u>: W98i

B98uuu. Schonberg, Harold C. "Letter From America." Gramophone 28:219 (March 1951)
"The effective sonata by Barber goes well: it is a virtuoso's paradise, a real contemporary showpiece. It has received a good press up to now, though one wonders how much of the praise is praise through default of contemporary composers of piano music." [RCA Victor RB 6554-5 (Great Britain)] See: D98k

B98vvv. -----. "Music: A Cliburn Recital." New York Times, October 5, 1963, p. 14.
"It was in the Barber sonata that he brought a good deal of individuality, however. Most pianists drive through this difficult work in a rather bleak manner, using little pedal, trying for big tone and big dynamics. Mr. Cliburn adopted a more relaxed approach and a quite varied one. In places his playing was sculptural, with an emphasis on clarity of line and finger work. In other places, notably in the second movement, he used touches of pedal that added an extra dimension. His tempo, too, was easier-going than is customarily encountered. And for one time in the recital he inserted a few nicely adjusted rubato effects. It all added up to a somewhat different view of the Barber sonata, and a more interesting one." See: W98jj

B98www. -----. "Music: Natural Pianist." New York Times, December 4, 1959, p.37.
"Zita Carno...is what musicians describe as 'a natural.' She plays the piano in an effortless manner and obviously is an all-around musician. Her style is neat and finished, her technique one of complete security. She is not a colorist, and she uses the pedal rather sparingly. What she stresses is clarity, logic, proportion." See: W98bb

B98xxx. -----. "Piano Debut Made by Howard Aibel." New York Times, November 4, 1959, p. 43.
"His well-regulated technique carried him easily through everything on the program, including the difficult Barber work. It was a pleasure to hear this easy-going, nonchalant kind of keyboard approach." See: W98z

B98yyy. Shupp, Enos E., Jr. "Concerto." New Records 35:5 (March 1967)
"Barber's Sonata is a jittery, compact, highly energetic affair that must be a real bruser for the performer. Miss Mitchell polishes it off with style and precision, making this a memorable disc." [Decca DL 10136, DL 710136] D98q

B98zzz. Simek, Julius Franz. "Thomas Brockman...Pianist." Musical America 79:263 (February 1959)
Brockman played the Barber Sonata "which, in the fluttering lightness of the Allegro vivace and the breath-

taking precision of the Fugue, was the highlight of the
concert." <u>See</u>: W98y

B98aaaa. Simmons, Walter. "Classical Recordings." <u>Fan-</u>
<u>fare</u> 5:68-69 (September/October 1981)
    "Barber's is a rather uncomfortable compromise between
the uninhibited romanticism of his youth and the brittle
neoclassicism that he often tried to adopt--sometimes with
unfortunate results--later on. In the <u>Sonata</u>, the consequence of this accommodation is a dilution of emotionali-
ty and a limp uncertainty of rhythmic flow. The effectiveness of the work can be optimized by accentuating its hard-
edged qualities--the impetuous rhythmic drive, the brittle
sonorities--and by letting the lyricism emerge as a natural
by-product as demonstrated by John Browning. But Brownridge, taking the opposite course and emphasizing the
softer qualities, does not present the sonata to its best
advantage, for the most part, although she does play the
slow movement quite eloquently." [Hyperion A 66016] <u>See</u>:
D98b

B98bbbb. "Sonata to Honor League." <u>New York Times</u>,
September 24, 1947, p. 20.
    News article announcing that Samuel Barber has been
commissioned by Irving Berlin and Richard Rodgers to write
a piano sonata to honor the League of Composer's twenty-
fifth anniversary. <u>See</u>: W98

B98cccc. Strongin, Theodore "Heukelekian Makes a Romantic Debut." <u>New York Times</u>, November 16, 1967, p. 60.
    "Mr. Heukelekian makes everything sound super-signifi-
cant. He gave the impression last night that he was always
at the edge of a big moment. At the drop of a hat he would
work up to a pianistic storm. In the last movement of the
Barber <u>Sonata</u> he pounded out a barrage that must have been
heard all the way to Timbuktu. He is definitely not the
restrained, icy, modern piano type." <u>See</u>: W98qq

B98dddd. Taubman, Howard. "Music: Exciting Recital."
<u>New York Times</u>, November 6, 1958, p. 45.
    "As an American, he [John Browning] disclosed a lively
identification with Samuel Barber's sonata, playing it with
brilliance and finding the sentiment in it." <u>See</u>: W98x

B98eeee. Tischler, Hans. "Barber's Piano Sonata, Op.
26." <u>Music and Letters</u> 33:352-354 (October 1952)
    "Brilliant and difficult though it is, this is no mere
display piece. It stands head and shoulders above any
other sonata written by an American composer in the past
thirty years, and is worthy of taking a place alongside the
great works of this category by reason of its Beethovenian
concentration, seriousness and mastership. The interesting
and arresting thing about this work is the combination of
thoughtfulness, masterly economy, brilliance and naturalness, which elicits an appeal both immediate and lasting.

The fusion of contemporary technique with that of the past thee centuries--of twelve-tone technique, contemporary harmonic materials, sonata-forms, passacaglia and fugue-- this thoroughly satisfying fusion stamps Barber's _Piano Sonata_, Op. 26 as a classic of our times." _See_: W98

B98ffff. Tischler, Hans. "Some Remarks on the Use of Twelve-Tone and Fugue Technics in Samuel Barber's _Piano Sonata_." _Journal of the American Musicological Society_ 5:145-146 (Summer 1952) [Read at Ann Arbor on April 19, 1952, at a meeting of the Midwestern Chapter of the American Musicological Society]
"After sporadic employment of twelve-tone rows in the first movement Barber bases the third one throughout on a twelve-tone row. Yet this is no twelve-tone composition; the row is transposed, shortened, lengthened, varied in texture, and opposed to melodic motifs not based on twelve-tone concepts. The row thereby gains a new flexibility." _See_: W98

B98gggg. Trimble, Lester. "Classical." _Stereo Review_ 27:79 (August 1970)
"In the Barber _Sonata_...there are occasions when some relaxation of forward drive would have allowed key phrases to speak with subtler impact. Nevertheless, these are first-rate performances, and no mistake about it. The reading, too, [by Robert Guralnik] is very fine." [Mace MXX 9085] _See_: D98f

B98hhhh. -----. "Classical." _Stereo Review_ 28:78 (February 1972)
"Samuel Barber's _Piano Sonata_ is one of those very rare birds--an _American_ work that has found its way securely into the piano repertoire. With this performance by John Browning, Desto has added to its fine and burgeoning catalog a stellar item, in terms of the music, the playing and the recorded sound. Browning's interpretation is splendidly thoughtful, imbued at every moment with personal conviction and insight...In short, this is one of the really top drawer recordings of the Barber Sonata: a virtuoso performance, but one in which virtuosity serves the music, rather than the other way around." [Desto DC 7120] _See_: D98c

B98iiii. Waldrop, Gid W. "New York Concert and Opera Beat." _Musical Courier_ 158:38 (December 1958)
"The Samuel Barber _Sonata_ had more than inherent brilliance. Few, if any of our current crop of young pianists can approach Browning in the matter of sensitive pianism." _See_: W98x

B98jjjj. Warrack, John. "Orchestral." _Gramophone_ 52:1801 (April 1975)
"John Browning is an old hand at Barber's music. and has a warm understanding of where the muscularity of con-

struction lies within the Romantic gestures of the work; for Barber's personal handling of serial techniques, so far from impeding the natural late-Romantic invention, do seem to help his organization and indeed to lend greater purpose to what can in other works seem rather soft. [Peerless PRCM 204] See: D98d

B98kkkk. Waters, Edward N. "Harvest of the Year: Selected Acquisitions of the Music Division." Quarterly Journal of the Library of Congress 24:54-55 (January 1967)

"In 1949 Mr. Barber composed a Sonata for piano, Op. 26, which has achieved great and deserved acclaim. Many virtuosos--for it is truly a virtuoso piece--have played it, and no less an artist than Vladimir Horowitz gave the first performance in Havana on December 9, 1949. When published in 1950 by G. Schirmer, Inc., a printed notice said: 'Commissioned by the League of Composers for its twenty-fifty anniversary.' It is more interesting to learn that the money for the commission came from two composers equally prominent in their own world of music: Irving Berlin and Richard Rodgers. Accompanying the holograph of the Sonata are a single leaf of holograph corrections (all of the fourth and last movement) and two reproductions of a copyist's manuscript showing further corrections. Final testimony of the Sonata's success is disclosed by an edition published in Moscow." See: W98

B98llll. Zaidan, Abe. "Pianist Browning Shows Artistry. Columbus (Ohio) Citizen-Journal, January 13, 1961, p. 11.

Review of the January 12, 1961 Ohio State University performance. "This is an artist who has strength to spare. In the Beethoven [Sonata in D minor, op. 31, no. 2] and Barber he played as though he was repaying a great debt to society. This was especially true of Barber's Sonata, which shifts from floodtides to meditation and back again in the frenetic medium of latter-day impulse and abandon." See: W98ff

B99. SUITE FOR CARILLON.

B99a. Salzmann, Eric. "Samuel Barber." HIFI/Stereo Review 17:77-89 (October 1966)

"In 1930, Edward Bok commissioned Barber to write a suite for the giant pink marble carillon he had constructed at the Mountain Lakes Bird Sanctuary in Florida." See: W98

B101. WONDROUS LOVE: VARIATIONS ON A SHAPE-NOTE HYMN, OP. 34.

B101a. Cohn, Arthur. "Recorded Classical Music." New York: Schirmer Books, 1981. 2164 p.

"The contrapuntal encounters of the four Variations show Barberesque fluency. The final one is the least conventional of the set. There is variational music aplenty in the world, much of it without a real note of music in it as it travels over the bar-lines. This is never true of Barber's handling of variation technique, which is always beautifully turned in its tonal enthusiasm." [p. 99] [Orion 76255] See: D101a, W101

B101b. Gehring, Philip. "A Survey of Contemporary Organ Music--America." Church Music no. 2:29-30 (1967)
This is "One of the finest organ works based on an American folk hymn...Barber begins by quoting the Dorian-mode melody with its original harmony...and follows this with four variations." See: W101

B101c. Greenleaf, Christopher. "Collections." American Record Guide 41:47 (March 1978)
The work is "...a gorgeous fantasia (for want of a better term) that would have sounded better on a Hook organ, or, even better, played by an orchestra. It is a totally orchestral work that Neville Marriner or Leonard Bernstein would do perfectly. Here it suffers from both insensitive playing and the blandness of the organ." [Repertoire Recording Society RRS 112] See: D101c

B101d. Lowens, Irving. "Recitals and Miscellany." High Fidelity 27:120 (July 1977)
"Thomas Harmon uses the Hradetzky [organ]...to excellent effect, and Barber's Op. 34 variations...have rarely sounded more beautiful." [Orion ORS 76255] See: D101a

B101e. McCandless, William Edgar. Cantus Firmus Techniques in Selected Instrumental Compositions, 1910-1960. Thesis (Ph.D.)--Indiana University, Bloomington, 1974. 309 p.
"Although the style of the piece is polyphonic, the number of voices is less consistent than in most Renaissance and Baroque works for organ; parts enter and drop out rather freely...Several features of the tonal organization of this work set it apart from the traditional chorale partita. Whereas Renaissance and Baroque composers normally maintain the cantus firmus in the same key throughout an entire set of variations, Barber changes its tonality with each variation." [p. 86, 87-88] See: W101

B101f. Rhoades, Larry Lynn. Theme and Variation in Twentieth-Century Organ Literature: Analyses of Variations by Alain, Barber, Distler, Dupré, Duruflé, and Sowerby. Thesis (Ph.D.)--Ohio State University, Columbus, 1973. 297 p.
"Barber's composition begins with a nearly literal four-voice reproduction of the shape-note hymn harmonization. Barber interchanges the tenor and soprano parts so that the theme melody in his setting appears in the upper-

most voice and the original soprano part appears in the
tenor line. The shape-note hymn, containing twenty measures, is reduced to ten measures through the use of halved
note values. These ten measures become the theme for the
beginning of Barber's Wondrous Love Variations..." [p. 87-
88] See: W101

    B101g. Smith, Rollin. "American Organ Composers."
Music (American Guild of Organists) 10:18 (August 1976)
     "Wondrous Love is a melody first printed in Southern
Harmony in 1835 and later in The Original Sacred Harp, an
1869 collection of hymn tunes whose pitches were indicated
by the shape of the note rather than by position on the
staff...Barber presents four highly evocative and original
variations." See: W101

Appendix I:

ALPHABETICAL LIST OF COMPOSITIONS

Numbers following each title, e.g. W61, refer to the "Works and Performances" section of this volume. Titles followed by an asterisk (*) do not bear opus numbers.

Ad Bibinem Cum Me Rogaret ad Cenam*, W13
Adagio for Strings, op. 11, W61
Adventure*, W62
Agnus Dei (see also Lamb of God)*, W14
Andromache's Farewell, op. 39, W26
Anthony O'Daly (Reincarnations), op. 16, W21
Antony and Cleopatra, op. 40, W1
At Saint Patrick's Purgatory (Hermit Songs), op. 29, W33
Au Clair de la lune*, W27
Ballade, op. 46, W93
The Beggar's Song*, W28
Bessie Bobtail (Songs (3)), op. 2, W51
A Blue Rose, op. 28, W63
Canzone for Flute and Piano, op. 38a, W84
Canzonetta, op. 48, W64
Capricorn Concerto, op. 21, W85
Choral Preludes for Christmas (Die Natali), op. 37, W74
Church Bell at Night (Hermit Songs), op. 29, W33
Le Clocher chanté (Mélodies passagères), op. 27, W41
Commando March*, W83
Concerto for Piano and Orchestra, op. 38, W65
Concerto for Violin and Orchestra, op. 14, W66
Concerto for Violoncello and Orchestra, op. 22, W67
Configurations, op. 38, W65
The Coolin (Reincarnations), op. 16, W21
The Crucifixion (Hermit Songs), op. 29, W33
Un Cygne (Mélodies passagères), op. 27, W41
Daisies, The (Songs (3)), op. 2, W51
The Dance*, W29
Death of Cleopatra (Antony and Cleopatra), op. 40, W4

Night Flight, op. 19a, W75
Nocturne (Songs (4)), op. 13, W53
Nocturne: Homage to John Field, op. 33, W97
Now I Have Fed and Eaten Up the Rose (Songs (3)), op. 45, W57
La Nuit*, W45
A Nun Takes the Veil (Songs (4)), op. 13, W53
Nuvoletta, op. 25, W46
O Boundless, Boundless Evening (Songs (3)), op. 45, W57
October Mountain Weather*, W47
October-Weather*, W47
An Old Song*, see "Preface"
On the Death of Antony (Antony and Cleopatra), op. 40, W2
On the Death of Cleopatra (Antony and Cleopatra), op. 40, W3
"One Day of Spring"*, W95
Overture to "The School for Scandal," op. 5, W76
Pas de Deux (Souvenirs), op. 28, W78
Petite Berceuse*, see "Preface"
Piano Concerto, op. 38, W65
Piano Sonata, op. 26, W98
The Praises of God (Hermit Songs), op. 29, W33
Prayers of Kierkegaard, op. 30, W20
Promiscuity (Hermit Songs), op. 29, W33
Puisque tout passe (Mélodies passagères), op. 27, W41
The Queen's Face on the Summery Coin (Songs (2)), op. 18, W56
Quintet, Act III, Scene II (Vanessa), op. 32, W11
Rain Has Fallen (Songs (3)), op. 10, W52
Reincarnations, op. 16, W21
The Rose Tree*, W6
Saint Ita's Vision (Hermit Songs), op. 29, W33
Schottische (Souvenirs), op. 28, W78
Sea-Snatch (Hermit Songs), op. 29, W33
Second Essay for Orchestra, op. 17, W77
The Secrets of the Old (Songs (4)), op. 13, W53
Serenade for Strings, op. 1, W88
Silent Night*, W74
Sleep Now (Songs (3)), op. 10, W52
Slumber Song of the Madonna*, W48
Solitary Hotel (Despite and Still), op. 41, W31
Sometime*, W49
Sonata for Piano, op. 26, W98
Sonata for Violin and Piano*, W89
Sonata for Violoncello and Piano in C Minor, op. 6, W90
Sonata in Modern Form, op. XVI, see "Preface"
Song for a New House*, W50
Songs (3), op. 2, W51
Songs (3), op. 10, W52
Songs (4), op. 13, W53
Songs (2), op. 18, W56
Songs (3), op. 45, W57
Souvenirs, op. 28, W78
A Stopwatch and an Ordnance Map, op. 15, W22
String Quartet in B Minor, op. 11, W91

Suite for Carillon*, W99
Summer Music, op. 31, W92
Sure on This Shining Night (Songs (4)), op. 13, W53
Symphony No. 1, op. 9, W79
Symphony No. 2, op. 19, W80
Themes, op. X, no. 2, see "Preface"
Third Essay for Orchestra, op. 47, W81
Three Sketches for Pianoforte*, W100
Thy Love*, W58
Thy Will Be Done, op. V, no.1, see "Preface"
To Be Sung on the Water, op. 42, no. 2, W23
To My Steinway (Three Sketches for Pianoforte)*, W100
Toccata Festiva, op. 36, W82
Tombeau dans un parc (Mélodies passagères), op. 27, W41
Twelfth Night, op. 42, no. 1, W24
Two Scenes (Antony and Cleopatra), op. 40, W4
Two-Step (Souvenirs), op. 28, W78
Under the Willow Tree (Vanessa), op. 32, W12
Vanessa, op. 32, W7
Variations on a Shape-Note Hymn (Wondrous Love), op. 34,
    W101
Violin Concerto, op. 14, W66
Violoncello Concerto, op. 22, W67
The Virgin Martyrs, op. 8, no. 1, W25
Waltz (Souvenirs), op. 28, W78
The Wanderer*, see "Preface"
The Watchers*, W59
With Rue My Heart is Laden (Songs (3)), op. 2, W51
Wondrous Love: Variations on a Shape-Note Hymn, op. 34,
    W101
Youth*, W60

Appendix II:

COMPOSITIONS IN ORDER
BY OPUS NUMBER

Numbers following each title, e.g. W61, refer to the "Works
and Performances" section of this volume. Titles bearing
opus numbers in the form of Roman numerals, generally
sketches, incomplete works, and juvenilia, follow the basic
list of works with opus numbers. Works lacking opus numbers are found at the end of this "Appendix."

Opus No.	Title
1	Serenade for Strings, W88
2	Songs (3), W51:
	Bessie Bobtail (Songs (3)), W51
	The Daisies (Songs (3)), W51
	With Rue My Heart is Laden (Songs (3)), W51
3	Dover Beach, W86
5	Overture to "The School for Scandal," W76
6	Sonata for Violoncello and Piano in C Minor, W90
7	Music for a Scene from Shelley, W73
8, no.1	The Virgin Martyrs, W25
8, no.2	Let Down the Bars, O Death, W18
9	Symphony No. 1, W79
10	Songs (3), W52:
	I Hear an Army (Songs (3)), W52
	Rain Has Fallen (Songs (3)), W52
	Sleep Now (Songs (3)), W52
11	Adagio for Strings, W61
11	String Quartet in B Minor, W91
12	Essay for Orchestra, W68
13	Songs (4)), W53:
	Nocturne (Songs (4)), W53
	A Nun Takes the Veil (Songs (4)), W53

Appendix II

Works Without Opus Numbers

Works Without Opus Numbers (continued)

Au Clair de la lune, W27
The Beggar's Song, W28
Commando March, W83
The Dance, W29
Dere Two Fella Joe, W30
Easter Chorale, W15
Fantasy in Purple, W32
God's Grandeur, W16
Horizon, W70
Incidental Music to "One Day of Spring," W95
Intermezzi (2) for Piano, W96
Invocation to Youth, W35
Lady, When I Behold the Roses, W37
Lamb of God (see also Agnus Dei), W17
Little Children of the Wind, W38
Longing, W39
Love Song (Three Sketches for Pianoforte),
    W100
Main Street, see "Preface"
Man, W40
Mother Goose Songs, W42
Music, When Soft Voices Die, W43
Mutations from Bach, W87
My Fairyland, W44
La Nuit, W45
October Mountain Weather, W47
October-Weather, W47
An Old Song, see "Preface"
"One Day of Spring," W95
Petite Berceuse, see "Preface"
The Rose Tree, W6
Silent Night, W74
Slumber Song of the Madonna, W48
Sometime, W49
Sonata for Violin and Piano, W89
Song for a New House, W50
Suite for Carillon, W99
Three Sketches for Pianoforte, W100
Thy Love, W58
To My Steinway (Three Sketches for Piano-
    forte), W100
The Wanderer, see "Preface"
The Watchers, W59
Youth, W60

INDEX

References within each citation are presented in the same order as found in this volume: page numbers in Roman numerals, e.g. ix, refer to the "Preface," page numbers in Arabic numerals, e.g. 11, refer to the "Biography," and these are followed by references to the "Works and Performances" section, e.g. W61, the "Discography," e.g. D61, and the "Bibliography," with references to general articles preceding references to the remainder of the "Bibliography," i.e. BG61 precedes B61a.

ABOUT THE COMPILER

DON A. HENNESSEE is Librarian Emeritus at California State University, Long Beach. He is the coauthor of *Women in Music* and *Nineteenth Century American Drama* (both with Don L. Hixon).